UN Territorial Administration and Human Rights

This book offers an original and insightful analysis of the human rights inadequacies that arise in the practice of UN territorial administration by analysing and assessing the practice of UNMIK. It provides arguments based on law and principles to support the thesis that a comprehensive legal framework governing the activities of the UN mission is a crucial prerequisite for its proper functioning. This is complemented by a discussion of several emerging issues surrounding the UN activity on the ground, namely, its legislative, judicial, and executive power.

The author offers an extensive and well-documented analysis of the UN's capacity as a surrogate state administration to respond to the needs of the governed population and, above all, protect its fundamental rights. Based on her findings, Murati concludes that only a comprehensive mandate can serve the long-term interests of the international community's objective to efficiently promote, protect, and fulfil human rights in a war-torn society.

UN Territorial Administration and Human Rights provides a detailed critical legal analysis of one of the major UN administrations of territory after the Cold War, namely, the UN administration of Kosovo from 1999 to 2008. The analysis in this book will be beneficial for international law and international relations scholars and students, as well as policymakers and persons working for international organisations. The analysis and the lessons learned through this study shed light on the challenges entailed in governing territories and rebuilding state institutions while upholding the rule of law and ensuring respect for human rights.

Gjylbehare Bella Murati is Assistant Professor of International Relations and International Diplomatic Law at Haxhi Zeka University, Kosovo. She holds a PhD in law from Ghent University, Belgium, an LLM from Essex University, UK, and a BA in law from the Universities of Prishtina, Kosovo, and Utrecht, the Netherlands. Previously she was an associate postdoctoral research fellow at the Human Rights Centre in Ghent, Belgium, research fellow at the Max Planck Institute for Comparative Public Law and International Law in Heidelberg, Germany, and a visiting lecturer at the European inter-university centre for Human Rights and Democratization in Venice Lido, Italy.

Post-Conflict Law and Justice
Series Editors: James A. Sweeney
Lancaster University
Matthew Saul
Inland Norway University of Applied Sciences

International law has great relevance in post-conflict contexts, but the complexity of its role, both as a supporting and restraining factor, can be underestimated. This series explores the role of law, and in particular international law, in securing 'justice' in post-conflict contexts. The remit of the series extends to matters of law connected to, for example: post-conflict legal reforms and the development of constitutions; the establishment of the rule of law; the place of international organizations in post-conflict; peace-keeping; transitional justice mechanisms (including criminal justice); and discussion of jus post bellum. It also seeks self-reflexive works on notions of post-conflict justice, transitional justice, and similar.

Available titles in this series include:

International Law and Post-Conflict Reconstruction Policy
Matthew Saul and James A. Sweeney

Silenced Victims of Wartime Sexual Violence
Olivera Simic

Sexualized Crimes, Armed Conflict and the Law
The International Criminal Court and the Definitions of Rape and Forced Marriage
Hannah Baumeister

Self-Determination, International Law and Post-Conflict Reconstruction
A Right in Abeyance
Manuela Melandri

Amnesty, Serious Crimes and International Law
Josepha Close

For more information about this series, please visit: www.routledge.com/Post-Conflict-Law-and-Justice/book-series/POSTCONLAW

UN Territorial Administration and Human Rights

The Mission in Kosovo

Gjylbehare Bella Murati

Routledge
Taylor & Francis Group
LONDON AND NEW YORK

First published 2020
by Routledge
2 Park Square, Milton Park, Abingdon, Oxon OX14 4RN

and by Routledge
605 Third Avenue, New York, NY 10017

First issued in paperback 2021

Routledge is an imprint of the Taylor & Francis Group, an informa business

Publisher's Note
The publisher has gone to great lengths to ensure the quality of this reprint but points out that some imperfections in the original copies may be apparent.

British Library Cataloguing-in-Publication Data
A catalogue record for this book is available from the British Library

Library of Congress Cataloging-in-Publication Data
Names: Murati, Gjylbehare Bella, author.
Title: UN territorial administration and human rights : the mission in Kosovo / Gjylbehare Bella Murati.
Description: Abingdon, Oxon ; New York, NY : Routledge, 2020. | Series: Post-conflict law and justice | Based on author's thesis (doctoral – Rijksuniversiteit te Gent. Faculteit Rechtsgeleerdheid, 2014) issued under title: The protection of human rights through a surrogate state administration : the United Nations interim administration in Kosova.
Identifiers: LCCN 2018061586 | ISBN 9781138103344 (hardback) | ISBN 9781315102825 (ebook)
Subjects: LCSH: United Nations Interim Mission in Kosovo. | Kosovo War, 1998–1999—Law and legislation. | Postwar reconstruction—Law and legislation—Kosovo (Republic) | Human rights—Kosovo (Republic)
Classification: LCC KZ6795.K68 M87 2019 | DDC 341.5/84—dc23
LC record available at https://lccn.loc.gov/2018061586

ISBN 13: 978-1-03-223620-9 (pbk)
ISBN 13: 978-1-138-10334-4 (hbk)

DOI: 10.4324/9781315102825

Typeset in Galliard
by Apex CoVantage, LLC

To my parents
Muharrem & Behija Murati

Contents

Acronyms and abbreviations

CEDAW	Convention on the Elimination of All Forms of Discrimination Against Women
CFK	Constitutional Forum of Kosova
CPT	European Committee for the Prevention of Torture and Other Cruel and Inhuman and Degrading Treatment
DARIO	Draft Articles on Responsibility of International Organisations
ECHR	European Convention on Human Rights
ECtHR	European Court of Human Rights
ERRC	European Roma Rights Centre
ESI	European Stability Initiative
EU	European Union
EULEX	European Union Rule of Law Mission in Kosovo
HRAP	Human Rights Advisory Panel
HRC	Human Rights Council
HRW	Human Rights Watch
IAC	Interim Administrative Council
IBA	International Bar Association
ICCPR	International Covenant on Civil and Political Rights
ICERD	International Convention on the Elimination of All Forms of Racial Discrimination
ICESCR	International Covenant on Economic, Social and Cultural Rights
ICG	International Crisis Group
ICO	International Civilian Office
ICTY	International Tribunal for Former Yugoslavia
IDP	Internally Displaced Persons
ILC	International Law Commission
ITA	International Territorial Administration
HPD	House and Property Directorate
HPCC	Housing and Property Claim Commission
JIAS	Joint Interim Administrative Structure (Kosovo)
JWG	Joint Working Group
KFOR	Kosovo Force
KTA	Kosovo Trust Agency

KTC	Kosovo Transitional Council
NCC	National Consultative Council
NGO	Non-governmental Organization
OIK	Ombudsperson Institution of Kosovo
OSCE	Organization for Security and Co-operation in Europe
PISG	Provisional Institutions of Self-Government
SG	Secretary-General of the United Nations
SRSG	Special Representative of the Secretary-General
UN	United Nations
UNHCR	Office of the UN High Commissioner for Refugees
UDHR	Universal Declaration of Human Rights
UNMIK	United Nations Interim Administration Mission in Kosovo
UNSC	United Nations Security Council
UNTAET	United Nations Transitional Administration in East Timor
WHO	World Health Organization

Preface

The interaction between United Nations peacekeeping missions and human rights is twofold.

The goal of the United Nation's peacekeeping mission is to put an end to the human rights abuses committed during hostilities and then to establish the foundation for a sustainable peace. All of this is conducted within narrow legal parameters established by the United Nations Charter and under the authority of the United Nations Security Council.

On 10 June 1999, the United Nations established the United Nations Interim Administration in Kosovo (UNMIK), empowering it with state – like functions. This endeavour necessitated the establishment of a system that was human rights compliant.

I became inspired to start researching this subject by my experience as an investigating lawyer at the Institution of the Ombudsperson in Prishtina, Kosovo. My daily professional experience, which involved investigating alleged human rights violations by the UNMIK authorities, has enabled me to identify the main deficits that arose from the functioning of the United Nations administration in practice.

Two scholars have helped me shape my thoughts: Ralph Wilde and Carstein Stahn. Both have enabled me to better comprehend the notion of international territorial administration from the international public law perspective. Moreover, their stimulating analyses have helped me identify the key elements that underpin the core argument developed in this research.

Ralph Wilde, Antony Anghie, and Roland Paris have in particular catalysed my thinking with their approach of drawing parallels between the practices of colonialism and today's United Nations missions. All three have tried to draw attention to the reincarnation of colonialism in today's United Nations enterprise.

Yet throughout this research, I had to carefully examine an ambiguous UN mandate that generated a need to look for a formula that would reconcile the interests both of the original sovereign (FRY) in preserving its title over the territory and of the majority of the population in achieving the independence of the country.

As a result, the entire system became a big laboratory that produced numerous experiments, which very often affected the human rights and freedoms of the governed population.

This study is the outcome of several years of arduous work that includes both field and desk research. Throughout this period I felt like I was being thrown in a secret mountain cave with the special task to discover the hidden gold of the United Nations' empire. Perhaps I was not able to find pure gold, but I was fortunate enough to identify the harmful elements that alter gold's atomic structure.

Introduction

The UNMIK's mandate in Kosovo

For more than 50 years, the United Nations was explicitly authorised to run trusteeships over former colonies. After the Cold War era, it became engaged in various territorial administrations, mainly in response to regional conflicts. Yet many of them were of a short-term character and mainly with limited administrative powers.[1]

Its two undertakings in Kosovo and East Timor represent the most comprehensive and yet most challenging missions the UN has ever mounted.[2] These undertakings were conceptualised as an extended form of peacekeeping operations and have brought to the surface new sets of issues in international law.[3]

Soon after their deployment, the UNMIK authorities found themselves in a difficult political environment that strongly influenced the development and strategies for the implementation of its mandate on the ground.

The comprehensive mandate required UNMIK to design legislation and establish mechanisms by which justice is claimed. In order to establish sustainable peace it had to maintain strong connection between peacebuilding and justice mechanisms.

Subsequently, UNMIK became the subject of serious critical scholarly investigation.

It sparked a very active debate among scholars and still occupies an important place in international discourse. Most of the literature on this far-reaching United Nations engagement has extensively covered the important questions in public international law as to the nature and scope of the UN's authority, its legal basis

1 For more about UN operations, see Michael O'Flaherty, *The Human Rights Field Operation, Law Theory and Practice*, Ashgate, 2007.

2 There is political disagreement over the name of the territory. Albanians refer to the territory as Kosova while for Serbia it is Kosovo or Kosovo and Metohija. The latter term dates since the abrogation of Kosovo's autonomy in March 1989. In order not to take a political stand, the appellation Kosovo will be used throughout this work, except when it comes to the citation of original titles used in international documents or books, which very often incorporate one or the other title, Kosovo or Kosova.

3 Carstein Stahn, *The Law and Practice of International Territorial Administration*, Cambridge University Press, 2008.

in the UN Charter and its limitations and accountability; however, not much has been said about the UN's experiments on the ground.[4]

My aim in this study is to explore the functioning of the UN's endeavour in practice, with a particular focus on the United Nations Interim Administration in Kosovo (UNMIK).

UNMIK was given the role of a surrogate state administration. UNSC Resolution 1244 empowered the Special Representative of the Secretary General (SRSG) to exercise all legislative and executive authority and to take responsibility for the administration of justice.[5]

The Resolution introduced a model of governance with no division of powers, as all three powers were concentrated in a single authority, the SRSG. In this regard, he was entrusted with exercising public authority over the mandated territory and with intervening in its politics, economy and legislation, as well as representing the territory outside its boundaries.

The aim of this study is to offer an all-inclusive analysis of the functioning of UNMIK. Particular emphasis is placed on the three powers exercised by the SRSG. The study encompasses all three phases of UNMIK's functioning, namely the initial phase, the capacity building and the transfer of competencies.[6]

The study's primary focus is on exploring the capacity of UNMIK, as a surrogate state, to respect, protect, and fulfil human rights.

In light of the context I have presented so far, this study argues that a comprehensive legal framework governing the activities of the mission was a crucial prerequisite for its proper functioning.

Addressing some critical conceptual issues

The notion of international territorial administration (ITA) reflects a divergence of opinion which has caused significant turmoil in the legal literature. Consequently, the whole concept has found little reception comfort in the international arena.

In this context, some scholars regard ITA as a relatively modern phenomenon, in terms of which the UN undertakes the duty of a surrogate state administration effectively to act as sovereign for an unlimited duration.[7] Others suggest that

4 Ralph Wilde, *International Territorial Administration, How Trusteeship and Civilizing Mission Never Went Away*, Oxford University Press, 2008. See Michael Bothe and Thilo Marauhn, UN Administration in Kosovo and East Timor, Concept, Legality, and Limitations of Security Council-Mandated Trusteeship Administration, in Tomuschat (ed.), *Kosovo and the International Community: A Legal Assessment*, Kluwer Law International, 2002; Berhard Knoll, *The Legal Status of Territories Subject to Administration by International Organizations*, New York: Cambridge University Press, 2008; Stahn, *supra* n. 3.

5 See UNSC Resolution 1244, adopted on 10 June 1999.

6 Emergency phase (1999–2000), the capacity building (2000–2005) and the phase that involved the transfer of competencies (2005–2008). For more information about the UNMIK's presence on the ground see, www.un.org/en/peacekeeping/missions/unmik/background.shtml.

7 Wendy S. Betts, Scot Carlson, and Gregory Giswold, The Post Conflict Transitional Administration in Kosovo and the Lessons Learned in Efforts to Establish a Judiciary and Rule of

although a new practice, today's ITAs should be seen not as a UN invention but rather as an endeavour that has existed for centuries, self-styled in accordance with the political demands of a particular situation.[8]

Ralph Wilde, a leading authority in the field of international territorial administration, for example, looks at the ITA concept through a so-called colonial comparator. He concludes that today's ITA activities include certain elements of colonial administration which, according to him, appear to be exercised in a different way, often called neo-trusteeship or postmodern imperialism.[9] Wilde argues that colonial administration should be viewed as a predecessor of international territorial administration, a shadow that continues to follow the creation and functioning of many international administrations today.[10] This opinion suggests that the origin of international territorial administration can be traced back to the period of colonialism, when the European powers asserted the right to civilise and exploit the territories of less advanced societies, justified as a duty of civilised nations to assist and protect people who had not yet reached the same level of development.[11]

Wilde suggests looking at the common characteristics of the establishment of ITA missions, such as the legitimacy of their policy institutions, legal authority, scope of activity and applicable law, and the identity of the actor, as according to him in many ways they resemble the colonial practice of administering territories.[12] In support, he points to the general control exercised by the colonial powers over local structures, which amounted to intrusive and extensive

---

Law, *Michigan Journal of International Law*, Vol. 22, 2001, p. 372; Michael Bothe and Thilo Marauhn, UN Administration in Kosovo and East Timor, Concept, Legality, and Limitations of Security Council-Mandated Trusteeship Administration, in Tomuschat (ed.), *Kosovo and the International Community: A Legal Assessment*, Kluwer Law International, 2002, p. 217, See also Berhard Knoll, *The Legal Status of Territories Subject to Administration by International Organizations*, New York: Cambridge University Press, 2008; Eric De Brabandere, *Post-Conflict Administrations in International Law*, Martinus Nijhof Publishers, 2009; Carstein Stahn, *The Law and Practice of International Territorial Administration*, Cambridge University Press, 2008.

8 Wilde, supra n. 4, Meir Ydit, *Internationalized Territories from the "Free City of Cracow" to the "Free City of Berlin"*, A.W. Sythoff, Leiden, 1961, p. 19.

9 Wilde, *supra* n. 4.

10 Ibid.

11 It has been widely claimed that due to their higher degree of civilisation, the civilised nations have a duty to protect the population from anarchy, bloodshed, and tyranny. Nele Matz, Civilization and the Mandate System under the League of Nations as Origin of Trusteeship, *Max Plank Yearbook of United Nations Law*, Vol. 9, 2005, p. 60, referring to British rule in India. See Henry H. Perritt, Structures and Standards for Political Trusteeship, *Journal of the International Law and Foreign Affairs*, Vol. 8, 2003, p. 391. For example, according to Anghie, Britain claimed that its venture was directed towards developing self-government in the colonies, but many scholars remained sceptical about this claim. Antony Anghie, Colonialism and Birth of International Institutions: Sovereignty, Economy, and the Mandate System of the League of Nations, *International Law and Politics*, Vol. 34, No. 513, December 2002, p. 554. See also Peter Malanczuk, *Akehurst's Modern Introduction to international Law*, Seventh Edition, Routledge, 1997, pp. 12–14.

12 Wilde, *supra* n. 4, pp. 442–447.

administrative conduct. The local structures were fully subordinated to the colonial authority through the appointment and removal of their officials, a common characteristic present in all UN missions.[13]

On the other hand, there are authors who argue that colonial-style behaviours are not only characteristic of UN missions, but are also a common characteristic of each international intervention, be it exercised by the UN, the European Union (EU) or any other international organisation.[14] For instance, Berman considers that the evolution of the international organisations demonstrates "the ability of the colonial imagination to reinvent itself under changing conditions".[15] Similarly, Paris argues that today's "peace-building resembles an updated version of the *mission civilisatrice*".[16] Verdirame takes a milder view; for him, "the UN administration constitutes a form of foreign rule, albeit outwardly benign rather than colonial".[17]

In addition, Chandler sees the establishment of ITA as a form of UN protectorate, which according to him is used as a tool for teaching or imposing democracy "on the basis that some cultures are not 'rational' or 'civil' enough to govern themselves". According to him, the divisive moral framework of the nineteenth century White Man's Burden has reappeared again, albeit recast in a liberal language of ethical foreign policy, protection of rights and civil society.[18]

13 Ibid., pp. 302–304.

14 See Michael Parenti, *To Kill a Nation, the Attack on Yugoslavia*, Verso, 2000, pp. 51–57; Bosnia David Chandler, *Faking Democracy after Dayton*, Second Edition, Pluto Press, 2000, pp. 1–4. Both authors refer to the international presence in Bosnia. Similarly, Jarat Chopra describes the UN endeavour in East Timor, stating: "comparisons with colonial administrations were unavoidable, and affirmed by various forms of segregation between expatriates and the Timorese". See Jarat Chopra, The UN's Kingdom of East Timor, *Survival*, Vol. 42. No 2, Autumn 2000; The International Institute for Strategic Studies. See also by the same author, Building State Failure in East Timor, *Development and Change*, Vol. 33, No. 5.

15 Nathaniel Berman, In the Wake of Empire, *The Grotius Lecture Series, American University International Law, Review*, Vol. 14, No. 6, p. 1531.

16 Roland Paris, International Peacebuilding and "Mission Civilisatrice", *Review of International Studies*, Vol. 28, 2002, p. 637. See also Roland Paris, *At War's Ends, Building Peace after Civil Conflict*, Cambridge University Press, 2004. Ford and Oppenheim refer to these new UN mission as neotrusteeship/mistrusteeship. See Christian Eric Ford and Ben A. Oppenheim, Neotrusteeship or Mistrusteeship? The "Authority Creep" Dilemma in United Nations Transitional Administration, *Vanderbilt Journal of Transnational Law*, Vol. 41, No. 1, January 2008.

17 Guglielmo Verdirame, *The UN and Human Rights, Who Guards the Guardians*, Cambridge University Press, 2011, p. 241.

18 See Chandler, *supra* n. 14, p. 3. For more about the UN's operation in Kosovo, see from the same author, David Chandler, *From Kosovo to Kabul and Beyond, Human Rights and International Intervention*, London: Pluto Press, 2006. It should be noted that protectorates are a form of administration dating from the colonial and imperial period of international politics. Nowadays, the term protectorate is considered to be pejorative and is no longer in use. However, some of its functions may be found in some international institutions; the common characteristic of all protectorates was the subordination of one party (the protected party) to the other party (the protector). For more about functioning of protectorates, see Michael Riesman, Reflection on State Responsibility for Violations of Explicit, Protectorate,

Similarly, Brooks states that the promotion of the rule of law by international actors amounts to a "fundamentally imperialist enterprise".[19] For Chesterman, a "modern colonial enterprise" has been installed in post-conflict territories.[20]

Yet we must interpret it in a fully integrated way. Let us begin simply by transplanting these arguments into the domain of international law. I put forward a rough sketch of what such views might imply. First, at this point it should be noted that colonial administrations reflect a matter of foreign control that mirrors today's belligerent occupation,[21] whereas an international administration is merely perceived as an administration of territory by a group of foreign states or an international organisation.[22] Given these facts, the only commonalities these two administrations may share involve the same type of activity, the territorial administration.

So in order to assess whether today's ITA involvement reproduces some of the key features of colonial government, it is necessary to sketch out the basic characteristics that accompany colonial administration. First to be noted is that the colonial policy of an earlier period consisted of two parts: colonial government and the colonial economy. Colonial government, which was directed by colonial officials, was mainly involved with the affairs of a colony at both the central and local levels, being responsible for legislation and overseeing the judicial system.[23] The local governments, which were run by traditional leaders (chiefs, kings) of the indigenous people, were allowed little real authority.[24] The local rulers were often engaged in political agreements/treaties allegedly designed to protect the interests of the colonised population, but in reality most of these treaties contained clauses for annexation or cession of territories to the European

---

Mandate and Trusteeship Obligation, *Michigan Journal of International Law*, Vol. 10, No. 231, 1989, pp. 233–244.

19 Rosa E. Brooks, The New Imperialism: Violence, Norms, and the Rule of Law, *Michigan Law Review*, Vol. 101, 2003, p. 2275.

20 Simon Chesterman, *You the People the United Nations, Transitional Administration, and State Building*, Oxford University Press, 2004, p. 47.

21 According to Ferraro an occupation is "a state of peaceful coexistence between the occupant and the local population and insisted on the former involving itself as little as possible in managing the lives of those temporarily under its rule "See Tristan Ferraro, *Occupation and Other Forms of Administration of Foreign Territory*, Report, Expert Meeting, International Committee of the Red Cross, p. 4, available at the following website: www.icrc.org/eng/assets/files/publications/icrc-002-4094.pdf.

22 Verdirame, *supra* n. 17, p. 230.

23 Colonialism is very often used synonymously with the term Imperialism. Both are forms of conquest that brought economical benefit to Europe. However, the colonialism refers to the conquests and expansions over other region, involving the great movement of the population to the new territory, establishment of the settlement, whereas imperialism means the creation of the empire, expansion into neighbouring regions, by exercising its power through sovereignty and military control. See, Margaret Kohn, Colonialism, *The Stanford Encyclopedia of Philosophy*, Edward N. Zalta (ed.), Fall 2011 Edition, available at: http://plato.stanford.edu/entries/colonialism/, See also, Anghie, *supra* n. 11, p. 513.

24 Colonialism in Africa, *Africa an Encyclopaedia for Students*, Vol. 1, Charles Scribner's Sons, 2002.

powers. Interestingly, all of them were styled as kings in an initial period prior to signing the treaty, implying that they had sovereign rights to sign such treaties pursuant to the validity of the customary international law at that time. Yet once the treaty had been signed, it turned them into subordinates and they were mostly regarded as "chiefs".[25] Moreover, the colonial territories were considered to be no-man's-land, their people were not recognised as societies with a right to self-determination, and they were therefore treated as outside the domain of international law.[26]

Although it is beyond the scope of this research to draw lines of comparison between colonial practice and today's international interventions, this narrow frame of reference will serve as guidance for assessing the specificities of the functioning of the UN administration in Kosovo and for establishing whether it contains any characteristics similar to those of colonial administration.

It is necessary to highlight, however, that without thorough analysis of the UN's functioning in practice it will not be possible to respond to the allegations.

A note on methodology

The methodology used in this study involves combined methods comprising historical, normative and comparative methods, which enable a qualitative assessment of the functioning of the international territorial administration in practice.

As UNMIK has been described as a unique case within the international institution- building regime, I consider that these methods are appropriate since they aim at finding and interpreting its specifics and moreover allow me to explain a problem and the background to it, and most importantly to assess and discuss both shortcomings and achievements. Each legal issue identified in this research is discussed in a concrete case study that examines the problem in depth.

The historical method is used to explain the variety of operations undertaken by the international community for the purpose of finding a temporary solution to internal matters that cannot be solved by states on their own. This method has enabled me to explore the concept of subjecting a territory to foreign power and its historical evolution through various models, and see whether UNMIK's functioning reflects any of the characteristics of its predecessors. It will help us to better understand what purposes international community involvement serves.

While the historical method looks at the roots of the international administration, the comparative method is used to assess the evolutionary account of the institutional appearance of various international involvements, respectively to draw analogies between different examples of international administrations and identify new characteristics that appeared through the process of their evolution.

25 Taslim Olawale Elias, *Africa and the Development of International Law*, Richard Akinjide (ed.), Martinus Nijhof Publisher, 1988, pp. 18–19, See also Brett Bowden, The Colonial Origins of International Law, European Expansion and the Classical Standard of Civilisation, *Journal of International Law*, Vol. 23, 2005. See, also, Mark Duffield and Vernon Hewitt (eds.), *Empire Development and Colonialism, the Present in the Past*, James Currey, 2009.

26 See Matz, *supra* n. 11, p. 58.

It puts emphasis on a similarity that accompanies their legal frameworks, structures and their operations on the ground. This will enable us to identify a central set of elements that accompanies an international administration.

The legal-normative approach is the major method used throughout the research. It traces the legal norms and judgements essential to the functioning of international administrations. In this regard, it has offered the possibility of identifying the shortcomings arising from the legal framework that governs such an endeavour, as well as identifying a correspondence between the existing legal framework and human rights law. It aims at discovering the legal gaps that accompany an instance of human rights violations by an international authority.

The analysis in this study is based on both primary and secondary sources, namely the legal framework that governs UN's activities, UNMIK's laws, case law (both national and international), and various reports (issued by both international and local agencies). Furthermore, it includes first-hand information obtained during my six-year experience of direct supervision of UNMIK's institutions while working as a senior lawyer for the Ombudsperson Institution in Kosovo. As an Ombudsperson's lawyer I was directly involved in processing claims of human rights violations, supervising the functioning of the legislative system, monitoring trials (including war crimes trials), and intervening on behalf of the victims. Thus, this research introduces an observation of how the UN authorities act in practice, namely the phenomenon of the abuse of the power and authority vested in them.

The research question: was UNMIK, as a surrogate state administration, capable of protecting the human rights of the people it governed?

The main research question of this study is whether UNMIK, as a surrogate state administration, was capable of protecting the human rights of the people it governed. A central element of this question pertains to accessing the capacity of the UN administration to perform state-like duties by virtue of being distinct from a state administration. In other words, it addresses the realistic challenges faced by an international administration in performing the entrusted functions. Each chapter carries sets of additional questions that build a path towards answering the main research question.

What Kosovars learned from UNMIK, and what UNMIK learned from Kosovars, will serve as concrete suggestions as to how the deficiencies that occurred during the UNMIK administration could be mitigated in present and future missions.

This study aims at contributing towards reshaping the international discourse regarding the administration of territory by the United Nations. By analysing its actions in practice, it attempts to demonstrate that such an endeavour requires a strict commitment to the rule of law and the protection of fundamental human rights. It argues that the model introduced by UNMIK is inimical to both the international legal framework of human rights and their protection in practice.

The structure

The overall structure of this study is the following:

The Introduction provides an overview of this study. The chapter starts off by presenting the context within which this study was conducted. This is followed by addressing some conceptual issues that are commonly used in the study. The research question that guides this study is briefly outlined. Finally, it offers an overview on the methodology in which the study was conducted.

It then proceeds to explain the historical circumstances that led to the establishment of the international territorial administration of UNMIK, such as the deployment of the verification mission and the violations of basic human rights that paved the way for the NATO air strikes. In addition, it examines the basic features that accompanied the deployment phase of the UNMIK administration. It offers an overall picture of United Nations engagement and to this extent provides a brief overview of the governance bundles under UNMIK and its judicial institutions, including the presence of Serbian parallel structures. In particular, it draws attention to the legal implications arising from UNSC Resolution 1244.

Chapter 1 focuses on analysing the scope of UNMIK'S legislative powers. It examines whether specific rules are enunciated in international law that provide strict limitations on UNMIK's law-making authority. And if so, where do these limits derive from? It explores the extent to which UNMIK is authorised to intervene in the domestic legal system. It also examines whether such legal intervention requires any consent from the original sovereign. Additionally, it looks at the legal nature of the UNMIK legislation.

Chapter 2 discusses the ability of the UN interim administration to construct and administer justice in a post-war setting. In particular, it focuses on assessing the effectiveness and the appropriate role of UNMIK in the process of promoting and establishing an independent judiciary in an internationally governed territory. It offers a brief background note on the theoretical framework behind the notion of judicial independence and impartiality, including the international standards relevant to establishing an independent judicial system. It goes on to discuss structural arrangements in Kosovo that differ in their specific attributes from the governance structures elsewhere. The aim is to discuss the sense in which the principles of judicial independence were employed by the UNMIK administration and to link judicial independence with the separation of powers in the Kosovo context.

Chapter 3 builds on the fourth chapter and enquires into the practice of UNMIK's judiciary. It sheds light on the shortcomings of the UNMIK justice system. It highlights the limitations placed on the judiciary. Particular emphasis is placed on the executive's interference with the course of justice through cases involving the use of executive orders in criminal and civil proceedings. It discusses the legal implications surrounding the impartiality of the international prosecutors and judges. It discusses the functioning of the quasi – judicial bodies established for the purpose of property restitution. Finally, it draws attention to the shortcomings arising from the fragile legislative framework governing these bodies and from their claim processing procedures.

Chapter 4 addresses the extent of UNMIK's mandate on the ground. It examines key issues that posed the greatest challenge to the implementation of UNMIK's mandate. In this context, it explores UNMIK's ability to offer equal protection within given boundaries. It raises the issue of competing jurisdictions, in particular in the northern part of Kosovo, where UNMIK failed to implement its mandate. It offers an overview of the parallel structures and their positions on determining certain civil rights of the population. The last part of this chapter draws attention to the legal implications arising from parallel systems of law and their general impact on the rule of law.

Chapter 5 examines the extent to which international actors have been subjected to ad hoc accountability mechanisms. Particular attention is given to the issues arising from the immunity regime for international organisations in general. In light of that discussion, it explores whether the immunity regime for international actors allows an interim administration to be controlled, and if so to what extent and with what type of control mechanism. It goes on to discuss the human rights mechanisms established by UNMIK, namely the Ombudsperson Institution and the Human Rights Advisory Panel.

The chapter discusses UNMIK's mandate, functioning, shortcomings etc. It explores the legal grounds for establishing an accountability mechanism. In this regard, it questions the existing mechanisms established by UNMIK. It assesses whether the established mechanisms provide an effective means of redress for alleged violations of human rights attributable to UNMIK.

Chapter 6 explores the existing options that provide legal grounds for holding UNMIK accountable for its wrongdoings before international mechanisms. It seeks an answer to whether international actors engaged in the administration of an entity are bound by the existing international human rights standards. In particular, it tries to identify who is responsible for UNMIK's wrongdoings: the United Nations, the SRSG, or a member state. It explores options that may lead towards international organisations being held accountable. It briefly sheds light on the responsibility of military troops and in this context, seeks an answer as to who should be responsible for the wrongdoings of military personnel, whether this be the state sending the troops or NATO.

The general conclusions lay out the findings of the research which give an overall estimation of UNMIK's performance. The chapter highlights both the positive and negative implications of UNMIK's practice. In this context it identifies the legal problems surrounding the implementation of its mandate, as well as providing recommendations for improvement of the legal framework for future international administrations.

The role of UNMIK in a post-war Kosovo

Since June 1999, the territory of Kosovo has been under the interim administration of the United Nations Mission in Kosovo (UNMIK), which engaged in the complex task of post-conflict peacebuilding. Established pursuant to Security Council Resolution 1244, UNMIK was empowered temporarily to exercise complete sovereignty over the territory of Kosovo, including performing basic civil administration functions, overseeing the development of provisional institutions for democratic and autonomous self-government (pending a political settlement), and protecting and promoting human rights.

The Special Representative of the Secretary General (SRSG) was entrusted with absolute legislative, executive, and judicial power over the administering entity, and as such enjoyed the maximum of civilian executive powers envisaged in UNSC Resolution 1244.

In light of the foregoing information, this chapter aims at highlighting the most important elements in the initial phase of the establishment and consolidation of UNMIK's administration. It offers an overall illustration of UN engagement and to this extent provides a brief overview of the various bodies established within the Joint Interim Administrative Structures (JIAS).

The UNMIK's mandate in Kosovo (UNSC Resolution 1244): general overview

The UNMIK administration was established on 10 June 1999, pursuant to Security Council Resolution 1244 invoking Chapter VII of the UN Charter. Accordingly, it was empowered to temporarily exercise complete sovereignty over the territory of Kosovo after the withdrawal of the FRY forces.[27]

The major tasks of UNMIK included promoting the establishment of substantial autonomy and self-government in Kosovo (pending a final settlement);[28] to perform basic civilian administrative functions as long as needed; to organise and oversee the development of provisional institutions for democratic and autonomous self-government pending a political settlement, including the holding of elections; to transfer its administrative responsibilities to the newly established institutions while overseeing and supporting the consolidation of those institutions; to facilitate a political process designed to determine Kosovo's future status;[29] to supervise the transfer of authority in a final stage from Kosovo's provisional institutions to institutions established under a political settlement; to support the reconstruction of key infrastructure and other economic reconstruction; to support humanitarian and disaster relief aid; together with international humanitarian organisations, to maintain civil law and order, including establishing local police forces; to protect and promote human rights; and to assure the safe and unimpeded return of all refugees and displaced persons.[30]

27 The FRY government had set up a so-called Committee for Cooperation established pursuant to UNSC Resolution 1244, Annex 6, para. 2, which was in charge in liaising with the international presence.

28 Taking full account of annex 2 of UNSC Resolution 1244 and the Rambouillet accords (S1999:648). About the implementation of Resolution 1244 see Sean D. Murphy, Reflection on ICJ Opinion on Kosovo, Interpreting Security Council Resolution 1244, in Michael Wood and Marko Milanovic (eds.), *The Law and Politics of the Kosovo Advisory Opinion*, Oxford University Press, Forthcoming, December 2014.

29 In accordance with the Rambouillet accords (S/1999/648).

30 UNSCR Resolution 1244, para. 11.

In addition to the civilian presence, the Resolution authorised the deployment of a military presence, the Kosovo Force (KFOR), which was responsible for maintaining and enforcing the ceasefire; for ensuring the withdrawal and preventing the return of Serbian forces, except for those allowed to return;[31] for demilitarising the Kosovo Liberation Army and other armed Kosovo-Albanian groups;[32] for liaising with the international presences; for supervising demining until the international civil presence was ready to take over those responsibilities; for establishing a secure environment for refugees and internally displaced to return in safety, for the international civil presence to operate and for humanitarian aid to be delivered; for ensuring public safety; for supporting and coordinating with the international civilian presence; for conducting border monitoring duties; and for ensuring the protection and freedom of movement of international organisations.[33]

The overall implementation of UNMIK's mandate was concentrated in the hands of the SRSG, who was vested with the power to control "the implementation of the international civil presence".[34] Additionally, the SRSG retained the final authority to interpret the Resolution.[35]

Until 2005, the overall implementation of UNMIK's mandate was concentrated in the hands of the SRSG, who was vested with the power to control "the implementation of the international civil presence".[36] Additionally, the SRSG retained the final authority to interpret the Resolution. Pillar I was in charge of Police and Justice and Pillar II of Civil Administration, both under the direct leadership of the SRSG, who represented the UN in Kosovo. Pillar III was responsible for Democratisation and Institution Building and was led by the OSCE; Pillar IV, led by the EU, was in charge of Reconstruction and Economic Development. Each pillar was placed under the direct supervision of the SRSG.[37]

31 Provided in point 6 of the Annex 2 of the UNSC Resolution 1244.

32 Pursuant to paragraph 15 of the UNSR Resolution 1244.

33 See UNSC Resolution 1244, para. 9.

34 UNSC Resolution 1244, para. 6.

35 UNMIK Regulation 2001/19 on the Executive Branch of the Provisional Institutions of Self Government in Kosovo, enacted on 13 September 2001.

36 UNSC Resolution 1244, para. 6.

37 In the first two years of UNMIK's operation (1999 to 2001), Pillar I was led by UNHCR, which was entrusted with humanitarian assistance. In 2000, Pillar I became responsible for rule of law functions. See UNMIK Police, *Saint Group, CIVPOL Language and Culture*, available at the following website: www.saint-claire.org/resources/UNMIK%20Police.pdf. From 2005, UNMIK started gradually to downsize its structures. Pursuant to UNMIK Regulation 2001/9 on the Constitutional Framework for Provisional Self-Government in Kosovo (15 May 2001), a number of competencies were transferred to local government institutions during the period 2005–2007. However, some major responsibilities remained in the hands of the SRSG until 2008. Those "reserved powers and responsibilities" included: "Exercising powers and responsibilities of an international nature in the legal field; Exercising authority over law enforcement institutions and the correctional service; Concluding agreements with states and international organizations in all matters within the scope of UNSCR1244 (1999); and External relations, including with states and international organizations, as may be necessary for the implementation of [the SRSG's] mandate". The third Pillar of UNMIK, the Organization for Security and Cooperation in Europe (OSCE) and

In light of this, Resolution 1244 empowered UNMIK to exercise public authority over the mandated territory and intervene in its politics, economy and legislation, as well as represent the territory outside its boundaries.[38] By becoming a state actor, UNMIK was empowered to enact laws, conduct judicial and law enforcement reforms, support civil society and establish transitional justice mechanisms aimed at creating a democratic system and strengthening the rule of law.

Acting as an "agent of necessity", UNMIK was entitled to enter into international treaties without being a state and as such to be subject to the rules arising from a particular treaty.[39] In this regard, numerous agreements were signed with international organisations involving police protection, investment, project finance, and extradition on behalf of the Provisional Institutions of Self-Government of Kosovo.[40] By carrying out such functions, UNMIK created rights and obligations for the Kosovo Provisional Institutions.[41]

Looking at UNMIK's mandate as a whole, it becomes clear that the main political objective for UNMIK was to promote the establishment "of substantial autonomy and self-government".[42] In this context, it took responsibility for establishing as well as overseeing the consolidation of the provisional institutions for democratic and autonomous self-government.

Subsequently, the SRSG was given far-reaching powers. His role amounted not just to exerting pressure on the local government but also in many instances to acting as the ruler.[43]

---

the Kosovo Force (KFOR), continue to perform their roles within the framework of UNSC Resolution 1244. See UNMIK report S/2012/603, issued on 3 August 2012.

38 UNMIK Regulation 2001/9, enacted pursuant to UNSC Resolution 1244.

39 On June 2005, the Legal Office of UNMIK sent a memo to Kosovo Prime Minister Bajram Kosumi explaining the multilateral strategy to expand Kosovo's subjectivity in international law. In its pertinent parts it states: "UNMIK represents the territory vis a vis the outside world, having assumed 'agency of necessity' in external relations". See Knoll, *supra* n. 4, p. 231.

40 On 9 September 2002, a Memorandum of Understanding on Police Cooperation was signed with Albania. Special Report, EU Monitoring Mission, Police Cooperation between Albania and UNMIK/Kosovo, CFSP/SEC/2110/02, 20 September 2002. On 7 April 2006, an Investment Protection Agreement was reached with Turkey. See Knoll, *supra* n. 50, p. 219.

41 Memo addressed to Kosovo Prime Minister Bajram Kosumi, Knoll, *supra* n. 4, p. 231.

42 UNSC Resolution 1244, para. 11 (a, c and d). Yet the meaning of this wording reflects an abstract legal dimension. As a result of this abstractedness, UNMIK was faced with a range of challenges that created significant difficulties for the implementation of its mandate on the ground. See Simon Chesterman, *You the People The United Nations, Transitional Administration, and State Building*, Oxford University Press, 2004, p. 131. However, seeking an antidote that would bring light to this confusion, Bernhard Knoll tries to establish a clear-cut distinction between these two wordings. He opines that while the very term autonomy "lacks fixed meaning in international law" and "substantive autonomy" may only connote an initial stage of democratic development, the notion of "self-government" has earned a clear legal meaning which implies "a collective entitlement to a higher level of self-responsibility within a larger political system", Knoll, *supra* n. 4.

43 According to Jarat Chopra, the SRSG's powers resemble those of "a preconstitutional monarch in a sovereign kingdom". See Jarat Chopra, The UN's Kingdom of East Timor, *Survival*, Vol. 42. No 2, Autumn 2000, The International Institute for Strategic Studies, p. 28.

The legal implications of UNSC Resolution 1244

Although perceived as absolute, sovereign powers can be limited in some particular cases. For instance, by being subject to an agreement between states in which sovereign powers are expressly conferred on another state for a limited period of time.[44] Moreover they can be formally removed from the previous sovereign and temporarily placed in the hands of an international organisation, as occurred in the past where the League of Nations played an important role in the process of transforming colonial territories into independent states. And recently, through the UN where sovereign rights were attained through Security Council resolutions, as the experience of Kosovo prominently demonstrates.[45]

In this regard, UNSC Resolution 1244 suspended the sovereign rights of the previous sovereign and consequently empowered an international administration to fully exercise sovereign rights over an entity and be fully charged with physically controlling the entire area.[46] Accordingly, the original sovereign was legally replaced by the temporary sovereign, which established new patterns of legal relations with the governed territory and its population.[47]

In light of this, the FRY[48] authorities cannot be held accountable for human rights violations committed on the territory of Kosovo as they no longer exercise jurisdiction over this territory within the meaning of Article 1 of the European Convention on Human Rights (ECHR).[49] In this context, the Resolution reconciles two conflicting objectives, namely the realisation of meaningful self-government supervised by the fiduciary powers of an international territorial administration and secondly, the preservation of the sovereign rights of the original sovereign, in this case FRY, which were secured by the Resolution itself.[50]

44 Examples include the lease of Kwang-Chou-Wan to France, the lease of Wei Hai-Wei to England, the Bay of Kiao to Germany and Port Arthur to Russia. See Daniel Sven Smyrek, *Internationally Administered Territories-International Protectorates*, Duncker and Humblot, 2006, pp. 42–43.

45 As well the case of UNTAET in East Timor, established pursuant to UNSC Resolution 1272 passed on 25 October 1999.

46 For more about the concept of "suspended sovereignty", see Alexandro Yannis, The Concept of Suspended Sovereignty, *European Journal of International Law*, Vol. 13, No 5. See also Christian Tomushat, Yugoslavia Damaged Sovereignty over the Province of Kosovo, in Gerard Kreijen, Marcel Brus, Jorris Duursma, Elizabeth De Vos and John Dugard (eds.), *State, Sovereignty, and International Governance*, Oxford University Press, 2002.

47 Yannis, ibid., p. 1039.

48 On 27 April 1992, Serbia and Montenegro established the Federal Republic of Yugoslavia (FRY) under a new constitution. On 4 February 2003, the FRY ceased to exist and was succeeded by a new state called simply Serbia and Montenegro. After the proclamation of Montenegro's independence on 21 May 2006, Serbia was obliged to proclaim its independence officially on 5 June 2006 as the successor state to the State Union of Serbia and Montenegro. However, Serbia was assumed to be the legal successor of the dissolved/divorced state.

49 Article 1 ECHR stipulates that "[t]he High Contracting party shall secure everyone within their jurisdiction the rights and freedoms defined in Section I of this Convention".

50 "Reaffirming the commitment of all Member States to the sovereignty and territorial integrity of the Federal Republic of Yugoslavia and the other States of the region, as set out in the

UNSC Resolution 1244 contains a range of ambiguous and contradictory provisions, which made it difficult for UNMIK to develop a clear modus operandi.

Beside a fundamental ambiguity regarding the preservation of the sovereignty of the original sovereign, a particular point in question arising from the Resolution is the sweeping and ambiguous authority vested in the hands of the SRSG. The ambiguity of the Resolution became evident in relation to the final status of Kosovo. The Resolution lays down the commitment of the international community to establishing "a substantial self-government for Kosovo, taking full account of the Rambouillet accords and the principles of sovereignty and territorial integrity of the Federal Republic of Yugoslavia",[51] thus failing to mention the eventual possibility of the territory acquiring independence.

Subsequently, the issue of the final political status and the termination of UNMIK's mandate became unidirectional, due to a sharp division between two parties who are in conflict.[52]

In addition, the Resolution did not clearly articulate the extent and limitations of the international administrator's authority. As a result, the SRSG, as the highest authority in Kosovo, was self-vested with enormous powers, turning the entire operation into a highly centralised administration.[53]

Designing the provisional institutions of Kosovo: the governance bundles under UNMIK

In the early days of the KFOR deployment, looting and violence, followed by both common and inter-ethnic crimes, were widespread and as such represented the greatest threat to public order and the welfare of the local population. Both public and private properties were looted. Though KFOR had the responsibility to maintain law and order until the civilian presence was established, it failed to act. Indeed, in some instances, KFOR forces reportedly refused to assist when both private houses and public enterprises/factories were plundered.[54]

The security situation did not improve even after the arrival of the international police force.[55] It was only in October 2000, when the first-ever free election was held, that the UN police succeeded in asserting a modicum of control.[56]

Helsinki Final Act and annex 2". See UNSC Resolution 1244. For an in-depth interpretation of the legal implications surrounding the sovereignty of the FRY in Kosovo, see Knoll, *supra* n. 4, pp. 98–99.

51 UNSC Resolution 1244. Annex 1.

52 The Albanian community requested independence, whereas the Serbian Government insisted on preserving its territorial sovereignty as guaranteed by UNSC Resolution 1244. Consequently, the implementation of UNMIK's mandate required the establishment of parameters that reconciled the demands of two parties, Albania and Serbia.

53 Regulation 1999/1 issued pursuant to para. 6 of Resolution 1244.

54 For an overview of the situation in the early days of post-war Kosovo, see International Crises Group's Balkan Report, *Starting from Scratch in Kosovo*, No. 83, 13 December 1999, p. 12.

55 Named by the local population as "coca cola" police, as their vehicles were painted in a distinctive red-and-white colour which resembled the colour of the Coca Cola drink can.

56 See International Crises Group's Balkan Report, *supra* n. 54, p. 4.

In this regard, one cannot fail to note that UNMIK was not prepared, nor was it capable of fully deploying its operation at a speed that would have enabled it to respond quickly to the situation on the ground.[57] The shortfalls that occurred during the deployment period caused irreparable damage to the political process. The power vacuum was used by Serbian extremists, the followers of the Milosevic regime, to establish parallel structures in the northern part of Kosova and to oppose the deployment of UNMIK's structures on the ground.[58]

The situation remains the same even today: neither UNMIK nor its successor European Union Rule of Law Mission (EULEX) succeeded in becoming fully operational in this area.

Throughout the political and institution-building chain of responsibilities, the SRSG was vested with the authority to establish a system of government in Kosovo and to obtain the means to enable this administered entity to carry out its state-like functions.

In this regard, within the framework of its executive competencies the SRSG was empowered with the role of designing and overseeing the development of the provisional institutions, pursuant to UNSC Resolution 1244, in order to establish a normal way of life for all inhabitants in the administered territory of Kosovo.[59]

At the departure of the Serbian forces, no formal political structures existed in Kosovo and the establishment of the executive branch (central and municipal), which involved the creation of effective and sustainable institutions, became the main goal of UNMIK's administration.

Pursuant to its mandate, a range of institutional structures were established, which functioned in tandem with the international actors.[60] The first stage of the institution building comprised the Kosovo Transitional Council (KTC), which was in charge of dealing with political matters,[61] and the Joint Advisory Council for Legislative Matters (JACLM), an advisory body empowered to deal

57 It should be stressed that persuading a society that had suffered deeply at the hands of state institutions and the law itself to buy into rule of law principles proved not to be a simple task. See Jane Stromseth, Post Conflict Rule of Law Building, Need for a Multi-Layered, Synergic Approach, *William and Mary Law Review*, Vol. 49, No. 4, 2008, p. 1443.

58 It was foreseen by UNSC Resolution 1244 that an agreed number of Yugoslav and Serbian personnel would be permitted to return to perform the following functions: Liaison with the international civil mission and the international security presence; Marking/clearing minefields; Maintaining a presence at Serb patrimonial sites; Maintaining a presence at key border crossings. See UNSC Resolution 1244, para. 4.

59 See UNSC Resolution 1244, para. 10, 11, (a, b).

60 Marcus Brand calls it improvised joint governance. See Marcus Brand, *The Development of Kosovo Institutions and the Transition of Authority from UNMIK to Local Self Government, Cluster of Competence, the Rehabilitation of Warn Torn Societies*, Centre for Applied Studies in International Negotiations, (CASIN), 2003, p. 6.

61 The highest consultative body of the JIAS, which acted as a sort of precursor to the Kosovo parliament. See Daniel Sven Smyrek, *Internationally Administered Territories-International Protectorates?*, Duncker and Humbolt, 2005, p. 191.

with legislative matters.[62] A few months later, in January 2000, the Joint Interim Administrative Structure (JIAS) was established, comprising both international and local actors. The highest body of the JIAS was the Interim Administrative Council (IAC), which acted as the executive board of the JIAS.[63] It consisted of the following members: the SRSG, as the supreme authority, the Heads of UNMIK Pillars, the KFOR Commander (COMKFOR) and representatives of the largest political parties at that time, Lidhja Democratike e Kosovës (LDK), Partia Demokratike e Kosovës (PDK), Aleanca për Ardhmërinë e Kosovës (AAK), Lëvizja e Bashkuar Demokratike) (LBD),[64] including representatives of the minority groups.[65]

The IAC was entrusted with the responsibility of designing policies for institutions as well as issuing recommendations to the SRSG for the enactment of new laws.[66]

The JIAS itself comprised a range of different administrative departments, which were later placed under the Council of Ministers. Though it had a mixed composition, the international actors' influence prevailed, which strengthened the executive power of the SRSG, who through his subordinates exercised absolute control over the executive institutions.[67]

Following the first local elections organised in 2000 and October 2002, municipal assemblies and municipal administrations were created.[68]

With the promulgation of the Constitutional Framework on 15 of May 2001, both the JIAC and the IAC were replaced by the Provisional Institutions of Self-Government (PISG), which comprised the Kosovo Assembly, the Kosovo Government, and the President.[69]

In 2001, the SRSG enacted an additional Regulation (Regulation 2001/19), which concerned the executive branches of the PISG, their structures and functions.[70] It consisted of the Prime Minister, ministries (the government), different executive agencies operating within ministries, and the civil service.[71] However, the SRSG retained the authority to assign international personnel to the ministries and executive agencies if deemed necessary.[72]

62 An in-depth description of the political institutions in the initial phase, as well as the subsequent establishment, is given by Blerim Reka, *UNMIK as an International Governance in Post-War Kosovo: NATOs Intervention, UN Administration and Kosovar Inspirations*, Shkup: Logos, 2003, See also Richard Caplan, *International Governance of War Torn Territories*, Oxford University Press, 2005, pp. 18–19.
63 Smyrek, *supra* n. 61, p. 191.
64 Leading political parties in Kosovo.
65 Reka, *supra* n. 62, p. 219.
66 Smyrek, *supra* n. 61, p. 191.
67 Reka, *supra* n. 62, p. 219.
68 For more about the establishment of local structures, see Seth G. Jones, Jeremy M. Wilson, Andrew Rathmell, and K. Jack Rilley, *Establishing Law and Order after Conflict*, Rand 2005, pp. 27–42.
69 Smyrek, *supra* n. 61, pp. 193–195.
70 UNMIK Regulation 2001/19, enacted on 13 September 2001.
71 Ibid.
72 Section 6 UNMIK Regulation 2001/19.

With the promulgation of the Constitutional Framework on 15 May 2001,[73] alongside local municipal authorities the major municipalities in Kosovo were run jointly with the international regional administrators, who were appointed by the SRSG[74] and enjoyed considerable discretion to supervise and control the functions entrusted to public services and local authorities and, in some cases, even to discharge those local authorities from their functions.[75]

It should be stressed that although it was assumed that there would be a joint exercise of executive functions, the SRSG administrators retained absolute power to perform many tasks of administration.[76] The local municipal authorities remained subordinated to them and were required to seek their prior approval for specific decisions or initiatives.[77] Consequently, the international administrators retained the authority to override any decision of the local municipal officials if taken independently.[78]

On the other side, the Serbian state established its own structures in the areas inhabited by the Serb minority, alleging that, based on UNSC Resolution 1244, it was entitled to carry out certain state functions.[79] In this regard, a range of parallel structures was established, including in public administration, security, the judiciary, and educational and health institutions. Interestingly, in some cases they operated even under the same roof as the PISG structures.[80]

The task of establishing the law enforcement unit was given to the Third Pillar of UNMIK, OSCE, which was assigned overall responsibility for creating a police force, the Kosovo Police Service (KPS).[81]

73 Promulgated on 15 May 2001 by UNMIK Regulation 2001/09.

74 In total, five Regional Administrators, each in charge of a region (Prishtine/Pristina, Peje/Pec, Gjilan/Gjilane Prizren and Mitrovice/Mitrovica). On 26 July, provisional local municipalities were established, making 27 communal "authorities" in total. At the same time, UNMIK established its own structure, comprising regional administrators, which became operational in October 1999. By that time the UNMIK presence was growing and becoming more assertive. Local representatives repeatedly stated that they would not accept being subordinated to the UNMIK administrators. After the first election, organised in November, new municipal mayors were elected. Yet they continue to co-govern with UNMIK's regional administrators until the declaration of Kosovo independence on 17 February 2008. For more about local administration in Kosovo, see International Crisis Group, *Waiting for UNMIK: Local Administration in Kosovo*, Balkans Report, No. 79, 1999.

75 Pursuant to UNMIK Regulation 1999/14, enacted on 21 October 1999, Section 2(1).

76 Issued not in accordance with UNSC Resolution 1244.

77 Pursuant to UNMIK Regulation 1999/14, enacted on 21 October 1999.

78 Ibid.

79 The FRY government has continued to claim that UNSC Resolution 1244 allows them to carry out certain public functions in Kosovo. Several letters were exchanged between the FRY government and the SRSG. Despite the fact that the claim is considered to be a violation of UNSC Resolution 1244, the FRY authorities have established their parallel structures in Serbian enclaves. For more about this, see Bernhard Knoll, pp. 184–186.

80 Organization for Security and Cooperation in Europe (OSCE), Mission in Kosovo, Department for Human Rights, Decentralization and Communities, *Parallel Structure in Kosovo*, Report, January 2007, p. 1.

81 Both the Constitutional Framework and UNMIK Regulation 2001/9 excluded the local authorities from exercising responsibilities regarding the development of the security

Initially, the enforcement unit comprised both the UNMIK police called CIVPOL and the NATO operational force KFOR. Later on, KFOR decided to withdraw gradually and the overall policing authority was transferred to the regional commands of the UNMIK Police. It numbered around 4,000 international police officers, who operated under the command of the Police Commissioner. The Police Commissioner was directly responsible to the SRSG. In addition, in the northern part of Kosovo, the FRY authorities established their own policing authority comprising so-called "bridge watchers" and police of the Serbian Ministry of Interior Affairs (MUP).

The UNMIK Police were tasked with patrolling and maintaining public order, investigating crimes, taking preventative measures, training local police to collect criminal intelligence, and performing border, immigration and traffic control.[82]

It was the first time that an international law enforcement force was given the power to arrest and detain individuals and to use firearms.[83] Throughout its existence, the UNMIK CIVPOL remained the primary policing authority in Kosovo, exercising a supervisory role over the local police unit, the KPC.

Accordingly, an oversight body for the KPS was established, the Police Inspectorate of Kosovo (PIK).[84] PIK was regarded as an independent civilian oversight mechanism that aimed at ensuring accountability and transparency within the KPS. It was assigned the task of investigating all allegations of serious misconduct by KPS officers of all ranks.[85]

To sum up, the law enforcement forces comprised the UNMIK Police, the Kosovo Police Service and the parallel (illegal) security force from Serbia, the so-called "bridge watchers" and the Serbian police (MUP).

However it should be stressed that whereas the PISG structures were operating under the absolute authority of UNMIK,[86] the Serbian parallel structures were directly subordinated to the Serbian government.

Judicial structures

The situation encountered by UNMIK in June 1999 was devastating. During the armed conflict, the majority of Kosovo's population had been expelled by the Serbian forces and lived in refugee camps, mainly in the neighbouring countries

---

infrastructure and this task was carried out exclusively by the international authorities under so-called reserved powers.

82 Additional information on the UNMIK police can be obtained from the UNMIK CIVPOL website: www.unmikonline.org/civpol/mandate.htm.

83 Caplan, *supra* n. 62, p. 51.

84 Established under UNMIK Regulation No. 2005/54, *On the Framework and the Guiding Principles of the Kosovo Police Service and Administrative Direction 2006/9 Implementing UNMIK Regulation No. 2005/54 On the Framework and the Guiding Principles of the Kosovo Police Service.*

85 Police Inspectorate of Kosovo, *Second Annual Report*, available at the following website: www.mpb-ks.org/repository/docs/Annual_Report_2007_Eng_Final.pdf.

86 UNMIK Pillar 1 Police and Justice.

of the region. However, shortly after the arrival of the KFOR troops the population started to return to their abandoned, burned, and looted homes, mainly in a spontaneous manner. Nothing was functioning. The previous law enforcement officials and judicial organs left the country and withdrew to Serbia proper. They took a large number of the court files with them, such as Kosovan cadastral records of title to land, court files, official court seals and stamps, records of births, deaths, marriages and divorces, and set up parallel courts in several towns in Serbia, each claiming to have the same competencies as they used to have prior to the NATO bombing.[87]

Violence, killings, the abduction of non-Albanians and alleged collaborators, looting, arson and usurpation of apartments belonging to Serbs became daily phenomena.[88] This emergency situation made it imperative for UNMIK to take urgent action towards establishing an emergency judicial system.

So judicial organisation was one of the key issues included in UNMIK's dynamic agenda. It therefore focused immediately on deploying strategies to change the legal and political legacies embedded in the nondemocratic institutions of a totalitarian regime. To this extent, it established a legal framework, adopted different institutional settings, established a police force, and conducted education and training of both judicial and law enforcement officials. The reconstruction was conducted with the active participation of various regional organisations and the technical assistance of the international community.[89]

The first action taken in this regard was to identify Albanian judges and law enforcement officials who had served before 1999.[90] On 28 June 1999, the SRSG issued a decree establishing the Joint Advisory Council on Provisional Judicial Appointment (JAC), whose mandate was to recommend the provisional appointment of judges and public prosecutors to serve for a three-month tenure.[91]

Provisional district courts and public prosecutor offices were set up in Prishtina, Prizren, Mitrovicë and Pejë. In addition, mobile units were established which

87 David Marshall and Shelly Inglis, The Disempowerment of Human Rights-Based Justice in the United Nations Missions in Kosovo, *Harvard Human Rights Journal*, Vol. 16, 2003, p. 101.

88 William O'Neil, *Kosovo: An Unfinished Peace*, Boulder, CO: Lynne Reinner Publisher, 2002, p. 75. O'Neil served as a human rights adviser to the SRSG. He argues that in order to avoid such a situation UNMIK should have declared martial law, "with carefully circumscribed limitations on certain human rights as permitted under international law".

89 The Organization for Security and Cooperation in Europe (OSCE) is directly involved in helping to re-establish the judicial system in Kosovo. For more details about OSCE activities in Kosovo, see the OSCE website: www.osce.org/kosovo/mandate.

90 Most Albanian judges who served before 1989 got their judicial position back after the arrival of UNMIK. However, those that had worked in the Serb-dominated judiciary during 1989–1999 were perceived as traitors and as such could not apply for a judicial position. For additional information, see O'Neil, *supra* n. 88, p. 75.

91 To this extent, 55 judges were appointed, among them 42 Albanians, seven Serbs, four Muslims, one Turk and one Roma. However, on the request of the Serbian Government soon after, the seven Serbian judges resigned and fled to Serbia proper. OSCE LSMS Report, *The System of Kosovar Judiciary*, July 2000, p. 11.

operated out of the Prishtina District Court to cover the areas where no courts were functioning.[92]

On 7 September 1999, two new regulations were promulgated to set up a regular judicial system, Regulation 1999/6 "On Recommendation for the Structure and Registration of the Judiciary and Prosecution Service" and Regulation 1999/7 "On Appointment and Removal from Office of Judges and Prosecutors". Subsequently, the Advisory Judicial Commission (AJC)[93] was established with the mandate to recommend candidates for judicial and prosecutorial appointments on a permanent basis; to recommend disciplinary measures, including the removal of judges and public prosecutors; and to investigate allegations of judicial misconduct by judges and make recommendations to the SRSG.[94] The AJC was later replaced by the Kosovo Judicial and Prosecutorial Council (KJPC), a mixed body composed of nine members, mainly internationals.[95]

By the end of December 1999, the AJC had selected 301 professional judges, public prosecutors and lay judges.[96] The majority of these newly appointed judges and public prosecutors lacked professional expertise and experience[97] due to the consequences of having been barred from practising law for ten years.[98] In addition, being trained in the "old communist school" they lacked working knowledge of basic human rights law and rule of law principles.

Soon after, a new Regulation 2000/15 was proclaimed establishing the Department of Justice, an administrative body responsible for the administration of justice.[99] Its mandate was to build a multi-ethnic, independent, impartial, and efficient judicial system. In addition, it was responsible for administering the correctional system, dealing with the issues of persons that went missing during the armed conflict in Kosovo, providing training for judges and prosecutors, etc.

The Department established a four-tier judicial system. One tier consisted of five district courts with the competence to adjudicate criminal cases that carried a sentence of more than five years' imprisonment, major property disputes, copyright disputes and patent disputes, as well as to hear appeals from the decisions of the municipal courts. A second tier comprised seventeen municipal courts with the competence to adjudicate on criminal cases that carry a sentence

92 See OSCE LSMS Report, *The System of Kosovar Judiciary*, July 2000, p. 12.

93 The previous body, JAC, ceased its activities on 10 September 1999.

94 UNMIK Regulation 1999/7, promulgated on 7 September 1999.

95 KJPC was established pursuant to UNMIK Regulation 2001/8, promulgated on 6 April 2001.

96 The initial oath-taking ceremonies were held in January 2000. See OSCE LSMS Report, *The System of Kosovar Judiciary*, July 2000, p. 13.

97 O'Neil, *supra* n. 88, p. 75.

98 In 1990, the majority of judges and prosecutors of Albanian ethnicity were forcibly dismissed from their jobs and replaced by judges and prosecutors of Serb ethnicity. For more information, see *Crisis in Yugoslavia, Serbian Prosecutions of Albanians in Kosova*, Albanian American Civic League, 1 July 1991.

99 The Department of Justice functioned under Pillar I, which was in charge of Police and Justice. After the proclamation of independence, its competencies were downsized and transferred to the Ministry of Justice and to the European Union Rule of Law Mission (EULEX).

of up to five years' imprisonment and to serve as courts of first instance for civil inheritance matters, labour relations and other civil matters.[100] In addition, the Department set up nineteen minor offences courts competent to adjudicate criminal cases punishable by a fine or up to two months' imprisonment. Furthermore, a Supreme Court was constituted which served as the highest judicial body, competent to hear appeals from district courts as well as administrative appeals against the Kosovo authorities, such as decisions by ministries and municipalities.[101]

In addition, one of the most interesting novelties of the UN Administration in Kosovo was the establishment of a hybrid court system.[102] The initial intention of the international community to establish the Kosovo War and Ethnic Crimes Court (KWECC), an internationally led, ad hoc tribunal, was abandoned after sets of negotiations between the international community and Kosovan representatives. The idea behind it was to establish KWECC, which was to have concurrent, primary jurisdiction over serious violations of international humanitarian law, including war crimes, genocide, crimes against humanity, and other serious crimes committed on political, ethnic, or religious grounds during the armed conflict in Kosovo, starting from 1 January 1998.[103] However, the whole idea was received with a degree of scepticism by both the domestic and international communities. While the domestic community feared mainly the potential complications of having an additional judicial layer between the domestic system and the International Criminal Tribunal for the Former Yugoslavia, which allegedly would be more likely to initiate criminal investigations against Albanians who had participated in armed conflict, on the other side the international community was mainly concerned about the security of court personnel and the cost of the court.[104]

On 27 May 2000, a hybrid court system option was chosen and systematically introduced,[105] enabling the appointment of international judges and prosecutors

100 It followed the previous model of the judicial system.

101 See Inglis and Marshall, *supra* n. 87, p. 102.

102 The hybrid courts exercise competence over persons who bear responsibility for serious violations of humanitarian law. A similar system was introduced into East Timor (Crimes panels of the District Court of Dili) and Sierra Leone (Court for Sierra Leone).

103 L. Tom Perriello and Marieke Wierda, *Lessons from the Deployment of International Judges and Prosecutors in Kosovo, the International Centre for Transitional Justice*, March 2006, p. 11. See also David Marshall and Shelly Inglis, The Disempowerment of Human Rights: Based Justice in the United Nations Missions in Kosovo, *Harvard Human Rights Journal*, Vol. 16, 2003, p. 95.

104 Tom Perriello and Marieke Wierda, *Lessons from the Deployment of International Judges and Prosecutors in Kosovo, the International Centre for Transitional Justice*, March 2006, p. 12.

105 In accordance with UNMIK Regulation 2000/6 on the Appointment and Removal from the Office of International Judges and International Prosecutors, promulgated on 15 February 2000; Amending UNMIK Regulation 2000/6 on the Appointment and Removal from the Office of International Judges and International Prosecutors, promulgated on 27 May 2000; and UNMIK Regulation 2000/64 on Assignment of International Judges/ Prosecutors and /or Change of Venue, promulgated on 15 December 2000.

to serve in domestic courts in Kosovo.[106] They formed part of the domestic judiciary and as such were grafted onto the domestic judicial system, applying a compound of international and national substantial and procedural law.[107] The involvement of the international judges came as a result of a continuing failure by local judges to conduct fair trials, in particular in serious cases involving minority victims.[108]

In this regard, the international judges served to mainly deal with war crimes, as well as cases involving ethnic crimes. However, very often they were engaged in matters characterised as politically motivated cases. It was left to their sole discretion to select and take responsibility for new and pending cases within the jurisdiction of the court to which they were appointed.[109] At the same time, a strict case-monitoring practice[110] was instituted that enabled international prosecutors to resurrect cases abandoned by their Kosovar counterparts.[111]

In addition to a hybrid court system, the UNMIK administration established a Special Chamber of the Supreme Court of Kosovo on Kosovo Trust Agency Related Matters, empowered to deal with disputes and claims related to the privatisation and economic restructuring process currently under way in Kosovo.[112]

106 A hybrid court system became a common practice in post-war society. For instance, it was also introduced into East Timor (the Serious Crimes Unit and Special Panels for Serious Crimes pursuant to Regulation No. 2000/15) and Bosnia and Hercegovina (the Special War Crime Chamber established pursuant to an agreement concluded between the Office of the High Representative of the International Tribunal for the Former Yugoslavia and the national authorities). See Office of the United Nations, High Commissioner for Human Rights, Rule of Law Tools for Post Conflict States, Maximizing the Legacy of Hybrid Courts, Report 2008, HR/PUB/08/02, p. 3. Furthermore, there are some cases where the United Nations was invited by a specific country to establish a hybrid tribunal within their judicial system. This was the case for the Special Court for Sierra Leone (based on an agreement between the United Nations and the Government of Sierra Leone concluded in 2002) and the creation of the Extraordinary Chambers in Cambodia to try the main leaders of the Khmer Rouge (under an agreement concluded in 2003 by the United Nations and the Government of Cambodia to create Extraordinary Chambers in the courts of Cambodia). For more about hybrid courts, see Office of the United Nations, High Commissioner for Human Rights, *Rule of Law Tools for Post Conflict States, Maximizing the Legacy of Hybrid Courts*, Report, 2008, HR/PUB/08/02, p. 3.

107 After the establishment of the new International Presence in Kosovo in 2008 (the European Union Rule of Law Mission in Kosovo "EULEX"), UNMIK judges and prosecutors were replaced by EULEX judges acting under the umbrella of the Assembly of EULEX judges, the self-governing body established pursuant to Art 4 of the Law on Jurisdiction, 2003/03 L 53.

108 O'Neil, *supra* n. 88, p. 88.

109 Section 1.2 of UNMIK Regulation 2000/64. The selection of the cases was performed in cooperation with the Head of the Judicial Department.

110 UNMIK Regulation 2001/2, amending UNMIK Regulation 2000/6, *On the Appointment and Removal of International Judges and Prosecutors*, 12 January 2001.

111 Michael Hartmann, *International Judges and Prosecutors in Kosovo*, Special Report 112, United States Institute of Peace, 2003, p. 2.

112 It was established by UNMIK Regulation 2002/13, which was later amended by UNMIK Administrative Direction No. 2006/17.

Under the regulation, a special chamber of the Supreme Court was created and had the primary jurisdiction to adjudicate the following claims:

(a) Challenges to decisions or other actions of the Agency undertaken pursuant to Regulation No. 2002/12, including the imposition of fines as provided for in section 27 of Regulation No. 2002/12;
(b) Claims against the Agency for financial losses resulting from decisions or actions undertaken pursuant to its role as an administrator of an Enterprise or Corporation;
(c) Claims, including creditor or ownership claims, brought against an Enterprise or Corporation currently or formerly under the administrative authority of the Agency, where such claims arose during or prior to the time that such Enterprise or Corporation is or was subject to the administrative authority of the Agency;
(d) Claims involving recognition of a right, title or interest in property in the possession or control of an Enterprise or Corporation currently or formerly under the administrative authority of the Agency, where such claims arose during or prior to the time that such Enterprise or Corporation is or was subject to the administrative authority of the Agency;
(e) Enforcement, upon application of the Agency, of the powers of the Agency exercised pursuant to Regulation No. 2002/12;
(f) Claims for rescission of transactions of a Socially-owned Enterprise undergoing a liquidation proceeding, as provided for in section 9.4 of Regulation No 2002/12; and
(g) Such other matters as may be assigned by law.[113]

In order to safeguard the proper functioning of the judicial system, the Judicial Inspection Unit (the "JIU") was created, with responsibility for conducting inspections, audits, and investigations within the system. It was an internal mechanism, established under the UNMIK Department of Justice. The JIU was primarily responsible for conducting investigations of misconduct committed by sitting judges, prosecutors and lay judges, either on its own initiative or upon request.[114]

Quasi-judicial structures of UNMIK

Among other consequences of the 1998–1999 Kosovo war and the following period, the issues surrounding housing and property rights[115] became a matter of particular concern for UNMIK. Thousands of houses were destroyed during

113 UNMIK Regulation 2002/13.
114 For additional information, see www.unmikonline.org/justice.
115 In the former Yugoslavia, two types of property were recognised: social, and privately owned.

the war and many of them were usurped.[116] Such a situation required an urgent response and a solution was found by establishing administrative mechanisms, the Housing and Property Directorate (hereinafter HPD),[117] which was entitled to receive and process property claims, and an independent quasi-judicial body, the Housing and Property Claims Commission (hereinafter HPCC), to adjudicate such claims.[118]

The UN Centre for Human Settlements (HABITAT) was given the task by the Secretary General of providing UNMIK with technical and legal support in the field of property rights. Accordingly, HABITAT pursued the role of an implementing agency, while UNMIK undertook the responsibility to provide policy orientation and to supervise and monitor HPD/HPCC activities.[119]

Both mechanisms were granted independence from the Provisional Institutions of Self-Government (PISG).[120] In addition, HPCC itself was independent of HPD, whose mandate was to "settle private non-commercial residential property disputes until the SRSG determines that local courts are able to carry out the mandate entrusted to the Commission".[121] Vested with the powers of a court, it had exclusive jurisdiction over certain categories of claims.[122]

HPD comprised two components, namely the Executive Director, tasked with responsibility for logistics, IT, public relations, and overall management of HPD, including fund-raising; and the Department of Coordination, which was responsible for field operations.

On the basis of UNMIK Regulation 2000/60,[123] HPD and HPCC were empowered to deal with matters involving residential property rights, categorised into three groups: Category A) encompassed claims by individuals who lost their property as a result of discriminatory laws after 1989; Category B) claims

116 Regarding residential property usurpation, it is necessary to stress that in some cases usurpation resulted as a consequence of the need for shelter, as many houses had been burnt during the war. In some other cases, usurpation of property was based on the claim that the alleged property had been taken unlawfully from Albanians during the Milosevic regime and as such they were entitled to have it back. In yet other cases, another motive was invoked (revenge, greediness). In the northern part of Mitrovica, the usurpation came as a result of revenge and to some extent as a need for shelter, since after the war many Serbs had to move to this part of Kosovo, leaving their residential property behind.

117 The HPD was an independent body established by UN-Habitat. Mechanisms established by UNMIK Regulation 1999/23 on the establishment of the Housing and Property Directorate and the Housing and Property Claims Commission (15 November 1999).

118 Pursuant to UNMIK Regulation 2006/10, the Housing and Property Directorate was replaced by the Kosovo Property Agency which assumed its responsibility on 4 March 2006.

119 See Leopold Von Carlowitz, Settling Property Issues in Complex Peace Operations/The CRPC in Bosnia and Herzegovina and the HPD/CC in Kosovo, *Leiden Journal for International Law*, Vol. 17, 2004, p. 609.

120 Chapter 11 section 1 para. (g) of the Constitutional Framework.

121 Section 2 UNMIK Regulation 1999/23.

122 Section 1.2 UNMIK Regulation 1999/23.

123 UNMIK Regulation 2000/60 on residential property claims and The Rules of Procedure and Evidence of the Housing and Property Directorate and the Housing and Property Claims Commission (31 October 2000).

by individuals who entered into willing but unofficial transactions subsequent to the annulment of Kosovo's autonomy, despite the existence of discriminatory legislation preventing the formalisation of sales;[124] and Category C) claims brought by internally displaced persons and refugees who were holders of residential real property prior to 24 March 1999 and did not enjoy possession of the property, where the property had not been voluntarily transferred.[125]

While HPD was involved just in providing general direction on property rights, HPCC retained the role of a quasi-judicial body to adjudicate on property right disputes.[126]

Both HPD and HPCC were succeeded by the Kosovo Property Agency (KPA), which was established by the promulgation of UNMIK Regulation 2006/10.[127] It retained the same mandate as its predecessors. It comprised three bodies, namely, the Executive Secretariat, the Kosovo Property Claims Commission (KPCC), and the Supervisory Board.[128]

Termination of UNMIK's mandate: nexus with successor mission EULEX

In 2005, the UN Secretary General appointed the former Finnish President, Martti Ahtisaari, as Special Envoy for the Kosovo status process, which was to determine the future political status of the UN-administered territory. On 15 March 2006, Mr Ahtisaari came out with the settlement proposal known as the Ahtisaari plan, which involved the internationally supervised independence of the country.[129] Almost a year later, on 17 February 2007, the Kosovo Parliament declared independence.[130]

124 Section 1.2 UNMIK Regulation 1999/23, Art. 1.2. b; UNMIK Regulation 1999/10 (13 October 1999) on the Repeal of Discriminatory Legislation Affecting Housing and Rights in Property.

125 Section 1.2 (c) UNMIK Regulation 1999/23.

126 Bjorn Vagle and Fernando de Medina-Rosales, *An Evaluation of the Housing s and Property Directorate in Kosovo*, NORDEM Report 12, 2006, p. 26.

127 UNMIK Regulation 2006/10 on the Resolution of Claims Relating to Private Immovable Property, Including Agricultural and Commercial Property.

128 Following the declaration of Kosovo independence, the UNMIK Regulations establishing KPA ceased to produce legal effects and were replaced by Kosovo Assembly Law No. 03/L-079 and Law No. 04/L-155. Additional information regarding KPA is available at the following website: www.kpaonline.org/about.asp (last accessed on 24 December 2013). It continues to retain its hybrid character, comprising both international and local staff. It is run by an international official.

129 See *Comprehensive Proposal for the Kosovo Status Settlement* S/2007/168/ Add.1, available at the following website: www.unosek.org/unosek/en/statusproposal.html.

130 See Kosovo Declaration of Independence, 17 February 2008, available at the following website: www.assembly-kosova.org/?cid=2,128,1635. The unilateral declaration of Kosovo independence continues to be a subject of debate. See Oisin Tansey, Kosovo: Independence and Tutelage, *Journal of Democracy*, Vol. 20, No. 2, 2009; Oisin Tansey, *Regime Building: Democratisation and International Administration*, Oxford University Press, 2009; Eric de Brabandere, *The Kosovo Advisory Proceedings and the Court's Advisory Jurisdiction as a*

The proposed settlement placed Kosovo under EU supervision, comprising an International Civilian Office (ICO) responsible for implementing the earlier-mentioned plan, and the EU's Rule of Law mission (EULEX), which was responsible for administering and developing the rule of law in the country. Pursuant to the settlement proposal, UNMIK was expected to fully cede power to the EU, but legal grounds for a structured transition were lacking.[131] The lack of unanimity within the UN Security Council on endorsing a further resolution which would establish the legal grounds for deploying a new EU mission in Kosovo brought new sets of problems to the functioning of the newly created state.[132] On 12 August 2008, the UN Secretary General made a decision on the basis of UNSC Resolution 1244 to reconfigure the UN presence in Kosovo. This was considered to be a temporary solution that would enable the deployment of a new EU mission.[133] However, it is not the aim of this chapter to elaborate on

---

Method of Dispute Settlement, The Hague Justice Portal, 2012; James E. Moliterno, What the ICJ's Decision Means for Kosovars, *German Law Journal*, Vol. 11, No. 8, 2010; Robert Howse and Ruti Teitel, Delphic Dictum: How Has the ICJ Contributed to the Global Rule of Law by Its Ruling on Kosovo?, *German Law Journal*, Vol. 11, No. 8, 2010; Thomas Burri, The Kosovo Opinion and Succession: The Sounds of Silence and Missing Links, *German Law Journal*, Vol. 11, No. 8, 2010; Richard Falk, Agora: The ICJ's Kosovo Advisory Opinion, the Kosovo Advisory Opinion: Conflict Resolution and Precedent, *American Society of International Law*, Vol. 105, No. 1, 2011.

131 See *Comprehensive Proposal for the Kosovo Status Settlement* S/2007/168/ Add.1, Annex IX, available at the following website: www.unosek.org/unosek/en/statusproposal.html.

132 The International Court of Justice in its Advisory Opinion on the *Accordance with International Law of the Unilateral Declaration of Independence in Respect of Kosovo*, rendered on 22 July 2010 in response to a question posed by the General Assembly, concluded that "the adoption of the Declaration of Independence of 17 February 2008 did not violate general international law, Security Council Resolution 1244 or the Constitutional Framework" for Provisional Self-Government in Kosovo. However, there are two opposing views when it comes to the legitimacy of Kosovo independence. The Serbian government, backed by Russia, argued that the declaration of independence was null and void because it lacked the agreement of Belgrade and hence that Kosovo would continue to remain a part of Serbia. On the other hand, the majority of EU countries and the US government argued that since UNSC Resolution 1244 did not include provisions on how the "final settlement" should be generated, the declaration of independence (which was based on the UN SE plan, and was recognised on that basis) had enabled Kosovo to enter into the *final phase* as per Article 11 of Resolution 1244, while the *interim phase* provisions of 1244, including those related to FRY sovereignty and territorial integrity, ceased to exist. See Joackim Rucker, Former UNMIK SRSG (2006–2008), *Kosovo Today*, Presentation at the University of Oxford, St. Anthony's College, January 2009, www.joachim-ruecker.de/PresentationOxford%2026Jan09.pdf; Knoll, *supra* n. 50, pp. 252–298.

133 "In line with the statement by the President of the Security Council of 26 November 2008 (S/PRST/2008/44) and my report of 24 November 2008 (S/2008/692), the European Union Rule of Law Mission (EULEX) operates under the overall authority and within the status-neutral framework of the United Nations". See UNMIK report S/2012/603, issued on 3 August 2012.

This modality came as a result of the series of talks on the status of Kosovo held between 2005 and 2008. They were initiated on the basis of the fact-finding report issued by the Special Envoy of the UNSG, Kai Eide, who concluded: "in the light of the limitations of

the structural arrangements of the EU mission, but rather to briefly shed light on some legal aspects of the relationship between the mission and UNMIK.

Pursuant to the Ahtisaari plan, the ICO[134] was established, whose main role was to supervise, monitor, and ensure effective and efficient implementation of the plan.[135] Apart from ICO, an additional layer of international presences was involved through EULEX,[136] which was strictly designed for rule of law matters. Both formally operated under the authority of a reconfigured UNMIK and at the same time retained a neutral stance towards Kosovo status.[137] The EULEX mission provided technical assistance and support to the Kosovan authorities in the rule of law area, in particular in judicial, police and customs matters. Though it was considered to be a technical mission, it retained a number of limited executive powers.[138]

At the same time, similar to the SRSG the International Representative was given a supervisory role to make appointments to certain senior government positions and to remedy actions taken by local authorities, such as by cancelling laws/decisions adopted by local authorities as well as by the sanctioning or removal of any public official.[139]

The new EU mission was given its authority by the UN and subsequently required to report to UN although this is a civil mission of European defence and security policy with a clear command chain from Brussels.[140] At present, UNMIK remains the nominal administrator in Kosovo, though with no real authority, an

---

the police and judicial system, there will be a need for a continued presence of international police with executive powers in sensitive areas. A continued presence of international judges and prosecutors will also be required to handle cases related to war crimes, organised crime, and corruption as well as difficult inter-ethnic cases. The currently ongoing reduction in the number of international judges and prosecutors is premature and should urgently be reconsidered. The result of such reductions would be a further loss of credibility of the justice system and of confidence in it among the population in general and the minority communities in particular. There is little reason to believe that local judges and prosecutors will be able to fulfil in the near future the functions now being carried out by international personnel". See Kai Eide, the Special UNSG Envoy, *A Special Review of the Situation in Kosovo*, UNDC/S2005.

134 Ahtisaari Plan, Article 1 (11).

135 Acting as the European Union's Special Representative.

136 The European Union's Common Security and Defence Policy (ESDP).

137 The very process of reconfiguring UNMIK lacked transparency and clarity. On 18 August 2008, an agreement was signed between UNMIK and EULEX on the transfer of certain parts of UN mission property to EULEX. It related to the transfer or sale of certain assets, vehicles, and facilities which were used by UNMIK. Due to the lack of transparency, the public still lacks clarity about the content of this agreement. For the majority of people, it was understood as a document which stipulated the details of the reconfiguration process. However, it was stressed by a UNMIK spokesperson that this was a purely technical agreement and that the signing of the Memorandum of Understanding between UNMIK and EULEX on the transfer of competences was a separate issue. It has still not been scheduled.

138 For additional information regarding EULEX's mandate in Kosovo, see www.eulex.eu.org.

139 Annex IX Articles, 2.2, 2.1. The International Civilian Office (ICO) closed in September 2012.

140 See SRSG's Report issued on 24.October 2008, S/2008/692. Para. 8.

authority which has been replaced by the EU presence. The new EU mission is widely rejected by the Serb minority and consequently UNMIK's authority continues to retain a certain level of responsibility, which is mainly concentrated on the Serbian enclaves. It focuses on assisting Kosovo's communities and engaging with a range of actors, local, regional, and international. It is committed at promoting security, stability, and respect for human rights in Kosovo and in the region. Since 2010, it has been actively involved in facilitating the participation of Kosovar institutions in regional multilateral fora, participation that has been continually impeded by those countries that have not yet recognised Kosovo.[141]

However, the absence of a legal basis for terminating the UNMIK mandate remains an ongoing enigma for the Security Council. Although the Resolution stated that the duration of the UNMIK mandate was to be for an initial period of 12 months subject to renewal,[142] it still remains in force in the absence of a revision, due to the lack of consensus between the West and Russia.[143]

The central question arising from this complex situation is what is the legal basis that enables the EULEX mission to function within UNMIK structures? Erica de Wet suggests looking at Article 53 (1) of Chapter VII, which provides the legal basis for the Security Council to authorise a regional organisation to establish a civil administration in a territory. In this context, the Security Council "shall, where appropriate, utilize regional arrangements or agencies for enforcement action under its authority".[144]

She argues that taking into consideration the geographic nature of the European Union, as well as the scope of competencies it exercises in the region, it qualifies as a "regional organization".[145]

Yet, she reminds us that the involvement of the regional organisations in the UN mission is not new, because the case of Kosovo demonstrates that regional organisations have been involved since the very beginning of UNMIK's functioning. This was done in compliance with UNSC Resolution 1244, which gives the SRSG the authority to establish a civil administration "with the assistance

141 See UNMIK, *Mandate and Structure*, available at the following website: www.unmikonline.org/Pages/about.aspx (last accessed on 24 December 2013).

142 See para. 19 of UNSC Resolution 1244.

143 According to the Chief Military Liaison Officer of UNMIK, Major Raul Cunha, the integration of EULEX into UNMIK's structures is possible through UN Resolution 1244, which will remain in force. One of the ways for EULEX to be in the field was obviously to be the pillar of police and justice, which already existed in UNMIK. That is basically what EULEX is: police and justice. What should not be possible to integrate inside UNMIK would be the post of the International Civilian Representative ICR. The only way would be for the ICR to be simultaneously the Special Representative of the Secretary General. See Andre Cuhna, *Eulex Inside UNMIK, Too Late?*, Observatorie Balcanie Caucaso, available at the following website: www.balcanicaucaso.org/eng/Regions-and-countries/Kosovo/EULEX-inside-UNMIK-too-late-41332.

144 Article 53(1) of the UN Charter, Chapter VII.

145 See Erica de Wet, The Governance of Kosovo, Security Council 1244 and Establishment and Functioning of the EULEX, *The American Journal of International Law*, Vol. 103, no. 83, 2009, pp. 85–89.

of relevant international organisations", which implied a so-called delegation of powers.[146] Subsequently, a number of functions were delegated to OSCE, the EU, and UNHCR, which formed a cornerstone of UNMIK's administration. So accordingly, Article 53 (1) and the specific reference enshrined in UNSC Resolution 1244 serve as a foundation for the functioning of the new mission, the EULEX.[147]

Nonetheless, it has been highlighted that as a result of the delegation of functions from the SRSG to EULEX, the SRSG retains the authority to override any decision taken by the EULEX authorities.[148]

Conclusion

The foregoing discussion has offered an insight into the structural arrangements of the UNMIK. It revealed the general issues that were found within the legal framework governing UNMIK activities in Kosovo. As may have been noticed, it did not engage in an in-depth critical analysis of the system, but focused mainly on explaining the challenges and barriers surrounding UNMIK's mandate so as to provide a foundation for analysing the most important issues arising from the legal developments of the UNMIK enterprise.

At the outset, the chapter focused on the design of UNSC Resolution 1244, namely the accumulation of legislative, executive, and judicial powers by the SRSG and the lack of a balance of powers that followed from such a course of action.

In this context, it tried to draw attention to the fact that as a result of the complexity and ambiguity of its mandate, UNMIK was obliged to be sufficiently elastic to be able to operate in a highly complex and conflictual environment.

Yet the greatest testimony to the "elasticity" of the UNMIK's mandate will undoubtedly come from the forthcoming discussion, which offers a clear picture of the functioning of this mandate in practice.

146 UNSC Resolution 1244, para. 10.

147 She argues that the regular reporting of the EULEX authorities to the UN Secretary General and the Security Council affirms both acceptance that the EU be subordinated to UN and that the Security Council represents the authorising source of its mandate. See de Wet, *supra* n. 145, p. 89.

148 Ibid., p. 90.

1 Making laws for others

Managing complexity

Introduction

The law that was applied to the territory of the former Yugoslavia did not rely sufficiently on accepted principles of international law. This problem was prevalent throughout the whole territory of former Yugoslavia. Nevertheless, the degree of unlawfulness proved to be much higher in Kosovo than in other federal units, especially after the abrogation of its autonomy in March 1989.

Empowered to exercise legislative power in the territory, soon after their deployment the UNMIK authorities embarked on a mission to build up a legal system which would strengthen the rule of law. However, this commitment faced innumerable challenges. It required the establishment of a legal framework which would enable citizens to regain trust in public administration and judicial organs, and protect and promote their human rights.

This chapter analyses sets of legal issues concerning the legislative power of UNMIK by examining its legal framework, its limitations, as well as the activities performed within the framework of its competencies. In particular, it examines the legal implications of actions taken during the initial phase. In addition, it discusses the law-making procedure, the legal nature of enactments promulgated by UNMIK's law-making body, their powers and the implementation process, as well as their compatibility with international human rights law.

Reconstructing the legal system: "the initial law-making process"

Transforming a weak and devastated country such as Kosovo into a "rule of law society" required a proper identification of problems, allocation of human and financial resources, and finally a proper strategic plan. Above all, the UN needed to create a legal framework within which these activities could be carried out.[1] Yet this undertaking highlights a number of gaps which caused extraordinary difficulties for achieving practical outcomes.

1 About common characteristics regarding the UN's involvement in reconstructing the post-war judicial system, see Carstein Stahn, Justice under Transitional Administration: Contours and Critique of a Paradigm, *Houston Journal of International Law*, Vol. 27, 2004–2005.

Given that UNSC Resolution 1244 failed to determine the applicable law in Kosovo, it caused confusion amongst both international and local actors as to which law should govern the administered territory. The confusion created a legal vacuum for several months.[2] Restricted by the narrow mandate set out in UNSC Resolution 1244, which secured the sovereignty of the FRY over the territory of Kosovo, the UNMIK administration insisted on the application of FRY laws.[3] On the other side, the local actors strongly opposed the application of FRY/Serbian laws, claiming that these laws belonged to an oppressive regime and that many of them contained discriminatory provisions especially designed for the purpose of oppressing the Albanian population.[4] Consequently, UNMIK found itself between a rock and a hard place. There were two options: "continuity", which implied the continuation of the discriminatory laws; and "reform", which required the enactment of new laws.[5]

Despite insisting on total discontinuity with the FRY/Serbian legal system, surprisingly, in the middle of the consultation process the local actors proposed the application of the pre-1989 laws, in particular the Kosovo criminal code, which was unlawfully revoked by the Serbian parliament during the Milosevic regime. Some judges even began to apply this code in court proceedings.[6] The proposal came as a result of frustration with the ongoing violence and the code's application was seen as a pragmatic choice that would speed up the process of establishing a justice system.[7]

Interestingly, the pre-1989 laws proposed by the Albanian lawyers were almost as inconsistent with international human rights standards as the laws of the post-1989 period.[8]

2 See International Crisis Group's Balkan Report, *Starting from scratch in Kosovo*, No. 83, 13 December 1999, p 12.

3 Russia has insisted on applying FRY laws. See Simon Chesterman, *You the People, the United Nations, Transitional Administration, and State-Building*, Oxford University Press, 2004, p. 166. In addition, it has been argued that the international community was largely unprepared to govern Kosovo. It was not clear which functions should be performed by international actors and which should be shared with local actors. See Jock Covey, Michael Dziedzic, and Leonard Hawley, *The Quest for Visible Peace, International Intervention and Strategies for Conflict Transformation*, US Institute for Peace Press, 2005, p. 166.

4 Blerim Reka, *UNMIK as an International Governance in Post War Kosova: NATOs Intervention, UN Administration and Kosovar Aspirations*, Shkup: Logos, 2003, p. 189.

5 See International Crises Group's Balkan Report, *supra* n. 2, p. 12.

6 See Rosa Ehrenreich Brooks, The New Imperialism, Violence, Norms, and the "Rule of Law", *Michigan Law Review*, Vol. 101, June 2003, p. 2292.

7 See International Crises Group's Balkan Report, *supra* n. 2, p. 12.

8 Regarding the criminal justice system, the Model Codes for Post-Conflict Criminal Justice offered by the United States Institute for Peace and the Galway Centre for Human Rights in collaboration with the UN Office on Drugs and Crime should be seen as a useful tool for future missions that can be implemented in transitional post-conflict situations. It takes into account the particular challenges presented by post-conflict societies and could enable those societies to move quickly towards re-establishing a criminal justice system. See Vivienne O'Connor and Colette Rausch (eds.), *Model Codes for Post Criminal Justice, Peace Building and Rule of Law*, United States Institute of Peace, 2007.

Designed under the Communist umbrella, they failed to meet basic human rights standards, in particular those related to property and civil law.[9]

However, on 25 July 1999, after a long debate, the first legal act (Regulation 1999/1)[10] by which the applicable laws in Kosovo were identified was promulgated under the authority of the SRSG.[11] In this light, it was decided that the applicable laws should consist of the laws of the Federal Republic of Yugoslavia, laws which were valid until 24 March 1999, to the extent that they did not conflict with the accepted standards of international human rights law.[12]

However, despite the fact that the applicable law had been determined, it was not possible to establish a functional legal system and ensure law and order for several months as no formal local government structures existed.

Consequently, in the aftermath of UNMIK's deployment different legal systems were applied: those belonging to the countries whose military troops were present in the territory, namely the US, Germany, France, and Italy.[13]

Nevertheless, it is difficult to identify in which circumstances these foreign laws were applied during this period.[14]

Making law without a democratic legislative body

As a result of the continuing resistance of domestic actors, in particular judges and prosecutors, to applying the existing FRY/Serb laws, in mid-August 1999, the Joint Advisory Council on Legislative Matters (JACLM), comprising both international and local actors, was established under the auspice of the SRSG, Bernard Kouchner.[15] The role of JACLM was to review the existing law, to propose and provide assistance in drafting legislation for the interim administration in the areas of criminal, civil, administrative, and commercial and property law,

9 See Ehrenreich Brooks, *supra* n. 6, *Michigan Law Review*, Vol. 101, June 2003, p. 2293.

10 Later amended by Regulations 1999/25 and 2000/54.

11 See Report of the Secretary General on the United Nations Interim Administration in Kosovo, 12 July 1999, UN Doc.S/1999/779, para. 35.

12 To this extent the following laws were applicable: Criminal Law of the Autonomous Province of Kosova, Criminal Procedure of the Federal Republic of Yugoslavia (SFRY), Law on General Administrative Procedure of SFRY, and several civil laws.

13 Military contingents were grouped into four regionally based multinational brigades. For more about the initial phase of international presence deployment, see Reka, *supra* n. 4, p. 186. Blerim Reka was a member of the Joint Advisory Council on Legal Matters (JACLM).

14 According to de Brabandere, in the cases where the establishment of a territorial administration has been preceded by military intervention the military forces should be governed by the laws of occupation. See Eric de Brabandere *supra* n. 1, p. 126.

15 Similarly in East Timor, a legislative body named the National Consultative Council (NCC) was assigned the task of providing advice and policy recommendations to the SRSG. By contrast with JACLM, which was an ad hoc body, the NCC was established by law, but did not possess so much power to amend draft regulations or to propose any regulation on its own and was often ignored by UNTAET. The NCC was established by UNTAET Regulation 1999/2. See Daniel Fitzpatrick, Developing Legal System in East Timor; Some Issues of UN Mandate and Capacity, *Austrian Review of International and European Law*, Vol. 5, 2000, p. 12.

and to advise the SRSG on legal matters.[16] It was divided into several working groups, each tasked with a specific responsibility.[17]

The creation of this ad hoc legislative body was welcomed by both international and local actors, and was seen as a tool which would help finally to put to an end the long debate over the applicability of FRY laws.[18] Nevertheless, despite expectations the JACLM was not able to stand on its own feet until the beginning of December 1999.[19]

On 12 December 1999, the SRSG adopted Regulation 1999/24, which modified the previous Regulation 1999/1 applying contemporary FRY/Serbian law. The Regulation determined that the applicable law should consist of the regulations promulgated by the SRSG, including subsidiary instruments, and the law which was in force in Kosovo on 22 March 1989 to the extent that it did not contradict internationally recognised human rights standards.[20] However, several months later, additional clarifications were provided by Regulation 2000/59, which identified the sources of law applicable in Kosovo: UNMIK Regulations, the law which was in force in Kosovo on 22 March 1989, and the law that applied in Kosovo between 22 March 1989 and 12 December 1999 to the extent that it was not discriminatory and not in contradiction with international human rights standards.[21] Though this regulation expressly states the supremacy of "SRSG Regulations" over 1989 law, unfortunately the hierarchy between other sources of law remained unclear.[22]

The manner in which the law was determined raised further issues, as it turned out to be rather difficult to apply in practice. Regulation 2000/59 itself failed to provide guidance on how to reconcile FRY/Serbian law with international human rights standards.[23] It drew no clear line as to which laws or parts of laws

16 See Reka, *supra* n. 4, p. 190.

17 Ibid.

18 "Dr Kouchner said the main task of the Advisory Group would be to review existing legislation and to draft new laws, which would eliminate all elements of discrimination; that is, the notion of apartheid. An example of this was the present "Law on Changes and Supplements on the Limitation of Real Estate Transactions", which prohibited Albanians from property transactions". UNMIK Press Release, 16 August, 1999.

19 See Reka, *supra* n. 4, p. 190.

20 See UNMIK Regulation 1999/24, section 1.1. The same legislative strategy and practice were utilised by UNTAET in East Timor. Like in Kosovo, it was decided to apply the legislation which was in force prior to the adoption of UNSC Resolution 1272, in this case Indonesian laws applicable in East Timor on 25 October 1999. However, as in Kosovo such laws required consistency with international human rights standards. This decision was regarded as a pragmatic choice since all East Timorese lawyers were familiar with the Indonesian laws. See para. 3 of UNTAET Regulation 1/1999; Fitzpatrick, *supra* n. 15, p. 12.

21 See UNMIK Regulation 2000/59, section 1.1.

22 See Carsten Stahn, The United Nations Transitional Administration in Kosovo and East Timor: A First Analyses, *Max Planck Yearbook of United Nations Law*, Vol. 5, 2001, Kluwer Law International, p. 156.

23 Scott N. Carlson, Wendy S. Betts, and Gregory Gisvold, The Post-Conflict Traditional Administration of Kosovo and Lessons Learned in Efforts to Establish Judiciary and Rule of Law, *Michigan Journal of International Law*, Vol. 22, No. 33, Spring 2001, p. 374.

were inconsistent with internationally recognised standards, which created confusion both for those who had designed the formula and for those who had to apply this formula in practice.[24]

Under the regulations mentioned earlier, domestic law would only continue to apply in Kosovo insofar as it did not conflict with human rights standards. In this regard the following international instruments were explicitly listed:

1 The Universal Declaration of Human Rights,
2 The European Convention for the Protection of Human Rights and Fundamental Freedoms and the Protocols thereto,
3 The International Covenant on Civil and Political Rights,
4 The International Covenant on Economic, Social and Cultural Rights,
5 The Convention on the Elimination of All Forms of Racial Discrimination,
6 The Convention on the Elimination of All Forms of Discrimination against Women,
7 The Convention Against Torture and Other Cruel, Inhumane or Degrading Treatment or Punishment, and
8 The International Convention on the Rights of the Child.[25]

Though drafted in ambiguous language, these regulations impose an obligation upon UNMIK to integrate the stated principles (even in the absence of formal adherence to the treaties) into domestic legislation and ensure its harmonisation with international human rights standards. Moreover, they impose an obligation upon UNMIK officials to exercise their functions in accordance with these principles: "In exercising their functions, all persons undertaking public duties or holding public office in Kosovo shall observe internationally recognised human rights standards".[26]

However, whether UNMIK Regulations constitute a legal source has been a subject of debate among legal scholars. In this regard, Alvarez considers that "[n]o one knows for sure whether the matter is a question of a legal duty or an *ex gratia* assumption of responsibility, or whether it applies to all of international organisations and with respect to all its operations, or even if all of international human rights law does apply to the UN, how it does so".[27] This assertion has

24 UNMIK Regulation 2000/59 says that the laws in force after 22 March 1989 are applicable if they cover "new grounds" and are not of a discriminatory nature; however, it raises the question what are these "new grounds"? See OSCE Report, *Property Rights in Kosovo*, January 2002.

25 See, UNMIK Regulations, 1999/1, 1999/24 and 2000/59.

26 Ibid.

27 Jose E. Alvarez, *International Organisations as Law-Makers*, Oxford University Press, 2005, p. 178. Alvarez notes that it was not the first time that the Security Council had used its Chapter VII powers to increase awareness of human rights protection. For example, in the case of Haiti UNSC Resolution 940 enshrined an obligation to treat human rights as "an integral part of the very definition of international peace and security". Similarly, UNSC Resolution 688 required respect for human rights in Iraq relating to the Kurdish and Shiite minority oppression.

been questioned by Cameron, who considers that Alvarez failed to notice that there is no equality among regulations, because some hold more weight than others. For instance, the Regulation on Immunity and Privileges of UNMIK and KFOR (UNMIK Regulation 2000/47) is widely viewed as binding, whereas the rest of the Regulations did not produce such an effect.[28] Thus in her view this assertion will remain open to discussion.

Yet despite the ambiguous language, the wording of the Regulations suggests that UNMIK was given the role of "a surrogate state and, as such, was institutionally bound not only to observe international human rights standards, but to implement them as well. These obligations, therefore, were not attached only to public officials in their official capacities, but to the institutions on behalf of which they exercised their public functions".[29]

The UNMIK laws

UNMIK introduced a legal system comprising regulations, administrative directions, and executive decisions which could not be repealed or altered by any other authority in Kosovo.[30] In addition, it enacted both a Criminal Code and Criminal Procedure Codes.

Initially, the very notion "regulation" brought much confusion, especially regarding the determination of its legal nature.[31] A few months later, it became clear that despite being called "regulations",[32] their legal nature was equivalent to the legal acts issued by the Assembly. It should be mentioned that the regulations had a double role: initially, they constituted only a law, whereas at a later stage they became a legal instrument for enacting the Assembly's law.[33]

In addition to the regulations, sets of administrative directions were issued as subsidiary acts for implementing the regulations. The procedure for their adoption was less complicated as they needed in principle only to be reviewed by the UNMIK Legal Adviser before being submitted to the SRSG for signature.[34]

28 See Lindsay Cameron, *Human Rights Accountability of International Civil Administrations to the People Subject to Administration*, Presentation for the International Conference: Accountability for Human Rights Violations by International Organizations, Brussels, 17 March 2007, Human Rights International Discourse, Vol. 2, Conference Reader, p. 9.

29 See Kosovo Ombudsperson Special Report Nr. 2, issued on certain aspects of UNMIK Regulation 2000/5 amending UNMIK Regulation 1999/24 on the Law applicable in Kosovo, para. 11, 30 May 2001.

30 Not even FRY/Serbian authority, which according to Resolution 1244 was still considered to have sovereignty over Kosovo.

31 Reka, *supra* n. 4, p. 202.

32 The very term regulation is of a broad scope. Usually, regulations are issued by internal bodies to regulate certain matters that arise from the law. For more about this, see Reka, ibid.

33 From the beginning of 2002, the Assembly was allowed to issue laws; however, its laws would become effective only if signed by the SRSG. Therefore, Regulations were used as a legal instrument simply to give legal effect to laws promulgated by the Assembly.

34 See Leopold Von Carlowitz, UNMIK Law Making between Effective Peace Support and Internal Self-Determination, *Archiv des Volkerrechts*, Bd. 41, 2003, p. 377.

At a later stage it became a tendency to try to avoid legislating by regulation and instead issue administrative directions.[35] With regard to subsidiary acts, it is necessary to stress that there was no definite terminology which precisely determined the nature of such normative acts. These acts have many different terms, such as administrative instructions, sub-acts, normative acts, guidelines etc. When it comes to their application in practice, the result is total confusion. For example, according to UNMIK Regulation 2000/19 on the Executive Branches of the PISG, the executive branches are entitled to issue administrative decisions and instructions, while the hierarchy and uniformity of the normative acts remains unclear.[36] Moreover, this matter became even more confusing after the enactment of Regulation 2000/59 on Applicable Law in Kosovo,[37] which declared that subsidiary instruments of UNMIK Regulations superseded domestic laws.[38]

The question of what constituted "subsidiary instruments" remained unclear and thus open to differing interpretations.[39] It is not difficult to assume that UNMIK's administrative directions fall under the category of subsidiary instruments, but controversy remains as to their power to supersede existing laws.[40]

In addition to the legal instruments described earlier, the SRSG also issued numerous executive decisions attempting to achieve a particular outcome or remedy a particular situation. Most of them were of a political dimension. In this regard, executive decisions were issued to detain individuals extra-judicially, to invalidate actions, agreements, and court decisions regarding the tender process for a second mobile phone operator in Kosovo, and for restitution of property. The legal implications surrounding executive decisions will be discussed in chapter five.

Taking into consideration the security situation in the early days of UNMIK, it does not come as a surprise that the restoration of a criminal justice system was one of the first tasks undertaken by JACLM. So, in September 1999 the Working Group on Criminal Law of JACLM began to work on a criminal code and a criminal procedure code.[41] During the drafting period they received assistance from various agencies, such as OSCE, UNICEF, the American Bar Association, and the Council of Europe, which enabled JACLM to complete its task in two years.[42] Provisional Codes were promulgated on 6 July 2003.[43]

35 The Kosovo Central Agency was established by administrative direction. Ibid.

36 OSCE Report, *The Implementation of Kosovo Assembly Laws*, Report II, December 2005.

37 Enacted on 27 October 2007, amending UNMIK Regulation 1999/24.

38 See section 1.1 of UNMIK Regulation 2000/59.

39 OSCE Report, *Property Rights in Kosovo*, January 2002.

40 Administrative directions are issued as subsidiary acts to implement regulations.

41 See Reka, *supra* n. 4, p. 190; see also International Crises Group's Balkan Report, *supra* n. 2.

42 See International Crises Group's Balkan Report, ibid.

43 It fulfils the modern criminal law criteria. The changes in law are designed essentially to bring the country into line with international human rights law standards. It introduced a new pre-trial investigative model, abolished the death penalty, extended the period of habeas corpus, improved the position of victims, increased protection for witnesses, etc.

It should be noted that alongside human security and basic order, it was of the utmost importance to set up a coherent legal framework relating to civil law, administrative law and commercial and economic law, and thereby to establish a secure environment for economic and commercial activities to develop.

The JACLM‘s group of local experts tried to draw attention to the importance of enacting such laws; however, their proposal was rejected by UNMIK.[44] Later, this reluctance caused many problems for the protection of property rights in general.[45]

It should be emphasised that in the first two years of UNMIK's functioning, actual law-making remained in the hands of UNMIK with little involvement of local actors.[46] Regulations were mainly drafted by UNMIK pillars and submitted for review to the Office of Legal Affairs at UN Headquarters in New York by the SRSG Legal Office and hardly ever to JACLM for consultation.[47] After the constitution of the Kosovo Assembly, local experts became more involved in the law-making process;[48] nevertheless, the international intrusion did not cease as the SRSG retained the same power, the position of a final arbiter. This empowered the SRSG to promulgate laws and to interfere directly in the legislative process by making corrections, amending laws and refusing to pass laws if he considered that such laws were in opposition to Resolution 1244 or the Constitutional Framework.[49]

The most challenging task performed by the UNMIK authorities appears to have been the drafting of the "Constitutional Legal Framework", the quasi-constitutional act for the Kosovar legal system. This came upon the repeated request of local authorities, which since the beginning of UNMIK's establishment

44 Reka, *supra* n. 4, referring to Esat Stavileci, Which Laws Should Be Drafted for the New Administration in Kosova?, *Kosova Law Review*, Vol. 4, No. 4, Winter 1999, p. 195.

45 Ibid.

46 Like local actors in Kosovo, members of the NCC in East Timor repeatedly complained about being prevented from giving their contribution to the UNTAET decision-making process. As a result, draft Regulations were presented as an accomplished act and could not be altered or repealed by the local authorities. See Fitzpatrick, *supra* n. 15, p. 14.

47 Reka, *supra* n. 4, p. 214, saying procedure of consultation with local experts was not respected; see also von Carlowitz, *supra* n. 34, p. 378.

48 The Assembly of Kosovo started to issue laws in July 2002.

49 After it became the responsibility of the Assembly, the process of promulgating laws was too long and complicated. The first draft laws were usually prepared by the legal department of the relevant ministry, which might decide to hold public consultations or elicit input from civil society. The draft was then further submitted to the Office of the Prime Minister, which established a working group to review the law. The working group had to include an UNMIK legal adviser and might include representatives from NGOs, municipalities and experts. Some, though not all, proposed legislation was referred by the working group to public debate and civil society input. The final stage required that all legislation be reviewed by the SRSG's office for compliance with the Constitutional Framework and international human rights instruments before being finalised. Moreover, corrections and amendments were often conducted without further consultation with the Assembly. See OSCE Report, *Assembly Law of Kosovo*.

had insisted upon having an interim constitution.[50] The proposal was accepted by the international actors but with a certain degree of caution. Preparations for a drafting process began in March 2000. A group of experts, comprising international experts only, was established to facilitate the process.[51]

The domestic legal experts felt ignored by not being consulted about the future model of the constitution. Directly thereafter, in October 2000, the Kosova Institute for Euro Atlantic Integration (KIEAI)[52] undertook an initiative to mobilise local community experts and subsequently established the "Constitutional Forum of Kosova" (CFK) with the task of drafting the "interim constitution for Kosova". Shortly after the creation of CFK came the establishment of the Joint Working Group (JWG),[53] an UNMIK body assigned with the task of drafting "a legal framework for self-governance in Kosova".[54]

In the end, they presented, as expected, two diametrically opposed models.

However, after several negotiating sessions between UNMIK and Kosovar political representatives, on 15 May 2001 the SRSG promulgated UNMIK Regulation 2001/9 on a Constitutional Framework for Provisional Self-Government in Kosovo.

In this regard, the concept of *pouvoir constituant* was completely absent, since the local actors were totally excluded from the constitution-making process.[55]

The Constitutional Framework established four institutions for self-government: the Assembly, the President, and the government and judicial

50 Reka, *supra* n. 4, p. 230.

51 Ibid.

52 Centre for legal research run by local legal experts.

53 The Joint Working Group, comprising both international and local representatives. While the Albanian representatives remained until the end, the Serb representatives left the JWG at an early stage of consultation.

54 Reka, *supra* n. 4, p. 231.

55 External influence on the constitution-making process has become quite frequent in transitional societies. Based on the degree of influence exerted upon the national actors, three different types of external influence have been identified, namely total, marginal and partial. It has been observed that in the case of ITA, as well as occupation, the influence of external factors is much stronger. Yet one can observe a clear distinction between such involvements. For instance, in East Timor the external influence in the constitution-making process was far less rigid compared to Kosovo. The UNTAET authorities were only involved with regard to the establishing of a framework for the process, and the actual constitution making and adoption remained with the Timorese. On the other hand, in Iraq, though international experts were required to remain aside during the drafting process, they continuously influenced the process, mainly through the United Nations and also United Kingdom officials. See; Tonny Brems Knudsen and Carsten Bagge Laustsen, *Kosovo between War and Peace, Nationalism, Peace-Building and International Trusteeship*, Routledge, Taylor and Francis Group, 2007, p. 123. See Philipp Dann and Zaid Al-Ali, The Internationalised Pouvoir Constituent-Constitution-Making under External Influences in Iraq, Sudan and East Timor, *Max Planck Yearbook of United Nations Law*, Vol. 10, 2006, pp. 423–463. See also Hilary Charlesworth, The Constitution of East Timor, *International Journal of Constitutional Law*, Vol. 1, 2003; Joel Colon-Rios, The Legitimacy of the Juridical, Constituent Power, Democracy and the Limits of the Constitutional Reform, *Osgoode Hall Law Journal*, Vol. 48, 2010; International Crisis Group, Unmaking Iraq, *A Constitutional Process Gone Away*, No. 19, September 2005, available at the following website: www.crisisgroup.org

systems, as well as a number of other institutions. It also laid down the areas in which the new government would be competent: economic and financial policy, fiscal and budgetary issues, trade and industry, education and culture, science and technology, health, environment, labour and social welfare, agriculture, and tourism.

While it transferred a broad range of areas to the newly elected authorities, key powers were reserved to the SRSG, such as external affairs, supervision of the local administration and the maintenance of law and order.[56] Above all, the SRSG could, on his own initiative or upon a request supported by two thirds of the members of the Assembly, effect amendments to the Constitutional Framework.[57]

Criticism has mostly centred on the title of the document, as well as its legal nature.

Given the limitations set by UNSC Resolution 1244 and the contradictory opinions of the parties involved, namely UNMIK, Albanian community representatives, and FRY, it is considered that the document reflects a compromise solution, which reconciles interests of all parties.[58]

The very title "Constitutional Framework" emerged from the fact that Kosova was not a state under international law but an entity under UN rule.[59]

However, the fact that Kosovo was not considered a state under international law should not have been used as an obstacle to the application of the notion of a constitution, since the notion constitution is not strictly connected to the rigid concept of statehood.[60]

Actually, in the past several constitutions were designed for different entities which were internationally governed territories, among them the Constitution of the Free City of Danzig, the "Permanent Statute" of the Free Territory of Trieste and the Draft Constitution of the City of Jerusalem.[61] In addition, both Kosova and Vojvodina, as former autonomous provinces of Yugoslavia, had their own constitution of 1974, which were unconstitutionally revoked in 1989 by the Milosevic regime.

Notwithstanding the ambiguity arising from the title, due attention should be paid to the substance of this legal document. Does it serve its purpose, which means does it represent the supreme law for Kosovar legislation? The fact that it was promulgated by UNMIK Regulation automatically placed it on the same rank as other Regulations and thus it is unclear whether it can be considered a supreme law.[62]

One may ask the additional question what is the Constitutional Framework's legal power in relation to the UNSC Resolution?

56 See Constitutional Framework, chapters 6, 6.1 and 8.1.

57 See Constitutional Framework, chapter 14.3.

58 See Carsten Stahn, Constitution without State? Kosovo under the United Nations Constitutional Framework for Self Government, *Leiden Journal of International Law*, Vol. 14, 2001, p. 543.

59 Ibid.

60 Ibid., p. 544.

61 Ibid.

62 Ibid., p. 546.

In this context, one should look at the wording of the Constitutional Framework, which states "The exercise of the responsibilities of the Provisional Institutions of Self-Government under this Constitutional Framework shall not affect or diminish the authority of the SRSG to ensure full implementation of UNSCR 1244(1999), including overseeing the Provisional Institutions of Self-Government, its officials and its agencies, and taking appropriate measures whenever their actions are inconsistent with UNSCR 1244(1999) or this Constitutional Framework".[63] Thus, it makes it clear that the Constitutional Framework could not be regarded as a supreme law as it is superseded by UNSC Resolution 1244. Furthermore, from the wording of the Constitutional Framework, it appears that the SRSG is its ultimate guardian.[64]

No supervisory body was established that could supervise the acts of UNMIK as regards their compatibility with human rights standards.

Although the Constitutional Framework foresaw the establishment of a Special Chamber whose task would be to determine the compatibility of adopted laws with the Constitutional Framework, it did not authorise this body to review cases involving alleged human rights violations.[65]

The establishment of such a supervisory body was viewed by the UNMIK authorities as unnecessary, since according to them UNMIK had its own internal mechanism, which was sufficient to fulfil the task.

In this regard, it has been stated: "UNMIK Regulation and Administrative Directives are examined for compatibility with international human rights standards both within UNMIK and by the Office of Legal Affairs at UNHQ in New York. Moreover, the office of the Legal Adviser has developed a practice of seeking, where appropriate, expert opinions from the Council of Europe on draft legislation under consideration".[66]

However, OSCE inquiries that have been conducted in relation to this matter proved that no such practice existed.[67]

The application of the initial legal formula in practice

As already stressed, failure to provide guidance as to reconcile FRY laws with international human rights standards led to confusion,[68] as both international and

63 See Constitutional Framework, Chapter 12.

64 Similar to Danzig and Saar territory.

65 The Constitutional Framework is no longer in force as it was replaced by the State Constitution, which came into effect on 15 June 2008.

66 Alexander Borg Olivier, UNMIK's Legal Adviser, *Nature and Operation of a Human Rights Advisory Panel in Kosovo*, Note, 25 May 2005, Quoted in Bernhard Knoll, *The Legal Status of Territories Subject to Administration by International Organizations*, Cambridge University Press, 2008, p. 385.

67 Accordingly, the draft laws were not subjected to a review of their compatibility with human rights standards from human rights experts or from human rights components of UNMIK. See OSCE Report, *Assembly Law of Kosovo*.

68 Scott N. Carlson, Wendy S. Betts, and Gregory Gisvold, The Post-Conflict Traditional Administration of Kosovo and Lessons Learned in Efforts to Establish Judiciary and Rule of Law, *Michigan Journal of International Law*, Vol. 22, No. 33, Spring 2001, p. 4.

local judges and prosecutors were unable to identify laws or parts of laws which were inconsistent with internationally recognised standards. As the international members came from different countries, it was often not easy for them to identify legal gaps in an "improvised law", particularly as regards discriminatory provisions that were considered to pose a serious obstacle to the rule of law.[69] On the other hand, local judges coming from the old communist school were totally unfamiliar with international human rights law and thus faced many difficulties in applying laws which had incorporated human rights standards.[70]

The failure of Regulation 2000/24 to clarify the relationship between international human rights law and applicable law led to human rights standards not being invoked by the international or domestic judiciary.

As a consequence, provisions of the FRY Criminal Code (CP) and Criminal Procedural Code (CPC) that were in breach of human rights laws were widely applied, which led to number of human rights violations, in particular of fair trial principles, the right to liberty, property rights and freedom of expression.

For example, Article 74 FRY CPC, which allowed the investigating judge to monitor and restrict a defendant's communications with his lawyer, was repeatedly applied by local judges. Such a restriction directly affected the ability of the defendant to adequately prepare his defence.[71] In addition, the FRY Code of Criminal Procedure did not envisage the right to a prompt adjudication of criminal charges,[72] which gave judges unfettered discretion to postpone trials and to prolong pre-trial detentions (Article 285FRY CPC).[73] As a result, individuals were subjected to indefinite detention.[74]

Moreover, the applicable law did not provide an effective remedy for the accused to participate in and initiate a review of his pre-trial detention. As a consequence, an individual subjected to an unreasonably long period of custody lacked independent domestic grounds for claiming that his detention was

69 See David Marshall and Shelly Inglis, The Disempowerment of Human Rights-Based Justice in the United Nations Mission in Kosovo, *Harvard Human Rights Journal*, Vol. 16, Spring 2003, p. 97. The authors mainly refer to the international judges who were acting pursuant to UNMIK Regulation 2000/64; however, the same should apply to the HPD and the HPCC panel.

70 Furthermore, taking into consideration that until recently Kosovo did not have an anti-discrimination law and that therefore most people, including the judiciary, were not familiar with issues involving discrimination, it is difficult to imagine how the presumption of discrimination was determined during the adjudication process.

71 See OSCE/ LSMS Report, A review of Kosovo Justice System, September 2000–28 February 2001, p. 13.

72 A right guaranteed under Article 6 (1) ECHR.

73 The length of proceedings in both criminal and penal cases continues to hamper the Kosovar judiciary. Judges continue the practice of postponing hearings without giving any valid reason. For additional information see Ombudsperson Annual Reports, 2005–2006–2007, available at the following website: www.ombudspersonkosovo.org.

74 See OSCE/LSMS Report, Report No. 3, Observations and Recommendations of the OSCE legal System Monitoring Section, Expiration of the Detention Period for current Detainees, p. 9.

unlawful.[75] In addition, it was quite common practice for a public authority to interfere with a sentenced individual's right to respect for his correspondence.[76] Article 107 of the Law on the Enforcement of Criminal Sentences guaranteed a right to correspondence with close family members only and any correspondence with other persons was subject to the permission of the respective prison director, who had discretion to decide upon such request. As a result, the right of sentenced individuals to correspond with the outside world was severely limited.[77]

In 2005, a group of young protesters from the *Vetëvendosje* movement[78] started to protest all over Kosovo in opposition to the decision of the international community to enter into negotiations with Serbia regarding Kosovo's future status. They organised peaceful protests whose purpose was manifested in the slogans "*Jo negociata – Vetëvendosje*" ("*No negotiations – Self-determination*"), which were sprayed on the walls of public and private buildings.[79] As a consequence, they were subjected to ill treatment and unwarranted arrests or alternatively received fines amounting to 150 euros.[80] Legal grounds for police intervention and court proceedings were found in the provisions of the Law on Public Peace and Order,[81] which had always been in contradiction with international human rights standards as they directly violated the right to freedom of expression and the right to freedom of assembly guaranteed by article 10 of the European Convention on Human Rights.[82]

75 See OSCE/ LSMS Report, *A Review of Kosovo Justice System*, p. 14; Kosovo Ombudsperson Institution, *Report Cele Gashi against United Nation Mission in Kosovo (UNMIK)*, Registration Nr. 256/1, available at the following website: www.ombudspersonkosovo.org. The latter report states: "Not only must an individual deprived of liberty have recourse to the courts to challenge the legality and the continuing necessity of the deprivation, but the courts themselves have an obligation to take a proactive role and at appropriate intervals to review every deprivation of liberty for its continuing necessity".

76 A right guaranteed under Article 8 paragraph 1 ECHR.

77 See Kosovo Ombudsperson's Special Report, Special Report Nr. 7, On the Compatibility of the with recognised international standards of certain provisions of the Yugoslav Law on Enforcement of Criminal Sentence (1977), available at the following website: www.ombudspersonkosovo.org.

78 The *Vetëvendosje* movement strongly opposed the negotiations as a form of resolving Kosovo's status. They called on the international community to recognise Kosovo's right to self-determination immediately. More details of this movement can be found on the following website: www.levizjaVetëvendosje.org.

79 The slogans on private buildings were written with the consent of the owners. Interview with Mr Glauk Konjufca, member of the *Vetëvendosje* movement, November 2005.

80 See the letter sent by the Ombudsperson to the SRSG, Mr Soren Jessen Peterssen, dated 25 October 2005, available at: www.ombudspersonkosovo.org.

81 The law is very old: it was enacted in 1981 and contains provisions which are not consistent with international human rights law.

82 Surprisingly, neither the law enforcement agencies nor the courts have so far considered the possibility that writing slogans on public buildings might amount to an offence arising from damage to property. See the letter sent by the Ombudsperson to the SRSG, Mr Soren Jessen Peterssen, dated 25 October 2005, available at: www.ombudspersonkosovo.org.

The scope of the legislative power of UNMIK

It is generally known that the legitimacy of a country's law-making bodies derives from its basic constitutional framework or constitutional settlement.

The law-making powers of the UN derive from the UN Charter. The General Assembly is given the legislative role as it has been empowered to "encourage the progressive development of international law and its codification".[83] In this regard, it is involved in making resolutions that address a variety of issues reflecting important international principles. As a result, many of them have been accepted as authoritative sources of international law.[84] In recent years, the Security Council has taken on a legislative role as well. Its resolutions have proven to be of universal character and impose immediate binding obligations on all states.[85] Together, they became involved in both the development and clarification of law.[86]

But can the UN legislate on behalf of a particular constituency? In light of the discussion presented here, one may ask whether specific rules are enunciated in international law, namely the UN Charter, that enables the UN to perform the role of an internal legislator. And if so where does this power derive from?

The law-making powers of these organisations derive from a constituent treaty and are attributed to them by the member states. In light of this, the scope of the law-making powers of international organisations is limited to internal matters only.[87]

UNSC Resolution 1244, among other things, calls upon UNMIK to provide security and maintain law and order throughout the territory of Kosovo,[88] which

83 See Article 13 (para. 1) of the UN Charter. Regarding the ongoing debate about the legislative powers of the General Assembly, see Jose E. Alvarez, *International Organisations as Law Makers*, Oxford University Press, 2005, pp. 67–74. See also Rosalyn Higgins, The United Nations and Law Making, *The American Journal of International Law*, Vol. 64, No. 4, 1970, pp. 37–48.

84 Higgins, Ibid. See also Gregory J. Kerwiin, The Role of United Nations General Assembly Resolutions in Determining Principles of International Law in United States Courts, *Duke Law Journal*, 1983, pp. 876–899.

85 UNSC Resolution, *1373 On Threats to International Peace and Security Caused by Terrorist Acts]*, adopted on 28 September 2001. See also UNSC Resolution 1540, *Regarding the Non-Proliferation of Weapons of Mass Destructions*, adopted on 28 April 2004. These measures were taken in response to global threats to international peace and security. See Eric Rosand, The Security Council as Global Legislator Ultra Vires or Ultra Innovative?, *Fordham International Law Journal*, Vol. 28, No. 3, 2004. See also Erika de Wet, *The Chapter VII Powers of the United Nations Security Council*, Oxford and Portland Oregon, 2004; Nicholas Tsagourias, *Security Council Legislation Article 2(7) of the UN Charter and the Principle of Subsidiary*, Working Papers, Series 2011, p. 5, Adam Smith Research Foundation.

86 Higgins, *supra* n. 83. See also Kerwiin, *supra* n. 84.

87 Jan Wouters and Philip de Man, *International Organizations as Law Makers*, Working Paper No. 21, March 2009, Leuven Centre for Global Governance Studies; Catholic University of Leuven.

88 UNSC Resolution 1244, para. 11 (a).

has been commonly understood to mean the recreation, reproduction and reconstruction of the Kosovar legal system.[89]

Looking at the legal grounds for the peacekeeping operations, which are Chapter VII of the UN Charter as well as the general framework governing the UNMIK administration, namely UNSC Resolution 1244,[90] there is no explicit provision that entitles UNMIK or its Special Representative to exercise legislative power.

It has been argued that the legal framework applicable to the legislative powers of UN missions derives from the nature of their creation.[91] With this in mind, one may assume that this implies the ability of an international territorial administration to adapt itself to the situation on the ground.

Generally speaking, there are no provisions that empower UN political bodies such as the General Assembly and the Security Council to legislate on behalf of a particular constituency. UNSC Resolution 1244, which constituted UNMIK, only calls upon UNMIK to provide security and maintain law and order throughout the territory of Kosovo.[92]

It is therefore difficult to assume that the authority of UNMIK to legislate derives from Resolution 1244. The wording "to maintain law" implies the duty to preserve the existing laws, ensuring their continuation.

One may ask whether this legal intervention requires any specific consent from the FRY authorities.[93] Or is the consent obtained through the Kumanovo agreement sufficient ground to guarantee UNMIK overall control over Kosovo? As noted earlier, UNSC Resolution 1244 lays down a normative framework for the UN's commitment to placing Kosovo under UN governance for an unlimited period of time. Yet in doing so it is also bound to ensure the sovereignty and territorial integrity of the FRY.[94] As already noted, the Resolution does not cede, transfer or convey sovereign title to UNMIK, but rather suspends it for an unlimited period and subsequently entitles UNMIK to exercise all sovereign rights within the Kosovo territory in the absence of

89 The legislative powers of UNMIK are set out in UNMIK Regulation 1999/1, which in its pertinent part says: "In the performance of the duties entrusted to the interim administration under United Nations Security Council resolution 1244 (1999), UNMIK will, as necessary, issue legislative acts in the form of regulations. Such regulations will remain in force until repealed by UNMIK or superseded by such rules as are subsequently issued by the institutions established under a political settlement, as provided for in United Nations Security Council resolution 1244 (1999), Section 4, UNSC Regulation 1999/1.

90 Endorsed pursuant to Chapter VII of the UN Nations Charter. The International Administration in East Timor was established in the same manner by UNSC Resolution 1272.

91 Kristen Boon, Legislative Reform in Post-Conflict Zones: Jus Post Bellum and the Contemporary Occupant's Law-Making Powers, *Michigan Law Journal*, Vol. 50, 2005, p. 11.

92 UNSC Resolution 1244, para. 11 (a).

93 *Reaffirming the commitment of all Member States to the sovereignty and territorial integrity of the Federal Republic of Yugoslavia and the other States of the region, as set out in the Helsinki Final Act and annex 2*", UNSC Resolution 1244.

94 Ibid.

the original sovereign.[95] In this regard, the UNMIK authorities were only obliged to refrain from any acts that might render FRY sovereignty rights meaningless in the long term,[96] which may readily be understood as refraining from intervening in FRY legislation.[97]

It has already been informed that during the initial phase of its establishment UNMIK ultimately decreed that FRY laws should be applied; however, as FRY laws proved to be highly discriminatory it found itself obliged to undertake an in-depth legislative reform and establish a new legal order. This was seen by the FRY authorities as a violation of its sovereignty.[98] However, UNMIK's legislative activity has been viewed by legal experts as a matter of necessity, both military and civilian, in enabling UNMIK to become fully operational.[99]

Thus during its entire existence UNMIK has been confronted with a fundamental tension between its narrow terms of mandate for governing the territory and its strategic priority to effectively re-establish the rule of law and the administration of justice over the territory.[100]

It should be stressed that this ambiguity caused difficulties for UNMIK in developing a clear modus operandi. Subsequently, it enabled the SRSG to take advantage of it and establish the legal grounds for endowing himself with the equivalent of sovereign powers to carry out all aspects of the UN's work in Kosovo, among them the power to override the national laws of the prior regime, to enact new laws in the form of regulations and to repeal existing national laws.[101]

95 According to Knoll, UNMIK was entitled to exercise full jurisdiction over the territory based on Chapter VII of the UN Charter that has been transferred to UNMIK as a subsidiary organ of the Security Council, Knoll, *supra* n. 66, p. 201. Yannis questions the legal capacity of the Security Council to declare sovereignty over a certain territory to be in abeyance. He particularly questions whether legitimate forms of coercive action can result in the suspension of all the rights of a sovereign state. In his view, the Security Council can undertake such an action as long as it serves the purpose of maintaining peace and security, as was the case with Kosovo. See Alexandros Yannis, The Concept of Suspended Sovereignty in International Law and Its Implications in International Politics, *European Journal of International Law*, Vol. 13, No. 5, 2003, p. 1039.

96 Knoll, *supra* n. 66, p. 98.

97 According to Resolution 1244, UNMIK was tasked with facilitating the political process regarding the future political status of the territory. UNSC Resolution 1244, para. 11.

98 Franz-Lothar Altman, The Status of Kosovo, in Dimitris Triantaphyllou (ed.), *What Status for Kosovo?*, EU-ISS Chaillot Paper No. 50, Institute for Security Studies, October 2001, pp. 19–22–34.

99 Such legal interventionism is regarded by local actors as arbitrary action undertaken by an unaccountable, appointed bureaucracy.

100 The legal implications arising from the ambiguity of the UNMIK mandate are discussed in chapters 3, 4 and 5.

101 The legislative power of the SRSG derives from UNMIK Regulation 1999/01, enacted by the SRSG. The ambiguity could have been overcome if the SRSG had taken the opposite course of action and established power-sharing control with domestic actors. The same model of governance was introduced into East Timor. Although different in terms of the goal of the mission (UNTAET had a clear goal when it comes to the final political status of

Caught between an indecisive and highly ambiguous mandate, UNMIK was obliged to conduct its legislative activity in an ad hoc manner designed to meet the requirements of the mission. Consequently, UNMIK's practice became associated with the behaviour of colonial power and belligerent occupation.[102]

Such an assertion deserves attention. Nevertheless it should be stressed that the objective of this section is not to discuss the normative distinction between colonialism or belligerent occupation and international territorial administration, but rather to identify those common characteristics that are relevant to the present argument.

So, do UNMIK legislative undertakings resemble the legislative action of a colonial government? In this context, the attention has been placed upon the manner of promoting the rule of law which is considered to resemble the practice of "fundamentally imperialist enterprise".[103]

Looking at the past, one of the most significant legacies of colonial practices was the importation and implementation of the coloniser's legal system.[104] To establish the basis for institutional stabilisation, the colonial government gradually transplanted its own legal system. Initially, laws supporting commerce and trade were the first to be introduced, whereas laws regulating domestic and private affairs were generally left to local authorities.[105]

This sums up that the legislative reform was an important component of colonial administration, whatever may have been the motive.

Boon argues that the balance between recognition of local legal orders and the extension of the coloniser's laws was delicate, as the primary limits on a colonial power's ability to change local laws were regarded as practical.[106] She further argues that even if the "colonizer retained absolute supremacy over the colonies, the colonial laws often stood side by side with traditional laws".[107] However, on the other side it has been argued that the colonial laws and institutions introduced by the colonisers were mainly concentrated on the protection of property and wealth (the main objectives of settlement), whereas little was done to protect

---

the territory), these two missions are very similar, in particular when it comes to the techniques applied regarding legal development. For more about the legal implications arising from the ambiguity of the international territorial administrations' mandate, see Christian Eric Ford and Ben A. Oppenheim, Neotrusteeship or Mistrusteeship? The "Authority Creep" Dilemma in United Nations Transitional Administration, *Vanderbilt Journal of Transnational Law*, Vol. 41, No. 1, January 2008.

102 Chesterman, *supra* n. 3, p. 47. Paris, International Peacebuilding and "Mission Civilasatrice", *Review of International Studies*, Vol. 28, 2002, p. 637; Boon, *supra* n. 91, p. 3.

103 See Ehrenreich Brooks, *supra* n. 6, p. 2275. See also Ralph Wilde, *International Territorial Administration, How Trusteeship and Civilizing Mission Never Went Away*, Oxford University Press, 2008, p. 297.

104 See Boon, *supra* n. 91, p. 3.

105 Ibid., p. 5.

106 Kristen Boon is referring to an in-depth analysis of French colonial practice. Ibid. See also M.B. Hooker, *Legal Pluralism: An Introduction to Colonial and Neo-Colonial Laws*, Oxford: Clarendon Press, 1975, p. 198.

107 Boon, *supra* n. 91.

the lives and well-being of the ordinary people.[108] The standards promoted by the colonial states aimed at securing their own interests, which were incorporated into laws and particular policies that reflected the subordination of the colony's economy and society.[109]

Relying on the foregoing discussion, it is difficult to draw a comparison between the legal performances of these administrations. A linkage can be found, however, if we look at the way in which these activities were performed. For example, both systems underline supremacy over the governed entity, which enabled them to retain enormous power to reorder and reconstitute local society. The legal bases for doing so are formless and lack clarity. Both claim to be knowledgeable and capable of devising rules for another people. They create laws for those "incapable of governing themselves", but do not subject themselves to the same laws.

So does such practice support the assertion of the scholars that "the contemporary practice of peacebuilding may be viewed as a modern rendering of the *mission civilisatrice* . . . an attempt to bring war-shattered states into conformity with the international system's prevailing standards of domestic governance"?[110]

I find it difficult, to build an opinion on such an observation, in particular if one takes into consideration the universality of the human rights norms that the ITA is attempting to diffuse into the national system of a war-shattered society. In particular if we leave aside the hypocritical attitudes in politics, limited efficiency of the human rights instruments and instead believe in sincere will that steam from these instruments.

As already mentioned, it has also been argued that the activities performed by UNMIK are similar to the powers accorded to a belligerent occupant.[111] Thus, in the eyes of some authors today's UN peace operations to some extent resemble a "modern occupation",[112] with some going as far as considering international organisations to be "a new set of occupiers".[113]

It has been argued that the analogy between ITA and administration by occupation retains much traction, because both actors resemble each other in the eyes of the local population and most of the time face the same challenges to acceptability, both within and outside the territory.

In order "to avoid the stigma of being seen as occupiers, they have developed their own legal and political coping mechanism".[114]

108 See Sidney Smith Bell, *Administration of Colonies by Great Britain*, Longman, Brown, Green, Longmans and Roberts, 1859, p. 448, An overall analyses of the British colonial administration.

109 See Wilde, *supra* n. 103, p. 388.

110 Roland Paris, International Peacebuilding and "Mission Civilisatrice", *Review of International Studies*, Vol. 28, 2002, p. 638.

111 Boon, *supra* n. 91, p. 3.

112 Harris regards ITA as a "modern occupation", Grant T. Harris, The Era of Multilateral Occupation, *Berkley Journal of International Law*, Vol. 24, 2006, pp. 4, 5.

113 Steven R. Ratner, Foreign Occupation an International territorial Administration: The Challenges of Convergence, *The European Journal of International Law*, Vol. 16, 2005, pp. 695–719, 698.

114 Ibid.

In light of this, it has been argued that UNSC Resolution 1244 incorporated some of the provisions of the Hague Regulations and Geneva Conventions, in particular those addressing the right of the foreign power to maintain public order and ensure the welfare of the people.[115]

However, such an assertion requires thorough scrutiny.

International law establishes clear obligations on the part of the occupying power towards the occupied territory.[116]

According to the provisions enshrined in Hague Regulation 1907 (Article 43) and Geneva Convention IV (Article 64), the occupying power is bound by the national law of the country.[117]

It should be noted that while the Hague Regulation has a general approach to this issue, unambiguously and without restriction referring to "the laws in force in the country", the fourth Geneva Convention[118] offers a more precise formulation by referring particularly to the criminal laws of the country. Although in principle it refers to criminal laws remaining in force, an exception to this binding obligation of national law is allowed if it is justified by military necessity,

115 See Tobias H. Irmscher, The Legal Framework for the Activities of the United Nations Interim Administration Mission in Kosovo: The Charter, Human Rights, and the Law of Occupation, *German Yearbook of International Law*, Vol. 44, 2001, pp. 353, 394. Chesterman argues that UNMIK's operation in Kosovo is governed through the military operation. See Chesterman, *supra* n. 3, p. 239. Blerim Reka further asserts that the initial undertakings of UNMIK in Kosovo were similar to those in post-war Iraq undertaken by the US as an occupying power, see Reka, *supra* n. 4.

116 Which means that the belligerent occupant is governed by the laws of war, in this case the Hague Regulations of 1907 and the Fourth Geneva Convention of 1949. The definition of "occupation" under international humanitarian law can be found in Article 42 of the 1907 Hague Regulations, which is reflective of customary international law: "Territory is considered occupied when it is actually placed under the authority of the hostile army. The occupation extends only to the territory where such authority has been established and can be exercised".

117 Art. 43. "The authority of the legitimate power having in fact passed into the hands of the occupant, the latter shall take all the measures in his power to restore, and ensure, as far as possible, public order and safety, while respecting, unless absolutely prevented, the laws in force in the country". As viewed by Edelstein, "[m]ilitary occupation is the temporary control of a territory by a state (or group of allied states) that makes no claim to permanent sovereignty over that territory". David M. Edelstein, *Occupational Hazards*, Ithaca: Cornell University Press, 2008, p. 3.

118 Art. 64. "The penal laws of the occupied territory shall remain in force, with the exception that they may be repealed or suspended by the Occupying Power in cases where they constitute a threat to its security or an obstacle to the application of the present Convention. Subject to the latter consideration and to the necessity for ensuring the effective administration of justice, the tribunals of the occupied territory shall continue to function in respect of all offences covered by the said laws. The Occupying Power may, however, subject the population of the occupied territory to provisions which are essential to enable the Occupying Power to fulfil its obligations under the present Convention, to maintain the orderly government of the territory, and to ensure the security of the Occupying Power, of the members and property of the occupying forces or administration, and likewise of the establishments and lines of communication used by them".

which means that the occupying power does not have to observe national law if its application constitutes a threat to its security or would become an obstacle to the application of international humanitarian law.[119] In addition, the protection of public order and the welfare of the inhabitants could be used as sufficient grounds for changes to the legislation.[120]

To sum up, the occupying power is under an obligation to administer the occupied territory within the context of existing legislation to the extent that it conforms to the law of occupation. Generally, this implies that the constitution, statutes and laws, international conventions and treaties should remain intact.[121] It follows that the primary responsibilities of the occupying power are to temporarily preserve basic public order and civil life, while respecting, unless absolutely prevented, the laws in force in the country without prejudicing a final outcome, as well as preserving local institutions and laws.[122]

Certain legislative changes are allowed only if they emerge from military necessity.[123]

So, how can we distinguish the legal performance of an occupying force and international territorial administration such as UNMIK?

Generally speaking, the significant difference between these two interventions lies in lawfulness of their undertakings. Whereas the legality of the ITA remains undisputed, the belligerent occupation continues to be regarded as unlawful and non-consensual in nature.[124] The visions of the two governing regimes stem from two different legal regimes, namely international humanitarian law and human rights law.[125]

119 Dieter Fleck, *The Handbook of International Humanitarian Law*, Second Edition, Oxford University Press, 2008, p. 287. See also the comment on Article 64 of Geneva Convention IV in Dieter Fleck, *The Handbook of International Humanitarian Law*, Second Edition, Oxford University Press, 2008, p. 286.

120 See Article 55 of the Hague Convention 1907. See Irmscher, *supra* n. 114, p. 390. See also Lindsey Cameron, Does the Law of Occupation Preclude Transformational Developments by the Occupying Power, in Marc Vuijlsteke and Floricica Olteanu (eds.), *Current Challenges to the Law of Occupation*, Collegium, No 34, Special Edition, College of Europe, 2006, pp. 60–67.

121 Cameron, ibid., p. 62.

122 Harris, *supra* n. 111, p. 4.

123 According to Dinstein, no fundamental changes are allowed and any enacted legislation should be subject to some qualification. See Yoram Dinstein, *Legislation under Article 43 of the Hague Regulations Belligerent Occupation an and Peace-Building*, Occasional Program on Humanitarian Policy and Conflict Research, Harvard University, Papers Series, No. 1, 2004. For more about military necessity, see Marten Zwanenburg, Legal Interoperability in Multinational Forces, a Military Necessity, in Marc Vuijlsteke and Floricica Olteanu (eds.), *Current Challenges to the Law of Occupation*, Collegium, No 34, Special Edition, College of Europe, 2006, pp. 101–108.

124 See Aleksandar Momirov, *Accountability of International Territorial Administrations, a Public Law Approach*, Eleven International Publishing, 2011, p. 116.

125 As Steven Ratner would say, "IHL should govern state occupations because it is minimalist, while human rights law should govern international organizations missions because it is ambitious". See Ratner, *supra* n. 113, p. 702.

Both actors bring about an immediate displacement of sovereignty in favour of the occupying force and both signify the fact that they are not sovereigns,[126] as well as preserve local institutions and laws.[127]

However, whereas an occupying power must operate within strict confines when making institutional changes and legal revisions, UNMIK lacks a clear framework to meet the objectives and needs of the interim administration. This insufficiency created a pool of uncertainty and perhaps the only way of escaping it was to borrow certain elements from the doctrine of *jus post bellum.*[128] This particularly happened in the early phase of UNMIK's deployment. In this phase UNMIK was willing to engage only in so-called "transformational change" that touched upon criminal legislation, and showed a total unwillingness to legislate in the civil and economic sphere. This came as a consequence of confusion arising from the absence of clear legal grounds. Because later on UNMIK's authorities fully engaged in a transformational process, legislative power passed into the hands of the SRSG, which resulted in a regime change and the setting up of new political institutions.[129]

These types of undertaking are not allowed to an occupying power. The law of occupation prevents the occupying power from remodelling the governmental structures of the occupied territory.[130]

So although these two forms of intervention may resemble each other, as they often share the same traits, it is difficult to prove that a UN administration stands on an equal footing with an occupying power.

This discussion helps us to understand that certain rules in international law can be used to manage the common implications arising from two different situations. But this does not mean that the law on occupation can be considered a valuable framework for the functioning of international administrations. Due to the lack of clear legal framework UN is obliged very often to establish strategic framework for making sense of intervention in post-war societies. In this context, such attitudes become oriented towards treatment of needs that lead to normalisation of situation. In doing so it legitimises the imposition of a particular normalcy in countries considered incapable to govern themselves.[131]

126 However, although international law emphasises that the occupation does not affect sovereignty, it recognises that the title of the territorial sovereign is considerably weakened and reduced to a "naked title" (*nudum ius*), as the occupied state is "undeniably, divested of possession". See Yoram Dinstein, *The International Law of Belligerent Occupation*, Cambridge: Cambridge University Press, 2009, p. 49, see also Momirov, *supra* n. 124, p. 116.

127 Harris, *supra* n. 111, p. 4.

128 Boon, *supra* n. 91, p. 7.

129 It has been extensively involved in selling socially own property.

130 Daniel Thurer, Current Challenges to the Law of Occupation, in Marc Vuijlsteke and Floricica Olteanu (eds.), *Current Challenges to the Law of Occupation*, Collegium, No. 34, Special Edition, College of Europe, 2006, p. 17.

131 Nicolas Lemay-Hebert and Gezim Visoka, Normal Peace: A New Strategic Narrative of Intervention, *Politics and Governance*, Vol. 5, No. 3, 2017.

What has gone wrong? Shortcomings in UNMIK's law

Although numerous UNMIK Regulations[132] explicitly required that domestic law should be in accordance with international human rights standards and, moreover, that all persons undertaking public duties or holding public office in Kosovo were to observe internationally recognised human rights principles and refrain from any discriminatory acts, the outcomes as well as the process by which the outcomes were achieved have exhibited a range of shortfalls.

In this regard, the following section focuses on shortcomings surrounding particular laws issued by UNMIK, which proved to be in contradiction with internationally recognised human rights principles.

In this context, we turn first to the text of the Constitutional Framework.

Though presented as a quasi-constitution,[133] it does not contain a separate chapter on the constitutional protection of human rights and fundamental freedoms. It only lists the main international treaties on human rights, stipulating that "the Provisional Institutions of Self-Government shall observe and ensure internationally recognized human rights and fundamental freedoms", including those contained in the international human rights instruments.[134]

The SRSG and the UNMIK administration were not bound by the Constitutional Framework and, moreover, the laws issued by the SRSG were excluded from the jurisdiction of the Special Chamber of the Supreme Court on constitutional matters. In addition, as already mentioned this chamber was never established.

It has been noted that several ad hoc Regulations were passed which were used as a tool to provide for a particular outcome in certain situations or to respond to isolated events.[135] So the legal intervention became evident on all fronts, in media, property, criminal justice, and so forth.

Thus, in response to the particular problems surrounding post-war ethnic revenge it was found to be an appropriate solution to impose certain restrictions on the freedom of the press, in particular on their reporting of news that revealed information involving war crimes.

For instance, following the murder of an UNMIK local employee of Serbian ethnicity, as a consequence of the statement issued in the daily newspaper *Dita* alleging that a person was involved in atrocities against the Albanian population, action was taken such as closing down *Dita* and a new Regulation 2000/4[136] on the Prohibition Against Inciting National, Racial, Religious or Ethnic Hatred, Discord or Intolerance was issued.

132 Among them, Regulations 1999/1 and 1999/24.

133 According to the ICJ Advisory Opinion, the Constitutional Framework possesses international legal character and together with UNSC Resolution 1244 forms part of international law. ICJ Advisory Opinion on Unilateral Declaration of Independence in Respect of Kosovo, 22 July 2010, p. 3.

134 The Constitutional Framework for the Provisional Self-Government of Kosovo is available at the following website: www.unmikonline.org/constframework.htm.

135 Marshall and Inglis, *supra* n. 69, p. 114.

136 Enacted on 9 February 2000.

The regulation incorporates a set of provisions against publicly inciting or spreading hatred or violence between national, ethnic, racial, religious, or other groups living in Kosovo. For this, it imposes a very high sentence.[137] The Regulation was subject to criticism both inside and outside Kosovo for directly affecting standards of freedom of expression, as it goes beyond the permitted parameters of freedom of expression recognised under international human rights law.[138]

Subsequently, legal analysts expressed their fear with regard to its implementation, especially its application in the judicial system knowing that the Kosovan system lacks impartiality and fairness. In this regard it has been argued that the Kosovan judicial system is "inadequate to apply such a sensitive Regulation, even where legitimate, with balance and impartiality; and that it is an inappropriate solution to the very complex problem of racism and intolerance in Kosovo".[139] Although this regulation has never been used in practice,[140] despite the critics similar provisions were incorporated into the provisional Criminal Code,[141] which inherited both the harshness and the lack of clarity of the regulation.

However, taking into consideration the level of ethnic hostilities that emerged after the conflict, one may assume that the legislator was obliged to reconsider the relationship between freedom of expression and freedom to endanger a relatively weak minority.[142]

137 See UNMIK Regulation 2000/4, Section 1: "1.1 Whoever publicly incites or publicly spreads hatred, discord or intolerance between national, racial, religious, ethnic or other such groups living in Kosovo which acts are likely to disturb public order shall be punished by a fine or by imprisonment not exceeding five years or both.

1.2 If the acts referred to in section 1.1 of the present regulation were committed systematically or by taking advantage of one's position or authority or if disorder, violence or other grave consequences resulted from those acts, the period of imprisonment may be extended to a term not exceeding eight years.

1.3 Whoever publicly incites or publicly spreads hatred, discord or intolerance between national, racial, religious, ethnic or other such groups living in Kosovo which acts are likely to disturb public order through coercion, jeopardising of safety, exposing to derision of national, racial, ethnic or religious symbols, damaging belongings of another, or desecrating monuments or graves, shall be punished by imprisonment for a term not exceeding eight years.

1.4 If the acts referred to in section 1.3 of the present regulation were committed systematically or by taking advantage of one's position or authority or if disorder, violence or other grave consequences resulted from those acts, the period of imprisonment may be extended to a term not exceeding ten years".

138 See the statement issued by Article 19, a London-based NGO, dated 20 March 2000, available at the following website: www.ifex.org/20fr/layout/set/print/layout/set/print/content/view/full/9945/ (accessed on 10 February 2010).

139 See the statement issued by Article 19, a London-based NGO, dated 20 March 2000, available at the following website: www.ifex.org/20fr/layout/set/print/layout/set/print/content/view/full/9945/ (accessed on 10 February 2010).

140 Marshall and Inglis, *supra* n. 69, p. 112.

141 The Provisional Criminal Code, enacted on 6 July 2003, establishes the same criminal liability for acts involving incitement or publicly spreading hatred or discord or intolerance between national, racial, religious or ethnic, religious or other groups living in Kosovo.

142 International law imposes a positive duty upon states as far as restrictions on freedom of expression are concerned. In this regard, the UN Covenant on Civil and Political Rights,

As Boyle argues, "there is a communal as well as an individual dimension to human rights and freedoms" and "the individual's right to promote racist views must not only be defended in terms of individual rights, but in terms of the communal interests in equality".[143] Consequently, a sensible society would be allowed to place limits on freedom of expression when it begins to endanger these latter interests.[144]

This suggests that possible misinterpretations of the regulation in practice could have been avoided with an effectively enacted administrative direction that provided clear guidance for the practical application of the Regulation.

Another similar legislative intervention was undertaken with regard to the sale of real property, Regulation 2001/17 on the registration of contracts for the sale of real property in specific geographical areas of Kosovo.

During the period between 1999 and 2001 the number of sales of real properties of Serbs/Montenegrins increased. The rapid sale of property soon became a matter of concern for the international community, whose aim was and still is the establishment of a multicultural society in Kosovo. In order to prevent the Serbian/Montenegrin minority from leaving Kosovo, UNMIK issued Regulation 2001/17, which forbids the selling of property in the areas inhabited by the Serbian/Montenegrin community.

It required that all contracts for the sale of residential property concluded between parties within the designated area should receive approval from the relevant UNMIK municipal administration before the competent court verified the sale.[145]

It forbade the competent court from registering a contract of sale for a property within the area without proof issued by a municipal administration.[146]

Article 20 reads: "Any propaganda for war shall be prohibited by law. . . . Any advocacy of national, racial or religious hatred that constitutes incitement to discrimination, hostility or violence shall be prohibited by law".

Article 10 (2) ECHR allows restrictions upon freedom of expression in cases involving hate speech, stating: "The exercise of these freedoms, since it carries with it duties and responsibilities, may be subject to such formalities, conditions, restrictions or penalties as are prescribed by law and are necessary in a democratic society, in the interests of national security, territorial integrity or public safety, for the prevention of disorder or crime, for the protection of health or morals, for the protection of the reputation or rights of others". Moreover, the International Convention on the Elimination of Racial Discrimination (ICERD) has gone even further and offers far-reaching standards of protection. According to Article 4 (a), there is an obligation upon states to declare as offences punishable by law the following categories: "1. dissemination of ideas based on racial superiority; 2. dissemination of ideas based on racial hatred; 3. incitement to racial discrimination; 4. acts of racially motivated violence; 5. incitement to acts of racially motivated violence; and 6. the provision of assistance, including of a financial nature, to racist activities".

143 Kevin Boyle, Overview of a Dilemma, in Coliver Sandra (ed.), *Striking a Balance, Hate Speech, Freedom of Expression and Non-Discrimination*, International Centre against Censorship and Human Rights Centre, University of Essex, pp. 1–8.

144 Ibid., pp. 5–8.

145 See Section 3 of UNMIK Regulation 2001/17.

146 See Section 4 of UNMIK Regulation 2001/17.

From a human rights perspective the Regulation proved to be incompatible with the recognised human rights standards, especially those enshrined in the European Convention on Human Rights.[147]

It directly violated the individual's right to peaceful enjoyment of possession,[148] the right to respect for private and family life and home,[149] the right to choose one's place of residence,[150] the prohibition against discrimination[151] and the prohibition against imposing restrictions on rights for purpose other than those prescribed.[152]

Furthermore it was in contradiction with its own law, namely UNMIK regulation 2000/60, which stipulates: "Any refugee or displaced person with a right to property has a right to return to the property, or to dispose of it in accordance with the law, subject to the present regulation".[153] The additional confusion that arises from this regulation is that it failed to provide a clear basis for its implementation in practice. It has been noted that the terminology incorporated in Regulations proved to be unknown. For example, some courts found it difficult to interpret the term "residential property".[154]

Another ad hoc intervention was made with regard to criminal justice.

On 22 December 1999, UNMIK Regulation 1999/26 on the Extension of Pre-Trial Detection was promulgated, authorising the SRSG to issue executive orders and order the detention of certain individuals. The Regulation proved to be in breach of international human right standards, namely Article 5 of the ECHR (paras. 1.3 and 3).[155]

Accordingly, several individuals against whom international prosecutors and judges found insufficient evidence to support their detention were detained for many months solely on the strength of such orders.[156] As a result of being exposed to wide criticism, the SRSG ultimately issued a regulation establishing an

147 The content of the regulation mentioned earlier has been criticised by the Ombudsperson Institution. For a detailed analysis, see the Ombudsperson's Special Report No. 5, issued on 29 October 2001, available on the following website: www.ombudsperson kosovo.org.

148 A right guaranteed by Article 1 of the Additional Protocol to the Convention.

149 A right guaranteed by Article 8 of the Convention.

150 A right guaranteed by Article 2 of Protocol No. 4 of the Convention.

151 A right guaranteed by Article 14 of the Convention.

152 A right guaranteed by Article 18 of the Convention.

153 UNMIK Regulation 2000/60.

154 OSCE Report, Property Rights in Kosovo, Department of Human Rights and Rule of Law, January 2002.

155 The legal applications arising from the executive orders are discussed in Chapter V.

156 For example, Afrim Zeqiri was held for 20 months in detentions based on executive orders. The executive orders were extended every thirty days. A similar situation applied to Cele Gashi and Avni Behluli. The SRSG, Bernard Kouchner, claimed "that the authority to issue such orders derived from 'security reasons'" and could be justified under UNSC Resolution 1244. Quoted in Simon Chesterman, *Justice under International Administration, Kosovo, East Timor and Afghanistan*, International Peace Academi, September 2002, p. 4.

international commission to review extra-judicial detentions,[157] including those which were subject to investigation by the Ombudsperson's Institution (OIK).[158] Nevertheless, in the view of OIK the establishment and nature of this commission still failed to meet the relevant international human rights standards.[159] The situation lacked legal clarity, sufficient independence and a necessary guarantee that its procedure would be conducted in an impartial manner.[160]

The common shortcoming that has accompanied these so-called ad hoc legislative processes is that very often the legislation failed to precisely determine the purpose of the law and the means of its implementation, which later caused difficulties to both the judicial and executive powers when implementing the law.

One such example is Regulation 2001/10 on the Prohibition of Unauthorised Border/Boundary Crossing,[161] enacted to address border crossing between Serbia and Kosovo during the uprising of Albanians in the southern part of Serbia. The Regulation aimed at providing KFOR with a legal basis for detention. This came as result of criticism of KFOR for previously carrying out hundreds of arrests and detentions.[162] This course of action was justified by UNMIK as an extraordinary tool that served to establish an environment based on the rule of law, as according to it the local judicial system had proved to be unable to respond adequately to ethnically motivated crime.[163]

Though it has not been applied often in practice, it failed to address the real issues of who can enter Kosovo proper and under what circumstances.[164]

Due to the unclear roles and responsibilities of PISG and UNMIK and the relationship between them (or for other reasons), legislation has in numerous cases contained serious gaps, overlaps, inconsistencies or even internal incompatibilities.

The limited involvement of civil society in the process of legislative and policy development has contributed to a lack of awareness and knowledge about the existing legislation among the general population.

All this has led to a situation with serious gaps in the development of subsidiary legislation. Only in a very few cases has the passing of laws in the Kosovo

157 Regulation 1999/26 on the extension of Periods of Pre-trial Detention was criticised for failing to adequately allow for independent and adversarial review of detention by a court.

158 See UNMIK Regulation 2001/18 on the Establishment of Detention Review Commission for Extra-Judicial Detentions based on Executive Orders, promulgated on 25 August 2001.

159 See OIK Special Report No 4, issued on 12 September 2001.

160 The Detention Review Commission was only used in one case. It convened on 20 September 2001 to determine whether the detention of three suspects in connection with the Niš bus bombing was justified. Following a review of the available information, the panel determined that the detention of the three suspects by executive order was justified. It stated that there were "reasonable grounds to suspect that each of the detained persons has committed a criminal act and that circumstances exist which suggest the strong possibility of flight". No appeal was allowed against this decision.

161 UNMIK Regulation 2001/10, enacted on 10 May 2001.

162 In the first phase, prior to the deployment of CIVPOL.

163 Marshall and Inglis, *supra* n. 69, p. 111.

164 Ibid.

Assembly been followed by even limited efforts to develop further binding instruments to ensure full and consistent implementation of the law.

Conclusion

The aforementioned examples highlight several instances in which UNMIK has shaped its domestic law-making in a way that ultimately damaged both its mission objectives and the rights of the governed population. Instead of building a coherent legal system, UNMIK pursued a selective approach and thus failed to properly address the social needs of the population.[165]

This approach caused serious shortcomings as very often the legislation failed to precisely determine the purpose of the law and the means of its implementation, which later caused difficulties for the executive power in implementing it. However the main weakness of this approach is that UNMIK's law-making system was not enabled to establish criteria for appraising the conformity of international governance with international standards of human rights.

Yet it is important to note that although an ad-hoc and non-democratic approach to resolving problems may be the only alternative for a post-conflict society, the experience in Kosovo shows that such a body might not be in a position to provide secure foundations upon which a new and inclusive order can be built.[166] In doing so, UNMIK brought into question its own efforts to promote democracy and the rule of law.

The difficulties inherent in exploring the full implications surrounding UNMIK's law-making power have provoked a great deal of thought accompanied by several important questions. Would the situation have been different if a firm legal framework governing the activities of international territorial administrations had been in place prior to its deployment? Given the narrow mandate of UNMIK, what other options could have been applied by UNMIK regarding the initial formula? Was the UN adequately prepared in both personnel and resources to carry out governmental functions? What would have been the consequences if FRY's law had not been followed by lawyers or judges?

In light of all of this, the experience of re-establishing the legal system in a post-conflict society such as Kosovo has shown that a comprehensive legal framework governing the activities of the peacebuilding mission is a crucial prerequisite for its functioning. Conversely, an ambiguous and deficient legal framework leads to unlawfulness and uncertainty.

165 Reka, *supra* n. 4, p. 204.

166 In his article *UNMIK: Lessons from the early institution – building phase*, Anthony Miller, who served as a legal advisor to UNMIK, discusses the difficulties surrounding the work of JACLM. In his view, UNMIK lacked substantial resources for making such a mechanism operationally effective. A lack of adequate premises and working equipment, and a shortage of qualified translators were some of the problems faced by JACLM. However, the problem was partially solved by the donations received from the American Bar Association's Central European and Eurasian Law Initiative (ABA-CEELI). For detailed information, see Anthony Miller, UNMIK: Lessons from the Early Institution: Building Phase, *New England Law Review*, Vol. 39, No. 9, 2004.

2 The paradigm of an independent judicial system under international administration

Introduction

Judicial independence is one of the most important principles of the court system.[1] As an integral part of democracy, it shields judicial process from external influences by providing full legal protection to all individuals going to court for whatever reason. It guarantees that the rule of law will be followed and not the rule of political will, with an independent judge able to decide the law free of outside influence.[2]

Used as a sophisticated instrument of oppression, the pre-war judiciary in Kosovo served as an important protector of Milosevic's power and of his political structures. The principles of the rule of law were pragmatically accepted; however, they lacked a degree of moral and practical integrity, as they were simply transformed into the rules that promoted a communist ideology as the guiding principle of the state.[3] The judiciary lacked independence as the judicial figures accepted a passive and subordinate role and as such exposed themselves to the direct control of the executive.[4] During this period, the judiciary experienced drastic changes, turning it into a factory of evidence owned by the unquestionable power of the sole political party.[5]

1 Simon Shetreet, Judicial Independence: New Conceptual Dimensions and Contemporary Challenges, in S. Shetreet and J. Deschênes (eds.), *Judicial Independence, the Contemporary Debate*, Dordrecht: Martinus Nijhoff Publishers, 1985, p. 591.

2 Hon. Myron T. Steele, Judicial Independence, *Widener Law Journal*, Vol. 18, No. 2, 2009, p. 300.

3 In the period between 1945 and 1990, there were five constitutions in Yugoslavia. For more about the constitutional law of the former Yugoslavia, see Ratko Markovic, *Ustavno Pravo i Politicke Institucije*, Sluzbeni Glasnik, 1998. See also Majda Strobel, *Ustavno Pravo SFR Jugoslavije*, Casopisni Zavod Uradni List S.R Slovenije, 1986.

4 Lenard J. Cohen, Post Federalism and Judicial Changes in Yugoslavia, the Rise of Ethno Political Justice, *International Political Science Review*, Vol. 13, No. 3, 1992, p. 312. See also Heike Krieger, *The Kosovo Conflict and International Law: An Analytical Documentation 1974–1999*, Cambridge University Press, 2001.

5 For more about Kosovo's position in Serbia and Yugoslavia, see Jusuf Fuduli, Kosovo and Bosnia: Different Products of Yugoslavia's Disintegration, in Larry Wentz (ed.), *Lessons from Kosovo, The KFOR Experience*, DoD Command and Control Research Programme (CCRP Publication Series), 2002, pp. 49–64.

Pursuant to its mandate, UNMIK took responsibility for the third branch of governmental functions and for re-establishing an independent, impartial, and multi-ethnic judiciary. To this end, it was responsible, inter alia, for establishing a judicial structure, setting up a court administration, appointing judges and prosecutors, and establishing a penal system.

However, the legacy of the Serbian regime inevitably left its mark on the country's legal culture. Together with the post-conflict situation, which involved various forms of violence and repression, the existence of a parallel court system became a strong impediment to the creation of an effective judicial system in post-conflict Kosovo.

This chapter aims to shed light on the ability of the UN interim administration to construct and administer justice in a post-war setting. In particular, it focuses on assessing the effectiveness and the appropriate role of UNMIK as an international interim administration in the process of promoting and establishing an independent judiciary in Kosovo.

It offers a brief background note on the theoretical framework behind the notions of judicial independence and impartiality, including the international standards relevant to establishing an independent judicial system. It goes on to discuss structural arrangements in Kosovo, which differ in their specific attributes from governance structures elsewhere. The aim is to discuss the senses in which the principles of judicial independence were employed by the UNMIK administration and to link judicial independence with the separation of powers in the Kosovo context.

While this chapter limits itself to examining key elements of the functioning of the judicial structure in Kosovo with reference to international standards governing judicial independence, it will briefly examine some of the key elements of the legal framework governing the independence of prosecutors relevant to the functioning of the public prosecution system. In the light of the conclusions reached, the chapter will question whether it is possible to establish an independent judiciary under a UN interim administration.

The notion of the independence and impartiality of the judiciary in legal doctrine

Though each has its specific meaning and requirements, the notions of "independence" and "impartiality" are closely linked and as such have been treated as inseparable by the international control organs.[6]

This section provides an explanation of the meaning and requirements of those two concepts and their interrelationship.

6 Manual, Human Rights in the Administration of Justice, *Independence and Impartiality of Judges, Lawyers and Prosecutors*, Professional Training Series No. 9, Office of High Commissioner on Human Rights, available at the following website: www.ohchr.org/Documents/Publications/training9Titleen.pdf, p. 119.

It is widely considered that the principle of judicial independence is deeply rooted in Montesquieu's doctrine of the separation of powers.[7] Montesquieu was among those who first noticed the importance of ensuring the independence of judicial power from the two other branches of government.[8] He considered that a true separation of powers existed when a clear demarcation of functions exercised by the three organs of government – the executive, the legislature and the judiciary – was ensured. As he eloquently stressed:

> When the legislative and executive powers are united in the same person . . . there can be no liberty. . . . Again, there is no liberty, if the judiciary power be not separated from the legislative and executive. Were it joined with the executive, the life and liberty of the subject would be exposed to arbitrary control; for the judge would be then the legislator.[9]

Montesquieu's view gained the support of many political theorists, among them Madison, who wrote:

> The accumulation of all powers, legislative, executive and judiciary, in the same hands, whether of one, a few, or many and whether hereditary, self-appointed or elective, may justly be pronounced the very definition of tyranny.[10]

It follows that any union of two powers would produce the same effect. In this context, when the legislative and judicial powers are accumulated, the laws are "uncertain", reflecting the "whims", "caprice" or "the prejudice of the judge"; and when the legislative and executive powers are accumulated, "the security and protection of the subject would be a shadow . . . the executive power would make itself absolute and the government end in a tyranny".[11]

Nevertheless, the application of the doctrine in its pure form is unworkable, in particular in a democratic system, as it proves difficult to ensure strict mutual independence of the public decision makers given that each branch of government will to some degree find itself engaged in all three activities.[12] As a consequence,

7 Shetreet and Deschênes (eds.), *supra* n. 1, p. 595.

8 It is asserted by historians that the idea of separation of powers did not originate with Montesquieu. They argue that he brought together earlier thinking on this subject and synthesised the doctrine. Richard Bellamy, The Political form of the Constitution, the Separation of Powers, Rights and Representative Democracy, in Richard Bellamy (ed.), *The Rule of Law and the Separation of Powers*, Ashgate and Dartmouth, 2005, p. 257.

9 Montesquieu, *The Spirit of Laws*, Cambridge University Press, 1989, p. 294.

10 Jeffry Madison, Federalist 47, quoted in, Kate O'Regan, Checks and Balances Reflections on the Development of the Doctrine of Separation of Powers under the South African Constitution, *PER/ PELJ*, Vol. 8, No. 1, 2005.

11 Oscar Handlin and Mary Handlin, *The Popular Sources of Political Authority: Documents on the Massachusetts Constitution 1780*, Cambridge: Harvard University Press, 1966, pp. 337–338.

12 Bruce Ackerman, The New Separation of Powers, in Bellamy (ed.), *supra* n. 8, p. 439. See also, John Braithwaite, On Speaking Softly and Carrying Big Sticks: Neglected Dimension

the doctrine was subjected to constant adaptation and as such combined with elements of different theories of mixed and balanced government, which further developed and clarified the doctrine.[13] While it has been widely argued that the purpose of the separation of powers is to protect the liberty of the individual through the division of power, some claimed that "[t]he system of separation of powers . . . constrains government, by making it harder for government to act"; nonetheless it "also helps to energize government and to make it more effective, by creating a healthy division of labor".[14] A common feature of this formulations is that a primary purpose of the separation of powers doctrine is to prevent the concentration of power in one branch of government.

Although not questioned as a concept, in reality a strict separation of powers does not exist in many countries, meaning that no judiciary is completely separated from the administrative and legislative bodies because this diminishes the potency of checks and balances, leading to inefficient communication between the branches of government.[15]

So far, no universal model of the separation of powers has been introduced that could serve as an example to democratic systems of government. Thus the degree of separation between the legislative and executive varies from country to country. For example, in the political systems of the USA, France and the Netherlands, members of the executive cannot be members of the legislature, whereas in the German system this is not a requirement. Moreover, in South Africa, which mirrors the Westminster model, an intertwined relationship between legislature and executive is allowed.[16]

However, many democratic countries have introduced a socially and politically balanced system based on mutually checking branches, where the powers allocated to various institutions are clearly defined in the constitution, a so-called system of checks and balances.[17] A system of checks and balances is understood as a mechanism that disciplines the legislative and executive branches of the state. In this regard, the term "checks" implies the right and responsibility of each governmental branch to monitor the activities of the others; and the term "balances" offers each branch the opportunity to use its constitutional authority to limit or restrain the power of the others.[18]

---

of a Republication Separation of Powers, *University of Toronto Law Journal*, Vol. 47, No. 305, 1997.

13 Ibid., p. 439.

14 Cass Sunstein quoted in O'Regan, *supra* n. 10.

15 Hadley Siers, *Separation of the Judiciary and Judicial Independence in Bangladesh*, 2004, available at: dhaka.net/School_Library/senior%20Projects/04_Hadley_judiciary.pdf.

16 O'Regan, *supra* n. 10. See also David Schoenbroad, Separation of Powers and Powers That Be: The Constitutional Purposes of Delegation Doctrine, *The American University Law Review*, Vol. 36, 1987.

17 Rene Ch. Verschuur, *Independence of the Judiciary*, Conference Paper, 2 June 2007, Belgrade, available at: www.medel.bugi.web.com. See also Irving R. Kaufman, The Essence of Judicial Independence, *Columbia Law Review*, Vol. 80, No. 4, 1980.

18 Torsten Persson, Gerard Roland, and Guido Tabellini, Separation of Powers and Accountability, *The Quarterly Journal of Economics*, Vol. 112, No. 4, 1997, pp. 1164–1167. See

The judiciary is the most vulnerable branch of government. Thus its protection requires the establishment of a clear equilibrium among its branches. But it should be emphasised that independence is not a one-time achievement. In this regard, the question arises as to what measures should be undertaken in order to provide a secure environment for courts.

In the view of some authors, the degree of judicial independence in a country depends not only on the constitution and the law of that country but also on the political structure and social climate as well as the tradition prevailing in that country.[19] This assertion is based on a comparison of different traditions, namely those arising from democratic and non-democratic or communist regimes. It is said that in common law countries that are known for their "strong tradition in favor of ignoring political considerations, in particular when it comes to judicial appointments", the commitment of society to judicial independence is far above the ground. By contrast, in non-democratic regimes, where there is no separation of powers, there is no such commitment.[20] The entire society appears to be locked in a "cloudy-minds fiction", driven by belief in dogmatic concepts.

Thus there is a common understanding that an independent judiciary is the key to upholding the rule of law in a society.[21]

In this regard, an independent judiciary became the cornerstone for the functioning of the modern state by ensuring that individuals' rights arising from modern legislation could be enforced through an effective and independent judicial system. It became true for all societies that a weak judicial system, where laws are not enforced deprived people of their individual rights and undermined the well-being of the community.[22]

Robert Stevens, A Loss of Innocence? Judicial Independence and the Separation of Powers, *Oxford Journal of Legal Studies*, Vol. 9, No. 3, 1999. See also Sam J. Ervin, Separation of Powers: Judicial Independence, *Law and Contemporary Problems*, Vol. 35, 1970.

19 Theodor Meron, Judicial Independence and Impartiality in International Criminal Tribunals, *The American Journal of International Law*, Vol. 99, 2005, p. 360. See also Shetreet and Deschênes, *supra* n. 1, p. 595. For a general overview of the functioning of judicial institutions in different European countries, see also Leny E. de Groot-van Leeuwen and Wannes Rombouts (eds.), *Separation of Powers in Theory and Practice: An International Perspective*, Nijmegen: Wolf Legal Publications, 2010.

20 Mauro Cappelletti, Who Watches the Watchmen? A Comparative Study on Judicial Responsibility, *American Journal of Comparative Law*, Vol. 13, No. 1, Winter 1983. Shetreet and Deschênes, *supra* n. 1, pp. 595–597. See also Gretchen Helmke and Frances Rosenbluh, Regimes and the Rule of Law, Judicial Independence in Comparative Perspective, *The Annual Review of Political Science*, Vol. 12, No. 345–366, 2009, p. 358.

21 Daniel C. Préfontaine, Q.C. and Joanne Lee, *The Rule of Law and the Independence of the Judiciary*, The International Centre for Criminal Law Reform and Criminal Justice Policy, Working Paper prepared for World Conference on Universal Declaration of Human Rights, Montreal, 7–9 December 1998.

22 However, it should be noted that there is tendency in the modern welfare state to limit individual rights by entrusting the public authorities with the power to make decisions affecting individuals' rights in such a way as to exclude them from court examination. See Arthur John Keeffe, Practising Lawyers Guide to the Current Law Magazine, *American Bar Association Journal*, Vol. 46, No. 459, 1948, p. 565.

The pre-war judicial legacy and its impact on post-war Kosovo

On 23 March 1989, Kosovo lost its previous autonomous status and all the powers it held within the Yugoslav Federation and was re-annexed to Serbia. It was given a provincial statute as its highest legal authority, which significantly reduced its previous legal status.[23] Subsequently, a series of laws were adopted to gradually dismantle the previous laws enacted by the Kosovo Assembly, leading to the complete de-institutionalisation of the Province (ibid, 232).3 Changes to the Serbian Constitution were passed which revoked the rights of Kosovo Albanians recognised by the 1974 Constitution.[24]

The Kosovo Albanians refused to obey these newly enacted laws and also to subordinate themselves to the new regime.[25] This resulted in a wave of arrests, unlawful detentions, disappearances, extrajudicial executions, house arrests, and politically motivated trials. The Kosovo judiciary turned into a highly politicised institution which was exposed to pressure from the Serbian Government.[26] This period was characterised by opaque trials, known as "telephone justice", wherein government officials sought to instruct judges by phone calls in order to have an influence on cases that mattered to them.

Whether and to what extent can the UNMIK judiciary be viewed as independent and impartial

The following section aims to offer a critical appraisal of judicial independence under UNMIK's administration by examining the structural independence of the judiciary as well as independence related to judicial performance. Its main focus is on analysing two separate aspects of the independence of the judiciary, the independence of the court system as a collective body and the independence and impartiality of individual judges.

The central issue which needs to be explored is whether the establishment of UNMIK's courts meets the criteria established by international standards.

Division of powers – a basic rule for the independence of the judiciary

Neither UNSC Resolution 1244 nor the Constitutional Framework contains an explicit clause on the principle of the separation of powers. While UNSC

23 Blerim Reka, *UNMIK as an International Governance in Post-War Kosovo: NATOs Intervention, UN Administration and Kosovar Inspirations*, Shkup: Logos, 2003, pp. 30–45.

24 Heike Krieger, *The Kosovo Conflict and International Law: An Analytical Documentation 1974–1999*, London: Cambridge University Press, 2001.

25 For more about passive resistance in Kosovo, known as Rugova's strategy, see Howard Clark, *Civil Resistance in Kosovo*, London: Pluto Press, 2000.

26 In a speech during a nomination ceremony on 28 May 1998, the Yugoslav Minister of Justice, Dragoljub Jankovic, addressed the newly appointed judges, saying: "Your duty is not only to protect the constitutionality and legislation of this country, but also to love this country, therefore do not forget your roots. . . . We will be fighting terrorism". See Ratko Markovic, *supra* n. 3, p. 215.

Resolution 1244 only dealt with the mandate of the UNMIK administration, the Constitutional Framework,[27] which regulates matters subject to the internal law of Kosovo, clearly demonstrates that there is no separation of powers in the UNMIK governance system. The Constitutional Framework identifies the institutions of the Interim Self-Government and their responsibilities relating to the administration of Kosovo with specific emphasis on the supervising role of the Special Representative of the Secretary-General relating to the Interim Institutions. In this regard, the responsibilities of the institutions of the Interim Self-Government include decision-making in the fields of economy and finance, culture, health, labour relations and social matters, transport, the postal service and telecommunications, agriculture and tourism.[28] However, authority over law and order was jointly exercised by the Interim Self-Government institutions and the international authorities.[29] The responsibilities reserved to the SRSG were those that involved dissolving the assembly and calling new elections after consultation with the president of Kosovo, monetary policy, control over the UNMIK custom service, exercising final authority concerning the appointment, removal from office and disciplining of judges and prosecutors, authority over law enforcement institutions, the correctional service and the Kosovo Protection Corps, concluding international agreements, external relations, and the control of minority rights.[30]

Furthermore, the SRSG retained the power to amend the Constitutional Framework either on his own initiative or upon the request of two thirds of members of the Assembly:[31] "[t]he exercise of the responsibilities of the Provisional Institutions of Self-Government under this Constitutional Framework shall not affect or diminish the authority of the SRSG to ensure full implementation of UNSCR 1244 (1999), including overseeing the Provisional Institutions of Self-Government, its officials and its agencies, and taking appropriate measures whenever their actions are inconsistent with UNSCR 1244 (1999) or this Constitutional Framework".[32]

This enabled the SRSG to use his authority and veto any decision taken by the Provisional Interim Self-Government Institutions and he used it on many occasions, among them in order to abolish the "Resolution on Territorial Integrity of Kosovo" issued by the Kosovo Assembly, to abrogate the "Memorandum of

27 UNMIK Regulation 2001/9 of 15 May 2001 on a Constitutional Framework for Provisional Self-Government.

28 See Chapter 5, 5.1, 5.2 and 5.7 of the Constitutional Framework.

29 See Chapters 6 and 7 of the Constitutional Framework.

30 See Chapter 8.1 and 8.2 of the Constitutional Framework.

31 Chapter 14 Section 3 of the Constitutional Framework. Furthermore, the Secretary-General stated that the Constitutional Framework contained "broad authority for my Special Representative to intervene and correct any actions of the provisional institutions of self-government that are inconsistent with Security Council resolution 1244 (1999), including the power to veto Assembly legislation, where necessary". Stated in his periodical report to the Security Council of 7 June 2001, (Report of the Secretary-General on the United Nations Interim Administration Mission in Kosovo, S/2001/565, 7 June 2001).

32 Chapter 12 of the Constitutional Framework.

Understanding" between the Kosovo Ministry of Economy and Finance and the Ministry of Economy of Albania,[33] to issue numerous executive orders related to justice, and so on. Furthermore, Section 1 of UNMIK Regulation 1999/1 on the authority of the interim administration explicitly states that the judicial administration is vested in the sole authority of the Special Representative:

> 1. All legislative and executive authority with respect to Kosovo, including the administration of the judiciary, is vested in UNMIK and is exercised by the Special Representative of the Secretary-General. 2. The Special Representative of the Secretary-General may appoint any person to perform functions in the civil administration in Kosovo, including the judiciary, or remove such person. Such functions shall be exercised in accordance with the existing laws, as specified in section 3, and any regulations issued by UNMIK.[34]

It should be noted that the scope of the judicial power was not defined anywhere in the Constitutional Framework. The part which refers to the justice system only affirms that court administration is conferred on the courts of Kosovo in securing the right of the SRSG to oversee and control the judiciary for the purpose of ensuring the implementation of UNSC Resolution 1244 and the Constitutional Framework.[35]

Hence, SRSG was given a supremacy over the courts and as such indirectly empowered to exercise the powers of a judicial administration. However, it is necessary to mention that the terms "judicial power" and "administration of justice" involve two distinct notions, with the first pertaining to the authority to render dispositive judgments and the latter consisting of the practices and offices that involve the management of the court system. In the context of Kosovo, the lack of a clear division between these two notions nourished confusion as to who had the judicial power in Kosovo. In the shadow of this uncertainty, the SRSG used his specific powers to interfere in *res judicata* matters[36] by taking, without explanation, any case from the Kosovar judiciary and requesting an international panel, as well as providing courts with the legal interpretation of enacted laws.[37] This shows that by virtue of considerable authority at judicial level, the SRSG had

33 Reka, *supra* n. 23, p. 146.

34 Section 1 of UNMIK Regulation 1999/1.

35 Sections 4 and 12 of the Constitutional Framework of Kosovo.

36 Article 171 of the Provisional Code of Kosovo foresees that an international prosecutor appointed by the SRSG may restart or continue the criminal proceedings 30 days after the first decision of the court was taken. For more about the SRSG's judicial powers, see Reka, *supra* n. 23, pp. 294–297.

37 Section 2 of UNMIK Regulation 1999/24 stipulates: "Courts in Kosovo may request clarification from the Special Representative of the Secretary-General in connection with the implementation of the present regulation. The Special Representative of the Secretary-General shall provide such clarification for the consideration of the courts in the exercise of their functions". UNMIK Regulation 1999/24, 12 December 1999. See also Section 2 of Regulation 2000/59.

unlimited access to the administration of justice as well as the power to directly exercise influence on judicial authorities. Overall, it coincidentally shows that the UNMIK administration is characterised by a model of governance with no division of powers, allowing a pervasive influence of one power (the SRSG) over the two other branches.

The requirement that a court/tribunal be established by law

The requirement that a court/tribunal be established by law lies at the heart of judicial independence.[38] The object of this requirement is to ensure that judicial organisations should be regulated by law and not by executive discretion, which means that the scope of the tribunal's jurisdiction should be specified by law.[39] The body envisaged to exercise this function must have a power to determine matters "on the basis of the rule of law, it should have powers to give a binding decision that may not be altered by a non-judicial authority".[40]

The concept of being "established by law" covers not only the existence of a tribunal, but also the composition of the bench in each case.[41]

In determining whether UNMIK courts meet the criteria of independent and impartial courts one should turn to the laws for establishing a court.

The court system in Kosovo was established by two Regulations, namely Regulation 1999/6 "On Recommendation for the Structure and Registration of the Judiciary and Prosecution Service" and Regulation 1999/7 "On Appointment and Removal from Office of Judges and Prosecutions". Undoubtedly, only law-making bodies which are democratically elected have the legitimacy to establish courts or tribunals, as was stressed by the European Commission on Human Rights: "The judicial organization in a democratic society must not depend on the discretion of the Executive, but should be regulated by law emanating from Parliament".[42]

As previously mentioned, the power to enact law in Kosovo lies in the hands of the SRSG, more specifically the SRSG's Legal Office. It was noted that the legislative power of UNMIK derived from the UN Charter by virtue of the Security

38 Human Rights Committee, Comment 13, Article 14, UN Doc. HRI/GEN/1/Rev. 1 at 14 (1994), para. 4, where the Committee found as follows: "The Committee notes the existence, in many countries, of military or special courts which try civilians. This could present serious problems as far as the equitable, impartial, and independent administration of justice is concerned. Quite often the reason for the establishment of such courts is to enable exceptional procedures to be applied which do not comply with normal standards of justice". Human Rights Committee, Comment 13, Article 14, UN Doc. HRI/GEN/1/Rev. 1 at 14 (1994), para. 4.

39 ECtHR, *Lavents v. Latvia*, Judgment of 28 November 2002.

40 ECtHR, *Sremek v. Austria*, Judgment of 22 October 1986 para. 36. See also ECtHR, *Van de Hurk v. the Netherlands*, Judgement of 19 April 1994, paras. 45–52, See also *Morris v. UK*, 26 February 2002, para. 73.

41 ECtHR Judgment, *Posokhov v. Russia*, Judgement of 4 March 2003, para. 37.

42 European Commission of Human Rights, Application 7360/76.

Council resolution that established it and that laws issued by such a body had a legal nature equal to that of the acts issued by the Assembly.[43] So notwithstanding the legal implications arising from the SRSG's legislative power, which significantly differs from the legislative power exercised elsewhere, it can safely be argued that UNMIK courts are "tribunals established by law", as required by the international standards. However, it will remain an open controversy whether a system that relies more or less on one person has the moral authority and integrity to institute an independent judiciary. The ensuing discussion will consider several other contributing elements accompanying judicial independence which play a crucial role in ensuring the independence of the judiciary, such as methods of recruitment, appointment, the removal of judges and prosecutors, lifetime tenure and the funding of courts. These are additional elements that safeguard a judicial branch.

The appointment of judges and their independence

Neither international treaty law nor soft law provides any specific criteria as to how judges should be appointed. The sole criterion for the selection of judges lies in their professional qualifications and their personal integrity.[44]

Although a certain degree of clarification of important issues in relation to judicial appointment has been provided by international judicial bodies, no clear guidance as to the manner of their appointment has yet been provided. The relevance of the manner of judicial appointment was recognised by the European Court of Human Rights, which stated that "in order to establish whether a tribunal can be considered 'independent' for the purposes of article 6 .1, regard must be had, *inter alia*, to the manner of appointment of its members and their term of office, the existence of safeguards against outside pressures and the question whether it presents an appearance of independence".[45]

The Human Rights Committee maintains that "governing the appointment of judges by the Government with approval of Parliament could have a negative effect on the independence of the judiciary". In this regard, it recommended that "specific measures be adopted as a matter of priority guaranteeing the independence of the judiciary and protecting judges from any form of political influence, through the adoption of laws regulating the appointment, remuneration, tenure, dismissal and disciplining of members of the judiciary".[46]

43 See Chapter III, section; the scope of the legitimate power of UNMIK.

44 "Persons selected for judicial office shall be individuals of integrity and ability with appropriate training or qualifications in law. Any method of judicial selection shall safeguard against judicial appointments for improper motives. In the selection of judges, there shall be no discrimination against a person on the grounds of race, colour, sex, religion, political or other opinion, national or social origin, property, birth or status, except that a requirement, that a candidate for judicial office must be a national of the country concerned, shall not be considered discriminatory". Principle 10 of the Basic Principles.

45 ECtHR, Judgment, *Incal v. Turkey*, 9 June 1998, Reports 1998-IV, p. 1571, para. 65.

46 UN doc. *GAOR*, A/50/40, paras. 288.

It further recommended that the system of "appointment of judges through elections be reconsidered with a view to its replacement by a system of appointment on merit by an independent body".[47]

As a result, many European countries have introduced a practice of conducting appointments through an independent commission, established by an independent body.[48]

With this in mind, I turn to examine the manner of appointing UNMIK's judges and to assess whether such a manner safeguards their independence.

Similar to other countries, the procedure for the appointment of domestic judges is conducted by the Kosovo Judicial and Prosecutorial Council (hereinafter KJPC), a so-called independent body established pursuant to Regulation 2001/8 (6 April 2001),[49] which plays the role of a consulting body (an advisory body with no real power) that gives advice and makes recommendations to the SRSG concerning the appointment of professional judges, lay judges and prosecutors. The SRSG then makes a final selection from a list of candidates proposed by the KJPC and endorsed by the Assembly, but reserves the right to remove local judges and prosecutors without any prior consultation with the KJPC.[50]

The majority of countries share a similar practice regarding the terms and practice of appointment of judges, with the formal appointment entrusted to the head of state[51] or to the minister of justice[52] and primarily based on the recommendation of a judicial council. In some countries, the appointment is made by the government[53] or by the head of state.[54] The involvement of the head of state has proved not to be a problem as long as such appointments are based on the recommendations of an independent judicial mechanism.[55] It appears that the effectiveness of such a process depends on the amount of the power guaranteed to the head of state in the whole process.[56] In this regard, the exclusive responsibility should lie with an independent body – the judicial council.[57]

47 Ibid., para. 301.

48 European Commission for Democracy through Law Opinion No. 403/2006, 22 June 2007.

49 Judicial Councils are a mechanism for selecting judges and prosecutors that can be found in many European countries. For more details, see *supra* n. 1, p. 14.

50 See David Marchall and Shelly Inglis, The Disempowerment of Human Rights-Based Justice in the United Nations Mission in Kosovo, *Harvard Human Rights Journal*, Vol. 16, 2003, p. 126, 97.

51 Albania, Armenia, Czech Republic, Georgia.

52 Italy.

53 In Sweden, judges are appointed by the government or by a public authority established by the government. See European Commission for Democracy through Law Opinion No. 403/2006, 22 June, 2007.

54 In the Netherlands, the Minister of Justice is in charge of political appointments and responsible for countersigning appointments. See European Commission for Democracy through Law Opinion No. 403/2006, 22 June, 2007.

55 Ibid.

56 Ibid.

57 Ibid.

As might be noticed, the executive power in Kosovo, the SRSG, can, in addition to involvement in judicial appointments, directly interfere with security of tenure, which does not accord with the international standards. Removal by such means is certainly an extremely rare practice, which brings us back to the time of colonialism when judges in the royal colonies held their office at the pleasure of the Crown, *durante bene placito regis*, instead of *quam diu se ben gesserint*, that is, during good behaviour (as long as they behaved well).[58]

Another issue that deserves attention is the tenure period for which judges were appointed, which has been a matter for concern since the creation of UNMIK. At the beginning of the mission, local judges were appointed for terms of six months; however, later on it was decided to extend their terms to the end of the UN mission.[59] Even if the term of office of the local judges was extended, it was still not a specified term, as nobody knew how long the UN administration would be in place. Such a practice was incompatible with international standards, which demands a fixed tenure until a mandatory retirement age or the expiry of their term of office.[60] Judges whose judicial career is not secure are more likely to be vulnerable to external influence, which may seriously interfere with the adjudication process. As stated by Sir Gerard Brennan, Chief Justice of Australia, "judicial independence is at risk when future appointment or security of tenure is within the gift of the Executive".[61] Judicial appointments by the executive can assure judicial independence only if security of tenure is guaranteed, if not permanently then at least for a reasonable period of time.[62] Thus short-term judicial appointments threaten the independent functioning of the courts. Where the head of state has the authority to appoint and remove judges and prosecutors, the judiciary is consequently relegated to an inferior position.

As already mentioned, the Kosovar judiciary included international judges, which required additional observation, especially with regard to the method of their selection and their security of tenure. The first question that requires an answer is whether judges who served on the UNMIK judiciary enjoyed sufficient security of tenure to act independently. The appointment of the international judges required a different method compared with the appointment of domestic judges. They were selected through an UNMIK-specific selection procedure and were finally appointed by the SRSG for six-month renewable terms, which was the standard term for all mission personnel working with the UN Department of

58 This was very common during the reigns of Charles II (1660–1685) and James II (1685–1688), when judges were removed for political reasons. See Joseph H. Smith, Independent Judiciary, the Colonial Background, *University of Pennsylvania Law Review*, Vol. 1105, 1975–1976, pp. 1105–1108.

59 See American Bar Association, *Legal Information for Kosovo*, available on the following website: www.abanet.org/ceeli/countries/Kosovo/legalinfo/html.

60 Points 11 and 12 of the UN Basic Principle on the Independence of the Judiciary.

61 Francis Gerard Brennan, The State of the Judicature, *Australian Law Journal*, Vol. 72, 1998, pp. 34–35.

62 See Meron, *supra* n. 19, p. 361.

Peacekeeping Operations.[63] However, the selection procedure lacked clarity since it was completely invisible to the outside world.[64]

They were elected for a fixed term subject to six months' renewable terms of office. Such short terms of office constituted a serious threat to judicial independence[65] and to the quality of the administration of justice. Due to the lack of security of tenure, both international and local judges became vulnerable to the influence of those who might affect their employment prospects.[66] In this regard, one may ask whether it would have been possible to provide an international judge with a longer tenure.

Let us now evaluate the practice of the appointment of international judges in international courts and tribunals and see if these conditions of judicial appointment also apply mutatis mutandis to international judges.

While the judicial appointment process in the International Court of Justice (ICJ) involves two actors, namely the General Assembly and the Security Council,[67] the judges of the ICTY and ICTR are subjected to a more complex procedure, which involves nomination by UN member states, then short-listing by the Security Council and finally election by the UN General Assembly.[68] In the case of the European Court of Human Rights, a government submits three candidates to the Council of Europe's Parliamentary Assembly, which then elects

63 Michael Hartmann, *International Judges and Prosecutors in Kosovo*, Special Report 112, United States Institute of Peace, 2003, p. 8. The method of appointment of international judges has been widely criticised by the Ombudsperson Institution in Kosovo. See OIK 5th and 6th Annual Report available at: www.ombudspersonkosovo.org.

64 Amended by UNMIK Regulation 2000/34 of 15 February 2000 and UNMIK Regulation 2001/2 of 12 January 2001. The method of appointment of international judges has been widely criticised by the Ombudsperson Institution in Kosovo. See OIK 5th and 6th Annual Report available at: www.ombudspersonkosovo.org.

65 "This is a serious matter of concern", said Marek Antoni Nowicki, Ombudsperson in Kosovo, who further stressed that "the short term appointments may affect their ability to act impartially". Interview with Marek Antoni Nowicki, conducted on 3 October 2005 in Prishtina.

66 Security of tenure involves a long-term appointment; it guarantees that a judge can be removed from his/her position only for good cause or a breach of ethical rules. For a detailed explanation, see *supra* n. 1, p. 19.

67 Pursuant to Article 7–10 of the ICJ Statute.

68 While the statutes of other international courts and tribunals have general qualification requirements, the ICC Rome Statute established detailed requirements for qualifications as a judge. The judges were to be chosen from among persons of high moral character, impartiality, and integrity, who possessed the qualifications required in their respective states for appointment to the highest judicial offices (art. 36.3(a)). Out of deference to the ICJ, which requires judges to be of "high moral character", the ICC, ICTY, and ICTR include the broader specification of "high moral character, impartiality and integrity". For an in-depth analyses of judicial independence in an international context, see Ruth Mackenzie and Philippe Sands, International Courts and Tribunals and the Independence of the International Judge, *Harvard International Law Journal*, Vol. 44, No. 1, 2003, p. 275. See also Statute of the International Criminal Tribunal for the Former Yugoslavia, Annex, Art. 13 bis. Statute of the International Criminal Tribunal for the Former Yugoslavia Article 12 bis.

the preferred candidate by voting; usually, the government's preferred candidate is elected.[69]

Judges are mainly appointed to serve for a fixed term of office, commonly three, six, or nine years with the possibility of re-election. In this context, the ICJ judges are elected to serve renewable terms of nine years in office,[70] the ICTY and ICTR judges four years,[71] and the ECtHR judges are appointed to serve non-renewable terms of nine years in office.[72]

Looking at the manner in which the appointment of international judges is conducted, one may expect these appointments to be influenced by the political consideration of a nominating state.[73] The very fact that they are nominated by a state and that their election practice is subject to little transparency leaves room for such speculation.[74] Given the fact that many candidates for international judgeships have previously served as ministers or legal advisers, former members of the diplomatic corps or even former parliamentarians of the nominating state, there are reasonable grounds for believing that such an established relationship may compromise judicial appointments.[75]

The practice of removal of ECtHR judges reveals some details that might confirm this assertion, in particular if we take into consideration the replacement of Austrian judge Willi Führman, a former Social-Democratic parliamentarian, after his party lost in the elections. A similar experience was that of the Moldovan judge Tudor Pantiru, where his newly elected government asked for his removal and openly declared that his post should be filled by "real patriots".[76] This was further confirmed by an independent source, who stated: "Even in the most established democracies, nomination often rewards political loyalty more

69 Eric Voeten, The Politics of International Judicial Appointments, Evidence from the European Court of Human Rights, *International Organization*, Vol. 61, 2007, p. 676.

70 Article 13 ICJ Statute.

71 Article 13 bis. ICTY Statute, Article 12.5 ICTR Statute.

72 Article 23 Protocol 14 of the ECHR, entered into force 1 June 2010. Prior to the adoption of Protocol no. 14, judges were elected for a six-year term, with the possibility of re-election.

73 Although it involved different procedures, this perception can also be valid in the case of UNMIK's system of judicial appointments, in particular when it comes to the extension of their terms.

74 "Almost nothing is known about the selection process at international level". Kate Malleson, Law Professor at Queen Mary University, London, in *System for Appointing Judges Undermining International Courts*, the Guardian UK, available at the following website: www.guardian.co.uk/law/2010/sep/08/law-international-court-justice-legal. See also Mackenzie and Sands, *supra* n. 68, p. 278.

75 In particular, the election of the ICJ judges proved to be highly politicised. For more on this, see Mackenzie and Sands, *supra* n. 68, p. 278. It has been observed by scholars that "these different career backgrounds have predictable behavioral implications. For example, the European Court of Human Rights (ECtHR) judges who were former diplomats show a much greater respect for the raison d'état than ECtHR judges who spent the majority of their careers in private practice or who were academics. This means that diplomats were both more likely to favor their own government in cases where it was a party to a dispute and that they were more likely to grant a wide margin of appreciation to states more generally". See, Voeten *supra* n. 69, p. 4.

76 Quoted in Voeten, *supra* n. 69, p. 676.

than merit".[77] As in the domestic context, security of tenure has proved to be a necessary element for securing the impartiality of judges. As noted earlier, international judges are assigned to serve a specific length of tenure. In this regard, taking into consideration the length of tenure, together with the political nature of the appointment and reappointment process, raises a reasonable degree of suspicion that in such circumstances judges are easily subjected to external pressure and that their independent judgment is liable to be affected.

Judge Meron, in particular, expresses his concern in considering that this practice may directly infringe the impartiality of a judge, as a judge who sits on an international court is to a certain extent apprehensive about the predictability of re-nomination by his government or re-election. As such, he may render decisions not in accordance with law, in order not to antagonise powerful UN member states and in particular his own state. In this context, the job uncertainty may oblige judges to be driven by their career and not by judicial conscience or a reading of the law.[78] This has led to recognition that the legal cordon that ensures the independence of an international judge is rather fragile. The very essence of such a reality enhances the probability of opting for "self-preservation" instead of observing standards of justice.

The foregoing discussion suggests that similar to hybrid court system, politics does shape the appointment process of the international judiciary as well. State governments may affect judicial behavior through the appointment process.

In the Kosovo context, one may note that in spite of the complexity of the situation caused by the political uncertainty, perhaps it would have been possible to ensure a longer specified term for international judges by assigning them at an initial stage to a reasonable period of time and avoiding the need for reappointment. Since the extension of both national and international judges fell under the sole discretion of the SRSG, it immediately gives a perception that such reappointments might have depended on the performance assessments of the SRSG's offices. In fact, some former judges have reported cases involving political interference they experienced during their stay in Kosovo, reflecting mainly the intention of halting an investigation or of influencing a desired outcome of judicial decisions involving persecution of "certain persons".[79] Moreover, some UNMIK officials admitted that outside pressure had existed, which according to them had obliged judges to give in to pressure.[80]

77 Ibid.

78 Meron, *supra* n. 19, p. 360.

79 A Swedish judge, Christer Karphammar, who previously worked as a judge and as a prosecutor in Kosovo, stated that he "directly knows of several cases in which UN and KFOR senior officials opposed or blocked prosecution of former Kosovo Liberation Army members, including some now in KPC (TMK). . . . The investigations were stopped at a high level". For the entire time he worked in Kosovo, "the judiciary was not allowed to work independently". Quoted in William O'Neil, *Kosovo: An Unfinished Peace*, Boulder, CO: Lynne Reinner Publisher, 2002, p. 91.

80 This refers to the case of Zoran Stankovic, a former Serb policeman, who was accused of taking part in the Racak massacre of January 1999. Quoted in O'Neil, ibid.

The foregoing examples illustrate that international judges may be exposed to a pressure to favour the political interests of their employing institution in specific cases, be it a government or the UN authority.

Budget, salaries, and court management

According to international standards, judicial matters should be exclusively within the responsibility of the judiciary, both at the level of the central judicial administration and at the court-level judicial administration.[81] In this context, the central responsibility for judicial administration should preferably be vested in the judiciary or jointly in the judiciary and the executive.[82] In this context, for a court to act impartially the system needs to establish a proper managerial capacity at every level: budget, personnel, court operations, relations with the executive branch, public relations and strategic planning.[83] From an institutional and functional standpoint, judicial independence can be undermined by a lack of financial and administrative independence.[84] In most countries, the executive power is fully responsible for the court budget, which poses an insidious threat to judicial institutional independence. Generally, funding approval is required from the legislative branch, as well as funding allocation from the executive through the treasury.[85]

A similar practice is followed in the context of the international judiciary, with the central responsibility for the court administration, including control over the budget, being placed in the hands of the organ which constitutes the court. In this context, the European Court of Human Rights is financed centrally by the Council of Europe, which itself is financed by the contributions of the member States. It does not have its own separate budget as it constitutes a part of the general budget of the Council of Europe, which is subject to the approval of the Committee of Ministers of the Council of Europe.[86] In the case of the ICC, the Assembly of the State Parties is the sole budgetary authority of the Court.

81 IBA Standards point 9.

82 IBA Standards point 8.

83 See Guidance for Promoting Judicial Independence and Impartiality, Office for Democracy and Governance, Bureau for Democracy, Conflict, and Humanitarian Assistance, p. 5, U.S Agency for International Development, Washington, DC 20523–3100, Revised Edition, January 2002, p. 38.

84 See Mads Andenas and Duncan Fairgrieve, Judicial Independence and Accountability, National Traditions and International Standards, in *Independence; Accountability, and the Judiciary*, The British Institute of International and Comparative Law, 2006, p. 24.

85 In Belgium, the legislature determines judicial salaries. Court services are financed centrally by the state; the Ministry of Justice prepares the budget. See Marcel Storme, *Country Studies*, Belgium, p. 43, in Shetreet and Deschênes, *supra* n. 1. In France, for example, the Ministry of Justice is responsible for the Justice budget together with the Finance Minister. For more on the Judicial System in France, see Grivart de Kerstratn, France Chapter 8, in Shetreet and Deschênes, *supra* n. 1, *Judicial Independence, the Contemporary Debate*, Martinus Nijhoff Publishers, 1985, p. 65.

86 See, Committee of Ministers of Council of Europe available at: /www.echr.coe.int/.

The Court is funded by the contributions provided by the State Parties as well as by contributions provided by the UN subject to the approval of the General Assembly. In addition, it may receive voluntary contributions.[87] International Criminal Tribunals are financed by the UN[88] but in contrast with the ICJ do not fall under the general programme budget. In addition, they also rely upon voluntary contributions of cash, equipment, and personnel. The main contributors are the United States, Italy, Japan, Germany, United Kingdom, France, Italy, Malaysia, Denmark, Netherlands, Canada, and various NGOs such as the Open Society Institute and the Rockefeller Foundation.[89]

The budget of the entire UNMIK judiciary and judicial operations fell under the competence of the Department of Judicial Affairs (DJA) and the Joint Interim Administrative Structure's Administrative Department of Justice (ADoJ), based on input received from the court's presidents. The prepared budget proposals were presented to the Central Fiscal Authority (CFA) responsible for the Kosovo Consolidated Budget and became final once they were approved by the SRSG.[90]

The courts were excluded from the consultation during the process of preparing the court budgets.[91] The administrative staff positions were decided by UNMIK and staff were employed using a title that very often did not correspond to the services actually performed.[92]

The greatest achievement of UNMIK was seen in its early stage when it had to give a response to the basic need to establish a functional court system. Though faced with limited resources, it managed, with the support of international donors, to equip the judiciary with computers, printers, vehicles, photocopy machines and even an initial stipend for the judges.[93]

However, later on the judicial system started to encounter serious problems due to the limited revenue-raising capacity and UNMIK's lack of a long-term

87 See Rome Statute, pp. 113–116.

88 Article 32 ICT Statute.

89 Cesare Romano and Thordis Ingadottir, *The financing of the International Criminal Court*, Project on International Courts and Tribunals (PICT), The Center on International Cooperation New York University; Brian Tittimore, New from the International Criminal Tribunals; ICTY, available at the following website: www.pict-pcti.org/publications/ICC_paprs/FinancingICC.pdf.

90 UMIK Regulation 1999/16 on the Establishment of Central Fiscal Authority of Kosovo and Other Related Matters.

91 Justice Rexhep Haxhimusa, a Supreme Court judge who opposed the policy, said: "An independent legal system is equally based on the degree of control over the budget of the court, decent salaries, and efficient management. In most countries, the Supreme Court proposes and administers the budget itself. But the Supreme Court in Kosovo is not even consulted for the employment of the court's administrative staff". Interview with Judge Rexhep Haxhimusa, 28 October 2005, Office of the Supreme Court, Prishtine.

92 Accordingly, the main criteria for selection of the local stuff was the knowledge of English language. Apparently, most of them did not possess a basic knowledge of functioning of the justice system. Interview with Judge Rexhep Haxhimusa, 28 October 2005, Office of the Supreme Court, Prishtine.

93 See O'Neil, *supra* n. 79, p. 81.

planning strategy was exposed. So from the very beginning the judicial system had to face low salaries for judges, prosecutors and judicial staff, which directly limited and still continues to limit the effectiveness of the judiciary. Consequently, a door was opened to corruption and other alternatives for providing an income.

The accountability of UNMIK's judiciary and its actors

There is a common opinion that no institution can operate without being accountable to society. All persons who utilise the public revenue are accountable to the public and judges cannot be an exception.[94] A number of non-binding instruments contain general principles that firmly establish the principle of judicial discipline and the removal of judges for failure, error, or misconduct.[95] The principle confirms that judges are equally accountable for their acts and omissions, whether conducted in a private capacity or under their authority as judges, in particular for malicious or corrupt acts and wilful abuse of judicial office.

While in Kosovo under UNMIK administration domestic judges could be subjected to disciplinary proceedings for specified misconduct/incompetence before KJPC, international judges remained untouchable and could operate without being accountable to society. The failure of UNMIK to establish a legal mechanism to address complaints involving international judges raised serious concerns with regard to the credibility and transparency of the judicial system as a whole.[96]

Generally speaking, Kosovar citizens lack and will continue to lack an effective mechanism for enabling individuals to initiate proceedings against any international authority that has violated their rights in order to obtain just compensation.

Conclusion

This chapter has examined the major challenges faced by UNMIK in attempting to establish an independent and functional judicial system in a post-conflict society.

It looked at the difficulty of securing the independence of the judiciary in a society shattered by the tradition of a totalitarian regime and civil war. The problems are endemic. Given the complexity of such an undertaking, which stemmed from the flawed legal framework, some of the challenges were inevitable.

In spite of its extensive efforts to establish an independent, impartial, and multi-ethnic functional judicial system based on human rights law principles of due process and fair trial, many shortcomings appeared during the period of UNMIK administration, illuminating the difficulties of administering justice

94 Shetreet and Deschênes, *supra* n. 1, p. 654.

95 Points 17, 18, 19 of the UN Basic Principle on the Independence of the Judiciary.

96 During the interview with Thomas Monaghan, the issue of the disciplinary mechanism by which complaints could be brought against international judges was raised. However, he was unable to provide a clear answer to the inquiry. Interview with Mr. Monaghan, 28 October 2004.

under international administration. The problem rests with the constituent document governing UNMIK, namely UNSC Resolution 1244, whose drafters failed to divide clearly the responsibilities arising from the SRSG's power. By concentrating all three powers into the sole authority of one person, the drafters disregarded the possibility that such an arrangement might enable this person to gain control of the passing, promulgation, and interpretation of the law as well as interfere in the course of justice. This could have been prevented by creating a system of checks and balances between UNMIK's pillars.

The injection of the international hybrid court as an additional layer within the existing judicial system proved to be an appropriate tool and as such has played an important role in bolstering the rule of law in post-conflict society. Yet, it should be emphasised that the effectiveness of those courts clearly depends on the degree of independence guaranteed to them. While the independence of the domestic judiciary is governed by clearly established rules, it is less apparent what the meaning of independence and impartiality in the context of the international courts should be.[97] To date, little has been done to promote the meaning and application of the principles of judicial independence in an international context. Consequently, the independence of the international judiciary should be treated in the same way as that of the domestic judiciary, which means following the same methods and adhering to the same standards of fairness and impartiality that apply to domestic systems.[98]

97 Mackenzie and Sands, *supra* n. 68, p. 275.
98 Ibid.

3 The paradox of UNMIK's justice system

Measuring the performance of UNMIK's courts and its quasi-judicial bodies

Introduction

It has already been highlighted that an independent judiciary is the strongest custodian of the rule of law and the best guarantor of a system of checks and balances. It guarantees that the executive branches will respect rule of law principles and act within an established legal framework, respect legal procedures, and institutions, and make sure that no one is above or can act in defiance of the law.[1] This chapter focuses on identifying the shortcomings surrounding the UNMIK justice system. It aims to shed light on the limitations placed on the shoulders of the judiciary. In this regard, it examines the SRSG's interference in the course of justice through cases involving executive orders used in criminal and civil proceedings. In addition, it discusses the legal implications surrounding the impartiality of the judicial system by highlighting the harmful effects a lack of impartiality causes for the fairness of the judicial process in general.

Additionally, it examines the functioning of the quasi-judicial bodies established for the purpose of property restitution. In this regard, it examines the legislative framework governing these bodies as well as the claim processing procedure. The aim is to assess whether the model introduced in Kosovo can serve as a future model for the post- conflict property restitution that may be required in the aftermath of armed conflict.

Executive interference in the course of justice

The following section aims at shedding light on the consequences that arise from the absence of a separation of powers on the ground. It highlights that in such a system the role of the courts remains uncertain. An attempt is made to sketch out examples of executive interference in the course of justice.

The practice of detaining criminal suspects in Kosovo under executive orders issued by the SRSG is the best example of this uncertainty.[2] Several individuals

1 Makau Mutua, Justice under Siege: The Rule of Law and Judicial Subservience in Kenya, *Human Rights Quarterly*, Vol. 23, 1991, p. 96, see also, Siri Glopen, Roberto Gargarella, and Elin Skaar (eds.), *Democratization and the Judiciary, the Accountability Function of Courts in New Democracies*, London: Frank Cass Publishers, 2004, p. 3.

2 In its Special Report No. 3, the OIK addressed the issue of the "Conformity of Deprivation of Liberty under Executive Orders with International Human Rights Law", in particular with

against whom international prosecutors and judges found insufficient evidence to support their detention were detained for many months solely on the strength of such orders,[3] issued pursuant to Regulation 1999/26, which extended the six-month detention period to one year, provided supporting reasons were given to the presiding judge or prosecutor.[4] The case of Afrim Zeqiri[5] is the best example to illustrate the way executive orders operated and in particular the legal implications arising from the practice.[6] On 29 May 2000, Afrim Zeqiri had voluntarily reported to the police after being informed that an arrest order had been issued for him on suspicion of having committed a murder. After being questioned by UNMIK police, he was arrested and sent to the detention centre in Bonsteel.[7] He was suspected of the murder of three Serbs and the attempted murder of two others in the village of Cernica. From 29 May until 25 July, he was held in detention based on judicial orders. The international investigating judge decided to suspend the case and terminate detention as it was found that there were no grounds for proceeding with the prosecution.[8] Nevertheless, the decision was not acceptable to the SRSG's office, so the following day on 26 July, the SRSG issued an executive order for the continuation of the detention for 30 days,[9] based on the aforementioned regulation. On 18 August, a second executive order was issued for another 30 days of detention. On the request of an international investigating prosecutor, the international judge issued a decision permitting extension of detention without specifying the exact detention period or providing any information about available legal remedies to challenge the detention time.[10] Two further executive orders were issued (13 January 2001 and 20 February 2001) and the grounds to support the ongoing deprivation of liberty included "the threat that the accused posed to public safety". Obviously, depriving someone of his liberty "based on a threat" falls outside the scope of Article 5 (1) of the European Convention on Human Rights as no such grounds for detention are

---

the Article 5 paragraph which guarantees an individual's right to liberty and security, issued on 29 June 2001, ABBACEELI, Judicial Reform Index, for Kosovo, April 2002, American Bar Association.

3 The European Court of Human Rights has long held that "in a democratic society subscribing to the rule of law, no detention that is arbitrary can ever be regarded as lawful". See e.g. *Winterwerp v. the Netherlands* judgment of 24 October 1979 and *N.C. v. Italy* judgment of 11 January 237.

4 UNMIK Regulation 1999/26, para. 1.1–1.3.

5 See UNMIK press release PR/394 dated 18 October 2000.

6 See Ombudsperson's report Afrim Zeqiri against UNMIK, issued on 30 May 2003.

7 Bonsteel belongs to the American KFOR and is situated in the area of Ferizaj.

8 See Ombudsperson's report Afrim Zeqiri against UNMIK, issued on 30 May 2003, paras. 20–21, 26–27 and 61.

9 Executive order was issued by Bernard Kushner, Second UNMIK SRSG, (15 July 1999–21 January 2001).

10 Both the International Covenant on Civil and Political Rights (Articles 9 and 14) and the European Convention on Human Rights (Article 6) guarantee the right to a fair trial and as such "preclude any interference by the legislature with the administration of justice designed to influence the judicial determination of the dispute". See the Ombudsperson's report *Afrim Zeqiri against UNMIK*, issued on 30 May 2003, paras. 26–27.

included in the exhaustive list set forth in this article.[11] Any expansion of this list by either a legislature or an executive authority constitutes a violation of Article 5 (1).[12] Notions such as "preventive detention" or general claims of concern for "national security", "public order" or similar terms that appear in other contexts in the Convention are not legitimate grounds for deprivations of liberty under para. 1 of Article 5 of the European Convention on Human Rights.[13] After a series of executive orders and judicial decisions had been issued, Afrim Zeqiri was finally released on 11 February 2002 because of the lack of evidence against him. The Kosovo Ombudsperson Institution issued a statement which made clear that "the practice of keeping a person in detention because of a lack of clear rules governing the detainee's situation, whereby a person may be deprived of his liberty for an unlimited period without *judicial* authorisation, is incompatible with the principles of legal certainty and the protection from arbitrariness, which are common threads throughout the Convention and the rule of law".[14] However, the case of Afrim Zeqiri was not the only one in which persons were detained based on executive orders. Almost the same procedure was applied in the case of Çelë Gashi, Avdyl Behluli, and Jusuf Veliu, which concerned the bombing of the *Niš Express bus*,[15] where around ten people were killed and a large number of others injured. These individuals were suspected of being involved in this incident. Three of them were detained without clarification of the legal basis for the detentions and remained in custody based on successive executive orders. In all three cases, it was found that their deprivation was not in conformity with Article 5 paras. 1, 3, and 4 of the Convention.[16]

It should be noted that where executive orders were used to detain individuals, all were already the subjects of ongoing criminal proceedings before competent courts and had already been released based on decisions by these courts.[17]

11 The European Convention establishes clear grounds under which a detention is permissible with a very narrow scope of margin of appreciation for States. In this regard, to be lawful any detention must fall within the scope of at least one of the fifteen purposes listed in paragraph 1 of Article 5 and may only be justified if it is based on the clearly established legal grounds of domestic law. It permits exceptions only in carefully prescribed circumstances by stating that any detention must have followed a "procedure prescribed by law" and second, it must have been authorised on the basis of one of the grounds listed in paragraphs 1 (a)–(f). In this regard, the deprivation of a person's liberty which does not take place in accordance with a procedure prescribed by law and is not in line with paragraphs 1 (a)–(f) is arbitrary and unlawful.

12 Ombudsperson's Special Report No. 3, *On Conformity of Deprivation of Liberty under Executive Orders with Recognized International Standards*, 2001.

13 Ombudsperson Special Report No. 3 referring to the ECtHR Judgement, *Jecius v. Lithuania*, 31 July 2000.

14 See the Ombudsperson's report *Afrim Zeqiri against UNMIK*, issued on 30 May 2003.

15 On 16 February 2001, a bus driving from Gracanica (Kosovo) to Nis (Serbia) was destroyed by a remote-controlled bomb near Podujeva (Kosovo territory) and as a consequence ten people were killed and several badly injured.

16 See OIK report *Cele Gashi, Avdyl Behluli and Jusuf Veliu* issued on 12 September 2001.

17 The European Court in its case law has on several occasions stressed that the fundamental importance of Article 5 of the ECHR is "securing the rights of individuals in a democracy

By reassessing the detention, the SRSG interfered in the area of judicial adjudication and consequently disregarded the authority reserved solely for the courts.[18] It should be noted that the ECtHR has established that executive interference is restricted even in a domain of its own institutional branch (the executive branch). For instance, the executive may only issue guidelines about the general performance of certain functions of its members, but not instructions on how specific cases are to be decided.[19]

This is because "the power to give a binding decision which may not be altered by a non-judicial authority to the detriment of an individual party is inherent in the very notion of a tribunal".[20]

As a result of being exposed to wide criticism, the SRSG ultimately issued a regulation establishing an international commission for the review of extra-judicial detentions, including those which were subject to the Ombudsperson's investigation.[21]

Nevertheless, the establishment and nature of this commission still failed to meet the relevant international human rights standards.[22] It lacked legal clarity, sufficient independence and a necessary guarantee that procedure would be followed in an impartial manner.

In addition, an executive decision was also used to close down the daily newspaper *Dita* because of the publication of an article leading to the death of an UNMIK employee of Serbian ethnicity, Petar Topoljski. On 27 April 2000, *Dita* published an article with a photograph of Topoljski along with serious allegations that he had been engaged in criminal activities during the war. Two weeks later, Topoljski was found dead. *Dita* alleged that prior to publication, it had tried to inform the UNMIK authority informally about the background of their employee, but allegedly UNMIK failed to pursue its concern.[23] On 3 June 2000, SRSG Bernard Kouchner issued an executive decision ordering the newspaper to close for eight days[24] on the ground that it violated the spirit of UNSC Resolution 1244. In normal circumstances, such an issue falls under the authority of a competent court that has the authority to determine the guilt or innocence of the person allegedly responsible for committing a prohibited act. Soon after, a

to be free from arbitrary detention at the hands of the authorities". See ECtHR Judgment, *Akdeniz and Others v. Turkey, Judgment*, 31 May 2001.

18 Review of the Criminal Justice System in Kosovo, OSCE Report 2001–2002, p. 34.

19 ECtHR Judgment, *Campbell and Fell v. the United Kingdom*, 28 June 1984, para. 79; *Sovtransavto Holdings v. Ukraine*, 25 July 2002.

20 ECtHR Judgement, *Van de Hurk v. Netherlands*, ECHR, 19 April 1994, para. 44–52. See also *Morris v. UK*, 26 February 2002, para. 73.

21 See UNMIK Regulation 2001/18 on the Establishment of Detention Review Commission for Extra-Judicial Detentions based on Executive Orders, promulgated on 25 August 2001.

22 See the OIK Special Report No. 4, issued on 12 September 2001.

23 The editor-in-chief of *Dita* said: "It is a task and obligation of every Albanian to reveal war criminals. If we do not do so now the forthcoming generations will never forgive us". Nicolas Wood, Kosovo, Newspapers Exposes of War Criminals Led to Murder, *The Guardian*, 21 June 2000.

24 Executive decision ED/2000/2.

new Regulation 2000/37 on the Conduct of Print Media in Kosovo was enacted governing the conduct of broadcast and print media. It established a Temporary Media Commissioner (TMC) with the task of implementing a regulatory regime for all media in Kosovo. The media commissioner was authorised to impose sanctions "on owners, operators, publishers, editors in chief, who operate in violation of the applicable law". Section 4 of Regulation 2000/37 states in its pertinent part that "owners, operators, publishers, and editors shall refrain from publishing personal details of any person, including name, address of place of work, if publication of such details would pose a serious threat to the life, safety or security of any such person through vigilance or otherwise". However, it failed to provide instructions on the procedure to be followed by the TMC in determining the existence of a violation and in imposing sanctions.[25]

Another practice of the SRSG's interference into the course of justice was that imposed by the executive decision (2004/25 of 20 October 2004) to cancel the tender process of a mobile phone provider. It was issued to invalidate all actions, agreements, and decisions taken by the local authorities, including the court decision issued by the Municipal Court in Prishtina.[26] The executive decision called for the cancellation of the tender process for the mobile phone provider after determining that the entire process was seriously flawed. It stated that "action to cancel the process was necessary in the best interests of Kosovo and its economic development, in particular its ability to attract investment".[27] The Municipal Court in Prishtina, which was called upon to determine the validity of a contract concluded between the Telecommunications Regulatory Authority (TRA) and the mobile company Mobikos, decided to disregard the relevant executive decision.

Yet soon after issuance of the Court's decision, UNMIK announced that the agreement between the TRA and Mobikos was null and void by virtue of the SRSG's executive decision.[28] It further stated that the Municipal Court's decision lacked a legal basis and as such was unenforceable.[29]

This discussion demonstrates that executive interference was not only present in the case of an ongoing procedure but as well in a case where a court had already made a determination of the legal matter. In yet another case, executive

25 Peter Krug and Monroe E. Price, A Model for Media Intervention/Content Regulation, in Post Conflict Zones, in *Forging Peace, Intervention, Human Rights, and Management of Media Space*, Indiana University Press, 2002, p. 157.

26 Decision P. br. 30/44/2004, issued on 16 of March 2005. The Rules of Tender that govern the tender process lack clarity as they do not contain clear provisions either regarding the jurisdiction of the court over possible disputes arising from the tender process or about the choice of law. See OSCE Report, *Privatization in Kosovo, Judicial Review of Kosovo Trust Agency Matters by the Special Chamber of the Supreme Court of Kosovo*, May 2008.

27 See UNMIK Press Briefing Notes, 23 March 2005.

28 Ibid.

29 Rebecca Everly, Reviewing Governmental Acts of United Nations in Kosovo, *German Law Journal*, Special Issue, What Future for Kosovo, Vol. 8, No. 1, 2007, p. 28.

orders were used to stop a court procedure initiated to declare void a political decision issued during the Milosevic regime. On 28 June 2002, the Municipal Court in Deçan issued two decisions voiding a 1997 Deed of Gift of the Serbian Government,[30] issued during the Milosevic regime, and affirming the right of the socially owned enterprise "Apiko" to the land, of which it was the registered owner in 1996, as well as of a tourist company "Iliria".[31] The Orthodox Monastery in Deçan lodged a complaint with UNMIK, alleging that these specific parcels of land belonged to them pursuant to the decision on the Deed of Gift by the Land Registry Office in Pejë/Peć of the Serbian Surveyor's Office,[32] as a restitution of land which, according to the representatives of the Monastery, was illegally confiscated from them after the Second World War. In 2008, the SRSG issued two executive decisions in a row, Executive Decision No. 2000/16, issued in April 2008, for temporarily setting aside entries relating to certain land parcels in the Municipality of Deçan and Executive Decision No. 2008/21, by which he set out detailed instructions for the implementation of ED 2000/16 and requested the cadastre office of the Municipality to inscribe certain changes in the cadastre books in favour of the Serbian Orthodox Monastery in Deçan.[33] Though the executive orders stated that they provided only a temporary settlement of the disputed land, they required the responsible authorities to inscribe certain changes in the cadastre books which, according to the relevant law, could only be incorporated by a valid court decision.[34] As may be noticed, executive orders served as tool to suspend the existing law and undermine the courts' authority as well as interfere in the course of justice. They mainly served to fulfil a political agenda. Although now abandoned as a practice, executive orders left a deep mark on the judicial system of Kosovo.

30 The Deed of Gift decision lacked a legal basis as a law regulating the restitution of land illegally confiscated from religious communities after the Second World War had never been enacted in Serbia.

31 Prior to it, on 6 March 2002 Fernard Saksik from the regional office of the Transitional Department for Trade and Industry wrote a letter to the relevant UNMIK authorities stating that the municipality and municipal court of Deçan could not be involved in matters related to companies with buildings on present-day monastery land. The involvement of Saksik in this matter lacked clarity as his department had nothing to do with the issues involved in this dispute.

32 Decision No. 952-901-1/97. Accordingly, a period of 15 days was set for appeals but no appeal was filed during the designated period. However, the interested parties in this case, representatives of "Apiko", a socially owned enterprise, could not appeal as it was impossible to expect that someone could turn down a political decision issued by a branch of the Milosevic regime.

33 Executive Decision No. 2000/21 para. 4.

34 It should be stressed that all disputes involving socially owned property fall under the jurisdiction of the Special Chamber of the Supreme Court on KTA Related Matters (UNMIK Regulation 2002/13). In this case, both Apiko and Iliria fell under the jurisdiction of the Special Chamber. According to the OSCE report, most of the time courts were confused about the jurisdiction of the Special Chamber. See OSCE, *Report, Property Rights in Kosovo, Department of Human Rights and Rule of Law*, January, 2002.

Shortcomings surrounding the efficiency of the justice system

This section looks at the shortcomings surrounding the responsibility of UNMIK's authorities to conduct proper investigations of violations involving its agents. In addition, it sheds light on breaches of ethical principles that are prejudicial to the administration of justice.

As already mentioned, the *Vetëvendosje* movement was the only one that openly opposed UNMIK's system, calling it an "anti-democratic regime". Since November 2005, the *Vetëvendosje* movement has campaigned through writing graffiti on public premises, marching on the streets, deflating the tyres of UNMIK's cars and organising massive demonstrations.

On 10 February 2007, the *Vetëvendosje* activists organised a protest calling for the rejection of the then recent proposals for the status of Kosovo issued by UN Special Envoy Martti Ahtisaari, which, according to *Vetëvendosje*, would lead to the ethnic division of Kosovo and indefinite international rule. As a consequence of the use of excessive force by UNMIK police, two people were killed and 82 others injured.[35]

Soon after, UNMIK's relevant authorities were called upon to establish an independent commission and ensure an independent and transparent investigation of this matter.[36] However, instead of establishing an independent commission to investigate the event, the investigations were carried out by a representative of the UNMIK Department of Justice, an international prosecutor, Robert Dean, and later on by the Police Inspectorate of Kosovo (PIK).[37] In his report on the police action case Dean reported that the deaths of two persons were caused by "improper deployment of rubber bullets by at least one and perhaps two Romanian gunners".[38] He also found that the rubber bullets were 13 years out of date and that there had been a breakdown in the UNMIK police's chain of command during the police action. Though the investigations have been completed, nobody has yet been brought to justice.[39] Instead, the responsible

35 Letter sent by the Acting Ombudsperson to the SRSG, dated 13 February 2007.

36 Ibid.

37 In this *Special Report 008/2007* (paras. 90, 91, 92) the OIK stated: "The preliminary investigations initiated by PIK were conducted by police organ and thus cannot be held to be completely independent". It further noted: "At the same time, the investigations conducted by an international prosecutor also cannot be deemed to be completely independent since international prosecutors and judges are appointed by the SRSG, who is also the final supervisor of the UNMIK Police and KPS".

38 See UNMIK Commission's established for investigating the death of the . . . reported dated 2 June 2008, Stated by Special Prosecutor Robert Dean, the UNMIK Department of Justice, 3 July 2007. Quoted in Amnesty International Press Release, AI Index: EUR 70/010/2007, News Service No: 130, 9 July 2007.

39 On 17 April 2007, Special Prosecutor Robert Dean submitted his interim report to the SRSG regarding the death and injuries of protestors during the 10 February 2007 protests. In his report, Prosecutor Dean concluded that the Romanian gunners attached to the Romanian Police Unit (FPU) were responsible for two deaths and two seriously wounded persons.

policemen were enabled to leave the country and evade justice by hiding behind their respective governments. In this regard, the European Court of Human Rights has held in numerous cases that States have a duty to provide an effective official investigation when individuals have been killed by the use of force. For instance, in the case *Kelly and others v. United Kingdom*,[40] the Court held that such investigations should ensure the effective implementation of domestic laws that protect the right to life and ensure the accountability of any State agents involved. The investigation must also be effective, i.e. capable of leading to a determination of whether the force used was justified and to the identification and punishment of those responsible. "Any deficiency in the investigation which undermines its ability to establish the cause of death or the person responsible will risk falling foul of this standard".[41] The investigation must also be conducted with promptness and reasonable expedition.[42] Finally, the investigation must be sufficiently open to public scrutiny to secure accountability in practice.[43]

Furthermore, the Court found that failure on the part of a prosecuting authority to give reasons for non-prosecution in a controversial incident involving the use of lethal force by the police may undermine public confidence in such a way as to amount to a breach of the right to life requirements of the ECHR.[44]

However, the very involvement of Prosecutor Dean in this process touched upon the meaning of the independence of the prosecutorial system in Kosovo because of the dual positions that he at that time exercised in two roles, one as an international prosecutor[45] and the other as the Acting Director of the Department of Justice, a political function of an executive nature. The Department of Justice was a component of the UNMIK structure, assuming the responsibility of the Ministry of Justice. With this in mind, one can only imagine how harmful it might be to justice if a political appointee were allowed to dictate which prosecutions were to be initiated or terminated, or how they should be conducted.[46] In October 2006, the parents of the victims submitted a complaint before the Human Rights Advisory Panel, the UNMIK oversight established mechanism.[47] The proceeding before the Human Rights Panel is discussed in Chapter VIII.

40 ECtHR, *Kelly and Others v. United Kingdom*, judgment of 4 August 2001 paras. 90 and 124.

41 Ibid., para. 96.

42 Ibid., para. 97.

43 Ibid., para. 98.

44 Ibid., para. 117.

45 Currently serving as a Prosecutor within the EULEX Rule of Law mission in Kosovo.

46 "The office of prosecutors shall be strictly separated from judicial functions". Provision 10 of Guideline on the Role of Prosecutor.

47 The Human Rights Advisory Panel was established in 2006 pursuant to UNMIK Regulation 2006/12 for the purpose of providing an effective means of redress for alleged violations of human rights attributable to UNMIK. Established by UNMIK regulation, run by members appointed by the SRSG and with a procedure subject to amendment by UNMIK, there is little hope that it can function independently. For more information, see Human Rights Watch, *Report Better Late Than Never*, June 2007.

Another example is provided by the proceeding initiated by UNMIK against the leader of *Vetëvendosje* movement, Albin Kurti, who was accused of organising a crowd that committed a criminal offence by calling for resistance and leading a group that prevented officials from performing their duties.[48] It is widely believed in Kosovo that this case was politically motivated by UNMIK to avoid prosecuting the persons who were really responsible for the violence on 10 February – the Romanian police unit acting under the umbrella of the UNMIK Police Commissioner – and in order to silence the opposition voice of the leader of the *Vetëvendosje* movement, Kosovo's most vocal critic of the country's international missions, UNMIK, EULEX and the ICO.[49] During the arrest, he was subjected to ill treatment and was held in detention for three days without a valid legal basis.[50] While in detention in 2007, Kurti was characterised as a category "A" prisoner, a categorisation reserved for Kosovo's most dangerous prisoners.[51] Only after the International Helsinki Federation (IHF) issued a public statement protesting against the denial of its attempt to visit Kurti in detention did the public learn that he had been categorised as an "A" prisoner.[52] Neither he nor his appointed defence council had been informed of this categorisation or its implications.[53] While the IHF was denied access to Kurti in detention, the American

48 Indictment No. PP 57-1, issued on 31 May 2007, which charges Kurti with three counts: Count 1) Attempt to cause "general danger" for participating in a crowd committing a criminal offence (Article 320 para. 1), Count 2) participating in a group obstructing official persons in performing official duties (Article 318, para. 1), and Count 3) Call to Resistance (Article 319 para. 1).

49 In a statement dated 10 December 2007, Amnesty International also described the case against Kurti as "politically motivated". Amnesty International Report, *Apolitically Motivated Prosecution?*, available at the following website: http/www.amnesty/au/news/comments/7098/. The Head of the Kosova Parliament, Jakup Krasniqi, asked the court not to delay the process but to end it and set Kurti free: "I do not agree with many things about *Vetëvendosje* or Albin Kurti's political views; however, he and everybody else in Kosovo should be free to express those views". Balkan Insight BIRN online publication available at the following website: http://birn.eu.com/en/79/10/2548/, However, the international administration strongly denied that claim. "Kurti is not being prosecuted for his political views. His political views are for independence of Kosovo, and that is the majority position here", said Robert Dean, the international prosecutor and acting head of UNMIK's Department of Justice. "The problem with Kurti is the way of expression. It's not the message, it's the manner". Balkan Insight BIRN online publication available at: http://birn.eu.com/en/79/10/2548/.

50 Kurti alleged that during the arrest, police failed to provide him with a valid copy of a court order. He received one on 13 February after being brought before a judge. Interview, July 2007, Detention Centre, Prizren.

51 The Acting Director of the UNMIK Department of Justice was not able to provide the Ombudsperson Institution, Amnesty International and other Human Rights Organisations operating within Kosovo with any document defining "category A" prisoners.

52 Letter published in the daily newspaper Koha Ditore on 15 May 2007.

53 "Alarmingly, Kurti's lawyer had not been informed of his client's categorization, raising further concerns about the application of the 'equality of arms' principle in Kosovo's UN-administered courts. (The idea behind equality of arms is that the defence and the prosecution operate on a level playing field so-to-speak because they both have access to the

diplomat William Walker (who enjoys high reputation among the Albanian population in Kosovo)[54] was guaranteed access to the detention centre, according to Kurti in order to persuade him to give up organising protests in the future.[55] The judicial proceeding itself has been a matter of concern as it was surrounded with many irregularities, which resulted in serious human rights violations as well as a breach of the judicial ethic. Immediately after his arrest, Kurti called upon all defence lawyers in Kosovo not to accept a court assignment in his case as he did not want to cooperate actively with UNMIK's court. However, his case required a mandatory defence as he was charged with a crime that exceeded ten years' imprisonment. Many of them complied with his request, some as a result of the pressure exercised by *Vetëvendosje* activists.[56]

Kurti was detained on remand, which meant that he had to stay in jail pending the investigation without the possibility of bail. He was kept in detention for seven months and under strict house arrest for four months, amounting to essentially the same deprivation of liberty as extended detention.[57]

The temporary defence counsel for Kurti, appointed by the court but not recognised by Kurti,[58] argued that the justification for keeping him under house arrest was vague. "The only legal basis that they are using to keep him under house arrest is the fear of repetition of similar offences, and they take it for granted that he is guilty of having committed these offences".[59]

Legal principles require that pre-trial detention only be invoked where strictly required and with due consideration of the rights of the accused. It should be noted that the ECtHR has found prolonged deprivation of liberty to be unjustified even in murder cases.[60]

Additionally, another irregularity has been detected in connection with the case that touched upon judicial integrity, independence and public respect for the

---

same information in the case before them.)", Head of the IHF, Julie Chadbourne, said in her letter published in the daily newspaper Koha Ditore on 15 May 2007.

54 William Walker served as a Head of the Kosovo Verification Mission OSCE in 1998–99.

55 Interview with Albin Kurti on 18 May 2008.

56 Koha Ditore and Bota Sot, Kosovo daily newspapers, Article *Avni Gjakova jep doreheqje*, 14 April 2010.

57 He was subjected to close surveillance by the police, who guarded his apartment for 24 hours. In addition, he was forbidden to appear in the media.

58 The defence lawyers would mainly accept one-day assignments in order to respond to the court's call. After the hearing they would announce their resignation. At each hearing the court was obliged to seek a new defence lawyer. After announcing the release of Kurti, Presiding Judge Ferdinando Buatier de Mongeot announced that the defence lawyers who refused to participate in the trial would face disciplinary measures. According to him the Kurti case proves "the incapacity of the Kosova institutions to secure the conditions for a fair trial and to administer justice". See *"The presiding Judge and politician with many orders"* at the following website: www.Vetëvendosje.org/en/news_post/the-presiding-judge-and-politician-with-many-orders-3/See also Press Release, Albin Kurti Found Guilty for Organising a Protest in Prishtina in February 2007, *Humanitarian Law Centre*, 17 June 2010.

59 Balkan Insight BIRN on line publication available at: http://birn.eu.com/en/79/10/2548/.

60 ECtHR, *I.A. v. France*, Judgement of 23 September 1998, paras. 104–111.

judiciary. It resulted from an improper interaction between prosecutor and judge during the proceedings.[61] In this case, the presiding judge failed to prove that he was an impartial guardian of fairness and justice,[62] whereas the prosecutor forgot that apart being obligated to seek justice he was also under an obligation to preserve the courts' reputation for impartiality in order to promote public confidence.[63] Permitting a prosecutor to interfere in panel matters violates fundamental principles of fairness and discredits the administration of justice in general.[64]

As has been highlighted, conduct rules are equally mandatory for judges and prosecutors and are based on ethical principles that serve not only an accused but society as a whole.[65]

In February 2008, after 11 months of holding the accused Kurti in pre-trial detention, the UNMIK panel suspended the proceeding against him due to the refusal of Kosovo's defence lawyers to accept the defence assignment and take part in this proceeding.[66] On 15 February 2010, an international panel composed of two EULEX judges and one local judge (presided over by a EULEX judge) decided to restart Kurti's trial. However, it was adjourned several times as the defence counsel, including the Head of the Advocacy Chamber,[67] continued to refuse court assignments. In the meantime, several human rights organisations

61 There was a certain moment during the hearings when the prosecutor approached the presiding judge and consulted him without the defence counsel being present and asked the judge "what do you want me to do next?", which gave the impression that this trial was based on a joint "prosecutor-judge" agreement, bringing into question the fundamental principles of fairness.

62 "In the performance of the judicial duties the judge must be impartial and must so be seen. The judge must perform his or her duties with restraint and attention to the dignity of the court and of all persons involved". Article 5, The Universal Charter of the Judge.

63 "Prosecutors, as essential agents of the administration of justice, shall at all times maintain the honour and dignity of their profession". See Provision 3 of the Guidelines for the Role of Prosecutor.

64 Moreover, the statement of UNMIK's prosecutor assigned to the case, that the schedule of the next hearing does not depend on the prosecution but rather on some external factors operating outside the judicial system, adds some suspicion as to fairness. The meeting with International Prosecutor Eli Koppel took place in the Prosecutor's office in Prishtina in May 2008.

65 Ross Cranston, *Legal Ethics and Professional Responsibility*, Oxford: Clarendon Press, 1996, pp. 1–6.

66 Kosovar lawyers consider that the consent of the defendant is the essential factor for a lawyer to accept an assignment. This act was perceived by the majority in Kosovo as an act of civil disobedience. However, from the legal point of view such an act is not reconcilable with the law, which, for certain cases, requires a mandatory defence. An interesting debate was initiated by some international lawyers regarding the legal implications of this act: "But imagine the situation if a defendant is charged with mass genocide or murder and if he does not want representation even though the representation is mandatory. Will Kosovo defence counsel refuse to represent the defendant? Will courts be forced to release a defendant until they can find an attorney? Clearly the Kurti trial is an open call to all defendants who are charged with serious crimes . . . refuse your defence attorney and if you refuse long enough, than eventually the case will be suspended", available on the following website: http://mrcheeseburger9000.wordpress.com/2008/02/07/albin-kurti-trial-suspended-indefinitely/.

67 See EULEX Press Release, 2 March 2010.

filed a petition with almost 200,000 signatures to the relevant authorities asking them to drop the charges against Kurti. Consequently, the prosecutor did decide to drop two charges against Kurti, namely, the third charge concerning the call to resistance and the charge of organising a crowd to commit a criminal offence. This left only the second count, leading and participating in a group obstructing official persons in the performance of their official duties. As this count carries a maximum sentence of three years, it did not require an accused to be represented by a defence counsel and enabled the panel to pursue the trial without a defence lawyer being present.[68] On 13 June, Kurti was arrested and the following day brought before the panel. He was found guilty of participating in and leading a crowd which obstructed official persons doing their official duty and was consequently sentenced to nine months in prison, but released the same day as he had already served 11 months in detention and house arrest in 2007.[69]

This section reveals much about the weakness of the administration of the justice, which was characterised by the failure of the responsible authorities to conduct an effective investigation into a case related to the involvement of UNMIK agents. It exposes the failure of UNMIK authorities to secure essential qualities of the justice system, such as efficiency, efficacy, and fairness. In addition, it illustrates the shortcomings arising from the lack of independence and impartiality of judges and prosecutors in conducting judicial proceedings before them. It shows that the uncertainty related to the preservation of the overall fairness and integrity of the process may severely affect the credibility and fairness of the system as whole.

Removal of the courts' jurisdiction for dealing with property rights

Property restitution occupies an important role in the peacebuilding process. Viewed as a form of restorative justice, it is considered to be an appropriate remedy that can enhance the rule of law in post-conflict society and promote reconciliation.[70] Such an undertaking contributes to the development of a body of "*ius post-bellum*" and strengthens the notion of new human rights, the "right to housing and property restitution", and the right of displaced persons to "return home".[71] These rights have been recognised as such by a sub-commission of the UN Commission on Human Rights in its guidelines that address legal and technical issues related to property restitution, known as the Pinheiro Principles.[72]

68 See Vetëvendosje Press Release, 14 June 2010.

69 Phone interview with Albin Kurti, 15 June 2010.

70 Megan J. Ballard, Post Conflict Property Restitution: Flawed Legal and Theoretical Foundations, *Berkley Journal of International Law*, Vol. 28, No. 2, 2010, p. 464.

71 Jose Maria Arraiza and Masimo Moratti, Getting the Property Question Right Legal Policy Dilemmas in Post-Conflict Property Restitution in Kosovo (1999–2009), *International Journal of Refuge Law*, Vol. 21, No. 3, 2009, pp. 423–424.

72 UN Principles on Housing and Property Restitution for Refuges and Displacement Persons, Economic and Social Council, E/CN.4/22005/17. Issued by the Special Rapporteur, Paulo Sergio Pinheiro.

The Pinheiro Principles call upon authorities to restore the rights of displaced persons, such as "housing, land and/or property of which they were arbitrarily deprived".[73] They highlight the importance of incorporating property restitution procedures into peace agreements.[74] In addition, they require states to ensure that national legislation related to housing, land and property restitution is internally consistent and compatible with the peace agreement and with international human rights, refugee, and humanitarian law.[75] Although the principles are mainly linked to the right to return, they do offer solid ground for restoration of property rights.[76]

On 28 January 2010, the Parliamentary Assembly of the Council of Europe issued Resolution 1708 on solving property issues of refugees and displaced persons. It calls upon states to take into account the Pinheiro Principles and ensure the restoration of occupancy and tenancy rights.[77]

Most importantly, both the Pinheiro Principles and Resolution 1708 have been cited by the ECtHR as a "relevant international document", which opened the door to a global level of acceptance.[78]

However, the model of property restitution in Kosovo was established on the premises of the restitution scheme introduced in Bosnia, which was run by the Commission for Real Property Claims (CRPC). As in Bosnia, responsibility for the restitution of property in Kosovo was entrusted to administrative bodies designed and administered by the international actors.[79] The Bosnian model was

73 Pinheiro Principles, Section 2.

74 It should be noted that the Pinheiro Principles reflect the practice of property restitution in Bosnia.

75 See para. 18.3 of the Pinheiro Principles.

76 Yet the Pinheiro Principles have been exposed to a range of criticism. It is argued that they are difficult to implement in practice. For more about the implementation of the Pinheiro Principles in practice, see Sara Pantuliano, *Uncharted Territory: Land Conflict and Humanitarian Action*, HPG Policy Briefs 39, 2009. See also, Megan J. Ballard, Post Conflict Property Restitution: Flawed Legal and Theoretical Foundations, *Berkley Journal of International Law*, Vol. 28, No. 2, 2010.

77 Resolution 1708 (2010) of the Parliamentary Assembly of the Council of Europe on Solving Property Issues of Refugees and displaced persons, paras. 9.10.10.4 and 10.5.

78 The Pinheiro Principles were cited in both judgments, while Resolution 1708 was cited in ECtHR, *Mago and others v. Bosnia and Hercegovina*, Judgement of 24 September 2012 See also ECtHR, *Dokic v. Bosnia and Hercegovina*, Judgement of 27 May 2010. The complainants invoked the inability to repossess their flats and to be registered as their owners. The flats have been allocated to them before the war under the scheme of "social ownership", in terms of which socially owned enterprises and other public bodies could allocate flats to their employees.

79 In Bosnia, the CRPC operated in parallel with municipal authorities. A successful claimant who received a decision from the CRPC was required to submit a request for enforcement to the municipal authority where the property was located. Many claimants would initiate proceedings before both mechanisms, the CRPC and the municipal housing office. See Paul Prettitore, *The Right to Housing and Property Restitution in Bosnia and Herzegovina*, A Case Study, Working Paper No. 1. Organisation for Security and Cooperation in Europe (OSCE), April 2003. See also, Rhodri C. Williams, *Post-Conflict Property Restitution in Bosnia; Balancing Repatriations and Durable Solutions in the Aftermath of Displacement*,

found appropriate due to the many commonalities between the two countries. As both countries belonged to the former Yugoslavia, they share the same nature and history of property rights, in particular the notion of "socially owned property" and the scope of "occupancy rights", including the notion of secondary occupants, which proved to be the most problematic for implementing restitution for third parties.[80]

Yet it should be noted that while the restitution of property in Bosnia had been foreseen in the Dayton Peace Agreement,[81] in Kosovo it lacked clear grounds. UNSC Resolution 1244 does not explicitly refer to property restitution, but mainly calls for UNMIK to take responsibility for ensuring the "the safe and unimpeded return of all refugees and displaced persons to their homes in Kosovo".[82] On the other hand, the Kumanovo Agreement is totally silent, as it does not incorporate a single provision on either the return or restitution of property. In addition, the legislation that governed property rights in Kosovo lacked clarity and consistency.

The following section discusses the legal implications arising from the model of property restitution introduced in Kosovo. It examines the processing of property claims before an ad hoc administrative body and a quasi-judicial body. The aim is to shed light on the shortcomings surrounding the functioning of these bodies.

Background information

As mentioned earlier, following the abrogation of Kosovo's autonomous status in 1989 the territory was placed under a specific regime resulting from a series of discriminatory laws[83] designed for a particular ethnic group, the Albanians, and it affected all aspects of their life, including their property. In 1991, two years after the abrogation of Kosovo's autonomy, new laws were enacted that governed property transactions, including the Law on Changes and Supplements on the Limitation of Real Estate Transactions[84] and the Law on the Conditions, Ways and Procedures of Granting Farming Land to Citizens Who Wish to Work and Live in the Territory of the Autonomous Province of Kosovo and Metohija.[85]

These newly enacted laws placed the Albanian population in a disadvantaged position compared to other minorities living in the province. Any property contract between members of different communities had to be approved by a Directorate of property rights, in this case the Ministry of Finance of the Republic of

---

Tesev, International Symposium on Internal Displacement in Turkey and Abroad, Istanbul, 5 December 2006.

80 Arraiza and Moratti, *supra* n. 71, p. 426. See also Paul Prettitore, *supra* n. 79.

81 Annex VII of the General Framework Agreement for Peace in Bosnia and Hercegovina, known as the Dayton Agreement, concluded in November 1995 near Dayton, Ohio, USA, and formally signed in Paris on 14 December 1995.

82 UNSC Resolution 1244, para. 11 (k).

83 Two of them were repealed by UNMIK. See Regulation 1999/10.

84 Passed on 18 April 1991, Official Gazette of the Republic of Serbia 22/91.

85 Passed on 20 July 1991, Official Gazette of the Republic of Serbia, 43/91.

Serbia.[86] This came about as a way for the regime to prevent Serb citizens from selling their property to Albanians, which according to them could greatly impact the ethnic composition in the province. However, despite these restrictions many informal transactions were undertaken between Serbs and Albanians.

Another problematic issue arising from the past was the status, purchase, and sale of apartments or flats in the 1990s. The laws of the social system incorporated the well-known socialist principle of social ownership, which means that property does not belong to individuals but is a common heritage of society. It allowed people to own structures but not land. In this way, one could only have user rights to the land. This set up a distinction between possession and ownership, but in actual fact the two amounted to the same thing.[87]

In 1992, the Serbian Parliament passed a law that allowed the privatisation of residential apartments. However, during that process a number of Kosovo Albanians lost ownership rights over privatised apartments because they had been dismissed from their employment with the socially owned enterprises (SOE) that were considered owners of the flats. Albanians who were dismissed from their employment were not allowed to purchase the apartments they lived in and as a result their apartments were privatised by other employees.[88]

Property restitution under the umbrella of UNMIK

As mentioned in a previous chapter, the restitution of property rights in post-war Kosovo was central to the realisation of the general objective of UNMIK's mandate. Through its mechanisms, namely HPD and HPCC, it undertook a role to interpret national legislation in the light of complex local conditions.

However, the main challenges confronting these mechanisms are threefold, notably the issues related to its independence, its capacity to interpret domestic norms and to ensure procedural fairness.

For instance, looking at the distinctive nature of HPCC's mandate, one may ask whether such an entity can be perceived as an independent body.

Although it formally assumed the role of an independent body, its practice suggests otherwise. HPCC worked in a panel composed of two international experts and one Kosovar expert, called Commissioners, who were appointed by the SRSG for a one-year renewable term.[89] As mentioned earlier, pursuant to the scheme established by the Secretary General UNMIK was required to establish cooperation with HABITAT and in addition to necessary assistance, provide

86 OSCE, Report, *Property Rights in Kosovo*, Department of Human Rights and Rule of Law, January, 2002; Sarah Aird, History of Human Rights Crisis, Part One of the Two Series on Kosovo Crisis, *Human Rights Brief*, Vol. 6, No. 2, Brief 30, 1999, p. 30.

87 Ibid.

88 See Edward Tavil, *Property Rights in Kosovo, a Haunting Legacy of Society in Transition*, International Centre for Transitional Justice, February 2009.

89 Section 2.2 UNMIK Regulation 1999/23.

policy orientation and supervise and monitor HPD and HPCC. In addition, due to lack of funds and adequate powers HPCC relied a lot on technical support from UNMIK. Moreover, the voluntary donors' contributions were administered through the UNMIK budget. In addition, the local staff were paid from the Kosovo Consolidated Budget, which was administered by the EU Pillar for Reconstruction and Development.[90]

Given the context, it can be safely argued that HPCC lacked institutional independence. Five factors lead to this conclusion: HPCC, as an UNMIK-established body, was faced with a complete absence of financial security; it lacked its own policy orientation; it was directly supervised and monitored by the establishing body; its members lacked security of tenure; and furthermore it lacked transparency in performing its adjudicative functions. As it had been given the power of a court, the structure of HPCC required a different design. Instead of being placed under the direct patronage of UNMIK it should have been fully detached from the UNMIK administration so as to put it in a position to render justice in accordance with the law.

This brings us to the second thread of challenges, capacity to interpret domestic norms.

The administration and adjudication of claims before the HPD/HPCC

The right to property[91] is often considered a complex and controversial right the parameters of which are difficult to establish.[92] It includes a wide range of economic interests, including movable and immovable property and tangible and intangible interests[93] and as such requires a proper degree of protection.

In the Kosovo context, the interpretation of property law was made especially complicated since it lacked an adequate legal framework. UNMIK's mechanisms relied on several bodies of laws that effect property rights. These include pre-1989 Yugoslav law, laws issued between 1989 and 1999 insofar as they did not conflict with the accepted standards of international human rights law, UNMIK regulations, and laws passed by the new Kosovo Assembly.

Two laws were repealed in their entirety as they proved to be discriminatory. UNMIK Regulation 1999/10 states that: "The following laws, which do not

90 IV Pillar of UNMIK Administration. See Leopold Carlowitz, Settling Property Issues in Complex Peace Operations/The CRPC in Bosnia and Herzegovina and the HPD/CC in Kosovo, *Leiden Journal for International Law*, Vol. 17, 2004, p. 609.

91 Article 1 of Protocol 1 offers a broad definition of property: "[e]very natural or legal person is entitled to the peaceful enjoyment of his possessions. No one shall be deprived of his possessions except in the public interest and subject to the conditions provided for by law and by the general principles of international law".

92 Theo R.G. van Banning, *The Human Right to Property Antwerpen*, Intersentia, 2002, p. 79.

93 Monica Carss-Frisk, A Guide to the Implementation of Article 1 of Protocol 1 to the European Convention of Human Rights, *Human Rights Handbook*, Vol. 4, 2001, p. 12.

comply with the standards referred to in section 2 of UNMIK Regulation No. 1999/1, are repealed in Kosovo":

> The Law on Changes and Supplements on the Limitation of Real Estate Transactions (Official Gazette of Republic of Serbia, 22/91 of 18 April 1991); The Law on the Conditions, Ways and Procedures of Granting Farming Land to Citizens Who Wish to Work and Live in the Territory of the Autonomous Province of Kosovo and Metohija (Official Gazette of Republic of Serbia, 43/91 of 20 July 1991).[94]

However, it has already been pointed out in a previous chapter that Kosovo lacked clear guidance as to how to identify which laws or parts of laws were inconsistent with internationally recognised standards, a deficiency which became problematic and created confusion in processing complaints.[95]

In addition, the legal framework governing property rights relations in Kosovo itself lacked clarity because of the existence of the two types of property, social and private, which led to confusion as to who was the holder of a property.[96] This resulted in total confusion as how to apply these laws in post-war Kosovo. In addition, some cadastral and court records were destroyed during the war and the rest were taken by the Serb Army to Serbia. The UN administration was unable to retrieve these records from Serbia.[97]

94 See UNMIK Regulation 1999/10.

95 The legal framework governing property rights in Kosovo consists of the following laws: Law on Basic Property Relations (Official Gazette of SFRY No.6/80), Law on Transfer of Real Property (Official Gazette of SAP Kosovo No.45/81 and 28/88), Law on Expropriation (Official Gazette of SAP Kosovo No. 37/71), Law on Construction of Annexes to Buildings and Conversion of Common Premises into Apartments) Official Gazette of SAP Kosovo No 14/88) Law on Construction of Facilities for Investment- Commercial Purposes (Official Gazette of SAP Kosovo No 5/86), Law on Co-Ownership of an Apartment (Official Gazette SAP Kosovo No 43/80 and 22/87), Law on Expropriation, (Official Gazette SAP Kosovo No.21/78 and 46 /86), Law on Forests (Official Gazette SAP Kosovo No 46/86 and 10/87), Law on Housing Relations (Official Gazette SAP Kosovo No 11/83, 29/86 and 42/86), Law on Land for Construction (Official Gazette SAP Kosovo No 14/80 and 42/86), Law on Registration of Real Properties in Social Ownership (Official Gazette SAP Kosovo No 37/71), Law on Transfer of Real Property (Official Gazette SAP Kosovo No 45/81, 29/86 and 28/88), UNMIK Regulation 2006/10, and UNMIK Regulation 2006/50.

96 The local experts had urged the SRSG to establish an advanced legal formula in civil and property rights area that would provide full protection to citizens. However, the response of the international actors was that "UNMIK lacked the institutional resources to establish an effective property rights regime". See, Reka, *supra*, Chapter 2, n. 23, p. 196. While some progress has been made, in the meantime instilling respect for property rights has continued to be problematic. After the proclamation of independence, the Kosova Parliament enacted sets of new laws related to property relations except the law of obligations.

97 See Edward Tavil, *Property Rights in Kosovo, a Haunting Legacy of Society in Transition*, International Centre for Transitional Justice, February 2009.

Under Regulation 1999/1, HPCC was obliged to uphold fair trial principles and to ensure the effective protection of individuals' rights to property in accordance with internationally recognised human rights standards.[98]

Accordingly, Regulation 2000/60 on Residential Property Claims and the Rules of Procedure and Evidence of the HPD/HPCC contained detailed provisions on substantial and procedural matters relating to the resolution of property disputes. In this regard, HPD assumed the responsibility of an administrative body to process property claims such as claims registration and mediation efforts, whereas HPCC was vested with the power of a quasi-judicial body, with an exclusive jurisdiction to adjudicate the property claims received by HPD.[99]

The procedure before HPD involved several stages: claim registration, notification, verification, rejection, mediation and the referral of cases to the Commission.

Prior to the submission of a claim, a claimant was required to be interviewed by a clerk/officer and then fill in a form and submit necessary documents. Soon after, the claimant, the respondent, and persons who had a legal interest in the dispute were notified about the process. The respondent was also required to submit a claim in reply to the claimant within the time limit foreseen by the Regulation.[100] After a thorough verification of the submitted documents, HPD considered the possibility of initiating mediation.[101] However, when a case was not settled by mediation the claim was submitted to the legal officer for review, who after thorough examination of the file had to write a referral report.[102] The referral report contained the basic findings, conclusion, and recommendations and once finalised, was subjected to an additional review by the case manager. After examination by the case manager, the referral report was forwarded to the Register Adjudication for a final review to assess whether existing rules had been followed and if so, the case was submitted to the Commission.[103] The claims were submitted electronically to the international members of the Commission as the commissioners were expected to do preparatory and supplementary work at their home base for most of the time. Basically, the Commission relied on the submissions received from HPD.

The proceedings before the Commission were carried out based on the written submissions. In this context, parties would not argue before the Commission, as oral hearings were excluded. In certain cases, the Commission used to delegate certain claims to the Register Adjudication, who submitted a claim to the local commissioner for review. In the case of any comments, it was sent to the full panel. It is necessary to point out that the Commission had developed cover decisions for claims involving similar legal issues. This was used for a so-called

98 UNMIK Regulation 1999/1, Section 2; UNMIK Regulation 1999/23, Section 2.6.
99 UNMIK Regulation 2000/60, Section 1.2.
100 Ibid., Section 8.9.
101 Section 10.
102 There is no information available regarding the practice of mediation.
103 UNMIK Regulation 2000/60, Section 7.8.

'mass-claims' approach, which involved collecting several cases at once that share similar facts and subsequently making a decision.[104]

In some cases, however, it could refer specific separate parts of claims to local courts or administrative bodies and it could also issue provisional measures of protection.[105] The final decisions issued by HPCC were binding and enforceable and not subject to any judicial or administrative review.[106]

The enforcement of the decisions was conducted through execution of evictions pursuant to an eviction order issued by the Directorate. The execution was assigned to the Enforcement Unit pursuant to HPD standard operational procedures.[107]

Finally, the third challenge confronting these quasi-judicial mechanisms concerns some procedural deficiencies that negatively impacted procedural justice.

Procedural deficiencies

The procedure before the HPCC was purely administrative and lacked transparency. The manner in which proceedings were handled clearly shows that the HPCC failed to ensure a fair trial to the parties involved and to address effectively the issues involving individuals' rights to property guaranteed under Article 1 of Protocol 1 to the ECHR.

The foregoing discussion shows that basically both parties in this case – claimant and respondent – were not able to participate in the hearing or at least give testimony. Article 6 ECHR states: "In the determination of his civil rights and obligations or of any criminal charge against him, everyone is entitled to a fair and public hearing". This means that in both civil and criminal cases a public hearing is necessary so that justice can be seen to be done.[108] A public hearing allows all parties to see the evidence of the other parties as a matter of basic fairness. However, an oral hearing may be unnecessary in cases where there are no contested facts and the court may fairly and reasonably decide on the basis of the parties' submissions.[109] In cases involving HPCC proceedings, commenting on the submissions of the other party was more than necessary and applicants should

104 See Anneke Smit, Housing and Property Restitution and IDP Return in Kosovo, *International Migration*, Vol. 44, No. 3, 2006, p. 68.

105 Section 1.2 UNMIK Regulation 1999/23.

106 Section 2.7 UNMIK Regulation 1999/23.

107 Information regarding proceedings before the HPD and HPCC is taken from Bjorn Vagle and Fernando de Medina-Rosales, *An Evaluation of the Housings and Property Directorate in Kosovo*, NORDEM Report 12, 2006, pp. 26, 52.

108 Article 6, Right to fair trial, Human Rights Review, 2012, p. 224, available at the following website: www.equalityhumanrights.com/uploaded_files/humanrights/hrr_article_6.pdf.

109 However, it is considered that the obligation to hold a hearing is not absolute if the relevant information cannot be conveyed in written submissions. See ECtHR, *Hakkansson and Sturesson v. Sweden*, Judgement of 21 February 1990, para. 66. See also, *Döry v. Sweden*, no. 28394/95, § 37, judgment of 12 November 2002; *Pursiheimo v. Finland* (dec.), no. 57795/00, judgment of 25 November 2003; *cf. Lundevall v. Sweden*, no. 38629/97, § 39, judgment of 12 November 2002.

have been given the opportunity to be heard on elements of personal experience regarding the deprivation of their property during the Milosevic regime, as well as in the aftermath of the Kosovo conflict.

In addition, the absence of a public pronouncement of a decision brings into the question the public character of the proceedings, which has proved to be an important principle safeguarding the fairness of the proceedings.[110] The ECtHR took the view that the principle

> protects litigants against the administration of justice in secret with no public scrutiny; it is also one of the means whereby confidence in the courts, superior and inferior, can be maintained. By rendering the administration of justice visible, publicity contributes to the achievement of the aim of Article 6 (1), namely a fair trial, the guarantee of which is one of the fundamental principles of any democratic society, within the meaning of the Convention.[111]

Regulation 2000/60 established that decisions issued by the HPCC were not subject to review by the courts and subsequently denied the right to access a court to affected individuals.

Such situations created significant problems for both claimants and respondents and many approached the Ombudsperson Institution seeking redress. Most of the complaints brought before the Institution involved the length of the proceedings, delays in delivering a decision taken by the HPCC and delays and failure in executing decisions.[112] Claims within "Category A", defined as "claims by individuals whose ownership, possession or occupancy rights to residential real property have been revoked on the basis of legislation which is discriminatory in its application or intent",[113] proved to be the most complicated ones.

UNMIK Regulation 2000/60 only specified rules on the procedures of the adjudicating mechanisms (HPD and HPCC). It failed to provide guidelines regarding the adjudication of claims involving loss of property during the discriminatory period.

Consequently, the HPD/HPCC panels had to apply legal provisions dating from before 1989 (pre-war laws), which were discriminatory and inconsistent with internationally recognised standards. Moreover, in the absence of property records the HPD and HPCC had to process the claim based on the statements of the parties.[114] In this regard, it became difficult to assess claims where

110 ECtHR J, *Pretto and Others v. Italy*, Judgment of 8 December 1983, Series A No. 71, p. 11, paras. 21, 22.

111 ECtHR, *Axen v. Federal Republic of Germany*, judgment of 8 December 1983, para. 25. This was an opportunity for UNMIK to reveal the truth about past injustices, which could have served to encourage the entire society to open a door to reconciliation.

112 HPD was experiencing a "severe funding crisis" and subsequently only limited resources for the processing of claims were available. See Ombudsperson Report, *Nazim Korqa and Others against HPD*, Registration No. 497/02.

113 Article 1.2, UNMIK Reg. 2000/60.

114 The majority of claimants were not in possession of the documents to prove their ownership.

complainants alleged to have been deprived of their property in a discriminatory manner (during the Milosevic regime), not only because of the complexity arising from the subtle actions of the discriminatory regime but also because of the absence of property records.[115]

Despite the complexity, HPD and HPCC officials were required to uphold a new regime of property relations based on the rule of law and international human rights standards. Given the situation, they were supposed to exercise an effective authority in order to respond properly to past injustices.[116] However, like the international judges they came from different countries and as such were faced with difficulties in identifying legislation which was discriminatory in its application or intent.[117] On the other hand, they could not rely on local members, since the majority of them had built their experience in the old communist period and as such were totally unfamiliar with international human rights law.[118]

The roughness of the process became more evident when it came to its execution.[119] The execution of decisions was delayed because the HPD and HPCC lacked the funds to employ eviction officers.[120] But even when this problem was addressed with the help of the UNMIK Police,[121] it was not resolved as very often illegal occupants of apartments and houses who were evicted later came back to threaten the rightful owners, or in the worst cases to burn or destroy the apartments or houses.[122] In many cases, the eviction was anyway delayed for security reasons.

Such ineffectiveness could be blamed on the failure of UNMIK Regulation 2000/60 on Residential Property Claims and the Rules of Procedure and

115 See OIK Report, *Osman Kozmaqi, Avni Kumnova, Fatmir Dragaj, Hamdi Zenelaj and Asim Rragoni against the HPD*. See also OIK Report, *Hatixhe Rexhaj Avdyli against the HPD*, available at: www.ombudsperson kosovo.org.

116 Arraiza and Moratti, *supra* n. 71, p. 449, issued on 11 February 2005.

117 See UNMIK Regulation 1999/23 on the Establishment of the Housing and Property Directorate and the Housing and Property Claim Commission. The HPD and HPCC officials were all required to have a good knowledge of property rights (property mass-claim adjudication), but not necessarily previous judicial experience. See vacancy note KPA-010 /011/012, March 2007 available at: www.kpaonline.org; see also Marshall and Inglis, pp. 97. The authors refer mainly to the international judges acting pursuant to UNMIK Regulation No. 2000/64; however, the same should apply to the HPD and HPCC panel.

118 As Kosovo did not have an Anti-Discrimination Law until 2005, society, including the judiciary, was generally not familiar with issues involving discrimination. Consequently, this also influenced the work of the HPD and HPCC. The lack of human rights knowledge and the complexity of the existing law might have led to the difficulties and eventual errors in determining the presumption of discrimination during the claim proceedings.

119 Most of the complaints involved the length of the proceedings and issues related to discrimination. See the reports *N. Korca against HPD* issued on 24 September 2004; *Ismet Ukqa and others against HPD*, issued on 12 November 2004; *Jusuf Gashi and others against HPD*, issued on 16 November 2004.

120 Leopold Carlowitz, Settling Property Issues in Complex Peace Operations/The CRPC in Bosnia and Herzegovina and the HPDCC in Kosovo, *Leiden Journal for International Law*, Vol. 17, 2004, p. 612.

121 Memorandum of Understanding between Police and HPD/HPCC December 2001.

122 Ombudsperson Institution in Kosovo, *Fourth Annual Report*, 2003–2004.

Evidence of the HPD and HPCC to foresee that the execution of HPD decisions would be "thwarted in such a tenuous and lawless manner".[123] The affected individuals thus did not have "normal recourse" to the remedy available to them to restore possession of the apartments and houses, since the law in force "did not foresee any further reaction if illegal occupants returned following their eviction".[124]

In the Hornsby case, the ECtHR pointed out that Article 6 embodies the "right to a court" and stated,

> that right would be rendered illusory if a Contracting State's domestic legal system allowed a final binding judicial decision to remain inoperative to the detriment of one party. It would be inconceivable that Article 6 should prescribe in detail procedural guarantees afforded to litigants . . . without protecting the implementation of judicial decisions; to construe Article 6 as being concerned exclusively with access to a court and the conduct of proceedings would be likely to lead to situations incompatible with the principle of the rule of law which the Contracting States undertook to respect when they ratified the Convention. . . . Execution of a judgment given by any court must therefore be regarded as an integral part of the 'trial' for the purposes of Article 6.[125]

Under Article 1 Protocol 1 "every natural or legal person is entitled to the peaceful enjoyment of his possessions". It places positive obligations on the authorities to provide effective protection for an individual's property rights. As it implicitly stressed in the case of *Scollo v. Italy*, such positive obligations may include the provision of necessary assistance in the recovery of property by means of eviction.[126]

Though it is argued that mass claims mechanisms are an exception to the domestic courts for the benefit of justice in exceptional situations,[127] the Kosovo experience proves that this might not be an appropriate option.[128] Although the matter required urgent action, it showed that urgency in resolving a situation should not validate the shortening of legal paths as it might negatively affect standards of fairness. The mass claims mechanisms should play an important role in the UN administration of territory in a way that ensures ITA compliance with international human rights standards. The foregoing discussion showed examples that led to some unwelcome results, particularly in the area of upholding fair trial principles. Thus it is of an utmost importance to develop clear guidelines that provide such ad-hoc mechanisms with a practical tool to reconcile their practice with human rights standards.

123 Ibid.
124 Ombudsperson Institution in Kosovo, *Fifth Annual Report*, 2004–2005.
125 ECtHR, *Hornsby v. Greece*, judgment of 19 March 1997, para. 40.
126 ECtHR, *Scollo v. Italy*, judgment of 28 September 1995, para. 26.
127 Arraiza and Moratti, *supra* n. 71, p. 449.
128 Vagle and de Medina-Rosales, *supra* n. 107, pp. 10–11.

Conclusion

This chapter has shown how daunting a task it is for a UN administration to safeguard the independence of the judicial system in the entity it governs. It illustrates that the lack of a clear division of powers may lead to an arbitrary and capricious justice. The functioning of an independent judiciary in a "managed judiciary" requires not symbolic commitments but complete adherence to international standards. Its independence is crucial to performing that role effectively. To achieve that, judges should not act as servants or agents of the two other branches of government but rather as a check upon the exercise of political power. They must be guaranteed that, irrespective of their ruling, no unpleasant repercussions will ensue for them. Instead of introducing special measures for overcoming political tensions, a UN administration should rather concentrate on introducing a special rule of law regime that can respond to the needs of the population. Special sets of institutional arrangements are allowed as long as they do not reduce the importance of the general concept of the separation of powers. Only strong, independent, and accountable judiciaries can provide full protection and the advancement of human rights and only fair and impartial judges can bring under control powerful individuals and institutions and provide remedies for violations of individual rights and freedoms. Only an independent judiciary can provide remedies from abuses of power and has the capacity to challenge the executive branch.[129]

129 Guidance for Promoting Judicial Independence and Impartiality, Office for Democracy and Governance, Bureau for Democracy, Conflict and Humanitarian Assistance, p. 5, U.S Agency for International Development, Washington, DC 20523–3100, Revised Edition, January 2002.

4 The extent of UNMIK's authority on the ground

Introduction

UNMIK was given full administrative powers to establish new institutional structures and ensure that new governance would provide equal protection to Kosovo inhabitants.[1] This was a so-called "pro-active project" in terms of which the UN asserts administrative control permanently taken from an existing authority.[2] Thus, UNMIK was required to establish new institutions that would serve the objectives of its mandate and mission.

The northern part of Kosova/a is mainly inhabited by the Serbian community, concentrated into four municipalities, Leposavic, Zubin Potok, Zvecan, and the northern part of Mitrovica.

The population of this area opposed the installation of the UNMIK administration from the beginning. It was followed by a range of attacks directed against both UNMIK structures and the Albanian population.[3] UNMIK's forces were not capable of subduing a hostile security environment and instead decided to evacuate for a couple of months, fearing for their own safety.[4] During this time so-called "bridge-watchers",[5] Serbian parallel security forces, took control of the

1 Ralph Wilde, From Danzing to East Timor and Beyond: The Role of the International Territorial Administration, *American Journal of International Law*, Vol. 95, No. 3, 2001, pp. 600–601.

2 Ibid.

3 After the gasoline bomb attack on the UNMIK police station in 2001, UNMIK had to withdraw its security forces from the north. Hans Binnendijk, Charles Barry, Gina Cordero, Laura Peterson Nussbaum, and Melissa Sinclair, *Solution for Northern Kosovo, Lessons, Learn in Mostar, Eastern Slavonia and Brcko*, Centre for Technology and National Security Policy, August 2006, p. 4. See also ICG Report, *Bridging Kosovo Mitrovica Divided*, No. 165, 13 September 2005, p. 23.

4 Both the UNMIK Police and KPS depended heavily on overall support from KFOR. But since there was no mutual cooperation between KFOR and UNMIK CIVPOL, the policing structures were exposed to continued attacks by the parallel security forces, which directly affected its efficiency on the ground. See ICG report, *supra* n. 3, p. 23. See also Binnendijk et al., *supra* n. 3, pp. 4–8.

5 Composed of former members of the Serbian paramilitary structures and MUP Serbia (in Serbian: Ministarstvo Unutrasnih Poslova). See the report of the Organization for Security and Cooperation in Europe, *Parallel Structure in Kosovo*, Report, Organization for Security and Cooperation in Europe, Mission in Kosovo, Department for Human Rights, Decentralizations and Communities, January 2007, p. 1.

entire area.[6] Moreover, a range of other parallel structures, namely court structures and public administration, were installed. The parallel structures comprised of individuals who used to work in a previous system.

This chapter aims at analysing the legal implications of the factual situation in the northern part of Kosovo. It tries to shed light on the major problems, dilemmas, and challenges faced by the UNMIK institutions in establishing the rule of law and ensuring full respect for human rights in this area.

It offers a brief overview of background factors that led to this situation by paying due attention to the legal implications of the competing jurisdictions, namely between the original and temporary sovereigns (respectively Serbia and UNMIK).

It shows that the failure of UNMIK to establish full security on the ground led to disorder and the installation of parallel state structures. In this regard, particular emphasis is placed on the legal implications of the dual legal system and the involvement of the myriad of authorities and their impact on individuals' enjoyment of human rights.

UNMIK's obligation to secure human rights protection to everyone within its jurisdiction

The following section sheds light on the legal implications of the reluctance of the responsible authorities to establish an institutional order. Through examples, it illustrates how this reluctance may have had a profound effect on fundamental human rights.

It explicitly focuses on cases that involved security, the right to life, the right to return, and the restitution of property, and the right to health. It argues that whatever the circumstances may be, UNMIK may not abstain from its duty to protect rights.

As already noted, human rights standards in Kosovo are disseminated through UNSC Resolution 1244, as well as numerous Regulations, including the Constitutional Framework that was promulgated by the SRSG. Resolution 1244, which has supremacy over Kosovar legislation, calls upon the UNMIK administration to protect and promote the human rights of the governed population.[7] Thus, UNMIK was under an obligation to ensure the effective implementation of its laws through its legitimate institutions in order to guarantee the exercise of human rights and to respond efficiently when they were violated.[8]

6 They could freely stop you on the street, demand to see your identity card and even deny you entry. Both UNMIK CIVPOL and KFOR were hesitant to interfere and offer you protection. ICJ Report, *supra* n. 3, p. 24.

7 UNSC Resolution 1244, section 11 (para. J).

8 Like a state, UNMIK was expected to be active in guaranteeing Convention rights. A state should undertake an active role in protecting human rights. Mere non-interference proved not to be sufficient in ensuring full enjoyment and effective implementation of human rights. See Alastair Mowbray, *The Development of Positive Obligations under the European Convention on Human Rights by the European Court of Human Rights*, Oxford and Portland Oregon: Hart Publishing, 2004, p. 221.

Looking at the phrasing of international human rights instruments, one may note that they unequivocally require a state to secure human rights to everyone within its jurisdiction. For instance, the ICCPR requires states to "*respect and ensure to all individuals within its territory and subject to its jurisdiction the rights recognized in the Covenant*".[9] In almost similar language, the ECHR requires states to "*secure to everyone within their jurisdiction the rights and freedoms defined in Section I of this Convention*".[10] Accordingly, a state assumes an operational responsibility to undertake some concrete actions to substantiate these rules in practice.[11] It becomes bound by the normative regime of a human rights treaty to put in place the institutional structures that will enable effective realisation of the rights enshrined in the treaty.[12] This means ensuring that the standards enshrined in those treaties are realised in the lives of ordinary people.[13]

While a large burden of the responsibility to give human rights weight in society lies on the shoulders of the legislators and courts,[14] it should be stressed that part of the burden is shouldered by the executive branches as well, since they are responsible in particular for ensuring the implementation of human rights in practice. It is commonly understood that the main task of the executive branches includes the enforcement of the law.[15]

As the executive wields the police power to enforce law and establish legal order in a given territory, it plays a very important role in criminal justice issues.[16] In this case, the executive branches become the primary duty bearers in society, as their main responsibility is to make human rights law workable.

9 ICCPR Article 2.

10 ECHR Article 1.

11 Vino Naidoo, *A Human Rights Perspective on Policy Implementation Process: Observation from the South African Public Service, Democracy and Governance*, 2003, available at: www.hsrc.ac.za/research/output/outputDocuments/2278_Naidoo_Humanrightsperspectiveonpolicy.pdf.

12 Michael K. Addo, *The legal Nature of International Human Rights*, Martinus Nijhoff Publishers, 2010, pp. 221–233. See also Beth Simmons, Civil Rights in International Law, Compliance with Aspects of International Bill of Rights, *Indian Journal of Global Legal Studies*, Vol. 16, No. 2, Summer 2009, pp. 440–451.

13 Christof Heyns and Frans Viljoen, The Impact of the Human Rights Treaties on the Domestic Level, *Human Rights Quarterly*, Vol. 23, No. 3, 2001, p. 470.

14 Mark Tushnet, The Political Institutions of Rights: Protection in The legal Protection of Human Rights, Sceptical Essays, in Tom Campbell, K.D. Ewing and Adam Tomkins (eds.), Oxford University Press, 2011, p. 297. See also Gennady M. Danilenko, Implementation of International Law in CIS States, Theory and Practice, *European Journal of International Law*, Vol. 10, 1999, p. 54.

15 This involves the authority to initiate legislation and establish legislative harmonisation, which is pursued through the enactment of secondary legislation, i.e. mainly administrative directives, policies and strategies, which make primary laws visible and workable in practice. See Daniel E. Brennen, Jr., *Constitutional Role of the Executive Branch, Checks and Balances, the Branches of the American Government*, USA: Thomson & Gale, Detroit, 2005. See also Hillarie Barnett, *Constitutional and Administrative Law*, Ninth Edition, New York: Routledge, 2011, p. 82.

16 They bear a primary duty to keep track of the primary laws, establish state structures, devise a justice system, maintain a prison system, establish public accountability mechanisms within each institution, etc.

With this in mind, we will turn to examine the factual situation in the northern part of Kosovo and look at the effectiveness of the institutional engagement of UNMIK's authorities in this specific area.

Failure to protect the right to life

As noted in the introductory part of this chapter, the northern part of Kosovo remains completely under the control of parallel structures. Even after 19 years of the international presence, neither UNMIK nor its successors, EULEX and the Kosovo government, have managed to establish an institutional presence in the northern part of the territory, which continues to remain under the partial control of the former sovereign.[17]

As a result, the inhabitants remained unprotected from crime and are continuously exposed to physical attacks.[18] For example, on 3 February 2000 several mobs rampaged through the streets of Mitrovica, throwing grenades into homes and going from door to door and killing people. Eight Albanians and one Turk were killed and dozens were severely injured, while the rest were expelled from their homes.[19] The UNMIK authorities knew at an early stage that the lives of the non-Serbian population were at risk in this area.[20] A series of attacks had been launched, including beatings on the street, looting, and harassment. Yet neither the UNMIK police nor KFOR intervened.

Moreover, after the incidents, no effective investigation was conducted into the circumstances surrounding the death of the victims. Although the Regional Investigation Unit was provided with the names of the alleged perpetrators, it failed to take appropriate action. As stressed by the UNMIK Human Rights Advisory Panel, "[t]he obligation to investigate is not of result, but of means. Critically, the authorities must have taken the reasonable steps available to them

17 In 2011, Serbia and Kosovo entered a negotiations mediated by European Union, but no visible progress towards the normalization of relations. Parties are exposed to lots of pressure from both USA and EE countries to reach an agreement. Recently a proposal of territorial swamp came out which is seen with doubts from many sides. While some consider that it may potentially end the stalemate which has persisted for so many years, others see it as a very dangerous idea. See, US-Backed Kosovo Land-Swap Border Plan under Fire from All Sides, 3 September 2008, available at: www.theguardian.com/world/2018/sep/03/us-backed-kosovo-land-swap-border-plan-under-fire-from-all-sides.

18 It came in response to an attack launched the same day by Albanian extremists in a Serbian café that injured a number of Serbs and killed one Albanian who was alleged to have been a Serbian collaborator. See United and Committed to Building Peace, *Mitrovica's Community Council for Peace and Tolerance*, Report, available at the following website: www.globalempowerment.org/policyadvocacy/pahome2.5.nsf/crresourceTrain/FC7A33CA3C936C6E88256E46008360DD/$file/CCPT.pdf (accessed on February 2011).

19 John Cerone, *Out of Bounds? Considering the Reach of International Human Rights Law*, Working Paper, Center for Human Rights and Global Justice, NYU School of Law, No. 5, 2006. French KFOR troops responsible for security in this area were unwilling to take effective action to provide security for non-Serbian individuals wishing to return to their homes. For more on this, see Paul Williams, Earned Sovereignty: The Road to Resolving Conflict over Kosovo Status, *Denver Journal of International Law, and Policy*, 2003, pp. 391–395.

20 Binnendijk et al., *supra* n. 3, p. 23.

to secure the evidence concerning the incident, including inter alia eyewitness testimony".[21] In addition, "where there is a plausible, or credible, allegation, piece of evidence or item of information relevant to the identification, and eventual prosecution or punishment, of the perpetrator of an unlawful killing, the authorities are under an obligation to take further investigative measures".[22]

The ECHR requires that the "domestic legal system must demonstrate its capacity to enforce criminal law against those who unlawfully took the life of another, irrespective of the victim's racial or ethnic origin".[23] The duty to investigate violations applies not only to cases concerning deaths that occurred at the hands of state officials, but also to any case in which the authorities are informed of a fatal incident.[24]

Thus, the UNMIK authorities were under a positive duty imposed by Article 2 of the ECHR to prevent and investigate the circumstances that led to the death of the victims.[25] As viewed by the ECtHR, state authorities are under an obligation to prevent and suppress criminal offences if it is established that they know or ought to know that the lives of individuals are at real and immediate risk from a third party. And they violate human rights if they fail to take measures within the scope of their powers which, judged reasonably, might be expected to avoid that risk.[26]

Consequently, due to the limited institutional engagement of UNMIK the non-Serbian population of this area was obliged to flee and seek shelter in the southern part of the town.[27] On the other side, the UNMIK authorities were obliged to give up on their goals and establish a sort of cooperation with the illegal parallel structures.[28] However, no such solution could solve the problem as neither UNMIK's nor the illegal parallel structures could adequately respond to the needs of the citizens, as they were acting under different sets of rules.[29] As a result, the area remained without a real governing authority.

Failure to restore the property of displaced persons

UNSC Resolution 1244 asks for "establishing a secure environment in which refugees and displaced persons can return home in safety".[30] Thus both the

21 UNMIK Advisory Panel Judgment, *Shaip Canhasi against UNMIK*, Case No. 04:08; Adopted on 12 November 2008. See also ICG Report, *supra* n. 3, p. 23. (referring to ECtHR, *Kelly v. United Kingdom*, paras. 94–98; ECtHR, *Orhan v. Turkey*, no. 25656/94, 18 June 2002, para. 92) and evidence from other key witnesses (ECtHR, *Önen v. Turkey*, No. 22876/93, judgment of 14 May 2002, para. 88; ECtHR, *Tahsin Acar v. Turkey*, No. 26307/95, judgment of 8 April 2004, paras. 230–232).

22 UNMIK Advisory Panel Judgment, *Shaip Canhasi against UNMIK*, Case No. 04:08; Adopted on 12 November 2008. Referring to the ECtHR, *Brecknell v. United Kingdom*, No. 32457/04, Judgment of 27 November 2007, paras. 71, 75).

23 ECtHR, *Nachova and Others v. Bulgaria*, Judgement of 6 July, 2005, para. 157.

24 ECtHR, *Ergi v. Turkey*, No. 23818/94, Judgement of July1998, para. 82.

25 See also ICG Report, *supra* n. 3, p. 23; Cerone, *supra* n. 18.

26 ECtHR, *Osman v. United Kingdom*, Judgement of 28 October 1998, para. 115.

27 As it could not rely on KFOR support. See ICG Report, *supra* n. 3, p. 23.

28 Ibid.

29 Kosovar Stability Initiative, Mitrovica: Two Realities, One City, *Policy Brief*, December 2009, pp. 6–7.

30 UNSC Resolution 1244, para. 9 (c).

international and national authorities are required to facilitate the return process.

As already discussed, owing to security reasons many individuals of Albanian and Turkish ethnicity had to withdraw from the northern area. Many houses were burnt or demolished, while apartments were occupied by individuals of Serbian ethnicity. Though a majority of the internally displaced individuals were in possession of a valid HPD decision that recognised the repossession of their property, many of them continue to remain deprived of their property due to the incapacity of the HPD to enforce its decisions.[31] The failure to execute its decisions was repeatedly justified on grounds of a lack of support from the UNMIK police, which were in charge of evicting illegal occupants.[32]

Yet the reconstruction of the demolished houses proved to be even more complicated than the repossession of apartments. For several years, many individuals were institutionally prevented from returning to their homes by being exposed to UNMIK's municipal's administrative directives, introduced by the UNMIK municipal office operating in the north.[33]

Similar to other municipalities in Kosovo, the municipality of Mitrovica was also co-run by the Municipal Administrator (an UNMIK official) and his officials. His role was to monitor, mentor and advise the municipal structures. He was entrusted with ensuring that municipal decisions complied with UNSC Resolution 1244 and the applicable laws, as well as ensuring that fundamental principles of human rights and equal treatment were respected, including the rights and interests of communities. In this regard, the Municipal Administrator retained a right to suspend and refer to the SRSG any decision he considered to be in conflict with UNSC Resolution 1244 or the applicable law. Moreover, together with the officials he was responsible for assisting to create conditions for the return of internally displaced persons and refugees and ensuring that there were peacebuilding and reconciliation programmes and activities.[34]

31 Involving the repossession of apartments and houses.

32 The previous chapter highlights the difficulties faced by the HPD authorities in executing their decisions, mainly through an eviction procedure. Owing to the lack of funds to employ eviction officers, who can perform evictions, the execution of decisions was subject to delay. However, it should be stressed that whereas the majority of decisions were executed with deals, on the other side, in northern Mitrovica, HPD was unable to ensure that their decisions would be enforced because of the authorities' concern that such attempts might lead to violence. For more information, see Ombudsperson Institution in Kosovo, 21 July 2008, Eighth Annual Report 2007–2008.

33 The same permission was not required in other parts of Kosovo. Neither Albanian nor non-Albanian returnees were required to re-obtain permission to construct. Moreover, most had benefited from various donors in the rebuilding of their demolished houses. For an insight into the difficulties faced by Albanian individuals wishing to return to their houses, see Muhamet Brajshori, UNMIK Active in North Mitrovica, *Southeast European Times, Prishtina*, 19 July 2011, available at the following website: http://setimes.com/cocoon/setimes/xhtml/en_GB/features/setimes/features/2011/07/19/feature-03.

34 See UNMIK Regulation 2000/45, *On Self Government of Municipalities I Kosovo*, Section 47, issued on 11 August 2000. See also UNMIK Regulation 2007/30, Amending UNMIK

To sum up, the primary role of the Municipal Administrator was to represent the SRSG and ensure compliance with UNMIK regulations and UNSC Resolution 1244.[35] To this end, he retained ultimate control over all matters affecting citizens' needs in the area. He could intervene whenever things proved to be incompatible with the applicable law. Yet despite this powerful mandate he could not exercise his powers over the authorities of parallel structures. Not only could he not exercise his powers over parallel structures but in many instances he attempted to comply with their requests. This can be illustrated by the failure to facilitate the return of displaced persons.

The first self-initiated attempts at reconstructing the demolished houses were undertaken in 2008, but with no major success, as they lacked UNMIK's institutional backup.[36] The individuals engaged in the construction widely claim that, allegedly, the construction permits issued by the Directorate for Urban and Rural Planning of the Municipality of Mitrovica (MP),[37] located in the southern part of the city,[38] were not recognised by the UNMIK Regional Administration in Mitrovica (RAM) and that consequently, they were required to apply for new permits from the RAM authorities.[39] It should be highlighted that in any case, RAM had no competence to issue construction permits, as this matter falls under the competence of the Municipal Office in Mitrovica.[40] Nevertheless, there are cases where individuals were given permission by RAM officials.[41]

Regulation 2000/45, *On Self Government of Municipalities I Kosovo*, issued on 1 October 2007, Section 47.

35 See United Nations Mission in Kosovo, available at the following website: www.un.org/peace/kosovo/pages/unmik12.html.

36 New Kosova Report, *UNMIK Blocking Return Process*, 5 November 2008, available at the following website: www.newkosovareport.com/200811051367/Politics/unmik-blocking-return-process.html.

37 Institutions established by UNMIK.

38 Brajshori, *supra* n. 33.

39 New Kosova Report, *supra* n. 36. See also Gazeta Express, *UNMIK-u rrenon nje shtepi shqiptareve ne very*, 18 July 2011, available at: www.gazetaexpress.com/index.php/artikujt/rubrika/C112/C6/gallery.php?cid=1,15,58369.

40 One may assert that MP has the authority to issue such permits as, for the moment, it is the only body run by democratically elected officials and as such is considered to be UNMIK's officially recognised institution. The UNMIK administration is only in charge of facilitating interaction between parties, which means providing a channel of communications for the parties involved. More details can be found on the following website: www.unmikonline.org/pages/mitrovica. Decision 07 NR 354/12-1, issued on 14 July 2011 by the inspection office, which bears an UNMIK stamp and was signed by a local person, Slavisa Milkovic, does not refer to applicable law in Kosovo. Taking into consideration that UNMIK does not have an inspection office within its structure, one can assume that this decision was issued by the parallel institutions and backed up by the UNMIK authorities. A copy of this decision was provided to the author by the Ombudsperson Institution in Kosovo.

41 Based on information received from the Ombudsperson Institution in Kosovo, of the six individuals who initiated the reconstruction of their houses in the northern part of Mitrovica, two claim to have obtained permission from the UNMIK administration, while four others are alleged to be in possession of permits issued by the Municipality of Mitrovica. Email communication with Sami Kurteshi, 2 September 2011.

Despite such complexity, few individuals attempted to pursue reconstructions on their own, but were automatically requested by RAM officials to cease construction and threatened with demolition of the structures.[42] Some were even arrested and held for hours at the police station. They claim to have been threatened with imprisonment if they returned to their homes.[43] The return of people to their previous homes was seen by RAM as a destabilising factor that might negatively influence the political situation in the region.[44]

On the other side, RAM did not use its power to stop construction undertaken by the Serbian parallel structures.[45] The Serbian Government is constantly engaged in the construction of collective settlements (residential premises, schools, sport halls, roads) and apparently their constructions are unsanctioned by UNMIK.[46]

42 Mrs Selaci and Mr Behrami, two citizens of Mitrovica who persistently tried to rebuild their houses, claim that the notifications were written in the Serbian language, which led them to conclude that this notification was issued by the Serbian parallel structures. Brajshori, *supra* n. 33.

43 According to Amnesty International, Ali Kadriu, a displaced ethnic Albanian, was beaten by UNMIK police when he attempted to rebuild his house in Suvi Dol/Suhadoll in north Mitrovica/ë. Amnesty International Report 2009, Serbia, The New Kosova Report states that Ali Kadriu was kept for four hours at the police station and threatened with imprisonment if he did not leave his property. New Kosova Report, *supra* n. 36.

44 According to former Regional Administrator Gerard Gallucci, who is known to the public to have been openly against the reconstruction of Albanian houses in the north, the reconstruction of those houses should not have been allowed as they were located in "inappropriate" areas, which he calls sensitive areas and as such should be negotiated with the local communities. Such an approach demonstrates the inefficiency of the UNMIK administration in responding to the needs of the population. It is not up to local communities to decide who should return to his/her home. See Galluci's Statement, *North Mitrovica and "Returns"*, available at the following website: http://outsidewalls.blogspot.com/search/label/construction. He shares his opinion with the leader of the Serbian community, Oliver Ivanovic, who says that the return of Albanians should be negotiated. Interview given to the Serbian Newspaper Press on Line, Povratak of Albanaca u Brdjane ugrozava obstanak Srba, available at the following website: www.pressonline.rs/sr/vesti/vesti_dana/story/64336/Povratak+Albanaca+u+Br%C4%91ane+ugro%C5%BEava+opstanak+Srba.html (last accessed on 22 December 2017). On the other hand, such interference has been viewed by the Ombudsperson Institution as a violation of basic human rights and freedoms. Commenting on the case of Ali Kadriu, the Ombudsperson stated that "the justification that home reconstruction endangers security [is] nonsense. 'It is the duty of the authorities to offer him security, and not stop him because of security'". New Kosova Report, *UNMIK Blocking Return Process*, November 2008, available at the following website: www.newkosovareport.com/200811051367/Politics/unmik-blocking-return-process.html.

45 According to the former leader of the Serbian Community in north Mitrovica, MP has no authority to deal with matters involving the northern part of Kosovo, as according to him, such an authority lies in the hands of the parallel structures. Oliver Ivanovic, Leader of Serbian community in North Mitrovica has been assassinated on 16 January 2017, Interview given to the Serbian newspaper Press on Line, Povratak of Albanaca u Brdjane ugrozava obstanak Srba, available at the following website: www.pressonline.rs/sr/vesti/vesti_dana/story/64336/Povratak+Albanaca+u+Br%C4%91ane+ugro%C5%BEava+opstanak+Srba.html.

46 The governing officials of the parallel structures continue to oppose the return of the Albanian population to this area. One of the reasons for such resistance may be the fear among

It should be stressed that the process of return generally faced many difficulties in the entire territory of Kosovo. Insecurity caused by hostile inter-ethnic relations, restricted freedom of movement, lack of confidence in the rule of law, failure to enforce decisions issued by HPD and HPCC, and lack of material and economic opportunities in the place of return continued to affect the return process adversely.[47] Yet it has been observed that, in contrast to the northern part, where the operating institutional structures are stalling and manipulating the return process, in other parts of Kosovo there is a certain commitment to and continuing institutional engagement in facilitating the return of the displaced.[48]

In the rest of Kosovo, a majority of displaced persons succeeded in recovering their property. However, many then opted to sell their property.[49] Although this option might not serve the objectives of return, they were at least given the opportunity to restore their property. It follows that in a situation where restitution in kind is barred by circumstances, other forms of restitution should take place, such as compensation or exchange of the apartments/houses between displaced persons.

This analysis has addressed the implications arising from both the right to return and the right to property restitution. The analysis further shows that the right to property restitution is grounded in the right to return which often requires political involvement. Such an approach narrows the options of the remedies that victims of forced displacement have.[50] Given the fact that the international law

---

many Serbs that they would lose control of their last urban area in Kosovo, since Mitrovica is an important administrative centre for the Serbian minority in Kosovo. See European Stability Initiative, People or Territory, A proposal for Mitrovica, 2004, p. 8. According to the Human Rights Report issued by the US Department of State, the Kosovo Property Agency KPA, which exercises the same functions as HPD, has issued 481 eviction orders in Mitrovice/Mitrovica, 299 of which are in north Mitrovica and 182 in south Mitrovica. These 481 eviction orders represent 83 percent of all pending evictions by KPA. It has been stressed that the inability of the KPA to enforce HPCC decisions for properties located in the northern part of Mitrovice/Mitrovica reflects a concern of the authorities that such attempts may lead to violence. For more information, see Human Rights Report: Kosovo, Bureau of Democracy, Human Rights and Labor, 8 April 2011, available at the following website: www.state.gov/g/drl/rls/hrrpt/2010/eur/154432.htm; International Crises Group, *North Kosovo, Dual Sovereignty in Practice*, Report No. 211, 14 March 2011, p. 5.

47 See Manual for Sustainable Return 2003.

48 Nevertheless, despite commitments this episode highlights many deficiencies, as potential returnees very often faced security risks before even returning to live in the property. Moreover, the general security of non-Albanians in the rest of Kosova/a proved to be very difficult for several years. Despite a commitment by the UNMIK police to provide them with a safe environment, many faced difficulties with freedom of movement and were constantly exposed to a range of violent attacks. See Anneke Rachel Smit, Housing and Property Restitution and IDP Return in Kosovo, *Journal Compilation, IOM International Migration*, Vol. 44, No. 3, 2006, Blackwell Publishing, Ltd, p. 76.

49 Yet, such attempts were limited by UNMIK Regulation 2001/17 for a certain period of time, forbidding minority owners, mainly those of Serbian and Montenegrin ethnicity, to sell their property. An extensive analysis of this Regulation is provided in chapter III.

50 See Megan J. Ballard, Post Conflict Property Restitution: Flawed Legal and Theoretical Foundations, *Berkley Journal of International Law*, Vol. 28, No. 2, 2010, p. 482.

lacks clarity as to what constitutes property restitution, by associating it with the notion of the "protection of property" or "possession",[51] these rights become the target of different manipulations. Thus it has been rightly observed that property restitution in post-armed conflict represents a new right that offers a remedy for forced displacement.[52]

Failure to protect the right to health

The following section serves as another example to illustrate violations arising from a failure of UNMIK's positive duty to protect individuals, in this case from the harmful effects of dangerous environmental pollution.

In the aftermath of the withdrawal of the FRY forces, many individuals belonging to the Roma minority[53] experienced severe violence, including murder, abduction, mass arson, and property destruction, based on the perception that they had been allied with the former Serbian machinery in the violence against the Albanian population. Consequently, most of them fled to neighbouring countries or withdrew into the Serbian enclaves.[54]

Those who previously lived in the "Roma Mahalla" settlement in the southern part of Mitrovica, around 130 families, were placed by UNMIK in sheltering camps in northern Kosovo in the areas called Cesmin Lug, Zhitkoc/Zitkovac and Kablar.[55]

51 Article 17 of the UDHR does not explicitly mention any limitations of the right to property. On the other side the right to property protection enshrined in the ICCPR (Article 17) and the ECHR (Article 1 of Protocol 1) appears as part of the non -discrimination clause and moreover protect a general right to property ownership. Yet it should be emphasised that to the certain extent the ECtHR has clarified this terminological ambiguity by underlining that: "by recognising that everyone has the right to the peaceful enjoyment of his possessions, Article 1 (P1–1) is in substance guaranteeing the right of property". See *Marckx v. Belgium*, Application No. 6833/74, Judgment of 13 June 1979, para. 63. See Ballard, *supra* n. 50, pp. 482–483. See also, Christophe Golay and Ioana Cismas, *The Right to Property from a Human Rights Perspective*, A Legal Opinion, Geneva Academy of International Humanitarian Law Human Rights, available at: www.geneva-academy.ch/docs/publications/ESCR/humanright-en.pdf.

52 Ballard, *supra* n. 50, p. 483.

53 The Roma community consists of Albanian Romany (Albanian-speaking) and Serbian Romany (Serbian-speaking). Some of them identify themselves as Ashkali, some as Egyptians and some as Roma.

54 Most of them sought refuge in the neighbouring countries Macedonia, Montenegro and Serbia. However, others sought refuge in western European countries, for example until recently Germany was sheltering around 50,000 Roma, Ashkali and Egyptians. See UNICEF, *Integration Subject to Conditions, a Report on a Situation of Kosovan Roma, Ashkaly, and Egyptian Children in Germany after Their Repatriation to Kosovo*, UNICEF Kosovo, 2010.

55 See the report issued by the Society for Threatened Peoples, a German non-governmental organization, *Dossier of Evidence Supporting the Call to Take Decisive Action to Implement Immediately an Emergency Evacuation and the Highest Level of Medical Treatment for All Roma, Ashkali and Kosovan-Egyptian Families in the Displaced Persons Camps of North Kosovo*, p. 8, available at the following website: www.gfbv.de/uploads/download/download/Dossier%20of%20Evidence.pdf.

These camps were established on land known to have life-threatening pollution.[56] The site itself belonged to the Trepça mining company, the biggest factory in the region, whose heavy metals, predominantly from the lead smelter, caused a high level of environmental pollution in the town and surroundings.[57]

This area had been known for its lead contamination since the late 1970s, particularly after the alarm raised by the Division of Epidemiology and Public Health of Columbia University, which found that its population experienced high concentrations of lead in the blood, which bears the risk of neurological damage.[58]

Soon after the establishment of these camps, UNMIK received warnings that the chosen location was built on ground polluted by nearby waste dumps containing large quantities of lead and this this risked serious health problems.[59] However, UNMIK's response was that the chosen location was a temporary solution that would last a few days. After visiting the camps, SRSG Bernard Kouchner declared: "As a doctor, as well as chief administrator of Kosovo, I would be derelict if I let this threat to the health of children and pregnant women continue for one more day".[60]

Nevertheless, despite the fact that these camps were intended to be temporary, they remained operational from July 1999 until October 2010.[61]

Consequently, this matter became the subject of a widespread and lengthy campaign by various health groups, including many international human rights

56 European Roma Rights Centre, Press Release, *Victims of Kosovo Poisoning Brings Law Suit at European Court of Human Rights*, 20 February 2006.

57 The Trepca mining and smelting complex was established in the 1930s and constituted the biggest mining company in Europe. It is rich in metals, including zinc, arsenic, lead, and cadmium. The factory provided employment for 15,000 workers in the past. See Marry Jean Brown and Barry Brooks, *Recommendations for Preventing Lead Poisoning among the Internally Displaced Roma Population in Kosovo*, The Centers for Disease Control and Prevention Atlanta GA, October 27, 2007. See also Organization for Cooperation and Security in Europe (OSCE) Background Report, *Lead Contamination in Mitrovice/Mitrovica Affecting the Roma Community*, February 2009.

58 OSCE, ibid.

59 Several health groups, as well as many international human rights organisations, demanded their immediate closure. Among them were Amnesty International, Human Rights Watch, the International Committee of the Red Cross, Mercy Corps, the World Health Organisation and the European Roma Rights Centre.

60 Quoted in *NATO troops seize mining complex*, published by International Action Centre, available at; www.iacenter.org/folder04/kos_mines.htm; also quoted by the ERRC team in their complaints written on behalf of Roma population and initiated before various national and international human rights mechanisms. Copies of the complaints were provided to the author by the ERRC lawyer, Dianne Post.

61 Some were moved to the new Osterode camp, the former military barracks of the French KFOR, while some were resettled to their former settlement in Roma Mahala. See Balkan Insight, *Blood Testing to Begin for Roma Lead Camp Children*, 24 November 2010, available at: www.balkaninsight.com/en/article/roma-children-to-test-lead-blood-contamination, See also The Sofia Echo, *UN Mission Closes Roma Camp in Kosovo*, 10 October 2010, available at: http://sofiaecho.com/2010/10/10/974136_un-mission-closes-roma-camp-in-kosovo.

organisations, which raised their voice about the hazardous effect of subjecting the families on a daily basis to toxic lead poisoning on an unprecedented scale.

In 2000, the UNMIK authorities conducted a medical survey of Mitrovica after an allegation that many UN police and French soldiers operating in this area were found to have high levels of lead in their blood.

The survey was conducted by the UN health officer, Dr Andrej Andrejew, whose results showed that lead poisoning affected most people living in the city of Mitrovica. He stressed that the worst affected were the Roma population living in the UN camps and therefore recommended the immediate closure of the camps and asked for the area to be fenced off to prevent access to the site.[62]

The World Health Organisation (WHO) conducted several assessments. In 2004, it issued a lengthy report analysing the effects of lead pollution on the Mitrovica region, finding that all those living around the industrial site had blood lead concentrations exceeding the permitted limits.[63] The results of the assessment showed that, due to their continuous exposure, Roma children had the highest blood lead levels of the entire population sampled.[64] It concluded that children and pregnant women were at greatest risk and urged their immediate removal from the camp.[65]

According to WHO's findings "88.23% of soils in the both camps are unsafe for human habitation and for gardening". It went further, stressing that "the child with the venous blood lead level of 74.4ug/dl represents a medical emergency, requiring immediate hospitalization for chelation therapy and other treatments. He or she needs the assistance of a physician experienced in chelation therapy".[66]

On the initiative of the WHO and the US Centers for Disease Control and Prevention, two rounds of oral chelation therapy were provided in 2006 through the Institute of Public Health, with approximately 40 children residing in Osterode camp receiving oral chelation therapy. According to Human Rights Watch researchers, the children of Cesmin Lug were not given the treatment, even though it was known that they were at the highest risk of lead contamination.[67]

62 Paul Polansky, *Roma Children Dying of Lead Poisoning*, New Kosova Report, 17 November 2008, available at the following website: www.newkosovareport.com/200811171411/Views-and-Analysis/roma-children-dying-of-lead-poisoning.html.

63 "Lead has chronic multi-system effects in the human body, but the most significant effect is on IQ levels where meta-analysis of numerous studies shows increases in blood lead from 10 to 20 micrograms/dl was associated with a decrease of 2.6 IQ points (1,2). These impacts are irreversible". World Health Organization (WHO), *Preliminary Report on Blood Lead Levels in North Mitrovica and Zvecan*, Main Office Prishtina, Institute of Public Health, July 2004.

64 Stated in World Health Organization (WHO), *Memorandum, Capillary Blood Lead Confirmation and Critical Lead-Related Health Situation of the Roma Camps Children*, 22 October 2004, available at the following website: http://kosovoroma.files.wordpress.com/2008/05/who-report-october-2004.pdf.

65 Ibid.

66 Ibid.

67 Osterode was considered a less contaminated environment. Human Rights Watch Report, *Kosovo: Poisoned by Lead, a Health and Human Rights Crisis in Mitrovica's Roma Camp*, June 2009.

In 2007, UNMIK stopped providing the affected children with treatment and necessary nutritional supplements on the basis of recommendations issued by WHO experts, who did not deem them to be necessary any longer.[68]

Two years later, in January 2009, WHO experts conducted a new assessment and subsequently issued a press release stating that lead poisoning in this area posed a severe risk to the population and calling on the relevant authorities to take measures to reduce toxicity and relocate the camp populations.[69]

It should be stressed that despite the known and documented health hazards arising from the lead toxicity, as well as the general demand for the immediate closure of these camps, no adequate measures were taken.[70]

According to Paul Polancky, Head of the Society for Threatened Peoples, as of November 2008 77 deaths had been registered in these camps that were caused by complications arising from lead poisoning.[71]

The reports issued by prominent human rights organisations have highlighted a range of serious human rights violations that have occurred in this regard, including the violation of the right to life, the prohibition against inhuman or degrading treatment, the right to health, the right to a healthy environment and the right to adequate housing.[72]

The European Roma Rights Centre (ERRC) initiated many complaints on behalf of the victims (143 camp inhabitants and 3 NGO workers), but without success. The case was dealt with before the Human Rights Advisory Panel in Kosovo and the European Court of Human Rights.[73]

68 In its letter of response to the UN Committee on Economic, Social and Cultural Rights regarding the steps taken to address problems in the camps, UNMIK stated: "These medical components were discontinued in 2007 as determined by WHO to no longer be of necessity". Quoted in Human Rights Watch Report, *supra* n. 67.

69 "Lead poisoning in this area poses a severe risk to the population of Mitrovice/a. WHO appeals for better coordination and communication between the health institutions and is ready to provide technical assistance . . . WHO asks for those who are still living in temporary camps to be relocated to a lead-safe environment as soon as possible, and particularly for Cesmin Lug Camp to be closed as a matter of urgency, in order to avoid another wave of newcomers. The area near the tailing dams should be declared a hazardous place for humans". See WHO Press Release, *WHO Calls for More Efforts to Reduce Lead Toxicity in Temporary Camps*, 31 January 2009.

70 See Balkan Insight and The Sofia Echo, *supra* n. 61. Though Osterode camp proved to be safer, it lacked basic living conditions, such as water, adequate hygienic conditions, and electricity.

71 Polansky, *supra* n. 62.

72 Human Rights Watch Report, *supra* n. 58; OSCE, *supra* n. 57; Amnesty International, *Kosovo: Protect the Right to Health and Life*, (AI) IndexEUR 70/011/2005, NR 189, published on 13 July 2005; Kosovo Ombudsperson, Ex Officio Report, 50/ 2010, *The situation of the Roma Ashkali Egyptian Community in the Camps of the Northern Part of Mitrovica and in Leposavic*, 23 February 2010.

73 In September 2005, a criminal complaint was filed with the Kosovo Prosecutorial Office against unknown perpetrators alleging criminal neglect resulting in continuing exposure to the hazardous environment, but not one action was taken by the Prosecutor. Email

Whereas the Strasbourg Court found itself not to be competent to review the case,[74] the Human Rights Advisory Panel, the quasi-judicial body established by UNMIK, issued two decisions.[75] The proceedings before the Human Rights Advisory Panel will be analysed in chapter VIII.

The factual situation in northern Kosovo demonstrates that the UNMIK mandate was deployed selectively. It shows how such selectivity affected UNMIK's realisation of its own objectives. By failing to assert its control over the area and establish institutions that would respond to population's needs, it opened the door to a range of violations. Thousands of people were left out of the institutional system of protection and as such exposed to violence and deprivation of property and, what is worst, compelled to live in a life-threatening situation. They have simply become victims of competing jurisdictions, exposed to the merciless forces of political compromise.

Competing jurisdictions: the spectrum of de jure *vs.* de facto *control*

The factual situation in northern Kosovo raises several questions. Do the present circumstances on the ground reflect an example of competing jurisdictions? If so, how can one define the relationship between the parallel structures and UNMIK? Is there a possibility of reconciling their interests for the benefit of human rights?

As already noted, by being proclaimed a temporary sovereign, UNMIK perpetually presumed to fully exercise all the competencies of a state authority.

This situation illustrates that these competencies prove to have been exercised within a limited domain. It is not clear whether this was caused by its powerlessness to exercise detailed control over the policies and actions of subordinated authorities, or simply by its reluctance to confront those that opposed its legitimacy.

This section attempts to discuss the legal implications of the situation, with an emphasis on the issues involving competition between jurisdictions. It seeks to provide an overview of the position of both competitors and to determine their ability to provide sufficient protection of those subject to their respective power.

As already said, according to UNSC Resolution 1244 FRY/Serbia was legally discharged of its positive obligations to secure rights guaranteed by the Convention on the territory of Kosovo.[76] Both UNSC Resolution 1244 and the

---

communication with ERRC lawyer Dianne Post. See also Human Rights Watch Report, *supra* n. 67.

74 On 21 February 2006, the Court sent a letter to the ERRC stating that it did not have jurisdiction to review cases involving UNMIK, since UNMIK was not party to the Convention. See ERRC, Press Release, European Court of Human Rights has no Jurisdiction in Kosovo Lead Poisoning Case, 3 April 2006, available at: www.errc.org.

75 Decision, *N.M. and Others v. UNMIK* (Case no. 26/08) Human Rights Advisory Panel, 5 June 2009 and the Second Decision 31 March of 2010.

76 "The State Governmental authorities of the Federal Republic of Yugoslavia and the Republic of Serbia understand and agree that the international security force ('KFOR') will deploy following the adoption of the UNSCR referred to in paragraph 1 and operate without hindrance

Kumanovo Agreement temporarily suspended its sovereignty over Kosovo, providing for the transfer of power from FRY/Serbia to the UNMIK administration.[77] To give effect to these provisions, FRY/Serbia was required to establish full cooperation with UNMIK institutions.[78] Though it retained *de jure* sovereignty over Kosovo,[79] the Serbian authorities forfeited the exercise of sovereign jurisdiction over the territory.[80] Its constitution and its laws were no longer applicable on Kosovan territory as they were gradually replaced by the supreme authority vested in the SRSG.[81]

Serbia was limited even in its attempt to organise elections, because this was seen to be an act of defiance against UNSC Resolution 1244 and a violation of the UN mandate over Kosovo.[82]

---

within Kosovo and with the authority to take all necessary action to establish and maintain a secure environment for all citizens of Kosovo and otherwise carry out its mission. They further agree to comply with all of the obligations of this Agreement and to facilitate the deployment and operation of this force". Para 2 of the Kumanovo Agreement.

77 "Resolution 1244 (1999) established an international civil and security presence in Kosovo –Temporary suspension of exercise of Serbia's authority flowing from its continuing sovereignty over the territory of Kosovo –Resolution 1244 (1999) created an interim regime. Object and purpose of resolution 1244 (1999)". The Advisory Opinion of the International Court of Justice regarding the Unilateral Declaration of Kosovo Independence, 22 July 2010, p. 3.

78 "Welcomes the acceptance by the Federal Republic of Yugoslavia of the principles and other required elements referred to in paragraph 1 above, and demands the full cooperation of the Federal Republic of Yugoslavia in their rapid implementation". Section 2 of UNSC Resolution 1244.

79 Guaranteed by UNSC Resolution 1244.

80 Marcus Brand, Institution-Building and Human Rights in Kosovo in the Light of UNMIK Legislation, *Nordic Journal of International Law*, Vol. 70, 2001, p. 463.

81 This could be compared with the situation of South West Africa (Namibia), which was mandated to South Africa for several years, but was later on placed under the trusteeship of the UN as a successor to the League. The decision was rejected by South Africa, which refused to surrender the territory to the UN and instead continued a *de facto* administration of South West Africa as its fifth province. The case appeared before the International Court of Justice, which was asked for an Advisory Opinion regarding the legal status of the territory of South West Africa. The Court was asked to give an Advisory Opinion of on the legal consequences for States of the continued presence of South Africa in Namibia, notwithstanding Security Council Resolution 276 (1970). In this regard, the Court gave its opinion "that the continued presence of South Africa in Namibia being illegal, South Africa is under obligation to withdraw its administration from Namibia immediately and thus put an end to its occupation of the territory". By Resolution 2145 of 27 October 1966, the UN General Assembly placed South West Africa under the direct responsibility of the UN and as such decided to end the mandate and terminate South Africa's right to administer the territory. In addition, several other resolutions were adopted, among them Resolution 276, which declared the presence of South Africa to be illegal. See ICJ Advisory Opinion of 21 June 1971. For more about the legal status of South West Africa, see chapter I.

82 Ruairi O' Connell, Deputy Head of the British Embassy in Kosovo, *Serbian Election in Kosovo, Statement*, 12 May 2008, available at the following website: http://webarchive.nationalarchives.gov.uk/20090320060633/blogs.fco.gov.uk/roller/oconnell/entry/serbian_elections_in_kosovo. See also Linda Karadaku and Igor Ivanovic, *Tension Protest marks Serbian Election in Kosovo*, saying that "The international community and Kosovo

Taking into consideration the consensual relationship established in the Kumanovo Agreement,[83] followed by UNSC Resolution 1244, the FRY (Serbian) authorities had accepted a temporary delegation of their sovereign rights to UNMIK.

In this light, the installation of its structures showed that Serbia failed to abide by the terms of the agreement as well as the obligations arising from UNSC Resolution 1244.[84]

As noted, it continues to exercise its sovereignty over a certain portion of the territory through its extended governmental institutions by widely undermining

officials have said they will not recognize any elections by the Serb government in Mitrovica". Quoted in *South East European Times*, 31 May 2010.

83 In the view of some authors, it was not a genuine consent, since it was rendered under military coercion, which is considered to be in violation of Article 52 of the Vienna Convention on the Law of the Treaties, which states that "a treaty is void if its conclusion has been procured by the threat or use of force in violation of the principles of international law embodied in the Charter of the United Nations". See Barbara Delcourt and Nina Wilen, International Administration of Foreign Territories and Sovereignty, an Impossible Equitation?, *Finish Yearbook of International Law*, Vol. 18, 2007, p. 68. See also Enrico Milano, Security Council Action in the Balkans: Reweaving the Legality of Kosovo's Territorial Status, *European Journal of International Law*, Vol. 14, 2003; Christopher J. Le Mon, Unilateral Intervention by Invitation I Civil Wars: The Effective Control Tested, *International Law and Politics*, Vol. 35, 2003. However, this view is present only among those legalists who do not regard the NATO intervention in Kosovo to be of a humanitarian nature and who still perceive sovereignty to be the absolute and permanent power of a nation state. The issue becomes more complex if viewed through the lens of the provisions enshrined in UNSC Resolution 1244, which provided an overall framework for the UNMIK operation. Taking into account its terminology, its subject matter, the number of votes which led to its adoption, and in particular the wording expressed in its Preamble ("Welcoming the general principles on a political solution to the Kosovo crisis adopted on 6 May 1999 (S/1999/516, annex 1 to this resolution) and welcoming also the acceptance by the Federal Republic of Yugoslavia of the principles set forth in points 1 to 9 of the paper presented in Belgrade on 2 June 1999 (S/1999/649, Annex 2 to this Resolution), and the Federal Republic of Yugoslavia's agreement to that paper"), it is difficult to identify the elements which may lead us to conclude that the undertaking lacked any party's genuine consent. However, even if the consent of those representing the FRY authorities in the Kumanovo Agreement might have been rendered by means of military coercion, the UNSC Resolution should be seen as a "tool" that provides a "legitimacy cure" to such coercion. In the view of Enrico Milano, nothing can legalise such an act. But he emphasises that due regard should be paid to the fact that besides a claim of imposition, the FRY authorities had never claimed that the Kumanovo Agreement was null and void under Article 52 of the Vienna Convention. Though it could so claim, it has never started any procedure under Article 65–68 Vienna Convention for the determination of such invalidity. Milano, *supra* n. 83, pp. 1020–1021.

84 Note that Resolution 1244 implies an act of creation of obligations, rights and powers, and therefore has a binding effect upon the parties. The binding force of Resolution 1244 has been reaffirmed by the ICJ in its Advisory Opinion, in which it stated: "Resolution 1244 (1999) was expressly adopted by the Security Council on the basis of Chapter VII of the United Nations Charter, and therefore clearly imposes international legal obligations". The Advisory Opinion of the International Court of Justice regarding the Unilateral declaration of Kosovo Independence, 22 July 2010, p. 32.

and obstructing the authority of those who gained power to temporarily exercise *de facto* jurisdiction (UNMIK).[85]

Yet apart from being reminded that such an endeavour brings into question the violation of the UN mandate, it was never prevented from doing so.[86]

Taking into consideration the complexity of the situation created on the ground, this raises the issue as to whether the power exercised by the Serbian authority proved sufficient to protect the rights of the inhabitants of the area.

Earlier in the discussion, it was explained that a domain of power was exercised by Serbian parallel structures as an attempt to expand its *de facto* jurisdiction in certain areas of Kosovo through its institutions. Based on the foregoing assessment, it appears that although they were in a position to determine certain civil rights and thus to influence the lives of the individuals living there, they may not have been able to protect their rights efficiently as the degree of such power proved to be quite limited, since the executive powers remained in the hands of the temporary sovereign, in this case UNMIK, that had established new legal dominion over the area. So the lack of executive power brings into question their ability to enforce laws through police action.[87]

Consequently, in the absence of the enforcement mechanisms the substantive rights remained nugatory.[88]

Nevertheless, it should be emphasised that whereas the parallel structures attempted to provide an existential minimum of protection (provide welfare services), albeit in a selective manner, the temporary sovereign authorities (UNMIK) reluctantly refused to do so.[89] It is difficult to say where this reluctance stemmed from, in particular if one takes into consideration the powers that were available for this purpose under UNSC Resolution 1244.[90]

85 According to Blacks Law Dictionary, seventh edition, *de facto* means "1. Actual, existing in fact; having effect even though not formally or legally recognized. 2. Illegitimate but in effect", whereas *de jure* means "Existing by right or according to law".

86 On the other hand not enough attention has been drawn during the last year to the problem of Mitrovica, where a lack of cooperation on the part of FRY with the United Nations Interim Administration Mission in Kosovo (UNMIK) continues and FRY maintains parallel structures. Council of Europe, Parliamentary Assembly, Amendment A, Doc. 9539, 10 September 2002. See also Valur Ingimundarson, Pitting Democratic Standards against Sovereign Rights: The Nature of International Rule in Kosovo, *New Balkans Politics*, No. 7/8, 2003.

87 As the MUP Serbia operates illegally in this part, they cannot be engaged as a enforcement agency.

88 Aaron X. Fellmeth, *Negative and Positive Human Rights*, Athens Institute for Education and Research 8th Annual International Conference on Law, Athens, Greece, 18–21 July, 2011.

89 Only to non-Albanians.

90 The UNSC Resolution calls upon UNMIK to "ensure public safety and order until the international civil presence can take responsibility for this task" (Section 9 (d)). In July 2011, for the first time an action was undertaken to establish a legal order in the northern part, in particular to extend control at the customs and police border. The action was undertaken by the Kosovo Police Special Unit, ROSU. They were helped by KFOR forces in transporting customs gates. However, soon after they had to withdraw in the face of the protest of the Serbian minority, who responded violently to the initiative. One of the police was shot dead and several injured. The official borders are closed for commercial traffic and controlled by

However, let us analyse UNMIK's position in this regard.

Pursuant to UNSC Resolution 1244, UNMIK was provided with the capacity of a sovereign to exercise substantive control over the activities of subordinated authorities within the administrative border of Kosovo. It comprised both civilian and military components. The civilian component was entrusted with state administration, while the military component, comprising both a contingent of international police and a military contingent (KFOR), was responsible for providing public security and establishing the rule of law.[91]

With this in mind, one may note that the UNMIK administration has at its disposal every means of exercising effective control throughout the territory.

Despite such capacity, it decided to hold a position of minimalist institutional engagement and justified it on the basis of exceptional circumstances, claiming to be prevented by parallel structures from exercising its authority.[92]

This raises another set of questions. May public authorities escape their responsibility where events take place on their territory that they are unable to influence? Or, may public authorities be held responsible for refraining from using their powers? Let us seek the answer from the Strasbourg jurisprudence. In this context, the ECtHR has, significantly, established that Article 1 of the Convention imposes a general duty on a state to secure compliance with the Convention throughout its territory and with regard to every individual (*Assanidze v. Georgia*).[93] In the view of the court, a state is responsible for events occurring anywhere within its national territory, even in the situation when a state encounters difficulties in exercising its jurisdiction[94] as a result of a separatist regime or military occupation by another state.[95]

KFOR. EULEX, which exercises its broad executive power, did not try to reverse the action of the Kosovo Police, nor did it support them. Soon after, it came out with the statement that "[t]he operation was not helpful. It was not done in consultation with the international community and the EU does not approve it. . . . It is essential now to calm the situation down and return to where we were. EULEX stands ready to assist the Kosovo authorities in doing this". See Balkan Insight, *Kosovo Police Pull Back from Serb Border*, 26 July 2011. The international community was widely divided regarding this matter. While the majority of European countries condemned the action and urged that the matter be resolved through dialogue, the US State Department, while calling for dialogue, equivocally stressed that the Kosovo had the right to extend its national authority and the rule of law to the northern area. See Security Council, Press release, Recent Violence called" stark reminder" of threats to security in Kosovo, Department of Public Information, 6604th meeting, 30 August 2011.

91 However, KFOR retained primary effective responsibility for overall control of security. For the evolution of NATO's role in Kosovo, more information is available at the following website: www.nato.int/cps/en/natolive/topics_48818.htm.

92 "The obstacles were mainly external in nature but there were also internal obstructions that developed as a result of many members of the international staff favouring Kosovo Serb demands and positions and acting less than impartially. There was extensive cooperation with the illegal parallel structures and their leaders. . . . "Regional Administrator Gallucci often undermined important aims and objectives that UNMIK tried to achieve" Interview with a high UNMIK official, 10 May 2011.

93 *Assanidze v. Georgia*, App. No. 71503/01, ECtHR, Judgment of 8 April 2004, para. 147.

94 Ibid., para. 146, referring to the Adjarian Autonomous Republic, where the State of Georgia has difficulties in exercising its jurisdiction.

95 *Ilaşcu and Others v. Moldova*, App. No. 48787/99, ECtHR, Judgment of 8 July 2004, para. 333.

However, one may ask what is the most efficient way to realise the values and rights in the case of competing jurisdictions. In this situation, when multiple authorities are involved the higher authorities (in this case UNMIK)[96] operating within the given borders "are under a duty to require their subordinates to comply with the Convention and cannot shelter behind their inability".[97] As such, they bear the positive obligations to take appropriate measures to respect rights and freedom within the territory (*Ilaşcu and others v. Moldova and Russia).*[98]

In this respect, UNMIK, as a higher authority, bears the primary responsibility for ensuring the rights and freedoms of the population in the northern part of Kosovo.

It is remarkable that the rights and freedoms of this population were nevertheless not sufficiently protected. They were deprived of the right to have an institutional order that secured and enabled them to realise their rights and freedoms.[99] In this respect, the UNMIK authorities deviated from their essential obligation to take positive measures to provide safety for everyone within their jurisdiction. As a consequence, the entire area was subjected to a dual system of governance, neither of which had real authority, in other words a phantom authority.

The following section will shed light on the legal implications of the dual legal systems and the functioning of parallel structures.

The effect of the dual legal system and the parallel court structures

One dimension completely left out of the picture by the UNMIK authorities in Kosovo was the need to address the legal implications of a multiple legal system, a situation of so-called legal pluralism.

As already noted, besides normative acts issued by UNMIK in the northern part of Kosovo Serbian laws are still present which often interact with or in some way rub against UNMIK's laws. The parallel courts apply the previous laws and laws currently applicable in Serbia. The Supreme Court of Serbia is the ultimate appellate body for the final judgments of the parallel courts.[100]

Though UNMIK declared void any decision issued under these laws, the denial of their validity did not end their existence; they continued to affect individuals' lives.[101]

96 The SRRS is the highest authority in Kosovo. UNSC Resolution 1244.

97 *Supra* n. 93, paras. 146–147.

98 *Supra* n. 95, para. 313.

99 As provided by the European Commission of Human Rights, "Convention does not allow vacuum in the protection of its rights and freedoms". Stated by the Commission in *Cyprus v. Turkey*, Decisions of 26 May, 1975, in. 2 Decisions and Reports 1975, para. 136.

100 Organization for Security and Cooperation in Europe (OSCE), Mission in Kosovo, Department of Human Rights and Democratization, *Parallel Structure in Kosovo*, 2006–2007, pp. 15–16.

101 Not all former laws were declared invalid, only those that contradicted human rights standards. See UNMIK Regulation 1999/1, Applicable Law in Kosovo.

Legal pluralism can generally be defined as "the state of affairs in which a category of social relations is within a field of operation of two or more legal norms".[102]

However, looking at it from the particular perspective of law, legal pluralism takes place whenever an individual is subjected to more than one body of law.[103] The phenomenon of legal pluralism has its roots in colonial times. Societies emerging from colonialism found themselves between two rails, preservation of their customary laws and adaptation to a new social environment designed by state laws. The problems begin when they start to disregard each other's legitimacy by denying a legal character to norms of the other law.[104] But post- colonial societies are not the only ones facing such problems, as today legal pluralism has become a part of stateless societies, societies emerged from conflict and even democratic societies which, in the name of democracy, seek to better accommodate social diversity. All of them share a common concern as to how to reconcile different bodies of norms within state law. A test suggested by Morse and Woodman can serve as a useful tool for addressing this social phenomenon. When a society is faced with legal pluralism it has several options, a) to employ negative measures and prohibit the observance of non-official laws in an imperative manner, b) to deny the validity of the acts arising from such laws, or c) to introduce a set of positive measures, such as recognising the consistent application of non-official norms to situations of fact. The latter option means that no adjustment of the state law in response to non-official laws, or incorporation of a non-official norm into the body of state law, is needed. A state may give to such norms the same legal effect as a state law by acknowledging in an expressive manner the incapacity of particular state institutions to perform certain functions and in this regard open the door to a non-official law to fill the gap.[105] However, in such a situation one should always bear in mind that whatever option is chosen, it should be constructed in a way that offers substantive and equal protection to all.

Given this perspective, there is a need to relate these ideas to legal experience in post-war Kosovo. As already noted, two parallel systems continue to claim absolute and exclusive jurisdiction over the territory. A number of public structures, including previous municipal courts in Kosovo, are still working under the auspices of the Serbian authorities, applying Serbian laws and are located in the northern part of Mitrovica town, Leposavic, Zvecan, and Zubin Potok, which are populated by the Serbian minority population.

At the same time, there is a parallel structure of district courts acting in Serbia proper, so-called courts-in-exile. Nowadays, they mainly deal with property issues. However, until 2003 they also used to exercise jurisdiction over criminal

102 Gordon R. Woodman, Legal Pluralism and the Search for Justice, *Journal of African Law*, Vol. 40, No. 152, 1996, p. 157.

103 Ibid.

104 Ibid.

105 Bradford W. Morse and Gordon R. Woodman, *Indigenous Law and the State*, Dordrecht: Foris, 1988.

and minor offences, which in some cases caused an overlap of jurisdiction and led to double jeopardy.[106] The double jeopardy principle, or *non bis in idem*, protects defendants from re-prosecution in the same jurisdiction for offences arising out of one event.[107] This situation would have caused general public confusion among the population living in the northern part, as nobody knew which court to turn to. It continues to lead to great confusion as it directly affects the rights of individuals and the rule of law.[108]

In 2000, one Kosovar Serb was arrested by the UNMIK authorities for a murder but due to security reasons which have not been specified, he was released after two days.[109] Several days later, he was arrested by the Serbian police in Kraljevo in Serbia, where he spent 16 months in pre-trial detention until he was released by the District Court in Kraljevo acting in its role as the District Court of Mitrovica. After his return to Kosovo, the UNMIK prosecutor from the Mitrovica prosecutorial office indicted him on the basis of the same, or substantially the same, facts and one week later he was arrested by UNMIK police and placed in custody. In February 2003, owing to a lack of sufficient evidence, the international public prosecutor withdrew the case and released him from pre-trial

106 Following an order issued in 2003 by KFOR, the parallel courts inside Kosovo stopped handling criminal cases. Nevertheless, the courts in exile operating within Serbia proper continued to deal with criminal cases, in particular those involving war crimes and inter-ethnic crimes, asserting jurisdiction over the accused individuals against whom indictments had been issued. As soon as they were found in Serbia, they were arrested and brought to trial. Several Kosovar politicians who used to serve as members of the Kosovo Liberation Army were indicted by the Serbian authorities, among them the previous and current Prime Ministers. Moreover, some trials have been held in absentia. For additional information, see Elena Baylis, Parallel Courts in Post Conflict Kosovo, *The Yale Journal of International Law*, No. 2, 2007.

107 Both the Criminal Code of Serbia and the Provisional Code of Kosovo prohibit re-prosecution. Furthermore, double jeopardy is prohibited under the ECHR (Article 4 of Protocol 7), which in its pertinent parts states: "No one shall be liable to be tried or punished again in criminal proceedings under the jurisdiction of the same state for an offence for which he has already been finally acquitted or convicted in accordance with the law and penal procedure of the state", as well as under the ICCPR (Article 14 (17)): "No one shall be liable to be tried or punished again for an offence for which he has already been finally convicted or acquitted in accordance with the law and penal procedure of each country".

108 See Ombudsperson Institution in Kosovo, Annual Report 2006, available at: www.ombudspersonkosovo.org.

109 The Radonja Ilic case is the best example for explaining the confusion. For an in-depth overview of this case, see Marcus Brand, Kosovo under International Administration, Statehood Constitutionalism and Human Rights, unpublished PhD dissertation, available at Vienna Public Library. See also Parallel Structures in Kosovo, OSCE, Department of Human Rights and Rule of Law, Report, 2003 and 2006–2007. It was not possible to obtain information regarding the outcome of this case. Kapllan Baruti, President of the District Court in Mitrovica, explained that the court had suspended its activities after the violent protest organised on 28 February 2008 by Serb mobs, who by force attempted to enter the court building, resulting in the death of a 25-year-old UNMIK police member from Ukraine. Since then, Albanian judicial organs have been prevented from entering the court building and as a consequence many cases have been put on hold.

detention. Soon after his release, the daughter of the victim, acting as an injured party, took up a private prosecution of the accused by filing an indictment against him for the criminal act of grievous bodily harm.[110]

Another similar case that involved the issue of double jeopardy was a murder case from 1999 involving another Kosovar Serb. Following an indictment issued by the Prosecutorial Office in Gjilan (Kosovo), the suspect had fled to Serbia proper, where an indictment for the same crime was issued against him by the parallel District Court of Vranje (Serbia), acting in its role as the District Court of Gjilan. The trial took place in Vranje on 20 August 2004 and he was sentenced to one year's imprisonment. As the sentence for murder appeared to be low, the Prosecutorial Office in Gjilan (Kosovo) issued an indictment on the basis of the same facts against the suspected/sentenced person, asking that the defendant be arrested upon his return to Kosovo.[111] There are several other cases that involved the same issue: in cases of alleged serious crimes suspected persons have often fled to Serbia proper, most likely hoping for a more lenient sentence if prosecuted in Serbia proper.[112]

As already mentioned, in addition to criminal justice the parallel courts in Serbia have also dealt with disputes arising from property rights. Looking at the number of cases brought before the parallel courts, it is alarming to notice the harmful influence this has had on the realisation of property rights, in many cases resulting in a loss of property for private individuals.[113] The Serbian government is strongly opposed to returning court files, cadastral records of title to land, official court seals and stamps and other relevant documents taken by the departing court structures.[114] As such, they continue to claim the same competences and jurisdiction over property disputes and subsequently to approve different certificates regarding property titles, which in some cases appear to be false.

Though their judgments are not considered valid by UNMIK and Kosovar institutions, they continue to cause many problems to the existing courts, particularly when it comes to the transaction of property, as very often parties come with the same documents alleging that they have ownership rights over particular property and the courts are not in a position to verify the authenticity of the documents.[115] Initially, the local courts took a stand against recognising documents

110 Until 2003 this case was still pending. Since Mitrovica courts are not functioning, it was not possible to obtain further information on the outcome of this case. Fax exchange communication, 25 February 2010.

111 See OSCE, *Parallel Structures, supra* n. 100.

112 Ibid.

113 Ibid.

114 Since April 2011, the Kosovo and Serbian governments have been engaged in negotiations sponsored by the EU representatives. The central issue that was dropped on the negotiation table of the parties was the return of the registry books (birth, marriage and death registry books) as well as the cadastral books of Kosovan citizens seized by the FRY machinery during the war. See Gjylbehare Bella Murati, Can Identity Cleansing Be Negotiated, *Prishtina Insight, Balkan Investigative Reporting Network (BIRN)*, No. 63, 6 May 2011, p. 20.

115 See Ombudsperson Institution in Kosovo, Annual Report 2006, available at: www.ombudspersonkosovo.org.

issued after 1999, on the assumption of falsification, but nowadays people are frequently provided with documents bearing stamps before the contested date.[116]

As a result of falsified documents and falsified contracts obtained from the parallel courts, the local courts issued several conflicting judgments. This came as a consequence of the fact that some judges working for the parallel courts accepted bribes to affirm contracts for the sale of real property with incorrect dates (prior to 1999) by using the old Yugoslav stamp.[117] As courts in Kosovo lack a proper mechanism for verifying the authenticity of documents submitted as evidence of property transfer, it frequently happens that the same property is sold several times to different individuals.[118]

Taking into consideration the consequences arising from such practices, it is difficult to understand the reluctance of both UNMIK and Kosovar institutions to coming up with a decision on the legal validity of decisions issued by parallel courts, especially between 1999 and 2002, when they were most active.[119] Though the "Standards before Status" policy[120] required that "parallel structures should be dismantled", the UNMIK authorities tried to avoid facing up to this problem.[121] The parallel structures have been active for fifteen years and as such have issued a large number of legal decisions and continue to do so.[122] One may ask what will happen if one day these structures are dismantled. What could be done with the legacy they leave behind? Can and should those judgments be recognised?

Notwithstanding concerns regarding these practices, the international actors call for mutual recognition of criminal judgments, stressing the importance of avoiding prosecuting individuals twice for the same set of facts. Nevertheless, it is considered that "in exceptional circumstances, such as new evidence or procedural irregularities, re-prosecution should be allowed".[123]

116 See Ombudsperson Institution in Kosovo, Annual Report 2007–2008, available at: www.ombudspersonkosovo.org.

117 Ibid.

118 The Ombudsperson Institution received numerous complaints alleging violations of the right to property and continued to insist and urge that the relevant authorities, in this case the courts and the Housing and Property Directorate, pay attention to the authenticity of the documents. For additional information, see Ombudsperson Institution in Kosovo, Annual Report 2007–2008, available at: www.ombudspersonkosovo.org.

119 See OSCE, *Parallel Structures, supra* n. 100.

120 In 2002, UNMIK adopted a policy called "standards before status", which can be classified as a set of conditions that needed to be fulfilled before starting negotiations on final status. The international creators of this policy came up with eight conditions that needed to be fulfilled by the Kosovo government before it would be able to move on to the status issue. One of these conditions involved the dismantling of all the parallel structures operating within Kosovo.

121 They were even operating under the same roof with the local courts, for example in the municipalities of Zubin Potok and Shterpce.

122 Just from 1999 until 2003, they heard around 8,780 cases including both civil and criminal matters.

123 See OSCE, *Parallel Structures, supra* n. 100.

Moreover, some go as far as recommending the creation of mechanisms to prevent duplicative litigation and ensure legal certainty for individuals who have already obtained decisions from parallel courts. In doing so, the establishment of a presumption of legality is proposed that will enable the affected individuals to appeal civil decisions and acts of the parallel courts. It is further considered necessary that UNMIK or its successor should establish a judicial review panel to determine the legality of decisions and acts not covered by the presumption. In cases where there are conflicting decisions by UNMIK and parallel courts, the creation of a mechanism is suggested that could resolve the issues arising from such situations.[124] In addition, other proposals were put forward which emphasised that parallel judgments should be recognised so as to promote legal certainty and fairness by allowing unconditional recognition of most parallel civil judgments.[125] However, given that the existing conflicts over jurisdiction are ultimately grounded in conflicting political claims regarding sovereignty over the territory, one should look towards introducing a model which would resolve the issue of recognition of judgments on purely legal, apolitical terms.[126]

To this end, it is considered that the best option would be to establish proper mechanisms that would maximise recognition of the judgments.[127] Such mechanisms would help to eliminate the risks of conflicting judgments and of unenforced decisions.[128]

In this context, the practice established by some states for recognising foreign judgments, arbitration awards and out-of-court settlements could serve as useful technical solutions for the recognition of parallel judgments, as they provide a possible way of overcoming the alleged tension over general jurisdiction.[129]

Though such a model might be practical, it should be taken into consideration that a central obstacle to such steps would be the political situation, in particular agreement by the Serbian government to cooperate in this matter. Even if in the near future consent is obtained from the Serbian government, it would be difficult to recover from the harmful effects they have caused. As already stressed, judgments and documents issued by the parallel courts appear to be of a conflicting nature, as they are based on false documents and evidence. In addition, it should be taken into consideration that some of the records were destroyed during the war and replaced by fakes, which were issued to the parties. Consequently, under these circumstances it will be difficult to determine the lawfulness of such judgments, in particular if we take into consideration the number of

124 Ibid.

125 See Baylis, *supra* n. 106, p. 5.

126 Ibid.

127 Ibid., p. 8.

128 Ibid.

129 Though in her proposal she also mentions the practice of enforcing foreign judgments, on the other hand she notes that such a solution might not be workable in Kosovo since the recognition of foreign judgments involves a state authority and therefore considers that either arbitration awards or out-of-court settlements could facilitate the process of recognition of Serbian parallel court judgments. Ibid., p. 27.

enforced judgments, which created a new reality on the ground. In 2004, the Housing and Property Directorate (HPD) established a liaison office in Belgrade with the purpose of assisting claimants in Serbia and Montenegro in their interactions with the HPD Head Office in Kosovo. Although the opening of this office was seen as a positive step for establishing cooperation with the Serbian judicial organs, it did not bring about any change as they were not allowed to have access to independent evidence, except that provided by the parties, which could have been obtained in different ways. The foregoing discussion has confirmed that denial of the validity of non-official laws is not the best alternative, as it may cause irreparable damage. On the other hand, it is difficult to imagine any other option. Despite all the consequences, there is no ground for keeping unjust laws that treat people differently and which pose an obstacle to the achievement of justice.

Conclusion

The foregoing discussion reveals the complex nature of the issues involved.

It has shed light on the major problems, challenges, and dilemmas that the international structures and their subordinates have encountered in their joint enterprise.

In addition, it has shown that the involvement of multiple authorities may be problematic, resulting in an overlap of competencies and neglect of the rule of law.

Yet, the reluctance of UNMIK to establish a baseline of institutional responsibilities can be viewed as a willingness to tolerate serious human rights violations. The parallel systems, and in particular the parallel courts, have precluded an environment in which all ethnicities could live with equal access to justice under the same law.[130] The broad executive authority of the SRSG, which proved to have been of a superior nature, was not exercised in an equal manner. The SRSG, who created a "cult of the almighty" in Kosovo, failed in this instance to accomplish his task to exercise his authority reflexively and secure institutional respect of human rights.

UNMIK's inability to institute a functional legal system in the entire territory has resulted in social disorder.

130 OSCE, *Parallel Structure*, *supra* n. 100, pp. 15–16.

5 Between immunity and accountability

The immunity and privileges of UNMIK

Introduction

Accountability encompasses a variety of norms, practices, and institutions whose main aim is to hold public officials answerable for their actions and omissions.[1] There are two types of accountability for transitional administrations: horizontal accountability, which entails the subjection of the administration to internal audits, and vertical accountability, which calls for subjection to the scrutiny of the secretariat or member states of international organisations.[2] In this regard, an international administration becomes subject to the political and administrative control of the body that established it, the UN Security Council. In addition, it may be subjected to the control and the oversight of the member states through the General Assembly, both as a plenary organ of the organisation and through various commissions or committees.[3]

Yet it remains exempted from judicial accountability.

The foregoing chapters have focused on discussing the implementation of UNMIK's mandate in practice in terms of its constituent document, the UNSC Resolution 1244. They have highlighted that UNSC Resolution 1244, as its constituent document, affirms the responsibility of UNMIK to uphold human rights standards on the ground.[4]

However, this responsibility stops when it comes to establishing a proper accountability regime that addresses the human rights violations committed by international actors. Because of the strictness of the immunity regime that shields international actors from court jurisdiction, both UNMIK personnel and KFOR members remained exempted from the jurisdiction of the local courts. Consequently, it prevented individuals from having access to remedies against wrongdoings by UNMIK's authorities.

1 Richard Caplan, *International Governance of War-Torn Territories, Rule and Reconstruction*, Oxford University Press, 2005, p. 197. See also Richard Caplan, *Who Guards the Guardians? International Accountability in Bosnia and Hercegovina*, available at the following website: www.dur.ac.uk/resources/law/LCD/Caplan-Durhamwebsite.pdf.

2 Caplan, *International Governance*, id. See also Caplan, *Who Guards the Guardians?*

3 Guglielmo Verdirame, *The UN and Human Rights, Who Guards the Guardians?* Cambridge University Press, 2011, pp. 336–337.

4 UNSCE Resolution 1244 para. 11 (j). "Protecting and promoting human rights".

The following chapter discusses the specificity of the accountability regime introduced in Kosovo. It provides a brief background on the immunity system of the international organisations. It seeks an answer as to whether the immunity regime of international actors allows an interim administration to be controlled and if so, to what extent and what type of control mechanism would be suitable.

In addition, it provides an overview of the accountability regimes of the mandate and trusteeship systems.

The final part discusses the existing accountability mechanisms established by UNMIK and their ability to provide an effective means of redress for alleged violations of human rights attributable to UNMIK.

Background information

Immediately upon its establishment UNMIK enacted Regulation 2000/47, which provides a far-reaching immunity regime for both KFOR members and UNMIK personnel, including locally recruited personnel.[5]

Accordingly, they all became immune from legal process for actions taken in an official capacity.[6]

Yet, while the UNMIK personnel became "untouchable", KFOR members could be subject to the exclusive jurisdiction of their respective sending states.[7]

It should be emphasised that the military personnel are not covered by the international legal framework that governs the immunity of international actors, namely Article 105 of the UN Charter and the Convention on Privileges and Immunities of the United Nations. Their immunity is granted by the Status of Force Agreements (SOFA) and Mission Agreements (MA) concluded between representatives of the military troops and a host state.[8]

Neither SOFA nor MA were concluded with FRY.[9]

5 "UNMIK personnel, including locally recruited personnel, shall be immune from legal process in respect of . . . all acts performed by them in their official capacity". Similar wording appears in respect of KFOR's immunity, stating that "KFOR personnel shall be immune from jurisdiction before courts in Kosovo in respect of any administrative, civil or criminal act committed by them in the territory of Kosovo". See UNMIK Regulation 2000/47, 1999. Section 3) 2.3.

6 Regulation 2000/47, 1999 "On Privileges and Immunities of international presences in Kosovo".

7 See UNMIK Regulation 2000/47, 1999. Section 2) 2.4.

8 See Frederick Rawski, Wave or Not to Wave, *Connecticut Journal of International Law*, Vol. 18, 2002, p. 108.

9 The UN faced a similar problem in East Timor. Prior to UNTAET deployment, there was an agreement between Indonesia and Australia (the Status of Forces Agreement), which provided certain privileges to Australian military and civilian staff who were working for the INTERFET mission. New Zealand, which had troops in East Timor, was not bound by this agreement and claimed that its personnel enjoyed immunity based on customary international law. After the arrival of UNTAET, no such agreement was signed with Indonesia, since when the UN continued to challenge Indonesian title over East Timor. Therefore, it is considered that UNTAET immunity relies on customary international law. See Eric De Brabandere, *Post-Conflict Administrations in International Law*, Martinus Nijhof Publishers, 2009, p. 107. See also UNTAET Regulation No. 2000/17 of 8 June 2000 and UNTAET Regulation No. 2000/19 of 30 June 2000.

The KFOR authorities refused the request of the FRY government to sign the SOFA, whose main aim was the reaffirmation of the FRY's sovereignty over Kosovo, and consequently decided instead to conclude the SOFA with UNMIK as the provisional authority.[10] In this regard, they were granted immunity from the jurisdiction of the courts in Kosovo.

Thus, both KFOR and the UN became immune from every form of legal process of the host country.

The immunity of the international organisations

The judicial accountability of international organisations is closely linked with the privileges and immunities that have been granted to international actors in order to allow them to carry out their functions effectively and independently.[11]

The immunity of the UN is primarily governed by the UN Charter and the Convention on Privileges and Immunities of the United Nations. According to Article 105, paragraph 1 of the UN Charter:

> The Organization shall enjoy in the territory of each of its Members such privileges and immunities as are necessary for the fulfillment of its purposes.[12]

The Immunities Convention further provides in its Article II, Section 2 that:

> The United Nations . . . shall enjoy immunity from every form of legal process except insofar as in any particular case it has expressly waived its immunity.[13]

This is so-called organisational immunity and it is considered to be grounded on the well established rules of diplomatic immunity enshrined in the Vienna Convention, which provides that "a diplomatic agent shall enjoy immunity from the criminal jurisdiction of the receiving state".[14]

10 According to the Kumanovo Agreement, "[t]he parties will agree a Status of Forces Agreement (SOFA) as soon as possible"; however, it was never respected. Kumanovo Agreement, Section (B) para 3. See also Saint Group, *UNMIK Police*, CIVPOL Language and Culture, available at the following website: www.saint-claire.org/resources/UNMIK%20Police.pdf (lastly accessed on 13 November 2013).

11 De Brabandere, *supra* n. 9, p. 107. See also Sam Muller, International Organizations and their Host States: Aspects of Their Legal, *Kluwer Law International*, 1995, p. 149; Emmanuel Gaillard and Isabelle Pingell-Lenuzza, International Organisations and Immunity from Jurisdiction: To Restrict or to Bypass, *International and Comparative Law Quarterly*, Vol. 51, 2002; Andrey Ladley, Peacekeeper Abuse, Immunity and Impunity: The Need for Effective Criminal and Civil Accountability on International Peace Operations, *Politics and Ethics Review*, Vol. 1, 2005.

12 Article 105 of the UN Charter.

13 Article II, Section 2 of the Convention on the Immunity and Privileges of the United Nations, 21 November 1947. See also Rawski, *supra* n. 8, p. 106.

14 Vienna Convention on Diplomatic Relations, 1961, Article 31.

Though the Convention refers to the functional immunity that is designed to ensure the independent functioning of international actors from nation states, which implies "immunity from suit", in practice it has been understood as an absolute immunity.[15] Although there are no customary international law rules that define the boundaries of privileges and immunities of international organisations,[16] the domestic courts have consistently regarded the absolute immunity of international organisations as a requirement under customary international law.[17] Despite the numerous cases that have dealt with the immunity of international organisations, no general or consistent practice or *opinio juris* has been established in this regard.[18]

Both domestic and international courts have on many occasions found that they do not have jurisdiction to hear cases against the United Nations owing to the far-reaching immunity granted to it by the UN Charter and by the Convention on the Privileges and Immunities of the United Nations.[19]

The ICJ played a central role in cementing the general rule of absolute immunity for international organisations. In its advisory opinion on the case of *Reparation for Injuries Suffered in the Service of the United Nations*, it maintained that the immunity provides that "the agent may perform his duties satisfactorily; he must feel that this protection is assured to him by the Organization, and that he may count on it. To ensure the independence of the agent, and, consequently, the independent action of the Organization itself, it is essential that in performing his duties he need not have to rely on any other protection than that of the Organization".[20] The same position was reinforced later on in the *Cumaraswamy* case, in which the ICJ made it clear that the interpretation of Article VIII, Section 29 of the General Convention should be understood to mean that "any claims against the United Nations shall not be dealt with by national courts".[21]

15 August Reinisch and Ulf Andreas Weber, In the Shadow of Waite and Kennedy, *International Organizations Law Review*, Vol. 1, 2004, pp. 61–62. Frederick Rawski considers that while Article 105 of the UN Charter limits immunities to a functional necessity standard, the Immunities Conventions expand the organization's immunity. See Rawski, *supra* n. 8, p. 111. For more about functional necessity, see Michael Singer, Jurisdictional Immunity of International Organisations: *Human Rights and Functional Necessity*, *Virginia Journal of International Law*, Vol. 46, No. 53, 1995–1996.

16 Aaron I. Young, Deconstructing International Organization Immunity, *Georgetown Journal of International Law*, Vol. 44, 2012, p. 354.

17 The proceedings initiated before domestic courts mainly comprise cases that involve employment-related disputes. See Reinisch and Weber, *supra* n. 15, pp. 61–62.

18 Young, *supra* n. 16, p. 356.

19 The Srebrenica case is a leading example. For detailed legal analysis of the Srebrenica case before international and domestic courts, see Oto Spijkers, The Netherlands' and the United Nations' Legal Responsibility for Srebrenica before the Dutch Courts, *Military Law and the Law of War Review*, Vol. 50, No. 3–04, 2011; Aleksandar Momirov, Dutch Courts and Srebrenica Ascribing Responsibility and Defining Legal Relevant Relationships, *Netherlands Yearbook of International Law*, Vol. 43, 24 June 2013.

20 See ICJ judgment, Reparation for Injuries Suffered in the Service of the United Nations, Advisory Opinion, I. C. J. Reports, 1949, p. 183.

21 See ICJ Advisory Opinion, *Difference Relating to Immunity from Legal Process of a Special Rapporteur of the Commission on Human Rights*, 29 April 1999, p. 89.

The pattern established by the ICJ has been followed by the ECtHR as well. In the case of *R. Waite and T. Kennedy v. Germany*, the ECtHR recognised that the "attribution of privileges and immunities to international organizations is an essential means of ensuring the proper functioning of such organizations free from unilateral interference by individual governments".[22] Similarly, in its *Behrami and Saramati* decision the ECtHR stated that denying the UN its immunity "would be to interfere with the fulfilment of the UN's key mission in this field . . . and with the effective conduct of its operations".[23]

Recently, the UN's immunity was challenged again when the ECtHR was given a very difficult task, to determine whether the United Nations and the government of the Netherlands were responsible for the failure of UNPROFOR to protect the civilian population in the "safe area" of Srebrenica in July 1995, which resulted in acts of genocide that killed 7,000–8,000 individuals. The inaction of UNPROFOR was regarded by the applicant as a failure of the UN to prevent genocide.

In its inadmissibility decision regarding the application by *Stichting Mothers of Srebrenica and others*,[24] the Court once again took the view that the organisational immunity of the UN was "a long-standing practice established in the interest of the good working of these organizations" and that as such it had a legitimate objective.[25] In order to justify the supremacy of the immunity rules, which arguably override the gravity of a claim such as genocide, the Court emphasised that

> international law does not support the position that a civil claim should override immunity from suit for the sole reason that it is based on an allegation of a particularly grave violation of a norm of international law, even a norm of *ius cogens*.

In this regard, it appears that the immunity of the international organisations proves to be above the *ius cogens* norms and consequently gives a legitimate purpose for restriction of the right to access justice effectively.[26] What becomes clear

22 The case involved two employees of the European Space Agency (ESA), who were dismissed from their jobs and lost their labour law dispute before the German courts due to the immunity of ESA. The employees lodged their complaint with ECtHR invoking Article 6 of the ECHR. See ECtHR, *Waite and Kennedy v. Germany*, Application No. 26083/94, Judgment, 18 February 1999, para 63.

23 *Behrami v. France and Saramati v. France* (dec.), nos. 71412/01 and 78166/01, ECtHR. 2007 (joint admissibility decision), para 149.

24 *Stichting Mothers of Srebrenica and Others v. The Netherlands*, App. No. 65542/12, ECtHR, 11 June 2013.

25 It did not depart from the statement reaffirmed in the case of *Waite and Kennedy*, *supra* n. 22, para 63.

26 Yet there are authors who are sceptical as to whether an obligation to prevent genocide falls within the category of *ius cogens* norms. See Manuel Ventura and Dapo Akande, *Mothers of Srebrenica: The Obligation to Prevent Genocide and Jus Cogens-Implication for Humanitarian Intervention*, Comments on EJIL talk, 6 September 2013, available at the following website: www.ejiltalk.org/ignoring-the-elephant-in-the-room-in-mothers-of-srebrenica-is-

here is that there is competition between two interests, namely the organisation's interest in preserving its immunity and individuals' interest in obtaining an effective remedy. It should be noted that the ECtHR uses a balancing approach most often to decide cases where conventionally protected individual rights conflict with governmental interests. In the present case, the Court did not make an attempt to determine thoroughly which interest weighed more, but instead went directly to the generally framed provisions of the legal framework governing the immunity of international organisations.

Taking into consideration that the "human rights rationale of providing access to court is equally cogent in the context of the immunity of international organizations",[27] one may find it difficult to understand such reasoning. This is an explicit recognition that the immunity of the peacekeeping mission is absolute, which increased the possibility of expanding the doctrine of restrictive immunity.

After the UN instantly enlarged its activities on a grand scale by even disguising itself in a state-like administration, a considerable debate arose as to whether such extraordinary circumstances might lead to some reasonable restrictions on the scope of the current immunity rules that cover international organisations, focusing on the possibility of their submission to the rule of law.

Spijkers considers that a limitation of the immunity regime is only possible if the organisation commits acts outside its functional scope, which means acts that are considered to be of a non-functional nature.[28] However, it remains unclear what the phrase "non-functional acts" implies.

Rawski considers that the drafters of the Immunities Convention aimed at providing a broad protection to UN officials and that their aim was further nourished by the ICJ, which interpreted the Convention's provision in a way that provided maximum protection to international organisations. He recalls the Court's interpretation of Article 105 of the UN Charter and Section 22 of the Convention in the *Mazilu* case,[29] in which the Court recognised that the provisions covered "all tasks entrusted to the person" regardless of whether they were performed on an official mission.[30] So it comes about that the law in question grants immunity to the conduct of a person who acts in an official capacity inside or outside the given

the-obligation-to-prevent-genocide-jus-cogens/. See also Dapo Akande and Sangeeta Shah, Immunities of State Officials, International Crimes: And Foreign Domestic Courts, *The European Journal of International Law*, Vol. 21, No. 4, 2011.

27 Reinisch and Weber, *supra* n. 15, p. 64.

28 Otto Spijkers, Immunity of the United Nations in Relation to the Genocide in the Eyes of the Dutch District Court, *Journal of International Peace Keeping*, Vol. 13, 2009, p. 203.

29 See ICJ Advisory Opinion on the Applicability of Article VI, Section 22, of the Convention on the Privileges and Immunities of the United Nations known as *Mazilu case*, issued on 15 December 1986.

30 According to the Court, "Section 22, in its reference to experts performing missions for the United Nations, uses the word 'mission' in a general sense". In this regard, "[t]he Court accordingly concludes that Section 22 is applicable to every expert on mission, whether or not he travels". See Mazilu case, *supra* n. 29, paras 51–52. See also Rawski, *supra* n. 8, p. 112.

institution. In this context, the immunity is given not to him/her as a person but to his/her acts.[31]

In light of this, Rawski asks whether a series of human rights violations may be considered to imply an official action performed as part of the UN's duty.[32]

As stated earlier, traditionally immunity and privileges are granted to the international organisation in order to secure it from the possible interference of the government of the state where the organisation is operating. Taking into consideration that UNMIK is exercising its government-like powers without any competitor within the entity, it raises the question from whose interference does it need to secure itself? Does government need to enact laws to protect itself against itself?[33] Or, should an internationally governed population be allowed to be run by an "untouchable, uncontrolled and unaccountable" regime?

Is a waiver of immunity an option?

At the present, there is a narrow road in the system that might be used to address certain wrongdoings of a UN official before the domestic courts. It can be reached through the immunity waiver procedure. The Immunities Convention Sections 20 provides that "[t]he Secretary-General shall have the right and the duty to waive the immunity of any official in any case where, in his opinion, the immunity would impede the course of justice and can be waived without prejudice to the interests of the United Nations".[34] Accordingly, the Secretary General is under a duty to waive immunity based on his personal assessment and failure to do so would be considered an impediment to justice.[35] Lifting immunity is

31 This comes in line with so-called modern immunity doctrine. See Carsten Stahn, *The Law and Practice of International Territorial Administration, Versailles to Iraq and Beyond*, Cambridge University Press, 2008 at p. 588.

32 He refers to the case of an UNMIK official who was accused of having been involved in genocide in Rwanda by separating Hutus from Tutsis while being on an official mission to organise the evacuation of the UN compound in Rwanda. Prior to UNMIK, he served in Angola and also in Rwanda. He was taken by the UN only after an extradition request initiated by the Rwandan government, seven years after the alleged acts were committed. See Rawski, *supra* n. 8.

33 "The rationale for classical grants of immunity, however, does not apply to the circumstances prevailing in Kosovo, where the interim civilian administration [the United Nations Mission in Kosovo – UNMIK] in fact acts as a surrogate state. It follows that the underlying purpose of a grant of immunity does not apply as there is no need for a government to be protected against itself". See Kosovo Ombudsperson Institution, *Special Report No. 1 On the Compatibility with Recognized International Standards of UNMIK Regulation No 2000/47 On the Status and Privileges and Immunities of KFOR and UNMIK and their Personnel in Kosovo and on the Implementation of the above Regulation*, para 23, 2001.

34 Article V, Section 20 of the Convention on the Immunity and Privileges of the United Nations, 21 November 1947.

35 As noted by the ICJ in the *Cumaraswamy* case, "the Secretary-General, as the chief administrative officer of the Organization, has the primary responsibility to safeguard the interests of the Organization; to that end, it is up to him to assess whether its agents acted within the scope of their functions and, where he so concludes, to protect these agents, including experts on mission, by asserting their immunity". See ICJ Advisory Opinion, *Difference*

usually based on the result of inquiries conducted by a UN-convened Board of Inquiry (BOI) comprising international staff appointed by the SRSG, the head of the mission. After completing its inquiry, the BOI sends its recommendations to the SRSG, who passes it on to the Secretary General. Recently, a new practice has been adopted through which the case is sent directly to the Department of Peacekeeping Operations, which follows up with the member state.[36]

In 2006, the Special Committee on Peacekeeping Operations issued recommendations which highlight the primary responsibility carried by national government to investigate acts of misconduct or serious misconduct committed by a member of its national contingent.[37] In this case, the United Nations retains an obligation to inform the government about the alleged misconduct and if the government does not show willingness to start an investigation or in case of any delay, the United Nations may, in cases of serious misconduct, initiate a preliminary fact-finding inquiry into the matter, until the government starts its own investigation. However, if the government decides to start its own investigation, it is obliged to inform the United Nations of that decision, including the identities of the officials concerned, and the United Nations is required to co-operate and facilitate the investigation.[38]

Though this seems to be a reasonable solution, no such practice was applied in Kosovo. An inquiry conducted for this purpose reveals that UNMIK seldom investigated alleged violations that involved its officials and KFOR members. It is noticeable that investigations have mainly been launched against violations by officials from less "powerful" or "influential" countries. In this regard, immunity has been waived in a few cases. For instance, an investigation was initiated into the case of an UNMIK police officer from Egypt who was accused of murder.[39] Surprisingly, he was stripped of his immunity shortly after the reported murder.[40]

An immunity waiver document issued in 2002 by Hans Corell, the Legal Counsel of the General Secretary Legal Affairs Office, reveals that immunity waivers could be obtained within a day and were issued upon the request of the UNMIK Legal Officer and the Police Commissioner.[41] Consequently, they

---

Relating to Immunity from Legal Process of a Special Rapporteur of the Commission on Human Rights, 29 April 1999, para 60. See also Rawski, *supra* n. 8, p. 114.

36 See Rawski, *supra* n. 8, pp. 114–115, 2002.

37 Report of the UN Special Committee Peacekeeping Operations and its Working group, Second resumed session 18 December 2006, General Assembly, Official Records, Sixty-Fifth Session, Supplement No. 19.

38 The fact-finding inquiry should include in its team a representative of a government. See, Report of the UN Special Committee Peacekeeping Operations and its Working group, resumed session 11 June 2007, General Assembly, Official Records, Sixty-Fifth Session, Supplement No. 19.

39 UNMIK police officer Sherif Abd Elaziz, who killed his interpreter.

40 See *UNMIK's Police-KFOR- OSCE-Press Briefing*, 9 January 2002, available at the following website: http://reliefweb.int/report/serbia/unmik-unmik-police-kfor-osce-press-briefing-9-jan-2002.

41 He was tried by an international panel. See Reuters News, *UN Police Officer Jailed for Kosovo Love Tryst Murder*, available at the following website: www.balkanpeace.org/index.php?index=article&articleid=12359 (lastly accessed on 5 November 2013).

enabled the domestic justice system to proceed with a criminal inquiry in a timely manner.[42] There was no particular involvement on the part of the SRSG or any inquiry board in the case at hand, which merely required the consent of the Police Commissioner and UNMIK's Legal Officer.[43] A similar procedure was applied in the case of an UNMIK police officer from Pakistan who was involved in prostitution.[44]

However, numerous cases that involved serious violations remained unpunished. For instance, cases involving trafficking in women that linked both UNMIK personnel and KFOR remained uninvestigated. Those involved in such cases were mainly repatriated home and the files closed.[45] Other cases implicated an Austrian police officer in torture, Rumanian police officers as responsible for the killing of two persons and injuring 80 more during the demonstrations of 10 February 2007 and Greek KFOR personnel whose tank run over a 17-year-old boy during the March 2004 riot, those involved in the death of a UNHCR employee, and many others.[46]

In the case of the Austrian police officer, immunity was lifted, but the accused managed to escape with the help of Austrian diplomatic representatives, who took him out of the country. It should be stressed, however, that the Austrian government had strongly opposed his arrest, which, it considered, put into question Austria's overall participation in the UN mission.[47]

42 "By waiving the legal immunity normally granted UN staff members in the field, Mr Annan opens the way for the Kosovo justice system to proceed in the criminal inquiry into the case". Charles Brayshow, Acting SRSG. For more, see *UNMIK's Police-KFOR-OSCE-Press Briefing*, 9 January 2002, available at the following website: http://reliefweb.int/report/serbia/unmik-unmik-police-kfor-osce-press-briefing-9-jan-2002.

43 The immunity waver issued on 8 January 2002. Document on file with the author.

44 See Report issued by Amnesty International, *Kosovo (Serbia and Montenegro) 'So does It Mean We Have the Rights?' Protecting the Rights of Women and Girls Trafficked for Forced Prostitution in Kosovo*, 6 May 2004, AI Index: EUR 70/010/2004, available at the following website: http://web.amnesty.org/library/print/ENGEUR700102004, pp. 41–42 (lastly accessed 1 February 2014).

45 About the cases regarding the involvement of UNMIK personnel and KFOR members in trafficking in women, see OSCE Report, Review of Criminal Justice System, *Themes: Legal Representation: Detention Trafficking and Sexually Related Crimes Municipal and Minor Offence Courts*, October 2001; Report issued by Amnesty International, *Kosovo (Serbia and Montenegro) 'So does It Mean We Have the Rights?' Protecting the Rights of Women and Girls Trafficked for Forced Prostitution in Kosovo*, 6 May 2004, AI Index: EUR 70/010/2004, available at the following website: http://web.amnesty.org/library/print/ENGEUR700102004, pp. 41–42 (lastly accessed 1 February 2014).

46 See International Crisis Group, *Collapse in Kosovo*, Report No. 155, 22 April 2004, available at the following website: www.crisisgroup.org/en/regions/europe/balkans/kosovo/155-collapse-in-kosovo.aspx (lastly accessed on 5 November 2013). The mother of the 17-year-old boy who was run over by the KFOR tank lodged an application against Greece before the ECtHR (App.32812/04), which was declared inadmissible.

47 See Serbia and Montenegro (Kosovo) The legacy of past human rights abuses AI INDEX: EUR70/009/2004 1 April 2004 at p. 12; IHF focus, www.refworld.org/pdfid/469243bd0.pdf, (lastly accessed 2 November 2013); Reuters News, *UN Police Officer Jailed for Kosovo*

Another case that received much attention is the death of a UNHCR employee, Benet Rexhepi, a 25-year-old man, who was killed in front of his house the day he offered his resignation from his post at UNHCR. His resignation was linked with his efforts to raise awareness within the UNCHR structure regarding alleged corruption. After failing to convince the authorities of the ongoing corruption within the organisation, he decided to offer his resignation. The same night, he was shot in front of his house. What raised suspicion that someone from UNHCR might be behind his death was an email that was sent from his UNHCR email account to his fiancée several days after the murder. This was reported to the UNMIK police as additional evidence in the hope that it might help the investigation. Apparently, the UNMIK authorities were unable to track down where the email came from due to the obstruction they encountered from UNHCR, which allegedly prevented them from entering premises on grounds of the organisation's immunity.[48] Moreover, they could not obtain the testimony of the co-workers of the victim.

Taking into account that UNHCR was one of the first pillars of UNMIK, it is difficult to understand its refusal to comply with the demands of UNMIK's courts.[49] Both belonged to the "UN Family" and were operating under the same legal framework, UNSC Resolution 1244.[50]

UNMIK's Department of Justice enjoyed a broad range of competencies equal to a Ministry of Justice. Given these competencies, one would have expected this body to advise the SRSG to intervene with the Legal Counsel of the General Secretary Legal Affairs Office and ask for the BOI to initiate an investigation or at least secure an agreement that guaranteed access to the UNHCR's premises. Such an act would have served justice and would have erased suspicion about the possible implication of UNHCR in the murder.

Even more complicated was the situation with cases that involved institutional abuse. Examples included the embezzlement of €3.9 m of Kosova /o Electric Corporation funds by senior German official Joe Truchler; the embezzlement of

---

Love Tryst Murder, available at the following website: www.balkanpeace.org/index.php?index=article&articleid=12359 (lastly accessed on 5 November 2013).

48 Benet Rexhepi, a UNHCR employee, was killed on 8 March 2008. See Summary of Press Briefing by UNMIK Spokesperson, 10 March 2002. Available at the following website, http://reliefweb.int/report/serbia/summary-press-briefing-unmik-spokesperson-10-mar-2000 (lastly accessed on 7 November 2013). Information regarding the Rexhepi case before the UNMIK authorities is on file with the author, who was in charged with the case in the capacity of Senior Investigating Lawyer in the Ombudsperson Institution in Kosovo from 2009 until 2012.

49 From 1999 to 2000, Pillar 1 of UNMIK was led by UNHCR, which was responsible for humanitarian assistance. Later, Pillar I became responsible for rule of law functions. See UNMIK background, available at the following website: www.un.org/en/peacekeeping/missions/unmik/background.shtml (lastly accessed on 20 November 20013). UNHCR operated under Resolution 1244, whose mandate was to supervise the "safe and free return of all refugees and displaced persons to their home".

50 For more about the "UN Family", see Henry G. Schermers, *International Institutional Law*, The Netherlands: Sijthoff and Noordhoff, 1980, pp. 837–864.

€300,000 by Kosovo Trust Agency Division Manager, Roger Reynolds; and allegations of corruption by Gerard Fischer, who held the position of Deputy SRSG and who allegedly signed a contract involving Postal and Telecom of Kosovo (PTK) without undergoing procurement procedures.[51]

The SRSG's determination to open grounds for possible waivers of immunity could have been influenced by the reluctance of the competent bodies to issue proper instructions, as was the case with the UNMIK Department of Justice, or by obstruction through political interference by the state concerned as well as by UN bodies, which may have refused such requests for a variety of reasons.

To what extent should an interim administration be controlled? Accountability mechanisms established by UNMIK

The proper functioning of an international administration requires the establishment of a balance between its functional independence and its institutional accountability.[52] While the scope of the power of international administration may differ from one operation to another, there is a common shortcoming that used to follow them, an accountability deficit in the system.[53]

In contrast to their predecessors, which did establish the legal grounds for an accountability regime within the system, the accountability regime of the new international territorial administrations, such as UNMIK and UNTAET, relies instead on some ad hoc arrangements that emerged as a response to the continuing critique accusing the mission of an accountability deficit. This critique came in a variety of forms, including from legal scholars, journalists, civil society, and intergovernmental organisations. Consequently, the administrations became associated with different images. Some associated them with "benevolent

51 Allegedly, Fischer was arrested but did not face trial and instead accepted another assignment. Regarding the case of Reynold, in 2009 the Kosova Government issued an international arrest warrant and lodged an extradition request with the UK authorities for Reynolds to be extradited to Kosovo. See Nicolas Lemay-Hebert, State Building from the Outside-In: UNMIK and Its Paradox, *Journal of Public and International Affairs*, Vol. 20, 2009, p. 81. See also Balkan Insight, Kosovo Seeks Extradition over Fraud Case, available at the following website: www.balkaninsight.com/en/article/kosovo-seeks-extraditions-over-fraud-case.

52 Stahn, *supra* n. 31, p. 598.

53 The first attempt to establish an institutional accountability mechanism for an international governmental authority was undertaken during the mandate regime. Similar practices existed under the trusteeship regime. The accountability regime of both the mandate and trusteeship systems, including *sui generis* administrations (Saar and Danzig), comprised the following forms: reporting, the right to petition, and the institutional judicial review. See Aleksandar Momirov, *Accountability of International Territorial Administrations: A Public Law Approach*, Eleven International Publishing, 2011, p. 83, *The Law and Practice of International Territorial Administration, Versailles to Iraq and Beyond*, Cambridge University Press, 2008 at p 84.

autocracy",[54] others with a new form of neotrusteeship or mistrusteeship,[55] or even with neo-colonialism.[56]

Initially, UNMIK followed the common UN culture of submitting reports to the Security Council.[57] Given the broad mandate of the UNMIK administration, which mirrored a state-like regime, numerous intergovernmental organisations, as well as international human rights organisations expressed their concern regarding the accountability gap in the mission.[58]

Legal scholars considered that the "a degree of accountability from the agency charged with holding governments worldwide to account" was expected.[59]

The pressure exerted upon UNMIK obliged its authorities to start an active search for a solution that would improve this unsatisfactory situation.[60] Initially, a Human Rights Oversight Committee was established, whose main task was to examine the compatibility of UNMIK regulations with international human rights law and to review the performance of politicians, the police, and the military and subsequently to issue recommendations to address any alleged shortcomings.[61] The Human Rights Oversight Committee was heavily criticised by

54 Simon Chesterman, *You the People, The United Nations, Transitional Administration, and State–Building*, Oxford University Press, 2004. p.153. The late SRSG Sergio Vieira de Mello, who served as the first SRSG both in Kosovo and East Timor, declared that he had been given the power to develop "a model for good governance through benevolent despotism". Quoted in Joel C. Beauvais, Benevolent Despotism: A Critique of UN State Building in East Timor, *International Law and Politics*, Vol. 33, 2001, p. 1102.

55 Christian Eric Ford and Ben A. Oppenheim, Neotrusteeship or Mistrusteeship? The "Authority Creep" Dilemma in United Nations Transitional Administration, *Vanderbilt Journal of Transnational Law*, Vol. 41, 2008.

56 Ralph Wilde, *International Territorial Administration, How Trusteeship and Civilizing Mission Never Went Away*, Oxford University Press, 2008.

57 UNMIK was requested to report every month to the Security Council, whereas UNTAET had to report every six months. See UNSC Resolution 1244, para 20; UNSC Resolution 1272, para 18.

58 The OSCE regularly issued reports regarding different human rights violations. See OSCE Mission in Kosovo, www.osce.org/kosovo/documents. Although one of the UNMIK's main pillars, its reports were not welcomed by UNMIK and were very often privately criticised by UNMIK. See William O 'Neill, *Kosovo: An Unfinished Peace*, Boulder, CO: Lynn Reinner, 2002 at p 52. In addition, both Amnesty International and Human Rights Watch regularly criticised UNMIK about the accountability gap of the mission. See Amnesty International, KFOR and UNMIK fail to uphold human rights standards in Mitrovica AI INDEX:EUR 70/14/00 13 March 2000. See also Human Rights Watch, Kosovo: EU Should Ensure International Mission is Accountable Success Will Depend on Effective Scrutiny of Human Rights Record, March 2008, available at the following website: www.commondreams.org/news2008/0310-02.htm; see, www.osce.org/publications/odihr/1999/11/17756_507_en.pdf.

59 See David Marshall and Shelley Inglis, The Disempowerment of Human Rights-Based Justice in the United Nations Mission in Kosovo, *Harvard Human Rights Journal*, Vol. 16, 2003, p. 117.

60 Chesterman, *supra* n. 54, p. 148.

61 HROC was established in 2008. It comprised the following members: the Deputy SRSG, the Heads of OSCE and the EU mission, the UNMIK Legal Adviser, the UNMIK Director of Office of Returns and Communities, the head of the UN High Commissioner for Human

the Human Rights Committee for performing its duty poorly.[62] In addition, it was viewed by the European Commission for Democracy through Law, (Venice Commission)[63] as lacking independence and, as such, as not suitable to act as an independent review body.[64]

A similar situation appears to have arisen with the UN-based claims review board, which was established to deal with "third-party claims for property loss or damage and for personal injury, illness or death arising from or directly attributed to KFOR, UNMIK or their respective personnel and which do not arise from 'operational necessity' of either international presence".[65] As it lacked transparency, it remained unclear to the public what types of cases were referred to this body for examination as well as the outcome of possible review.[66]

In addition, as will be discussed in the next chapter, UNMIK periodically reported to different international mechanisms, which reflected a new mode of interaction between an international territorial administration and an international oversight body.[67]

It remains unclear in which context the submission of these periodic reports was conducted. It was understood as a way of securing the continuation of the treaty obligations of the host state, in this case the FRY.[68]

Rights, the Chief of the UNMIK Office of Gender Affairs, the Head of OSCE Human Rights and Rule of Law, and the Deputy Commander of KFOR.

62 See Human Rights Committee, *Consideration of Country Report, UNMIK in Kosovo*, Initial Report 14 July–28 July 2006.

63 Venice Commission is an advisory body of the Council of Europe. It is composed of independent experts that provide legal advice to its member states on constitutional matters. More about Venice Commission see www.venice.coe.int/WebForms/pages/?p=01_Presentation.

64 As its performance remained closed to the public, it was never clear whether it ever exercised the role of an internal mechanism.

65 Established pursuant to General Assembly Resolution (GA RES. 52/247), 17 July 1998. In line with this Resolution, UNMIK Regulation 2000/47 was enacted (Regulation on immunity of UNMIK's personnel), which in Section 7 referred to the establishment of a claims commission whose task would be to deal with "third party claims for property loss or damage and for personal injury, illness or death arising from or directly attributed to KFOR, UNMIK or their respective personnel and which do not arise from 'operational necessity' of either international presence".

66 See Human Rights Watch, Report *Better Late Than Never*, Number 2, June 2007, pp. 17–18. See also Kosovo Ombudsperson Institution, First Annual Report, 18 July 2001 and Second Annual report 10 July 2002.

67 It has been perceived as a step forward towards the improvement of UN accountability and as such recommended as a model to be served to future territorial administrations. See Ivan Ingravallo, UN Territorial Administrations: Between International Humanitarian Law and Human Rights Law, in Robert Kolb and Gloria Gaggioli (eds.), *Research Handbook on Human Rights and Humanitarian Law*, United Kingdom: Edward Elgar Publishing, 2013, p. 404.

68 See Momirov, *supra* n. 53, pp. 236–237. This assertion is only valid for the human rights treaties ratified by FRY prior to UNMIK's arrival, for instance ICCPR, ICESCR and CEDAW, but not for the Framework Convention for the Protection of National Minorities, which came into play later. Serbia became party to the FCNM on 11 May 2001, whereas Kosovo

However, it should be noted that this continuation of the host state's obligations was exercised selectively, because it excluded the possibility of submitting individual petitions before these bodies.

The Ombudsperson Institution

The OIK was established by UNMIK Regulation 2000/38 on 30 June 2000 "for the purpose of enhancing the protection of human rights in Kosovo".[69] The role of the Institution was confirmed by the Constitutional Framework for Kosovo, which gave it an important position in the new post-war legal order.[70]

As an independent entity, the OIK has a mandate to engage in human rights and rule of law issues, both with the international administration[71] and with emerging local institutions.

The jurisdiction of the OIK covers issues concerning human rights violations and actions constituting abuse of authority. The main reference instruments are the European Convention on Human Rights and its Protocols and the International Covenant on Civil and Political Rights. While the OIK does not have the power to issue binding decisions, its findings are presented in the form of special reports, which cover general situations and individual case reports on an individual complaint or ex officio.

It does not have a mandate to review cases involving violations committed by the KFOR authorities. Although the regulation in question provides for the signing of an agreement between the OIK and the KFOR authorities that might subject KFOR to the scrutiny of the OIK, such an agreement was never reached.[72]

Consequently, all complaints which involved the KFOR authorities were forwarded to KFOR's claims commission. Regrettably, no information is publicly available about the functioning of this mechanism and the public remains deprived of information about the number of claims initiated and processed before this body.[73]

The OIK is considered to be the most effective mechanism for the protection of human rights in Kosovo today. To this extent, it is directly involved in monitoring, protecting, investigating and reporting on human rights violations by public institutions. Although the OIK refrains from commenting upon draft

---

was subjected to the FCNM obligations pursuant to the specific monitoring arrangements signed between UNMIK and the Council of Europe in 2004.

69 UNMIK Regulation No. 2000/38 on the Establishment of the Ombudsperson Institution in Kosovo (30 June 2000).

70 The institution was led for five years by the International Ombudsperson, Polish human rights lawyer Marek Antoni Nowicki.

71 Under the old Regulation 2000/38, the OIK had a mandate to investigate complaints against administrative bodies (UNMIK).

72 "In order to deal with cases involving the international security presence, the Ombudsperson may enter into an agreement with the Commander of the Kosovo Forces (COMKFOR)". See Article 3.4 of UNMIK Regulation 2000/38.

73 See Ombudsperson Institution in Kosovo Annual Report 2001–2002.

laws, when it comes to already promulgated laws it has proved to be very vocal. It always limits itself to comments addressing the compliance of the adopted regulations with international standards.

The independence of the OIK is ensured by Section 2 of Regulation 2000/38, which provides that "[t]he OI shall act independently. No person or entity may interfere with his/her functions". This was confirmed by Regulation 2006/06 section 2.1, using similar wording.

After the promulgation of the new UNMIK Regulation 2006/6,[74] the mandate of the Institution became constricted and, consequently, removed its automatic right to review and redress acts of omissions/decisions constituting an abuse of authority or a violation of human rights by UNMIK. Regulation 2006/6, which excludes UNMIK from the OIK's jurisdiction, has weakened the institution in the eyes of citizens who vested their hopes in it to seek justice for acts committed by UNMIK officials.[75] Paradoxically, the Regulation foresaw a possibility of concluding bilateral agreements between the OIK and the UNMIK authorities or of promoting so-called "orderly cooperation".[76]

Consequently, the OIK was awkwardly squeezed between its narrow mandate and the wide expectations coming from the victims of possible violations.

Faced with such a legal cocktail together with the lack of accountability of the actors involved, it continued to struggle to build paths towards promoting and protecting human rights in Kosovo.[77] The OIK has promoted human rights in Kosovo but is nonetheless not an effective remedy for human rights protection.[78]

74 UNMIK, Regulation No. 2006/6 on the Ombudsperson Institution in Kosovo (16 February 2006).

75 See Ombudsperson Institution in Kosovo, *Fifth Annual Report* (2004–2005) addressed to the Special Representative of the Secretary-General of the United Nations (11 July 2005).

76 The Regulation has been subject to criticism by the Ombudsperson, who, immediately after being informed of its promulgation, sent a letter to the SRSG in which he expressed his concerns/comments about the decision to narrow the mandate of the Institution. "[W]e consider it problematic that the OIK no longer has automatic jurisdiction over UNMIK bodies, given that there are still a considerable number of areas that remain under reserved powers, in particular matters pertaining to the protection of minority communities. One specific example of this would be Northern Mitrovica, where the PISG do not operate and concerns would need to be brought directly to the attention of UNMIK", said the Acting Ombudsperson. The letter was sent on 22 February 2006 and is available on the OIK website: www.ombudspersonkosovo.org.

77 It was not clear for a long time whether the Acting Ombudsperson, who was appointed by the SRSG, could exercise his oversight functions over UNMIK following the long transition period from an internationally to a locally appointed Ombudsperson. Despite the fact that the Acting Ombudsperson had required clarification on this matter from the SRSG, he did not received an answer until the Human Rights Watch officials raised it with the SRSG's office and urged them to provide the Ombudsperson Institution with an answer. Finally, on 9 November 2007 it was clarified that the Acting Ombudsperson would continue to exercise his functions and responsibilities over UNMIK upon the appointment of a new Ombudsperson.

78 About the process of Kosovanisation of the Ombudsperson Institution, see Christopher P.M. Waters, "Kosovanizing" the Ombudsperson: Implications for Kosovo and Peacekeeping, *International Peacekeeping*, Vol. 15, No. 5, 2008.

Regardless of the legal, financial, and cultural settings in which the OIK works and regardless of the current state of democratisation in today's Kosovo, the OIK has been persistent in seeking ways to defend Kosovans' rights against unfair acts perpetrated by both the UNMIK administration and local actors.

Being the only non-judicial mechanism for promoting human rights in Kosovo, the institution has been trying to enhance its sphere of activity from that of a transitional watchdog guarding against maladministration. It has been supervising with the utmost care, trying to prevent the authorities from violating the law to the detriment of human rights. Thus although denied the authority to correct UNMIK official abuses, it at least raises its voice whenever it comes across a violation.

The institution was highly critical of UNMIK and contributed enormously towards a better understanding of UNMIK's mandate. Through its criticism, it tried to raise awareness among the population of ongoing violations and progressively stood to defend the rights of victims.[79]

The Human Rights Advisory Panel

In 2004, the Venice Commission proposed the establishment of human rights mechanisms through which Kosovars could bring their claims against UNMIK and the KFOR authorities, stating: "It is necessary that the UN system itself develop mechanisms which must ensure the respect for the limitations on UN action, as they derive from general international law (in particular human rights law), in individual cases".[80] Although it recognised that establishing such a mechanism might conflict with the very character of UNMIK and KFOR as international organisations, it emphasised "that in Kosovo UNMIK and KFOR carry out tasks which are certainly more similar to those of a State administration than those of an international organization proper. It is unconceivable and incompatible with the principles of democracy, the rule of law and respect for human rights that they could act as State authorities and be exempted from any independent legal review. Yet, due consideration must be given to their legal nature".[81]

The suggestion came after five years of UNMIK's effective engagement on the ground. Within the framework of this discussion, different options were considered. Initially, there were two options on the table. The first suggested the extension of the jurisdiction of the ECtHR in respect of UNMIK and/or KFOR through an agreement signed between the Council of Europe and the UN or

79 The OIK was among the first to point to the negative effects of the immunity of international institutions upon the people of Kosovo. Through its commitment, it tried to make people understand that UNMIK cannot be perceived as an Almighty Authority but instead is called upon to promote and protect their rights.

80 European Commission for Democracy Through Law, *Opinion on Human Rights Possible Establishment of Review Mechanisms Kosovo*, adopted by the Venice Commission on its 60th Plenary Session, 11 October 2004, para 78.

81 Ibid., para 91.

UNMIK.[82] The second option, which was proposed by the Legal Affairs Committee of the Parliamentary Assembly, involved establishing a special Human Rights Court for Kosovo, similar to the Human Rights Chamber for Bosnia and Herzegovina, a hybrid court that would comprise local (Albanian and Serbian) and international judges appointed by the European Court or its President. Accordingly, this court would serve as a kind of predecessor to the European Court.[83]

Unfortunately, both options proved to be difficult to implement and financially expensive.[84] Subsequently, a new proposal emerged for setting up a provisional mechanism of review of human rights violations allegedly committed by UNMIK. Its mandate would be to examine complaints lodged by individuals whose rights and freedoms had been breached by acts, Regulations, decisions etc. by UNMIK, but only in cases where the Ombudsperson had found human rights breaches.[85] The proposal envisaged that a panel would be set up for a fixed term comprising independent international experts with demonstrated expertise in human rights. Further, it was suggested that the mandate of the panel should cease as soon as a judicial body with jurisdiction over UNMIK, such as the Human Rights Court for Kosovo, was established.[86]

Subsequently, the Parliamentary Assembly issued a Resolution recommending the establishment of an advisory panel or human rights commission.[87] One year later, on 23 March 2006, the Human Rights Advisory Panel (HRAP) was established pursuant to Regulation 2006/12.[88]

The HRAP was given a mandate to examine complaints from any individual or group of individuals concerning alleged human rights violations committed by or attributable to the UNMIK authorities.[89] It had jurisdiction over complaints relating to violations that occurred after 23 April 2005, including violations that

82 A major problem confronting this option was that the UN as a worldwide organization would need to be placed under the jurisdiction of the ECtHR, a regional human rights mechanism, while a mechanism of supervision by the Human Rights Committee already existed. Moreover, even if the United Nations agreed to subject itself to the jurisdiction of the ECtHR, a range of different issues would arise, in particular the ability of the United Nations or NATO to confer jurisdiction *ratione personae* on the Strasbourg court. Such an endeavour would be contrary to Articles 33and 34 of the ECHR (complaints can be directed only against a state), as neither the United Nations nor NATO can be regarded as a state. On this, see also *supra* n. 80, paras 80–81.

83 *Supra* n. 80, para 104.

84 Ibid., paras 108–114.

85 Ibid., paras 115.

86 European Commission for Democracy Through Law, *Opinion on Human Rights Possible Establishment of Review Mechanisms Kosovo*, adopted by the Venice Commission on its 60th Plenary Session, 11 October 2004, para 119.

87 Council of Europe Parliamentary Assembly, Resolution 1417 (2005) at para 5, issued on 25 January 2005.

88 For more on the history of the creation of HRAP, see Bernhard Knoll, *The Legal Status of Territories Subject to Administration by International Organizations*, Cambridge University Press, 2008, pp. 381–393.

89 See UNMIK Regulation 2006/12, section 1.2 3.

occurred prior to this date where the facts give rise to a continuing violation of human rights.[90] The HRAP had no jurisdiction over KFOR troops.

After examining the complaint, the HRAP would issue an opinion on the given violation which may include recommendations to the SRSG.[91] It should be noted that these recommendations were of an advisory nature and their implementation was at the sole discretion of the SRSG, who retained the exclusive authority to decide whether to act on them.[92]

The HRAP could only determine whether UNMIK is responsible for a violation but could not order compensation or specific relief.[93] Moreover, although the nomination of its members was made by the President of the ECtHR, their actual appointment was effected by the SRSG.[94]

It is important to mention that the legal framework that governed the HRAP was designed to comply with the terms of the UN Conventions on Privileges and Immunity of international staff as well as to determine clearly the relationship of the HRAP with the Ombudsperson Institution.[95] Most importantly, the Regulation failed to provide grounds for reviewing UNMIK's acts regarding their compliance with human rights instruments.[96]

However, three years later, on 16 October 2009, Administrative Direction No. 2009/1 was issued as a modification of Regulation 2006/12, which retroactively affected the procedural rights of the parties.[97] The Direction imposed the following:

1 proceedings before the HRAP should be non-adversarial (section 1);
2 Any complaint to the HRAP that is or may in future become in future the subject of a claim under the UN Third Party Claims Process should be deemed inadmissible (section 2). For any new admissibility determination,

90 See UNMIK/REG/2006/12, 23 March 2006 section 2.
91 See UNMIK/REG/2006/12, 23 March 2006 section 17.
92 See The Annual Report 2012 of the Human Rights Advisory Panel, issued in March 2013, para 33.
93 See The Annual Report 2010 of the Human Rights Advisory Panel, para 1.
94 The tenure of HRAP members is two years and can be renewed for further terms of two years. See UNMIK Regulation 2006/12 section 5.1.52.
95 The adoption of Regulation 2006/12, which created the HRAP, resulted in the restriction of the previous Ombudsperson's power to investigate human rights violations attributed to UNMIK. It was one of the main requirements posted by the UNMIK authorities that UNMIK Regulation 2006/12 should be designed in light of the UN Convention on Privileges and Immunity of International Staff. Moreover, its mandate should not undermine or duplicate the role of the Ombudsperson Institution. More about it see, Bernard Knoll, *supra* n. 88, pp. 384–385.
96 Initially, UNMIK had agreed to allow the HRAP to examine the conformity of UNMIK's acts with the human rights standards enshrined in the ECHR and its protocols. Bernhard Knoll, referring to the note of UNMIK's Legal Adviser, issued on 21 July 2005. See Knoll, *supra* n. 95, p. 386.
97 Administrative Direction No. 2009/01of 17 October 2009 Implementing UNMIK Regulation No. 2006/12 on the Establishment of the Human Rights Advisory Panel Rules of Procedure.

the HRAP is required to refer such new determination to the SRSG, for further comments;

3 A claim deemed admissible should be revisited in light of the Direction (section 2). This meant that the HRAP was required to reconsider its earlier decision declaring the complainants' case admissible in light of the new Direction;

4 A complaint received after 31 March 2010 must be deemed inadmissible (section 5).

Although Administrative Direction No. 2009/1 was justified by UNMIK as a tool that provided guidance for the interpretation of certain provisions of Regulation 2006/12, in fact, it was viewed by HRAP members as an amendment of the Regulation.[98] Accordingly, "it significantly limited the Panel's role and mode of functioning".[99]

This so-called "interpretive guidance" of Administrative Direction 2009/01 narrowed and weakened the mandate of the HRAP, making it even more fragile than before. For instance, it requested that "public hearings of the Human Rights Advisory Panel shall be conducted in such manner and settings that allow a clear sense of non-adversarial proceedings to be conveyed to all participants and to the public at large including to any media presence in case such presence is permitted by the Advisory Panel".[100] This shift from an adversarial to a non-adversarial approach brought into question the mutual trust of the parties involved in the proceedings. In particular, it made victims of violations feel alienated and powerless towards the UNMIK system in general.[101] It favoured the violator over the victims of the violations as it enabled the SRSG to interfere arbitrarily in the course of justice.

Yet the most bizarre aspect of Administrative Direction No. 2009/1 is that it explicitly requested that the Third Party Claims Process, the United Nations Internal Oversight Mechanism, should serve as an "available avenue", meaning that it should be exhausted by the potential human rights victims before submitting a complaint to the HRAP.[102] Regardless of the widely known fact that the UN Third Party Claims Process has no reasonable chance of success, both the HRAP and the potential victims were compelled to consider the UN Third Party

98 The members did not welcome these changes and expressed the hope that the new framework would not affect the performance and activities of HRAP. See HRAP Annual Report 2009.

99 See Human Rights Advisory Panel's Annual Report 2009.

100 Administrative Direction No. 2009/01of 17 October 2009 Implementing UNMIK Regulation No. 2006/12 on the Establishment of the Human Rights Advisory Panel Rules of Procedure, para 1.1. See also Human Rights Advisory Panel's Annual Report 2009.

101 See Press release issued by Lëvizja Vetëvendosje, *The Case at the Human Rights Panel 2007–2010*, available at the following website: www.Vetëvendosje.org/en/the-case-at-the-human-rights-advisory-panel/ (lastly assessed on 7 December 2013).

102 See UNMIK Regulation 2000/47.

Claims Process to be an accessible and appropriate remedy.[103] In this regard, the HRAP was stripped of jurisdiction for determining itself whether the United Nations Third Party Claims Process fulfilled conditions that could be regarded as an effective remedy.[104]

It should be noted that the UN Claims Commissions are an internal body of the UN comprising three or more UN officials in charge of the whole proceedings, including the investigation, processing and final adjudication of the claims. These bodies are not established as standard procedures in the initial phase of establishing a peacekeeping mission; usually, they are set up "when the need arises".[105] Moreover, the system does not have a second judicial instance for settling disputes in cases when the parties are not able to reach an agreement.[106]

Taking into consideration the narrowness of its mandate as well as the form of adjudication adopted by this body, it is difficult to comprehend that it could constitute "a remedy before a national court within the meaning of Article 13". It is of the utmost importance that the remedy must be "effective" in both practice and law, meaning that there must not be undue interference by the state.[107] Additionally, when recourse to remedies is known to be inadequate or ineffective the applicant may be exempted from complying with the rule of exhausting domestic remedies, in particular where "an administrative practice consisting of a repetition of acts incompatible with the Convention has been shown to exist, and is of such a nature as to make proceedings futile or ineffective".[108]

Additionally, the modification brought about by Administrative Direction No. 2009/1, resulted in the suspension of the examination of the merits of complaints which were initiated prior to its enactment.[109] It required that no new complaints were to be accepted by HRAP after 31 March 2010, thereby creating serious obstacles for those who were eligible to resubmit complaints before HRAP.[110]

The legal constraints imposed on HRAP can be illustrated by two high profile cases dealt with before this body, *Balaj and others v. UNMIK*[111] and the Roma Poisoning case initiated by *N.M. and others v. UNMIK*.[112]

103 See Human Rights Advisory Panel Annual Report 2010.

104 The response of HRAP was that it was within the discretion of the SRSG to determine the regulatory scheme for HRAP and that it had no jurisdiction to examine challenges to the legal basis of its own functioning. See Human Rights Panel Annual Report 2010, para 55.

105 See Verdirame, *supra* n. 3, pp. 224–226.

106 Ibid.

107 *Aksoy v. Turkey*, App. No. 21987/93, ECtHR, Judgment, 18 December 1996, para 52.

108 Ibid.

109 See Human Rights Advisory Panel Annual Report 2010.

110 Ibid.

111 HRAP, *Balaj and Others v. UNMIK*; Decision Case No. 04/07 (first admissibility decision 6 June 2008; second decision on admissibility 31 March 2010). The complaint was lodged by the relatives of the deceased Mon Balaj and Arben Xheladini, who were killed by UNMIK policemen during the protest of 10 February 2007 organised by the Vetëvendosje movement, as well as two wounded individuals, Zenel Zenelaj and Mustafa Nerjovaj.

112 HRAP, *N.M. and Others v. UNMIK*, Decision Case No. 26/08 first admissibility decision 5 June 2009; second decision on admissibility, 31 March 2010.

On 11 October 2007, *Balaj and others* filed a complaint alleging that a number of human rights violations had been committed by UNMIK, including the right to life, the right to an effective remedy, and the right of peaceful assembly. On 6 June 2008, the HRAP issued an admissibility decision in the complainants' case, declaring the case admissible.

Shortly before the public hearing, the SRSG informed the HRAP that UNMIK's representatives would not attend the hearing for security reasons and instead required the hearing to be held in private.[113] Consequently, on 19 March 2009 the hearing took place in private, but the representatives of the applicants requested an adjournment of the hearing so that it could be held in public, stating that they would not participate in a closed hearing.

Soon after, Administrative Direction 2009/1 was adopted, introducing changes to the nature of public hearings before the HRAP.[114] By way of this direction, the SRSG used its power to alter the HRAP's procedure and direct the HRAP to find claims such as the complainants' inadmissible.[115] As already discussed, in light of this direction the HRAP was required to reconsider its earlier decisions declaring the complainants' case admissible, conduct the hearing in private, and apply a non-adversarial system.[116]

In a complaint introduced on 12 November 2009, the applicants challenged Administrative Direction 2009/1. They submitted that it breached their right to a fair trial as the SRSG was seeking to reopen the issue of admissibility, prevent adversarial proceedings, and direct the HRAP on the correct interpretation of the law. The applicants also reserved the right to argue that the SRSG had no power to issue the direction as Regulation 2006/12 did not allow the SRSG to do this.[117]

On 31 March 2010, the HRAP issued a decision on the admissibility of the complainants' case, applying Administrative Direction 2009/1. It stated that it had no jurisdiction to deal with the arguments raised by the complainants concerning the illegality of Administrative Direction 2009/1. Consequently, it issued a decision declaring the complaint inadmissible and at the same time instructed the applicants to submit a new complaint after completing proceedings before the UN Third Party Clams Commission.[118]

Yet a proceeding before the UNMIK Claims Review Board was already initiated in 2007, and therefore continued throughout the applicants' case. During the

113 UNMIK claimed that it could not guarantee security prior to and during the hearings. It remains unclear what this fear was about. The application and the accompanying documents of the case Balaj and others v. UNMIK are on file with the author.

114 See Section 1 of the Administrative Direction 2009/01.

115 On 30 October 2009 and 18 January 2010, the SRSG submitted to the Panel that the complainants' case must be declared inadmissible as it was the subject of the UN Third Party Claims Process because the complainants were still negotiating with the UNMIK Claims Review Board.

116 See Section 2 of the Administrative Direction 2009/01.

117 Information provided by the applicant's lawyer, Mr. Jesse Nicholls.

118 HRAP, *Balaj Xheladini, Zeneli Nerjovaj v. UNMIK*, Decision Case No. 04.2007, issued on 11 May 2012.

entire process, the applicants repeated that even if they accepted compensation, they would continue the proceedings that were pending before the HRAP.[119]

In December 2010, agreement was reached with the UNMIK Claims Review Board and financial compensation solely for economic loss was determined for each applicant. The applicants were requested to sign forms including words stating that compensation was "in full and final settlement of all claims of every nature and kind whatsoever resulting from" the deaths and injuries sustained on 10 February 2007.[120]

Soon after, the applicants approached the HRAP with a request to continue with the proceedings of their case. Subsequently, the HRAP issued a decision stating that it would reopen the applicants' case and consider the merits of the case in full. Though the SRSG insisted upon the HRAP not reopening the case, his claim was rejected by the HRAP.[121]

In the HRAP's opinion, the applicants continued to have "victim" status, which gave rise to the reopening of the complaint and its consideration on its merits. Because the victims had not received written apologies for the events of 10 February 2007, the compensation that they had received was not based on acknowledgement of a violation of applicants' human rights, but was limited to compensation solely for economic loss, and not the applicants' pain, suffering and moral anguish or for punitive or other moral damages.[122] At the time of the writing, this case was still pending before the HRAP.

It should be stressed that despite being exposed to so much obstruction, the HRAP succeeded in having the case declared admissible.

The same problem as *Balaj and others* was encountered by the applicants in the case *N. M and others*, known as the Roma poisoning case.

In July 2008 *N. M and others* filed a complaint with the HRAP alleging that they were victims of violations with specific reference to the right to life, the prohibition of inhuman and degrading treatment, respect for private and family life, the right to a fair hearing, the right to an effective remedy, the right to adequate housing, etc.

119 Ibid., para 23.

120 Ibid., para 27.

121 The SRSG submitted that no new complaint could be filed with HRAP and therefore argued that it was mandatory for HRAP to deem it inadmissible as it came after 31 March 2010. HRAP, repeating its earlier decision of 31 March 2010, stated that this was not a new complaint, as the complaint had already been filed on 11 October 2007, and to treat it as a new complaint would render it permanently inadmissible, which would be unacceptable in the circumstances. In addition, the SRSG claimed that HRAP could only deal with a matter submitted to HRAP within six months of the final decision in the other available avenue of redress. In this case, that avenue was the Claims Process with UNMIK. The SRSG stated that this six months commenced when the final offer was made by UNMIK. HRAP stated that the time would run from the signing of the release forms, not the offers being made. In any event, the Panel rejected the premise of the SRSG's submissions, holding that the six-month requirement did not even apply to a request to reopen proceedings. That only had to happen within a "reasonable" period and the applicants had complied with this requirement. See *Balaj Xheladini, Zeneli Nerjovaj v. UNMIK*, *supra* n. 118, paras 38–49.

122 Ibid., paras 70–71.

On 5 June 2009, the complaint was declared partly admissible and partly inadmissible.[123]

Two months later, the SRSG raised an objection regarding the admissibility of the complaint, invoking the non-exhaustion of available avenues.[124]

As in the *Balaj and others* case, the complainants were required to initiate a procedure before the UN Third Party Claims Process as an accessible and sufficient avenue. Consequently, on 31 March 2010, the entire complaint was declared inadmissible by the HRAP on account of the non-exhaustion of available remedies.[125]

Although aware of an existing interlinkage between the substantive and procedural aspects of complaints, the HRAP viewed it as inappropriate to consider them separately, having taken into consideration that the substantive complaints were to be dealt with by the UN Third Party Claims Process, a condition enshrined in Administrative Direction 2009/01.[126]

The HRAP considered that the decision highlighted the requirements of exhaustion of remedies and as such, appeared to apply temporary restrictions on admissibility. In this regard, it would allow the complainants to resubmit their claim before the HRAP once the process had been concluded before the UN Third Party Claims Process.[127]

It should be noted that before submitting a complaint to the HRAP, the compensation claim was already under examination before the UN Third Party Process.[128]

123 HRAP found the complaint to be admissible on multiple counts (involving substantive aspects). However, two persons named in the complaint who died before the complaint was filed and three others, namely workers that used to visit camps on a semi-regular basis, were not characterised as complainants. Consequently, the complaints made by them were declared inadmissible *ratione personae* pursuant to section 1.2 of the Regulation. See *N.M. and Others v. UNMIK*, Decision Case No. 26/08 first admissibility decision 5 June 2009; second decision on admissibility, 31 March 2010, paras 25–27.

124 Ibid., para 14.

125 Even though it clearly confirmed that none of them fell within the domain of the UN Third Party Claims Process.

126 As they do not reflect acts, omissions or situations that result in personal injury, illness or death, or in property loss or damage.

127 Human Rights Advisory Panel, 5 June 2009. See, also Human Rights Advisory Panel Annual Report 2010.

128 On 10 February 2006, the European Roma Rights Centre (ERRC) lodged a claim on behalf of the victims before the United Nations in New York, based on the UN Third-Party Claims Process, requesting the following: "Medical and rehabilitation expenses and loss of earnings for all claimants, transportation expenses associated with injury, illness or medical care for claimants who paid such expenses; burial expenses for those whose family members have died, legal expenses for all claimants, the maximum payment of $50,000 USD per person because the damage from the lead poisoning is so severe, affects the vital organs, especially impacting intelligence levels and is irreversible". See ERRC claim para 227 (on file with the author).

Yet the processing of the claim exceeded the time limit, with a lengthy delay. Only after five and a half years were the applicants informed by the UN Third Party Process that their claim had been rejected on the grounds that it involved complaints against the UNMIK administration and was not an individual claim.[129]

So although UNMIK Administrative Direction 2009/1 foresaw the possibility of complainants reopening the proceedings before the HRAP once the UN Third Party Claims Procedure had been concluded, this was not possible as the same Direction provided that the cut-off date for submission of complaints before the Panel was 31 March 2010.[130] In this regard, it appears that any future complaint would automatically be rejected given that the compensation claim before the UN Headquarters authorities had ended in August 2011.[131]

Conclusion

The foregoing discussion reveals the existence of a vacuum in the system of protection of rights and freedoms in Kosovo. The legal constraints posed by the conventional law that shields an international organisation and its agents from judicial accountability leave the rights of the individuals subjected to an international administration insufficiently protected. The functional immunity of UN officials remains intact even in a situation where the UN establishes a state-like administration and where no host state governmental structures are present. Consequently, the immunity turns into a shield that protects UN officials from its own structures. The unwillingness to search for reasonable restrictions on its own jurisdictional immunity has become a lock that keeps the rights of the whole population chained.

The attempt to resolve the tension between human rights standards and the UN's immunity through the creation of *ad hoc* accountability mechanisms did not bring a suitable solution.

The SRSG's interference significantly limited the functioning of these mechanisms, in particular the functioning of the HRAP.

Consequently, the HRAP was obliged to keep a balance between, on the one hand, executive interference and, on the other, a minimal amount of institutional independence, which made its functioning extremely difficult.

The mechanism that provides a remedy must be independent of the body alleged to have committed the violation.[132] The extensive involvement of UNMIK, not only in establishing the institutional infrastructure of the HRAP

129 On 15 August 2011, the applicants were informed of the rejection of the claim. Email communication with Ms. Dianne Post, the ERRC lawyer, 20 September 2011.

130 Section 5 of UNMIK Administrative Direction 2009/1.

131 This was one of the main concerns of the Human Rights Panel. See Human Rights Advisory Panel Annual Report 2010.

132 *Khan v. United Kingdom*, App. No. 35394/87, ECtHR, judgment 12 May 2000, paras 46–47.

but also in the appointment of its members, as well as its direct interference by way of modification of the legislative provisions, turned the HRAP into an official field service of UNMIK.[133]

In this light, the rights of the people administered by UNMIK amount to no value as there is no adequate human rights mechanism to ensure the active and effective protection of their rights. It is unacceptable for any governing administration to operate in such a legal vacuum.

133 "Since the panel is created by UNMIK law regulation and its procedures are subject to amendment by UNMIK, it is hard to see how the panel can be considered independent". See Human Rights Watch Report, *Better Late Than Never: Enhancing the Accountability of International Institution in Kosovo*, June 2007, p. 16.

6 Holding UNMIK accountable for human rights violations

Introduction

The role of the United Nations has significantly expanded since the 1990s with respect to its involvement in post-conflict societies. It has shifted from general supervision to direct governance, assuming a wide range of state-like tasks.[1] Yet this innovation has created considerable tension as to the applicability of human rights law to such structures.

In this regard, a range of questions has been raised related to the UN's practical capability for performing this role, as well as the availability of feasible alternatives to the United Nations to take appropriate responsibility for its actions and decisions and to become more accountable to the people it governs. Particular interest has been shown in whether ITAs, as political entities, carry international responsibility for their acts.

As already indicated in the previous chapter, the UNMIK authorities remain exempted from the jurisdiction of the domestic courts. Human rights mechanisms established for the purpose of maintaining the accountability of UNMIK proved to lack real power.

The following chapter addresses the general issues surrounding the human rights obligations of international organisations. It explores the responsibilities of the United Nations when it undertakes the role of a surrogate state.

The fact that the UNMIK administration assumed state-like powers has opened the door for a discussion as to whether its responsibility in the sphere of human rights protection is equal to that of a state government.

1 "In interim administration missions beginning in the late 1990s, such as the United Nations Interim Administration Mission in Kosovo (UNMIK) and the United Nations Transitional Administration in East Timor (UNTAET), the United Nations (UN) performed ever more specialized governmental functions at all administrative levels in the mission area. In these cases, civil affairs became a civil administration responsible for directly managing all aspects of civilian life while simultaneously working to devolve its responsibilities to local authorities. It should be strongly emphasized, however, that governance mandates are the exception rather than the norm in peacekeeping". See *Handbook on United Nations Multidimensional Peacekeeping Operations*, published by Peacekeeping Best Practice Unit, *Department of Peacekeeping Operations*, United Nations, 2003, p. 44.

Thus this chapter examines whether international authorities engaged in the administration of an entity in which they exercise state-like powers are bound by the existing international human rights standards.

Therefore, this chapter identifies the primary rules governing international territorial administrations. Based on the existing case law, it will try to assess the degree of control exercised by the UNMIK authorities and see if it is sufficiently broad to be compared with the degree of control exercised by a state government.

Is human rights law binding on international territorial administration?

The novelty brought by the establishment of international territorial administrations with extraordinary state-like powers has decisively proven that human rights violations are not only a pathology of a state government but can also affect non-state actors.[2] By exercising functions giving them direct power over individuals, the international territorial administrations become responsible for the violation of the rights of the people they govern. However, the privileges and immunity principles that shield the UN from the jurisdiction of the host country narrow the possibility of bringing a successful lawsuit in a domestic court against UN officials.

It has been observed that every international administration has been accused of having been involved in human rights violations of the population they governed.[3]

UN-established administrations were regularly treated as functional entities governed by the laws and principles applicable to international organisations even where they exercised governance functions in the role of a "surrogate state (e.g., in terms of privileges and immunities, legal obligations and intra-institutional power-sharing).[4] They were governed by internal laws that determine the institutional and procedural limitations of the international organisations and the mechanisms for supervision and monitoring of their activities (reporting, financial and administrative control, judicial review).[5] However, these laws proved not to be sufficient for establishing an adequate accountability regime. On the other hand, the domestic laws of the governed entity, the UNSC resolutions, as well as the ITA's regulations enacted for the purpose of administering the territory, reflected an ambiguous language, which enabled the ITA's actors to shield themselves.[6]

2 Guglielmo Verdirame, *The UN and Human Rights, Who Guards the Guardians*, Cambridge University Press, 2011, p. 55.

3 Ibid., p. 243.

4 For an overall overview of human rights violations that occurred in past ITA missions, see *supra* n. 1, pp. 243–244. See also C. Stahn, *Accountability and Legitimacy in Practice: Law-making by Transitional Administrations*, 11 *International Peacekeeping*, available at: www.esil-sedi.org/english/pdf/Stahn.PDF.

5 International Law Association, *Accountability of International Organisations*, Final Report, Berlin Conference, 2004, p. 20.

6 Although UNSC Resolution 1244 empowers the administration to "protect and promote human rights", in practice only local actors were to abide by it, whereas the international actors remained exempted from responsibility in terms of human rights violations.

Consequently, a range of questions arose about the possibility of applying existing human rights law to international territorial administration, particularly from the specific perspective of protecting individuals. Do ITAs as political entities bear international institutional responsibility for their acts? If so, is it similar to the responsibility of a state? Can the extraterritorial application of human rights conventions serve as an option for holding ITAs accountable? Or can ITAs carry on the treaty obligations of the previous government and continue to provide protection to the inhabitants they govern?

Despite the fact that the list of subjects of international law has been greatly expanded in recent decades, embracing non-state actors such as individuals, non-governmental organisations and multinational corporations, it appears that when it comes to the international human rights framework the state remains a dominant subject with regard to duties and rights in the international system. International organisations, including the two largest organisations, namely the United Nations and the Council of Europe,[7] which are directly involved in drafting and overseeing the implementation of these conventions in practice, have no direct human rights obligations under the existing international human rights framework.[8]

It has been submitted that the UN Charter, together with the international covenants and the Universal Declaration of Human Rights (UDHR), should be seen as the constitution of the organisation and as such should be applicable to UN peacekeeping operations.[9] Nevertheless, this submission was rejected by scholars, who considered that such an assertion lacked legal recognition since neither the international covenants nor the UDHR were conceptualised by the United Nations and its member states as a constitution that could serve the organisation.[10]

7 The EU is considered an exception as it has become a signatory party to the UN Convention on the rights of persons with disabilities. Moreover, the entry into force of the Treaty of Lisbon has brought additional challenges as it empowers the EU to accede to the European Convention for the protection of Human Rights and Fundamental Freedoms. See Jan Wouters, Eva Brems, Stefaan Smiss, and Pierre Schmitt (eds.), *Accountability of International Organizations for Violations of the Human Rights of Staff*, Intersentia, 2010, p. 5.

8 Chittharanjan Felix Amerasinghe, Accountability of International Organizations for Violations of the Human Rights of Staff, in Jan Wouters, Eva Brems Stefaan Smiss and Pierre Schmitt (eds.), *Accountability for Human Rights Violations by International Organizations*, Intersentia, 2010, p. 527. See also Ralph Wilde, International Territorial Administration and Human Rights, in Nigel White and Dirk Klaasen (eds.), *The UN, Human Rights and Post-Conflict Situations*, Manchester University Press, 2005, p. 152.

9 See Pierre Marie Dupuy, *Constitutional Dimension of the Charter of the United Nations Revisited*, Vol. 1, Max Planck Yearbook of United Nations Law, 1997. It should be noted that Dupuy reminds us that the perception that “the UN Charter has become the constitution of the international communities” is an expression that entails in part a metaphorical dimension. See also Boris Kondoch, Human Rights Law and UN Peace Operations in Post-Conflict Situations, in Nigel White and Dirk Klaasen (eds.), *The UN, Human Rights and Post-Conflict Situations*, Manchester University Press, 2005, p. 37.

10 Kondoch, challenging the view of Dupuy. Ibid., p. 37.

In addition, it has been argued that the human rights obligations of UN peacekeeping operations derives from their mandate, which provides the legal basis for the functioning of the UN peacekeeping operations, namely the specific clause enshrined in their mandate that requires human rights observance.[11]

However, it is evident that neither UNSC resolutions establishing an ITA nor internal documents that regulate the functioning of UN peacekeeping operations (rules of engagement, rules of conduct for peacekeeping) contain a provision that confirms the application of human rights instruments to UN peacekeeping operations.[12] Moreover, it has been observed that current models for status of forces agreements and participation agreements, known as Status of Force Agreements (SOFAs) and Status of Mission Agreements (SOMA), continue to lack a clear legal framework and do not contain a specific clause that refers to human rights obligations.[13] As a result, in practice they cause friction between the UN peacekeeping mission and the host state.[14]

Consequently, many legal scholars were motivated to explore the precise extent of the international obligations which are incumbent on the governing structure of an international territorial administration. In this context, it has been recognised that the UN "is bound transitively by international human rights standards as a result and to the extent that its members are bound", meaning that "the United Nations is bound by a type of functional treaty succession by international organizations to the position of their member states".[15]

Traditionally, there are two possible scenarios that may involve the responsibilities of international organisations for internationally wrongful acts: a) when it is found that a member country has direct or indirect involvement in the act or decision of the international organisation; and b) when the complaint refers to a structural gap in the internal dispute-settlement mechanism.[16] It follows

11 Ibid., pp. 33–36.

12 Eric de Brabandere, *Post-Conflict Administrations in International Law*, Martinus Nijhof Publishers, 2009, p. 96.

13 Participation agreements define the duties of peacekeeping operations and its members, while Status Force Agreements (SOFAs) are bilateral or multilateral agreements that define the legal position of the military and civilian personnel operating on the territory of the receiving country. Participation agreements contain the basic rights, privileges, and immunities of UN officials, including regulations on property and dispute settlement. See Aurel Sari, Status Forces and Status Mission Agreements under ESDP, the EU's Evolving Practice, *European Journal of International Law*, Vol. 19, No. 1, 2008.

14 Scott Sheeran and others, UN *Peace Keeping and the Model of Status Forces Agreement, United Nations Peace-Keeping*, Law Reform Project, Essex School of Law, February 2011, available at the following website: www.essex.ac.uk/plrp/.

15 This is called the hybrid conception, which incorporates both an internal conception, which claims that the binding character flows from the membership of the organization, and an external conception, which claims that the state "brings in" the human rights norms and makes them binding within the borders. See Frederic Megret and Florian Hoffmann, The UN as Violator? Some Reflections on the United Nations Changing Human Rights Responsibilities, *Human Rights Quarterly*, Vol. 25, No. 2, 2003, pp. 317–319.

16 Cedric Ryngaert, Responsibility of Member States, in Connection with Acts of International Organisations: Assessing the Recent Case Law of the European Court of Human Rights, *International and Comparative Law Quarterly*, Vol. 16, October 2011, p. 1006.

that Member States cannot be held liable, concurrently or subsidiarily, for the acts that involve international organisations solely by virtue of their status of being member of the organisations. Moreover, states cannot incur responsibilities for eventual structural lacunae within the internal accountability regime of an international organisation[17] In this light, the following discussion will proceed to examine the scenario that involves UN's responsibility in an ITA context. After the emergence of the recent practice of international territorial administrations, which in many ways resembled a state administration, it became clear that there was a need to demonstrate the legal implications arising from this new renewal and development of international law. In this regard, it has been suggested that the whole matter should be taken beyond a traditional state-centred approach of international law.[18] This debate has focused on addressing the world's overall challenge arising from the changing role of states and non-state actors in international law.[19]

In this regard, it has been emphasised that the immense growth and unprecedented scope of activities exercised by non-state actors such as international organisations in the past two decades have demonstrated that there is an immediate need to extend the current normative human rights framework to non-state actors.[20]

The adoption of the Draft Articles on Responsibility of International Organisations (DARIO), which came into play recently, marked a historic occasion as it provides a strong framework for promoting the responsibilities of international organisations.[21] It enshrines a multiple attribution rule that provides a ground of responsibility for both a state and an international organisation (Article 5).

It is necessary to note that during their adoption, the International Law Commission (ILC) was faced with numerous challenges which did not favour the applicability of human rights law to international organisations. Several states

17 "There is no general rule of international law whereby States members are, due solely to their membership, liable, concurrently or subsidiarily, for the obligations of an international organization of which they are members", 1996 resolution of the Institut de Droit International, quoted in Ryngaert, *supra* n. 16, p. 997.

18 Christina Voigt, The Role of General Principles in International Law and Their Relationship to Treaty Law, *Retfaerd Argang*, 31, No. 2/121, 2008, p. 4. The development of national and international governmental organisations has influenced the "very path of making international law" by offering different statements, resolutions, draft codes, and numerous instruments that clarify the content of international law. See Theo Van Boven, Distinguishing criteria of Human Rights, in Henry J. Steiner, Philip Alston, Ryan Goodman (eds.), *International Human Rights in Context, Law: Politics, Morals*, Third Edition, Oxford Press, 2008, p. 161.

19 Eric de Brabandere, *State Centrism and Human Rights Obligations, Challenging "Stateless" Approaches towards Direct Corporate Responsibility*, International Law Association, Research Seminar on non state actors, 26–28, 2009 Leuven, Belgium, available at: http://ghum.kuleuven.be/ggs/projects/non_state_actors/publications/de_brabandere.pdf.

20 Ibid. For more about the expanding scope of international law, see Andrew Clapham, *Human Rights Obligations of Non-State Actors*, Oxford University Press, 2006.

21 Draft Articles on Responsibilities of International Organizations, Adopted by the International Law Commission at Its Sixty-Third Session, 2011.

argued that "there was no customary international law on the responsibility of international organizations" and that the entire matter lacked institutional practice.[22] Despite numerous difficulties, the ILC succeeded in launching 66 articles referring to the responsibilities of international organisations, which make clear that an international organisation can incur responsibility. It should be underlined that as a non-binding document they have not yet reached a central place in international law. Although cited by the Strasbourg judges as relevant international law,[23] they were not used as guidance to determine the attribution of conduct. Thus there is a general assumption that their application in practice may not be easy.[24] An overview of doubts regarding the application of DARIO's principles in practice will be provided under the section which discusses the notion of delegation of powers. However, it should be underlined that DARIO's principles are not included in the legal analysis in the following sections.[25]

Does innovation in recent ITA practice affect existing human rights law?

The foregoing section has mentioned two possible scenarios that may incur the responsibility of the Member States for the acts of international organisations. The following discussion will focus on discussing the situation when an international organisation assumes state-like powers.

That the very establishment of recent ITA practice in Kosovo and East Timor has brought an innovation to the area of international law is an indisputable fact. It is the first time in history that an international organisation has undertaken the role of a surrogate state and could exercise it for a long period of time.[26]

The organisation's far-reaching immunity from the national legal system makes it impossible to initiate a successful proceeding before the domestic courts. Moreover, taking into consideration that existing international mechanisms are designed to deal with states only, any possibility of bringing the UN before such mechanisms remains minimal.

22 Verdirame, *supra* n. 2, p. 92.

23 ECtHR, *Agim and Bekim Behrami v, France and Ruzhdi Saramati v. France Germany and Norway, (Behrami and Saramati)*, Admissibility Decision of 2 May 2007.

24 "The diversity of international organizations may affect the application of certain articles, some of which may not apply to certain international organizations in the light of their powers and functions". See ILC Draft Articles on Responsibilities of International Organizations, with commentaries, para 7.

25 The DARIO principles have been questioned by many scholars for their "over-reliance" on the ILC's State Responsibilities Articles and as such failed to include practical examples. See Ryngaert, *supra* n. 16, p. 999.

26 Its precedents did not have the opportunity to administer a foreign territory fully. See Michael J. Matheson, United Nations Governance of Post Conflict Societies, Symposium: State Reconstruction after Civil Conflict, *The American Journal of International Law*, Vol. 95, No. 76, 2001, p. 81.

Following UNMIK's establishment, the first suggestion that came on stage was the possibility of extending the treaty obligations of human rights conventions from the original to the temporary sovereign. Unfortunately, it brought more controversy than clarification.

For instance, the Human Rights Committee considered that

> the rights guaranteed under the Covenant belong to the people living in the territory of a State party, and, once a people are accorded the protection of the rights under the Covenant, such protection devolves with the territory and continues to belong to them notwithstanding changes in the administration of territories.[27]

Conversely, in its report submitted to the United Nations Human Rights Committee (HRC), the UNMIK authorities made it clear that though they had been subjected to the HRC's reporting procedure as an international human right mechanism, this "does not imply that these treaties and conventions are in any way binding upon UNMIK".[28] This presumption arose from UNMIK's own interpretation of UNSC Resolution 1244, as well as Article 103 of the UN Charter, which according to the UNMIK authorities form legal grounds that prevail over obligations under any other international agreement in case of conflict.[29]

The Venice Commission also issued interpretative guidance which is totally opposite to that issued by the HRC. It considered that the human rights treaties concluded by the original sovereign were no longer applicable to an internationally administered territory where the original sovereign did not exercise its sovereign rights. In this context, it has been stated that "it cannot, in particular, be maintained that the Convention, as well as the jurisdiction of the European Court of Human Rights in Kosovo, applies because Serbia and Montenegro has ratified the Convention and because UNMIK should be seen as a 'care-taker' for Serbia and Montenegro, having assumed the obligations by Serbia and Montenegro under the European Convention of Human Rights or having succeeded in those obligations".[30]

27 Human Rights Committee, Consideration of Reports Submitted by State Parties under Article 40 of the Covenant, Concluding Observations Kosovo (Serbia), CCPR/C/UNK/CO/1, 87th Session, 14 August 2006.

28 See *Report to Human Rights Committee*, UNMIK, para 123–124. For an extensive analysis, see Lindsay Cameron, *Human Rights Accountability of International Civil Administrations to the People Subject to Administration*, Presentation for the International Conference: *Accountability for Human Rights Violations by International Organizations*, Brussels, 17 March 2007, Human Rights International Legal Discourse, Vol. 2. Conference Reader, pp. 10–11.

29 Bernhard Knoll, *The Legal Status of Territories Subject to Administration by International Organizations*, New York: Cambridge University Press, 2008, p. 361.

30 European Commission for Democracy through Law (Venice Commission), *Opinion on Human Rights Possible Establishment of Review Mechanisms Kosovo*, adopted on its 60th Plenary Session, 8–9 October 2004, para 78.

The rationale behind this position is the following: "Such a theory would not be limited to the Convention, and indeed not to Kosovo. It implies the assertion that all UN interim administrations would have to respect all treaties which the state on whose territory they operate has concluded, and continues to conclude. Such a rule would contradict the need for the UN to establish and implement a mandate".[31]

Yet, it seems that the Commission's opinion had an impact on the application of the ECHR only, since the other international instruments continued to apply. For instance, UNMIK was asked to produce reports on the compliance of domestic standards and practices with covenant rights arising from the ICCPR. In addition, the monitoring committee of the ICESCR asked UNMIK to report on the human rights situation pursuant to its obligations under UNSC Resolution 1244.[32] Moreover, UNMIK also concluded an agreement with the Council of Europe by which it accepts being subjected to the European Committee for the prevention of Torture and Other Cruel and Inhuman and Degrading Treatment.[33] In addition, pursuant to the agreement reached between the Council of Europe and UNMIK, the UNMIK authorities continued to report to the Council of Europe Advisory Committee on National Minorities.[34]

31 Ibid., para 78. This is in line with the argument presented by Bernard Knoll, who argues that UNMIK's reluctance to accept treaty obligations signed after Milosevic's removal (or the installation of UNMIK) is in conformity with Article 43 of the 1907 Hague Regulations (law in force), which entails that the UNMIK authorities are not bound to respect laws enacted by the absent territorial sovereign. Knoll, *supra* n. 29, p. 361.

32 See Human Rights Committee, *Concluding Observations*, 14 August 2006, CCPR/C/UNK/CO/1. As stated by the Human Rights Committee, "the Committee decided that the provisions of the *International Covenant on Civil and Political Rights* (ICCPR) were still applicable in Kosovo". See Human Rights Committee, Consideration of Country Report, *The United Nations Interim Administration of UNMIK* (initial report); 87th Session, Geneva, 10 July–28 July 2008. See also Human Rights Committee, Concluding Observations of Committee on Economic, Social and Cultural Rights documents submitted by UNMIK, 1 December 2008.

33 On 23 August 2004, UNMIK concluded an agreement with the Council of Europe to implement the Convention for the prevention of Torture and Other Cruel and Inhuman and Degrading Treatment. It should be emphasised that with regard to its implementation, there were some delays on the ground as the KFOR authorities refused to allow the European Committee for the Prevention of Torture and Inhuman or Degrading Treatment or Punishment to access detention facilities that were under their control. See Ombudsman Institution in Kosovo, Fifth Annual Report (2004–2005), addressed to Special Representative of the Secretary General of the United Nations, p. 27. The CPT's report to UNMIK reveals no information regarding its visit to KFOR's detention centres. It says that in July 2006, arrangements were made with NATO to allow the CPT also to visit KFOR's detention facilities. See the European Committee for the Prevention of Torture and Other Cruel and Inhuman and Degrading Treatment (CPT) Report to *International Interim Administration in Kosovo (UNMIK) on the visit to Kosovo, carried out by the European Committee for the Prevention of Torture and Other Cruel and Inhuman and Degrading Treatment (CPT) from 21to 29 March 2007*, CPT/Inf, 2009/03, published on 20 January 2009.

34 Agreement concluded on 23 August 2004.

Thus, it is difficult to understand why the Venice Commission has taken such a strict position, which does not go in favour of human rights protection. Cameron finds the Commission's stand acceptable because when UNMIK arrived the then FRY was not party to the ECHR, although Serbia, as its successor, ratified the Convention in 2004.

Yet one may note that the author failed to detect that a similar scenario appears to arise regarding the applicability of other human rights instruments. For instance, the ICCPR was ratified by Serbia in 2001, two years after the establishment of the UNMIK administration in Kosovo.[35] Moreover, Serbia is not considered to be a SFRY successor because according to the Arbitration Commission of the Conference for Peace in Yugoslavia, known as the Badinter Arbitration Committee, the new states that were created as a result of the dissolution of Yugoslavia cannot claim to be the sole successor of the former Yugoslavia or the former membership of the Socialist Federal Republic of Yugoslavia in any international organisations.[36]

So both instruments are present on the same territory that corresponds to the same factual situation and it is difficult to understand why the ECHR should be considered an exemption.[37] Like the ICCPR, the ECHR provides the same spectrum of protection. The only reason why the applicability of the ICCPR and other instruments is seen as less complex than the ECHR might possibly be because of the specificities arising from the individual complaints system of the ECHR, which compared to the ICCPR requires a more concrete enforcement mechanism. Moreover, the ECHR is a regional human rights instrument and is central to the operation of the Council of Europe. It has become a precondition for the Council of Europe's membership, whereas the ICCPR enjoys more

35 This was not the first time that the HRC requested a successor state to submit a report notwithstanding that it had not acceded to the ICCPR. For instance, on 7 October 1992 the Chairman of the HRC requested the governments of the Republic of Bosnia-Herzegovina, the Republic of Croatia, and the Federal Republic of Yugoslavia (Serbia and Montenegro) to submit reports to the Committee. See Johannes Chan, State Succession to Human Rights Treaties, Hong Kong and International Covenant on Civil and Political Rights, *International and Comparative Law Quarterly*, Vol. 45, No. 4, October 1996.

36 The Badinter Arbitration Committee was established on 27 August 1991 by the Council of Ministers of the European Economic Community. For more about the Badinter Arbitration Committee, Opinions 9 and 10, see Alain Pellet, The Opinions of the Badinter Arbitration Committee a Second Breath for the Self-Determination of Peoples, *European Journal of International Law*, Vol. 3, 1992. See also Danilo Turk, Recognition of States: A Comment, *European Journal of International Law*, Vol. 4, 1993.

37 Mansson sees the exemption of UNMIK from human rights treaty obligations to be right because such an undertaking might bring into question the sovereignty rights of the original state. However, subjecting UNMIK to the treaty control of ICCPR and other human rights instruments proved not to be an act of infringement of Serbia's sovereignty. Katarina Mansson, Implementing the Concept of Protection of Civilian in the Lights of Humanitarian Law and Human Rights Law: The Case of Monuc, in Roberta Arnold and Noelle Quiniver (eds.), *International Humanitarian Law and Human Rights Law: Towards New Merger of International Law*, Martinus Nijhoff Publisher, 2008, p. 562.

independence within the UN system and the complaints procedure is under the sole competence of the HRC.[38]

In light of these considerations, one may highlight that the prospect of holding UNMIK accountable for its wrongdoings is minimal. This problem is exacerbated by the fact that the UN civilian missions do not appear alone but are nowadays accompanied by military contingents. Consequently, it becomes difficult to determine eventual responsibility for the wrongdoing.

Despite the complexity, legal scholars continue to seek options for initiating proceedings for human rights violations occurring under the umbrella of the UN's peacekeeping and peacebuilding operations. In this regard, much of the following section is focused on discussing the complexity of the reality that surrounds the development of a credible accountability system for the victims affected by the ITA's wrongdoings.

To what extent is customary international law binding on international territorial administrations?

The current limitations arising from international human rights treaties make it unachievable for international territorial administrations to be directly bound by their norms.[39] In this regard, one may turn at customary international law as an auxiliary source that fills in the gap when no specific treaty norm governs the matter at issue.

Customary international law forms a constituent element of international law, as some of the fundamental rules of international law derive from customary law.[40]

Some authors consider customary law to be a "gap-filler of international law",[41] while others believe that customary international law has become a *Deus ex machina* of international law.[42] The important feature of customary international

38 For more about the differences between the ICCPR and the ECHR, see Magdalena Forowicz, *The Reception of International Law in the European Court of Human Rights*, Oxford University Press, 2010, pp. 152–153.

39 On 1st June 2010, the EU accessed to the ECHR. The accession became a legal obligation under the Treaty of Lisbon, which entered into force on 1 December 2009. Since 7th July 2010, there is an ongoing debate regarding the modalities on the accession, namely negotiating the relationship between the European Court on Human Rights and the Court of Justice of the European Union. Although EU's accession to the ECHR should be considered a significant step towards enforcing human rights laws in Europe, yet it is still to be seen whether the future accession agreement will oblige the EU's missions to fully uphold to the ECHR regime, for instance the current EULEX mission in Kosovo.

40 Vojin Dimitrijevic, Customary Law as an Instrument for the Protection of Human Rights, *Insituto per gli Studi di Politica Internacionale*, WP 7, 2006, pp. 14–15.

41 Jan Wouters and Dries van Eackhoutte, *Giving Effect to Customary International Law through European Community Law*, Working Paper No. 25, The Institute for International Law, K.U Leuven, June 2002, p. 14.

42 See Samuel Estreicher, Rethinking the Binding Effects of Customary International Law, *Virginia Journal of International Law*, Vol. 33, 2003, p. 5.

law is that for different from treaty rules, it applies even to states that did not consent to its rules.[43]

According to D'Amato, a custom reflects universality, since "custom is, traditionally at least, the only source of international law that yields universal norms".[44]

The traditional theory of customary international law highlights that the existence of a rule of customary international law requires the presence of two essential elements, namely state practice (*usus*) and *opinio juris*.[45]

The theory has been legitimised by the judgement of the International Court of Justice (ICJ) in the *North Sea Continental Shelf* case:

> Although the passage of only a short period of time is not necessarily, or of itself, a bar to the formation of a new rule of customary international law on the basis of what was originally purely conventional rule, an indispensable requirement would be that within the period in question, short though it may be, State practice, including that of states whose interests are especially affected, should have been both extensive and virtually uniform in the sense of the provision invoked. Not only must the acts concerned amount to settled practice, but they must also be such or be carried out in such a way, as to be evidence of a belief that this practice is rendered obligatory by the existence of a rule of law requiring it. The need for such a belief, i.e. the existence of a subjective element, is implicit in the very notion of the opinio juris sive necessitatis. The states concerned must therefore feel that they are conforming to what amounts to their legal obligation. The frequency or even habitual character of the acts is not in itself enough.[46]

It follows that a rule comes about "through the emergence of a general, uniform, consistent and settled practice, more or less gradually joined by a sense of legal obligation(a belief in legal obligation), the *opinio juris*".[47] State practice is given priority in this process, which shows that the formation of a rule of customary international law originates from the activities performed by the state.[48]

According to Buergenthal and Murphy,

> the practice of states' means official governmental conduct reflected in a variety of acts, including official statements at international conferences and

43 Dimitrijevic, *supra* n. 40, pp. 14–15.

44 Anthony D'Amato, *Human Rights as a Part of Customary International Law: A Plea for Change of Paradigms*, Faculty Working Paper, Northwestern University School of Law Scholarly Commons, 2010.

45 Robert Jennings and Arthur Watts, *Oppenheim's International Law*, Vol. 1, Ninth Edition, Oxford University Press, pp. 26–28, See also Malcolm Shaw, *International Law*, Sixth Edition, Cambridge University Press, 2008, pp. 73–75.

46 ICJ, *North Sea Continental Shelf*, ICJ Reports, 1969, paras 74 and 77.

47 When the states believe that they have a legal duty to think so. See Malcolm Shaw, *International Law*, Sixth Edition, Cambridge University Press, 2008, pp. 73–75, 419.

48 Ibid., p. 74. See also, Grigory Ivanovich Tunkin, Remarks on the Judicial Nature of the Customary International Norms, of International Law, *California Law Review*, Vol. 49, No. 3, August 1961, p. 419.

> in diplomatic exchanges, formal instructions to diplomatic agents, national court decisions, legislative measures or other actions taken by governments to deal with matters of international concern. Inaction can also be deemed a form of state practice.[49]

With this in mind, I proceed to examine the process of elevating human rights norms to norms of customary international law.[50] So which norms in existing human rights treaties form the basis of customary international human rights law?

The substance of the United Nations Charter can serve as a point of departure for tracing the passage of the international customary law of human rights. In this regard, scholars agree that the Charter has given an international dimension to human rights. As argued, its norms reflect the values of the "international community", which have been widely accepted by the vast majority of states.[51]

In addition, scholars place particular emphasis on the Universal Declaration of Human Rights (UDHR). They unequivocally argue that the UDHR generates customary international law and as such has played an important role in strengthening international custom.[52]

The International Court of Justice referred directly to the UDHR's principles and confirmed that the fundamental principles enunciated in the UDHR provide proof of the existence of universal human rights.[53]

The UDHR has paved the way for the adoption of numerous human rights conventions, which have been ratified by over half of the world community and which taken together have greatly contributed towards the formation of the customary rules of human rights.[54] Yet there are authors who try to draw attention to distinctions

49 Buergenthal and Murphy, *Public International Law in a Nutshell*, Fourth Edition, West Academic Publishing, Minnesota, 2007.

50 For more about the evolution of customary international law, see Tunkin, *supra* n. 48.

51 Namely in its preamble and articles 1.3 and 55c, which encourage "respect for human rights and for fundamental freedoms for all without distinctions as to race, sex, language, or religion". For additional analysis, see Michael K. Addo, *The Legal Nature of International Human Rights*, Martinus Nijhoff Publishers, 2010, pp. 139–143.

52 Bruno Simma and Philip Alston, The Sources of Human Rights Law, Custom, Jus Cogens, and General Principles, *Australian Yearbook of International Law*, Vol. 85, No. 12, 1988–1989, p. 84.

53 It stated that "wrongfully to deprive human beings of their freedom and to subject them to physical constraint in conditions of hardship is in itself manifestly incompatible with the principles of the Charter of the United Nations, as well as with the fundamental principles enunciated in the Universal Declaration of Human Rights". See International Court of Justice (ICJ), *The Teheran Hostages Case, the United States v. Iran*, Case Concerning United States Diplomatic and Consular Staff in Teheran, judgement 24 May 1980, para 42. Moreover it has been argued that the UDHR has been accepted as an authoritative part of customary international law. See The Van Boven, Distinguishing Criteria of Human Rights, in Henry J. Steiner, Philip Alston and Ryan Goodman (eds.), *International Human Rights in Context, Law: Politics, Morals*, Third Edition, Oxford Press, 2008, p. 161.

54 However, despite the polarisation among scholars on the question of whether the UDHR forms part of customary international law, the vast majority agree that it reflects customary international law. See Chittharanjan Felix Amerasinghe, Accountability of International

between different provisions of the UDHR, claiming that the rights promoted in the UDHR are not given equal weight in practice because not all of them have reached the status of international custom. The majority agrees that the prohibition of slavery, genocide, torture, mass killings, prolonged arbitrary imprisonment, and systematic racial discrimination have become customary international law.[55]

However, there are authors who refer to an extensive list of customary law norms, including the right to self-determination, the right to humane treatment of detainees, the prohibition of retroactive penal measures, the principles *ne bis in idem*, the right to equality before the law, the right to an independent and impartial trial, the right to presumption of innocence and many others.[56]

That the grounding of some international human rights law norms has found a solid base in customary law is an undeniable fact. Customary international law is legally binding regardless of whether a state has expressly accepted it. In this context, one may ask whether customary rules oblige international organisations as well.

Relying on the principle established by the ICJ in the *Reparations for Injuries* case, in which it upheld the position that international organisations are bound by obligations arising under general rules of international law, their constitution and the agreements to which they are parties,[57] de Brabandere advances a presupposition that international organisations can be bound by customary international law.[58]

Organizations for Violations of the Human Rights of Staff, in Jan Wouters, Eva Brems, Stefaan Smiss and Pierre Schmitt (eds.), *Accountability for Human Rights Violations by International Organizations*, Intersentia, 2010, p. 528. In Simma's and Alston's view there is still a split between scholars on whether the UDHR has gained the status of customary law. While the majority are in favour of a customary law of human rights based on the UDHR, there are scholars who consider that only parts of the UDHR have gained the status of custom in international law. An in-depth analysis is provided in Bruno Simma and Philip Alston, The Sources of Human Rights Law, Custom, Jus Cogens, and General Principles, *Australian Yearbook of International Law*, Vol. 85, No. 12, 1988–1989, pp. 86–92.

55 In Schachter's view, there are provisions that have not yet achieved the status of customary law, such as freedom of expression, equality between men and woman, and the right to work. See comments of Oscar Schachter in Bruno Simma and Philip Alston, The Sources of Human Rights Law, Custom, Jus Cogens, and General Principles, *Australian Yearbook of International Law*, Vol. 85, No. 12, 1988–1989, p. 92. See also, Romualdo P. Eclavea, Larissa J. Erkman, Edward K. Espring and Tracey Bateman Farell, *Force and Effect of International Law, American Jurisprudence*, Second Edition, The Lawyers Co-operative Publishing Co., 2010. Moreover, in its Advisory Opinion regarding Reservations to the Convention on the Prevention and Punishment of the Crime of Genocide, the ICJ referred to the principles of the Convention as "principles which are recognized by civilized nations as binding on States, even without any conventional obligations". See International Court of Justice Report, *Reservations to the Convention on the Prevention and Punishment of the Crime of Genocide*, 19, 1951.

56 Teodor Meron and Richard Lilich came out with an extensive list of rights, claiming that all of them are well-established customary law norms. Bruno and Alston referring to Meron's and Lilich's comments, See Bruno and Alston *supra* n. 55, pp. 92–93.

57 ICJ Advisory Opinion, *Reparation for Injuries Suffered in the Service of the United Nations*,11 April 1949, para 90.

58 Eric De Brabandere, *Post-Conflict Administrations in International Law*, Martinus Nijhof Publishers, 2009, p. 98.

He goes on to state that all those international human rights standards that have gained the status of international customary rules are binding on international organisations.[59]

Yet one of the most prominent aspects of the application of customary rules is that unlike treaties, it is difficult to determine the existence of rules of customary international law. Therefore, any attempt to establish the precise scope and content of such rules might be vague and uncertain.[60]

Subsequently, the ambiguities inherent in defining and using customary international human rights norms have sparked heated debates regarding their application in practice, before both domestic and international courts. Although customary international norms are often invoked by international bodies, it should be noted that such bodies have limited jurisdiction. Their jurisdictions mainly depend on state consent that is obtained either through a treaty or through a special agreement.[61] Due to the lack of a legislative body in the international system, the international courts lack clear guidance as how to apply customary norms in practice.[62]

It is therefore very uncertain whether an individual can submit a complaint before international mechanisms relying solely on customary human rights norms.[63]

However, let us move to the recent practice of the UN and see whether the innovation brought by this new type of practice in international law means that international organisation, in this case the UN, can form customary rules for themselves.

This automatically leads us to several questions. For instance, how widespread must practice be for it to lead to a new custom? What if the UN authorities are not willing or capable of putting that process into force? Or what if the practice of a current ITA is not in accordance with human rights principles? What are the consequences of such practice?

It has been argued that Article 38 of the ICJ Statute does not restrict international custom to being a product of state practice only, since it does not contain

59 Ibid., p. 99.

60 See Wouters and Eackhoutte, *supra* n. 41.

61 Paul Stephan, Disaggregating Customary International Law, *Duke Journal of Comparative and International Law*, Vol. 21, No. 191, 2010, p. 194. "The problem with custom is that, under the present state of doctrine, it is impossible to respond explicitly and definitively, or precisely, to these institutional design variables. Rather, the doctrine of custom, unlike treaty law, cannot be self-consciously adapted to particular types of cooperation problems". See also, Joel P. Trachtman, Persistent Objectors, Cooperation, and the Utility of Customary International Law, *Duke Journal of Comparative International Law*, Vol. 21, No. 221, 2010.

62 As Antony D'Amato would say, "the ICJ has been better at applying customary law than defining it". See Anthony D'Amato, Trashing International Customary Law, *American Journal of International Law*, Vol. 101, 1987, p. 81. See also Noora Arajarvi, Customary International Law and the Principle of Legality in International Criminal Courts, *Tilburg Law Review, Journal of International and European Law*, Vol. 15, No. 2, 2011, p. 167.

63 It should be noted that not all customary international law norms reached the level of peremptory norms.

an explicit reference to states or nations.[64] In this context, through their practice international organisations may provide new grounds that may in time acquire the character of customary law.[65]

Many intergovernmental organisations are (to some extent at least) international legal persons in their own right and are capable of performing acts which contribute to the formation of international law.

According to the Committee for Formation of Customary Law, international organisations can contribute to the formation of customary law. It states that "the depositary practice of the UN Secretary-General, as well as that of national chancelleries, and the military activities of that organization can contribute to the formation of customary rules relating to conduct during armed conflicts".[66]

Estreicher submits that today's customary law rules are no longer a state-centred, "bottom-up process" as they are made by academics, non-governmental organisations and other international groups.[67]

In addition, Schermers argues that the development of custom is relatively fast in international organisations. In his opinion, international organisations express themselves through resolutions which underline customary rules. In this regard, he considers that the development of such customary rules does not require any specific confirmation because they develop through the procedural field.[68]

But let us see whether this opinion can apply to the sphere of international organisations, namely the activities of the ITA, taking into consideration that such activities mainly originate from UNSC resolutions. In this regard, it raises a question as to whether UNSC resolutions can possibly have an effect on international customary law. Yet this question requires a look at the thematic and legal effects that the resolutions produce.

64 Robert Jennings and Arthur Watts, *Oppenheim's International Law*, Vol. 1. Ninth Edition, Oxford University Press, pp. 26–28, 47. See Also Noora Arajarvi, *From State Centrism to Where? The Formation of Customary International Law and Non–State Actors*, available at: http://ssrn.com/abstract=1599679.

65 Jennings and Watts, *supra* n. 64, p. 47. See also Arajarvi, *supra* n. 64; Peter Malanczuk, *Akehurst's Modern Introduction to International Law*, Seventh Edition, Routledge, 1997, pp. 39–45.

66 See the Statement of Principles Applicable to Formation of General Customary International Law, Final Report of the Committee on Formation of Customary (General) International Law, International Law Association, London Conference 2000, section 11.

67 See Samuel Estreicher, Rethinking the Binding Effects of Customary International Law, *Virginia Journal of International Law*, Vol. 33, 2003, p. 15.

68 Henry G. Schermers, *International Institutional Law*, Sijthoff and Noordhoff, the Netherlands, 1980, p. 1192. See also Jennings and Watts, *supra* n. 64, p. 46. D'Amato opposes this opinion. In his view, resolutions of the United Nations cannot be treated as a source of law, because this would result in the United Nations becoming a world legislature. According to him UN resolutions can only help interpret the provisions enshrined in the UN Charter. Anthony D'Amato, *Human Rights as a Part of Customary International Law: A Plea for Change of Paradigms*, Faculty Working Paper, Northwestern University School of Law Scholarly Commons, 2010.p. 4.

The very term "resolution" is considered to be generic, as it appears in two different forms, recommendations and decisions, and as such has been seen as lacking variable meaning in the Charter.[69]

The ICJ refers to "decisions" as binding resolutions, whereas "recommendations" appear to be of a non-binding nature. It follows that a resolution has a binding nature if it is capable of creating obligations for its addressee. On the other side, declarations are considered to be a sub-category of resolution.[70]

There are three basic types of legal effect that a resolution can produce: a) it can create obligations, rights and/or powers (substantive effects); b) it can make determinations of fact (e.g. that an alleged fact is true) or determine legal situations (e.g. that an obligation was violated), which trigger substantive effects ("causative effect"); and c) it provides how and when the substantive effects operate (so-called "modal effects").[71]

Moreover, it is considered that when unanimously adopted some resolutions may have equal legal force as treaties concluded in simplified form.[72] Nevertheless, it has been emphasised that the very fact that a resolution is unanimously adopted by a universally representative body such as General Assembly does not mean that it reflects an *opinio juris* or gives rise to a new customary law. Thus, it has been suggested that several elements need to be addressed in order to assess the legal significance of a resolution, namely the practice to which the resolution relates, the legal force of the resolution under a given treaty establishing the organisation, the course of debate and *travaux préparatoires*, showing the extent to which the resolution indicates a uniform trend. These elements help to assess whether a resolution expresses an *opinio juris*, since according to Jennings and Watts, there is a difference between voting and acting in practice. A state may vote for the adoption of a resolution but on the other side may act differently in practice, simply because very often it may find itself unable to adopt any practice related to the matter.[73] A similar approach was taken by Mendelson, who stated that "as a matter of principle, there is no reason why Assembly resolutions should not in appropriate circumstances be treated as evidence of the *opinio juris* of states (or at least those voting in favour), bearing in mind there is no particular form prescribed by the law for the expression of such beliefs".[74] Based on this assertion, Arajarvi concludes that resolutions represent international practice reproduced by international organisations acting in their own capacity, not as the representative of a state.[75]

69 See Marko Divac Oberg, The Legal Effects of Resolutions of the UN Security Council and General Assembly in the Jurisprudence of the ICJ, *The European Journal of International Law*, Vol. 16, No. 5, 2006, p. 880.
70 Some consider that declarations constitute a separate category. Marko Divac Oberg, p. 880.
71 Oberg, *supra* n. 69, p. 880.
72 Jennings and Watts, *supra* n. 64, p. 48.
73 Ibid., p. 49.
74 Quoted in Arajarvi, *supra* n. 64, p. 11.
75 Ibid., p. 23.

As the previous chapters show, the establishment of ITA is closely linked with UNSC resolutions. Besides expressing a political view regarding certain situations, most of the text of a resolution expresses an *opinio juris* regarding the rules enunciated through the resolution itself. In UNMIK's and UNTAET's cases, the UNSC resolutions reflect constituent documents that enable an international organisation to disguise itself in the form of surrogate state administrations, which means taking the role of a legislator and adopting laws that regulate all aspects of daily life within the given territory, acting as an executive authority as well as exercising judicial functions.

The foregoing discussion leads to the conclusion that international organisations can form customary international human rights rules for themselves.[76]

Yet de Brabandere reminds us that due regard should be paid to the element of time, which plays an important role in the process of forming international customary law norms. Since the recent practice of UN-run administrations has been relatively new, according to him it has not reached a sufficient level to pass "the time test" foreseen to be necessary for a certain conduct to become a customary rule. He strictly limits his analysis to the cases of Kosovo and East Timor, leaving out of scope the practice of previous international administrations as, according to him, they did not sufficiently contribute to the formation of the customary norms of human rights, since in many cases that practice proved to be of a short-term character or simply resulted in failed attempts.[77]

Before moving to the next section, I would like to recapitulate the argument of this section.

Customary law, although important, is not as effective as treaty law. It is an unsettled concept. Customary international law rules may result from the practice of international organisations. However, it remains unclear whether such rules will have general application or be binding upon international organisations only. Yet whatever contribution UNMIK's practice may have made to customary international law, there is no possibility for individuals in Kosovo to use customary international law to initiate complaints before international bodies because today's customary law does not contain a rule that allows complaints against a non-state entity such as an international administration. So in this context, it might not be a useful instrument to solve these types of problems. Thus any hope of remedy depends on conventional law. The following section shows how this degree of rigidity crept into the ECtHR in its development of a new logic of interpretation of the convention, maintaining a strict reservation from customary rules.

76 This is in line with the argument presented by Eric de Brabandere, *supra* n. 58, p. 99.

77 Referring to both the UN administration in West Irian, which was of a short-term character, and an attempt to establish UN administrations for Trieste and Jerusalem. Eric de Brabandere, *supra* n. 58, p. 99. See also Cameron, *supra* n. 28. p. 5.

The European Court of Human Rights: a source of hope or toothless human rights tiger?

The following section engages in discussing the issues that shape the engagement of the ECtHR with the reviewability of UNMIK's acts.

The opportunity to protect individuals from alleged human rights violations conducted by Troop Contributing Countries (TCC) was given to the European Court of Human Rights in the joined case *Behrami and Saramati*.[78]

The *Behrami case* involved complaints against KFOR and UNMIK concerning the death of one child and serious injuries inflicted on his brother as a consequence of cluster bomb explosions.

Both Behrami children were playing in an area of Mitrovica and found several undetonated cluster bombs which were dropped in 1999 during the armed conflict in Kosovo. One of them was killed instantly and the other severely injured.

The Behrami family brought an application against France invoking Article 2 (right to life) with the allegation that the mine clearance or site marking had been the responsibility of the French KFOR, whose troops controlled the area where the cluster mines were found, and that France thus bore responsibility under the ECHR for the failure to mark or defuse the undetonated cluster bombs.[79]

The *Saramati case* involved the complaint of an individual, Ruzhdi Saramati, who was arrested by UNMIK police officers in 2001 and later subjected to extrajudicial detention by KFOR for a period of several months. The applicant claimed that he had been arrested on the basis of an order issued by the KFOR commander, who at the time of arrest was a Norwegian national and later on a French general. Consequently, Ruzhdi Saramati lodged an application against two countries, Norway and France, taking into consideration the nationality background of the KFOR commanders. He invoked Article 5 (right to liberty and security) in conjunction with Articles 6 (fair trial) and 13 (right to a remedy) of the European Convention of Human Rights, claiming that he did not have access to a court and was subjected to illegal detention. He argued that he fell under the jurisdiction of Norway and France, since his arrest and detention were based on orders issued by the Norwegian and later the French Commander of KFOR.[80]

The case involved the attribution of conduct on the basis of the factual control exercised by the respective states (France, Germany, and Norway) through their military troops as well as on the basis of the institutional (control) link between the military troops and the organisation to which they belonged.

Although the Court was tasked with determining whether the alleged violations were committed within the jurisdiction of the respondent state,[81] it explicitly decided to change the route, stating that the overall task in the given cases was to

78 ECtHR, *Behrami and Saramati*, Admissibility Decision of 2 May 2007.

79 Ibid.

80 Ibid.

81 As foreseen by Article 1 of the ECHR.

examine not whether the respondent states exercised extraterritorial jurisdiction in Kosovo but far more centrally, "whether it is competent to examine under the Convention those States' contribution to the civil and security presences which did exercise the relevant control of Kosovo".[82]

Having so decided, the Court purposely skipped ruling on the extraterritorial obligations of the contracting states under the ECHR, instead choosing to approach the case from the point of view of linking the attribution to the mandates granted to UNMIK and KFOR.[83]

The reason for doing so appears to be the Court's reluctance to decide on issues involving state jurisdiction and norm conflict.

One of the central mistakes of the Court in this case was that it excluded the possibility of dual attribution, which goes contrary to Article 5 of DARIO, which forms part of the relevant law and practice in the decision of the Court.[84]

Article 5 of DARIO enshrines a multiple attribution rule that provides a ground for determining the responsibility of both a state and an international organisation involved in an operation and consequently enables the same act to be potentially attributable to both entities.[85]

Thus it remains unclear what legal basis the Court applied in the decision.[86]

Consequently, as it will be discussed later, it ended up with ambiguous sets of analyses, which proved to be contrary to the established rules of responsibility in international law.[87]

Although the Court ruled the case to be inadmissible, the reasoning it used in its admissibility decision is worthy of assessment, in particular its approach regarding the notions of delegation of powers and of the ultimate overall control test.

82 See *Behrami and Saramati Decision*, para 71. See Kjetil Larsen Mujezinovic, Attribution of Conduct in Peace Operation, "the Ultimate Authority Control Test, *The European Journal of International Law*, Vol. 19, No. 3, 2008, p. 511.

83 In this regard, the Court admitted that the requirements for the extraterritorial application of human rights had been met. See Marko Milanovic and Tatjana Papic, As Bad as It Gets: The European Court of Human Rights' Behrami and Saramati Decision and General International Law, *International and Comparative Law Quarterly*, Vol. 58, No. 2, 2009. The same opinion is shared by Kjetil Mujezinovic Larsen, who considers that although the Court knew that the requirements for extraterritorial applications had been met, but purposely decided to change the approach. See Larsen Mujezinovic, *supra* n. 82, p. 511.

84 The Draft Article 5 of DARIO and Article 6 of the Articles on State Responsibilities have been explicitly mentioned as "relevant law and practice", but were not addressed further in the decision. See *Behrami and Saramati* decision, paras 34–35; See also Larsen Mujezinovic, *supra* n. 82, pp. 512–513.

85 Article 5 of DARIO reads: "The conduct of an organ of a State or an organ or agent of an international organisation that is placed at the disposal of another international organisation shall be considered under international law an act of the latter organisation if the organisation exercises effective control over that conduct". See also Caitlin A. Bell, Reassessing Multiple Attribution: The International Law Commission and Behrami and Saramati Case, *International Law and Politics*, Vol. 42, No. 501, 2010, pp. 503–504.

86 See Larsen Mujezinovic, *supra* n. 82, pp. 512–513.

87 See Bell, *supra* n. 85, pp. 503–504. See also Milanovic and Papic, *supra* n. 83.

The notion of delegation of powers

In both applications, the applicants hold KFOR (as opposed to UNMIK) to be the relevant responsible organisation for the alleged violations, contending that they fell under the jurisdiction of respondent states within the meaning of article 1 of the ECHR.[88]

In this context, three legal issues were subject to the Court's examination. The first was the determination of which entity, KFOR or UNMIK, had a mandate to detain and demine in Kosovo at the relevant times. Secondly, it dealt with the issue of attribution and in this regard it examined whether the impugned action of KFOR (detention in *Saramati*) and inaction of UNMIK (failure to demine in *Behrami*) were attributable to the United Nations. Thirdly, it considered whether it was competent *ratione personae* to review any action or omission found to be attributable to the United Nations.[89]

As to the allegations regarding detention, the Court found that "issuing detention orders fell within the security mandate of KFOR", but that its omissions were attributable to the UN, "an organization of universal jurisdiction fulfilling its imperative collective security objective".[90] Accordingly, KFOR "was exercising lawfully delegated Chapter VII powers of the UNSC, so that the impugned action was, in principle, 'attributable' to the UN".

In relation to the issues that involved demining, the Court found that the impugned actions and omissions could be attributable to KFOR but not to the UN, since KFOR's role in the demining process was limited only to provide assistance to UNMIK. As to the allegations that involved demining, the Court responded that they were also attributable to the UN, since UNMIK was a subsidiary organ of the UN.[91] Yet when it comes to KFOR, NATO retained only operational control over KFOR troops.

Overall, it came to the conclusion that the alleged human rights violations were attributable to the United Nations and not to the respondent countries, and therefore the Court was not competent *ratione personae* to examine the relevant actions.

88 Though the Court found itself in the realm of Article 5 of International Commission's Draft Articles on Responsibility of International Organizations, it did not take into account the substance of the Article. Article 5 enshrines a multiple attribution rule that provides a ground of responsibility for both a state and an international organization involved in an operation. However, the Court concluded that NATO alone bore the weight of responsibility. See *Behrami and Saramati*, para 73. See also Bell, *supra* n. 85, 2010, pp. 503–504.

89 *Saramati and Behrami*, para 121.

90 Ibid., para 152.

91 The Court found that "issuing detention orders fell within the security mandate of KFOR and that the supervision of de-mining fell within UNMIK's mandate". In that respect, the Court considered that KFOR's failure to secure and provide information to UNMIK regarding the site where the detonation had taken place did not alter the mandate of UNMIK. See paras 122–126 and 140–141 of the *Behrami and Saramati* decision.

Scholars find it difficult to understand why the Court decided to link attribution with the mandate of KFOR and UNMIK.[92] In particular, the Court's interpretation of the notion of the delegation of powers has provoked responses from many scholars.[93]

In the Court's view, both UNMIK and KFOR were established pursuant to Chapter VII of the UN Charter.[94]

In this regard, UNMIK was acting as a subsidiary organ of the UNSC, while KFOR was exercising lawfully delegated Chapter VII powers of the UNSC.[95] Both were acting based on the delegation of powers.

Though invoking Chapter VII, which constitutes the foundation for the delegation of powers, the Court failed to consider whether such delegation was accompanied by sufficient overall control by the UNSC over KFOR. As noted, although the delegation of powers rests in the hands of the UNSC, it must ensure that it retains the right to issue decisions that have the power to override the decisions of its delegate at any time.[96]

Given this, one may ask whether the UNSC is in a position to issue binding decisions of a military nature that regulate the operational conduct of the KFOR mandate. Or does UNSC retain the right ultimately to override decisions issued by the KFOR commander?

According to the Kumanovo Agreement, the "KFOR commander is the final authority regarding interpretation of the Agreement and the security aspects of the peace settlement it supports. His determinations are binding on all Parties and persons".[97]

The Court based its reasoning on UNSC Resolution 1244, which required that a security international presence with substantial North Atlantic Treaty Organization participation must be deployed under unified command and control. Yet the language used in UNSC Resolution 1244 did not explicitly mention who would exercise such "unified command".[98] In reality the "unified command" was exercised by the NAC, the supreme NATO body, comprising NATO members.[99]

92 Milanovic and Papic, *supra* n. 83.

93 *Behrami and Saramati*, paras 140–141. See also, Milanovic and Papic, *supra* n. 83.

94 Ibid., *Behrami and Saramati*, para 129.

95 Ibid., paras 140–141. See also, Milanovic and Papic, *supra* n. 83.

96 Daan Sarooshi, *The United Nations and the Development of Collective Security: The Delegation by the Security Council of Its Chapter VII Powers*, Oxford University Press, 2000, pp. 37–41. See also Erica de Wet, *The Chapter VII Powers of the United Nations, Security Council*, Oxford and Portal Oregon, 2004, pp. 314–324.

97 See Article V of the Kumanovo Agreement.

98 "The international security presence with substantial North Atlantic Treaty Organization participation must be deployed under unified command and control and authorized to establish a safe environment for all people in Kosovo". See Annex 2 para 4 of UNSC Resolution 1244.

99 Daniel Sven Smyrek, *Internationally Administered Territories-International Protectorates*, Duncker and Humblot, 2006, pp. 184–185.

It has been noticed that in the official statements and correspondence by NATO member states and NATO itself, the KFOR authorities have consistently been referred to as a "NATO- led force".[100]

It is necessary to emphasise that the wording "unified command" reflects the political compromise achieved during the negotiations for establishing the UN administration in Kosovo. In order to overcome the Russian and FRY refusal to have the same military force that bombed the country involved in the peacekeeping mission, the parties agreed to incorporate the specified wording into UNSC Resolution 1244.[101]

So, the wording "North Atlantic Treaty Organization participation" was used as a political tool to convince Milosevic and his allies to sign the Kumanovo Agreement.[102]

It is difficult to understand the Court's approach in *Behrami and Saramati*, in particular if we take into consideration the previous case law, in which the delegation of powers was strictly linked from the state to an organisation.[103] For example, in *Waite and Kennedy v. Germany*, instituted by German citizens against the European Space Agency (ESA), the Court explicitly stressed the following:

> [W]here states establish international organizations in order to pursue or strengthen their co-operation in certain fields of activities, and where they attribute to these organizations certain competences and accord them immunities, there may be implications as to the protection of fundamental rights. It would be incompatible with the purpose and object of the Convention, however, if the Contracting states were thereby absolved from their responsibility under the Convention in relation to the field of activity covered by such attribution. . . . [A] material factor in determining whether granting ESA immunity from German jurisdiction is permissible is whether the applicants had available to them reasonable alternative means to protect effectively their rights under the Convention.[104]

The transfer of power to an international organisation was further clarified in the *Bosphorus* case, in which it was maintained that the Convention States might

100 Ibid., pp. 184–185.
It has been noted that NATO was explicitly mentioned only in Annex 2, para 4 of UNSC Resolution 1244. The rest of the Resolution refers to the international security presence. See *supra* n. 99, Daniel Sven Smyrek, *International Administered Territories-International Protectorates*, Duncker and Humblot, 2005, pp. 184–185.

101 Smyrek, *supra* n. 99, pp. 184–185.

102 By contrast with UNSC Resolution 1244, the Rambouillet Accords explicitly provided that NATO forces would be deployed in Kosovo, consisting of ground, air and maritime units from NATO and non-NATO nations operating under the authority and political control of NAC (Chapter VII, Article 1 para 1b). Quoted in Smyrek, *supra* n. 99, p. 185.

103 *Matthews v. the United Kingdom*, App. No. 24833/94, ECtHR, judgement of 18 February 1999, *Waite and Kennedy v. Germany*, App. No. 26083/94, ECtHR, judgement of 18 February 1999. See also *M and Co v. Federal Republic of Germany*, ECtHR Decision on Admissibility, 9 February 1990.

104 *Waite and Kennedy*, paras 67–68.

transfer their sovereign power to an international organisation "as long as the relevant organization is considered to protect fundamental rights, as regards both the substantive guarantees offered and the mechanisms controlling their observance, in a manner which can be considered at least equivalent to that for which the Convention provides".[105]

Similar findings appear in the judgment of *Matthews v. the United Kingdom* when deliberating on a complaint brought by a British citizen residing in Gibraltar against her exclusion from participating in the election to the European Parliament. The Court found that even in cases where there was a transfer of competencies to an international organisation, in this case the European Commission, the rights guaranteed by the Convention continued to be secured.[106] It reaffirmed that "[t]he Convention does not exclude the transfer of competencies to international organizations provided that Convention rights continue to be 'secured'. Member States' responsibility therefore continues even after such a transfer".[107]

Given all this, it follows that even in cases where powers are transferred from Member States to international organisations, the protection of the individual from human rights violations committed by the Member State remains intact. Yet the Court failed to clarify "at what point Member States' responsibility for the wrongful acts of an international organisation is triggered". For instance, is responsibility taken on simply by transferring competencies or does this only occur in case an international organisation fails to offer equivalent rights protection?[108] Moreover, it failed to provide a clear reasoning as to who incurs responsibility in a joint enterprise designed for overall operation of two organisations.

Effective/overall test vs. ultimate authority and control test

Another confusion resulting from the *Behrami and Saramati* decision is the determination of the degree of control exercised by the actors deemed to have been responsible for the alleged violations.

It should be emphasised that whether or not an act of a violation can be attributed to an outside power depends on how one defines the exercise of control. This needs to be effective so that the power which exercises it has effective control over abuses, meaning that it can prevent violations of human rights.[109]

105 ECtHR, *Bosphorus Hava Yollarim Torizm ve Ticaret Anonim Sirketi v. Ireland*, App. No. 45036/98, judgement of 30 June 2005.

106 *Matthews v. the United Kingdom*, p. 138.

107 Ibid., para 157.

108 Ryngaert, *supra* n. 16, pp. 1001–1002.

109 Interestingly, Dannenbaum considers that the core issue of this problem is not effective control over territory or victims, but effective control over the actors that commit the violations. See Tom Dannenbaum, Translating the Standard of Effective Control into a System of Effective Accountability: How Liability Should be Apportioned for Violations of Human Rights by Member State Troop Contingents Serving as United Nations Peacekeepers, *Harvard International Law Journal*, Vol. 51, Winter 70, 2010, pp. 80, 189–190.

There are two known tests in international jurisprudence that have emerged for the purpose of determining the degree of control exercised by foreign powers in order to attribute their responsibility. They are the effective control test, which was set out by the International Court of Justice (ICJ) in the *Nicaragua* case; and the overall control test, laid down in the *Tadic* case by the International Tribunal of Former Yugoslavia (ICTY).

The *Nicaragua* case was concerned with the responsibility of the US regarding the military and paramilitary activities of the opposition group Contras, operating in and against Nicaragua.[110]

In light of this, the Court addressed the question whether the Contras could be regarded as agents of the US. In this regard, it asserted that the United States would be held responsible if such "acts could be attributed to the United States only if that State had effective control of the operations in the course of which the alleged violations were committed".[111] It held that in order to meet the test, the state should exercise sufficient control in all fields, such as financing, organising, training, supplying and equipping the Contras, the selection of its military or paramilitary targets, and the planning of the whole of their operations. Accordingly, there are three types of person involved in such operation, a) those who do not have the status of *de jure* organs of a state but nevertheless act on behalf of that state, b) those totally dependent on the foreign state and paid, equipped, generally supported by and operating according to the planning and direction of organs of that state, and c) persons who, although paid, financed and equipped by a foreign power, nonetheless retain a degree of independence of that state.[112] It follows that acts committed by the first group will clearly be attributed to the foreign power.[113]

The rules set up in the Nicaragua case were reaffirmed by the ICJ in the case *Concerning the Application of the Convention on the Prevention and Punishment of the Crime of Genocide*.[114] In addition, they are considered to be part of customary international law.[115]

As noted earlier, the overall control test emerged from the case law of the ICTY, namely the *Tadic* case.[116]

Both Trial Chamber II[117] and the Appeals Chambers[118] were tasked with the classification of the conflict in Bosnia and Herzegovina and in this context, stated that the attribution of conduct does not require the "effective control" of a foreign power, because the "overall control" of a military organisation (or army) is

110 ICJ, *Military and Paramilitary Activities, Nicaragua. v. U.S*, 14 June 1986, p. 27.
111 Ibid., para 115.
112 Antonio Cassese, The Nicaragua and Tadic Test Revisited in Light of the ICJ Judgment on Genocide in Bosnia, *EJIL*, Vol. 18, 2007, p. 652.
113 Ibid.
114 ICJ, *Bosnia and Herzegovina v. Serbia and Montenegro*, 26 February 2007.
115 Ibid., para 398.
116 ICTY, *Prosecutor v. Dusko Tadic*, Jurisdiction Appeal, No. IT-94–1-AR72, 2 October 1995.
117 ICTY, *Tadic, Trial Chambers II, Opinion and Judgement*, 7 May 1997.
118 ICTY, *Prosecutor v. Dusko Tadic, Appeals Chambers, Judgement*, 15 July 1999.

sufficient to trigger the responsibility of the state. Essentially, it appears that the overall control test requires that the given state wields its "overall control over the group, not only by equipping and financing the group, but also by coordinating or helping in the general planning of its military activity".[119]

The concept of effective overall control was further developed by the ECtHR itself through the notion of the extra-territorial application of human rights.[120]

The issue of effective overall control came to the surface for the first time in two cases involving Turkey's action in Northern Cyprus, namely *Loizidou v. Turkey*[121] and *Cyprus* v. *Turkey*.[122] In both cases, the Court had to determine the degree of control exercised by Turkey, which meant assessing whether the territory of the Turkish Republic of Northern Cyprus was within the extraterritorial jurisdiction of Turkey due to the large presence of Turkish troops on the ground and if so, whether the acts and omissions of the authorities of the Turkish Republic of Northern Cyprus were imputable to Turkey.

In this context, it has been recognised that the "effective overall control" of the relevant territory means the exercise of power through military action, be it lawful or unlawful.[123]

It further recognised that the extraterritorial exercise of jurisdiction by a state includes the situation where a state, through effective control of the relevant territory and its inhabitants, exercises *de facto* control similar to the one exercised by the government of the Contracting State on its own territory.[124]

Both in the *Loizidou* case and *Cyprus v. Turkey*, the Court stated that the exercise of effective control by the state requires military action (whether lawful or unlawful) which is exercised directly through its armed forces or through a subordinated local administration.[125]

119 However, the Appeals Chamber considered that the *Nicaragua* case was an inappropriate test for the VRS case. This test appeared to be contrary to the logic of the law of state responsibility and at variance with state and judicial practice. Idem, paras 115 to 162. The *Nicaragua* case addressed the issue of state responsibility for wrongful acts, while the *Tadic* case dealt with the applicability of humanitarian law as well as the classification of armed conflict. See Marco Sassoli and Laura M. Olson, International Decision: Prosecutor V. Tadic (Judgement): Case No. IT-94-1-A. 38 ILM 1518 (1999): International Criminal Tribunal for the Former Yugoslavia, Appeals Chamber, July 15, 1999, *The American Journal International Law*, Vol. 94, July 2000.

120 On the extraterritorial application of human rights treaties, see Virginia Mantouvalou, Extending Judicial Control in International Law: Human Rights Treaties and Extraterritoriality, *International Journal of Human Rights*, Vol. 9, No. 2, 2005. See also Sarah Miller, Revisiting Extraterritorial Jurisdiction: A Territorial Justification for Extraterritorial Jurisdiction under the European Convention, *The European Journal of International Law*, Vol. 20, No. 4, 2010.

121 ECtHR, *Loizidou v. Turkey*, App. No. 15315/89, ECtHR judgement of 18 December 1996.

122 ECtHR, *Cyprus v. Turkey*, App. No. 25781/94.judgement of 10 May 2001.

123 *Loizidou v. Turkey*, 1996, para 52 and *Cyprus v. Turkey*, paras 62, 77–80.

124 Ibid.

125 *Loizidou v. Turkey*, 1996, para 62.

In this context, the structure and extent of ground forces involvement in (control over) an area does not play a significant role. It is, rather, the degree of dependency between an area and a foreign state, which results in continuing support being provided by the foreign state to the area that enables its survival.[126]

This criterion was applied in the *Bankovic v. Belgium and others* case[127] with the purpose of determining the responsibility of the NATO countries regarding the bombing of the Serbian state television headquarters (Radio Televizija Srbije), which killed at least 16 civilians and wounded 14 others. The relatives of the victims brought a case before the ECtHR invoking an extraterritorial application of the Convention. The Court found that the NATO aerial bombing of the Serbian TV station in Belgrade did not imply the effective control test that was enunciated in *Loizidou v. Turkey*, as suggested by the applicants, because according to the Court the aerial involvement of NATO countries was not regarded as effective territorial control, which would have justified the imposition of the obligations arising from the ECHR.[128]

In the Court's view, effective control of the relevant territory and its inhabitants abroad not only requires a military presence, but most importantly the foreign power should exercise some of the public powers normally exercised by the government.[129]

In the *Bankovic* case the Court employs higher standards for an exercise of jurisdiction for the purpose of applying the ECHR, as it not only requires as a precondition territorial control (the presence of ground forces) but also the exercise of public power equivalent to a state government.[130]

In this regard, if we look at *Issa and others v. Turkey*,[131] the deployment of 35,000 ground troops in Iraq, accompanied by heavy military equipment such as tanks, helicopters and F16 fighter aircraft, proved insufficient to secure effective control over the given area.[132] In the Court's view the mere presence of the troops does not, in itself, presume the imputability of the Turkish troops, but

126 Joanne Williams, Al Skein: A Flawed Interpretation of Bankovic, *Wisconsin International Law Journal*, Vol. 23, No. 4, p. 705.

127 ECtHR, *Bankovic et al v. Belgium et al*, Grand Chamber Decision 12 December 2001.

128 *Bankovic*, para 71.

129 It automatically excluded the aerial space above the country from the state's jurisdiction. *Bankovic*, para 355.

130 In the *Bankovic case*, the Court relied strictly on the definitions of the notion of jurisdiction provided by legal Scholars such as Oppenheim, Cassesse, Brownlie, and Higgins, who considered that jurisdiction is mainly linked to territoriality. See *Bankovic* paras 59–61. See also Williams, *supra* n. 126, p. 688.

131 *Issa and others v. Turkey*, App. No. 31821/96, ECtHR judgment, 16 October 2004. The Court stated that *"a State may be held accountable for violation of the Convention rights and freedoms of persons who are in the territory of another State but who are found to be under the former State's authority and control through its agents operating – whether lawfully or unlawfully – in the latter State. Accountability in such situations stems from the fact that Article 1 of the Convention cannot be interpreted so as to allow a State party to perpetrate violations of the Convention on the territory of another State, which it could not perpetrate on its own territory"*. See para 71.

132 Williams, *supra* n. 126, p. 706.

strictly requires verifying whether at the relevant time Turkish troops were operating in the given area.[133] It follows that effective control requires "a structured relationship normally existing over a period of time".[134]

Recently, the Court came out with an even more restrictive finding in *Al Skeini v. United Kingdom.*[135]

The case of *Al-Skeini and others v. UK* was brought by six applicants, close relatives of five Iraqi citizens who were killed by British troops and another who died as a consequence of being exposed to brutal maltreatment in a British detention centre in Basra (southern Iraq). It has been observed that the *Al-Skeini* case confirms once again that the ECHR only applies extraterritorially on an exceptional basis and is strictly linked to the degree of control exercised by a foreign power.[136] In this context, the degree of control is not only measured by the exercise of public power by a foreign power which is required to be equivalent to a state government, but also by the military strength of the given state, in this case British troops.[137]

Nevertheless, what is most important to elucidate is that the *Al-Skeini* case has brought to the surface a new strand of the meaning of jurisdiction, the personal model of jurisdiction which arises in cases when the state exercises authority or control over an individual.

Though it has been viewed as a desertion by the Court of the spatial model that emerged from *Bankovic*'s ill-conceived *espace juridique* concept,[138] it seems more that the Court has embraced both the personal model of jurisdiction and the spatial.[139]

133 Olivier De Schutter, Human Rights, Globalization and Jurisdiction: Lessons from the European Convention on Human Rights, *Baltic Yearbook of International Law*, Vol. 6, 2006, p. 198.

134 Submission of the British Government in *Bankovic v. Belgium Case*, cited in Williams, *supra* n. 132, p. 706.

135 ECtHR, *Al-Skeini and Others United Kingdom*, App. No. 55721/07, ECtHR judgement of 7 July 2001.

136 Ibid. See also. Cedric Ryngaert, Clarifying the Extra- territorial application of the European Convention on Human Rights, Utrecht Journal of International and European Law 57–60, available at: http://dx.doi.org/10.5334/ujiel.ba, p. 58.

137 *"In these exceptional circumstances, the Court considers that the United Kingdom, through its soldiers engaged in security operations in Basrah during the period in question, exercised authority and control over individuals killed in the course of such security operations, so as to establish a jurisdictional link between the deceased and the United Kingdom for the purposes of Article 1 of the Convention". Al-Skeini and others United Kingdom, supra* n. 139, para 149.

138 The spatial model is based on the effective overall control of an area that links jurisdiction with the legal space of the Contracting States for the purpose of applying the Convention. In the *Bankovic* case, the Court considered that "the Convention is a multilateral treaty operating in an essentially regional context and notably in the legal space (*espace juridique*) of the Contracting States" (para 80 of the Judgment). For an in-depth analysis of the extraterritorial application of the ECHR, see Ryngaert, *supra* n. 136, p. 58. See also Samantha Miko, Al-Skeini v. United Kingdom and Extra-Territorial Jurisdiction under the European Convention for Human Rights, *Boston Colleague International and Comparative Law Review*, Vol. 35, No. 3, 2013.

139 The relatives of the applicants were considered to fall within the state's jurisdiction because the British soldiers were exercising authority and control as well as some kind of public power in the Basra region. See *Al-Skeini v. UK*, para 149.

As one may note, the very shaping of an effective control test depends on the factual circumstances in the given case. The Court's reasoning in its decision on *Behrami and Saramati* has brought even more confusion since it came out with a new term, ultimate authority and control.

It found that the UN Security Council is the one that "retained ultimate authority" over the security of the UN mission in Kosovo and that effective command of the relevant operational matters was retained by NATO. Yet, it failed to explain explicitly what is the scope and content of such authority.

According to the International Law Commission, there is a customary law presumption that the wrongdoings of UN peacekeeping operations are attributable to the UN, as it is presumed that the UN exercises effective control over the states contributing troops. Nevertheless, it is considered that this assertion can always be rebutted if it is proven that a troop-contributing state has exercised effective control over the conduct of its troops.[140] In this light, although the contributing states place their troops at the disposal of the UN in support of UN peacekeeping operations, it cannot be automatically assumed that the UN exercises overall control over the troops, but may rather take the role of a coordinator which unifies and coordinates the operation.[141]

So as already noted, it was a general assumption that KFOR forces were operating on delegated powers.[142] However, the Court had to determine whether this delegation of powers was "sufficiently limited so as to remain compatible with the degree of centralization of UNSC collective security constitutionally necessary under the Charter".[143]

This meant, in practice, establishing the capacity of the UNSC to have influence over the two realities of its implementation, namely KFOR and UNMIK.[144]

In order to prove that, the Court had to set up new dimensions, which it called "the ultimate authority and control test".

In light of this, it tasked itself with the question "whether the UN Security Council retained ultimate authority and control so that operational command only was delegated".[145] It found the answer in UNSC Resolution 1244. Accord-

140 Alexander Breitegger, Sacrificing the Effectiveness of the European Convention on Human Rights on the Altar of the Effective Functioning of Peace Support Operations: A Critique of Behrami and Saramati and Al-Jedda, *International Community Law Review*, Vol. 11, 2009, p. 159.

141 Ibid.

142 As distinct from KFOR, UNMIK was a subsidiary organ of the UN and as such it was easier for the Court to establish a link between UNMIK and the UN. See Verdirame, *supra* n. 2, pp. 107–108.

143 See *Behrami and Saramati* decision para 132. See also Verdirame, *supra* n. 2, p. 108.

144 See *Behrami and Saramati* decision, para 132.

145 While it noted that UNSC Resolution 1244 failed to identify the precise article of Chapter VII under which the UNSC was acting, it went on to interpret UNSC Resolution 1244, holding that the UNSC's power to retain ultimate authority and control in delegating its security powers derived from UNSC Resolution 1244 itself. It considered that "Chapter VII allowed the UNSC to delegate to 'Member States and relevant international organisations'. Secondly, the relevant power was a delegable power. Thirdly, that delegation was

ing to the Court, the UNSC retains ultimate authority and control over the security mission and delegated to NATO (in consultation with non-NATO member states) the power to establish an international presence, KFOR.[146]

However, looking at UNSC Resolution 1244, which governs the establishment of the military presence in Kosovo, it is difficult to justify this assertion.

There is no explicit wording in Resolution 1244 that stipulates that the UNSC will exercise ultimate authority over the security presence (KFOR). The UNSC authorised the security presence and that is all. The wording of the Resolution states only that the SRSG, as the appointee of the UNSC, would be in charge "to control the implementation of the international presence".[147]

The relationship between UNMIK and KFOR was based on mutual cooperation and was strictly of a consultative nature.[148] Moreover, the Helsinki Agreement clearly states that the North Atlantic Council (NAC) was not under the ultimate authority of the UNSC, but rather cooperated with it on a consultative basis.[149]

The situation with the civilian component was different. It is apparent that its four pillars, led by specified agencies, namely the UNHCR, the OSCE and the EU, functioned under the unified command of the SRSG,[150] who exercised the "overall authority to manage the mission" as well as to "coordinate the activities

---

neither presumed nor implicit, but rather prior and explicit in the Resolution itself Fourthly, the Resolution put sufficiently defined limits on the delegation by fixing the mandate with adequate precision as it set out the objectives to be attained, the roles and responsibilities accorded as well as the means to be employed. Fifthly, the leadership of the military presence was required by the Resolution to report to the UNSC so as to allow the UNSC to exercise its overall authority and control (consistently, the UNSC was to remain actively seized of the matter, Article 21 of the Resolution). The requirement that the SG present the KFOR report to the UNSC was an added safeguard since the SG is considered to represent the general interests of the UN". See, *Behrami and Saramati*, para 134. See also, Verdirame, referring to para 133 of the Court decision; Verdirame, *supra* n. 2, p. 108.

146 See *Behrami and Saramati* decision para 135.

147 UNSC Resolution 1244, para 6.

148 See Constitutional Framework for Provisional Self-Government in Kosovo, UNMIK Regulation 2001/09; Section 8.2. The SRSG was to coordinate closely with the International Security Presence (KFOR). Moreover, in its Periodic Report to the Security Council, the Secretary General states: "A Political Violence Task Force, staffed jointly by senior staff of UNMIK police and the Kosovo Force (KFOR), established a Kosovo-wide network of officials to coordinate activities between UNMIK police and KFOR at the local, regional and central levels". See Report of the Secretary General on the United Nations Interim Mission in Kosovo, S/200/1196.

149 See interpretation of the "Agreed Points on Russian Participation in KFOR", known as the Helsinki Agreement concluded on 18 June 1999, provided by Smyrek; *supra* n. 99, pp. 184–185.

150 However, one may also question the extent of the control exercised by the SRSG over the international organisations, knowing that each of them was functioning according to a mandate established by the highest body of organisation to which they belonged. For instance, the OSCE mandate was established by OSCE Permanent Council Decision Nr. 305 of 1 July 1999, and is subject to annual extension.

of all UN agencies and other international organizations operating as part of UNMIK".[151]

In this regard, the Court failed to consider the complexity of the UN mission and as a result, it established a legal regime that does not properly and justly attribute responsibility for the wrongdoings that occurred on the international governed territory.

Subsequently, the Court's reasoning in *Behrami and Saramati* was the subject of discussion in the seventh report of Special Rapporteur Gaja of the International Law Commission, who observed that "had the Court applied the criterion of effective control set out by the Commission, it would have reached the different conclusion that the conduct of national contingents allocated to KFOR had to be attributed either to the sending State or to NATO".[152]

The Court's reasoning caused confusion as it appears that effective control applies only if a contracting party occupies a foreign territory, as was the case with Northern Cyprus and Iraq, but not where a group of states was authorised by the UN to administer a foreign territory.[153]

Owing to this judicial inconsistency today, legal scholars have differing opinions when it comes to the standard of effective control exercised by foreign troops. Some opine that the peacekeeping troops are under the effective control of the United Nations,[154] while others consider that since contributing states retain operational command and control, they bear the international responsibility for the conduct of their troops.[155]

But recently, some authors have called for multiple attribution, arguing that troop-contributing countries should be accountable and responsible together with the United Nations for conduct committed by their peacekeeping forces.[156]

The test of ultimate authority and control appears to be unknown in the case law.[157]

151 See, UNMIK Police, Saint Group, *CIVPOL Language and Culture*, available at the following website: www.saint-claire.org/resources/UNMIK%20Police.pdf.

152 Giorgio Gaja, Special Rapporteur of the International Law Commission, *Seventh Report on Responsibility of International Organizations*, International Law Commission,¶ 26, U.N. Doc. A/CN.4/610, 27 March 2009.

153 See Mujezinovic Larsen, *supra* n. 82, p. 523.

154 "Ordinarily, the members of national contingents, while remaining in the service of their state, become for the period of their assignment to the force international personnel under the authority of the U.N.". Moshe Hirsch, *The Responsibility of International Organisations Towards Third Parties, Some Basic Principles*, Martinus Nijhoff Publisher, 1995, p. 66.

155 See Daphna Shraga, The United Nations as an Actor Bound by International Humanitarian Law, in L. Condorelli et al. (eds.), *The United Nations and International Humanitarian Law*, Paris, Editions Pedone, 1996, p. 330.

156 See Christopher Leck, International Responsibility in United Nations Peacekeeping Operations: Command and Control Arrangements and the Attribution of Conduct, *Melbourne Journal of International Law*, Vol. 10, 2009. See also Mujezinovic Larsen, *supra* n. 82, pp. 513–514.

157 "The precise meaning of the term 'ultimate authority and control' I have found somewhat elusive". Lord Carshwel, quoted in *Al-Jedda v. UK*, App. No. 27021/08, ECtHR judgment 7July 2011, para 148.

According to Larsen Mujezinovic, it can be found neither in the commentaries on the Draft Articles in State Responsibilities nor in the Draft Articles on the Responsibilities of International Organizations.[158]

He submits that the Court failed to provide an explanation as to why it adopted "ultimate authority and control" instead of overall or effective control, which has been widely accepted as a common test in international case law and as such became part of customary international law.[159]

Nevertheless, the "ultimate authority and control" test was further mentioned in *Al Jedda v. United Kingdom*, a case which involved deliberation regarding the actions of UK troops in southern Iraq, namely the unlawful deprivation of liberty of Mr Hilal Abdul-Razzaq Ali Al-Jedda by UK forces at the British temporary detention facility in Basra.[160]

Yet the *Behrami and Saramati* test proved not to apply to the situation in southern Iraq[161] and consequently the Court determined that Al-Jedda's detention could not be attributable to the United Nations as, according to the Court, the UN Security Council had neither effective control nor ultimate authority and control over the acts and omissions of troops within the multinational force and that Al-Jedda's detention was therefore not attributable to the United Nations.[162] Yet, as in *Behrami and Saramati*, the Court failed to define the specificity of what the "ultimate authority and control" test involves.

158 However, the term itself can be found in the legal literature concerning the legality of delegations from the Security Council. See Larsen Mujezinovic, *supra* n. 82, p. 521.

159 As already stated, the doctrine of the effective control test was first laid down in the *Nicaragua* case by the ICJ and was adopted by the ILC in its Draft Articles on State Responsibility (Article 8). By contrast, the overall control test emerged from the case law of the ICTY, namely *Prosecutor v. Tadic*. The overall control test requires that the state wield "overall control over the group, not only by equipping and financing the group, but also by coordinating or helping in the general planning of its military activity". See *Prosecutor v. Tadic*, paras 131–137. A detailed analysis of the difference between the ultimate control test and the effective control test is provided in Mujezinovic Larsen, *supra* n. 82, pp. 519–522.

160 *Al-Jedda v. United Kingdom*, App. No. 27021/08, ECtHR judgment 7 July 2011.

161 In its submission, the UK government had strongly relied on *Behrami and Saramati* in trying to draw a parallel between UNSCR Resolution 1511, which authorised the UK military presence in Iraq, and UNSC Resolution 1244 (UNMIK), arguing that the actions of its troops on the ground were not attributable to the UK, but to the UN. See *Al-Jedda v. United Kingdom*, para 64.

162 The Court found that the United Kingdom had jurisdiction under Article 1 ECHR in respect of civilians killed during the British occupation of southeast Iraq. Tobies Thienel considers that the reason behind this finding is the fact that the United Kingdom troops were deployed in Iraq before the UN installed its structures. Moreover, the UNSC Resolution on the UN's mission in Iraq recognised that the UN was not operational on the ground in Iraq. See Tobies Thienel, *Issues of Attribution in Al-Jedda and Srebrenica: The Cases Compared*, available at the following website: http://invisiblecollege.weblog.leidenuniv.nl/2011/08/28/issues-of-attribution-in-al-jedda-and-sr/. See also *Al Jedda* para 84. An in-depth analysis of the Court's reasoning in Al-Jedda is provided by Jelena Pejic, The European Court of Human Right's Al-Jedda Judgment: The Oversight of the International Humanitarian Law, *International Review of the Red Cross*, Vol. 93, No. 883, September 2011.

Although Chapter VII, namely Articles 24–26 and 41–42, does not explicitly include such terminology, practice shows that in some cases particular measures taken by the Council have resulted in deviation from customary international rules or treaty law.[163] This can be demonstrated by the types of measures taken by the Security Council in the last few decades, which often had an impact not only on the states or entities which were its direct target but also on other states which had trade relations with the targeted states. States are obliged to accept such interference in order to give weight to the enforcement measures exercised by the Security Council. The ability of the Security Council to exercise an omnipotent power in the modern world could be justified by its responsibility to act efficiently in the interest of international peace and security.[164]

Scholars argue that although the UN might assume exclusive control over the military troops, in practice it never exercised full control.[165] This assertion has been built upon premises established by the Capstone doctrine, which is considered to be the doctrinal foundation for UN peacekeeping operations. It says that "in the case of military personnel provided by Member States, these personnel are placed under the operational control of the United Nations Force Commander or head of military component, but not under the United Nations command".[166]

In this regard, it is difficult to accept that the UNSC exercised the highest possible degree of control in the given situation, or to regard UNMIK as alone bearing the responsibility for the alleged violations.

163 See Erica de Wet, *The Chapter VII Powers of the United Nations Security Council*, Oxford and Portland Oregon, 2004, pp. 181–183.

164 Moreover, the ability of the Security Council to affect the rights of member states under international law lies in Article 103 of the UN Charter, which provides that when the obligations of the member states under the Charter conflict with a treaty, the Charter is to prevail and the members are under an obligation to accept and carry out Security Council decisions. Idem, de Wet, pp. 181–183. See also Dapo Akande, The International Court of Justice and the Security Council: Is There a Room for Judicial Control of Decision of Political Organs of United Nations? *International Comparative Law Quarterly*, Vol. 46, No. 2, 1197, pp. 318–320.

165 Boris Kondoch, The Responsibility of Peacekeepers, Their Sending States, and International Organizations, in Terry Gill and Dieter Fleck (eds.), *The Handbook of the International Law and Military Operations*, Oxford University Press, 2010, p. 521. See also Hilaire McCoubrey and Nigel D. White, *The Blue Helmets: Legal Regulation of United Nations Military Operations*, Dartmouth Publisher, 1996, pp. 144–147.

166 Quoted in Kondoch, Idem, p. 521. This might be supported by the fact that in the case of the European Committee for Prevention of Torture, despite an agreement concluded with UNMIK that guarantees the Committee access to detention facilities it was not allowed to visit the military detention facilities of KFOR. Subsequently, it had to conclude additional arrangements with the NATO authorities in order to be able to visit them. See The European Committee for the Prevention of Torture and Other Cruel and Inhuman and Degrading Treatment (CPT) Report to *International Interim Administration in Kosovo (UNMIK) on the visit to Kosovo, carried out by the European Committee for the Prevention of Torture and Other Cruel and Inhuman and Degrading Treatment (CPT) from 21to 29 March 2007*, CPT/Inf, 2009/03, published on 20 January 2009.

What can we learn from the Behrami and Saramati *decision?*

It should be emphasised that for the first time an international court showed that the conduct of a United Nations agent, in this case UNMIK might be attributable to the United Nations. Yet the Court failed to clarify the legal basis it applied in this decision.[167]

In this light, the conduct of peacekeepers may in principle be attributed to the international organisation that establishes the peacekeeping operation and has operational control over the force. The attribution will in most cases be based either on the institutional link or the control link.[168] Although such a stance might deserve loud applause, the question of exposing of such conduct to legal scrutiny (the accountability) remains vague.

Interestingly, there are authors who fear that if the Court's reasoning in *Behrami and Saramati* becomes established law, it may have a negative impact on the overall involvement of the United Nations in peacekeeping operations. It is argued that such a rule would reduce the UN's willingness to participate in peacekeeping missions out of fear of the possibility of being held solely responsible for wrongdoing conducted jointly with Member states and over which the UN may not have had effective control.[169] Accordingly, it has been noted that though the ECtHR declined jurisdiction over the United Nations, other courts (be they international, regional, or domestic) may accept the challenge and adjudicate the issue of responsibility for wrongful acts attributed to the UN.[170]

However, there are authors who hold the opposite view. In their opinion, the *Behrami and Saramati* decision will serve as a precedent for both national and international courts to refuse to review cases that involve human rights violations committed both by state members acting under UN authority and by the United Nation as an international organisation.[171]

This is what has happened. After the *Behrami and Saramati* decision, the ECtHR rejected numerous applications, stating that it did not have jurisdiction to review cases involving UNMIK, since UNMIK was not party to the Convention.[172]

167 Mujezinovic Larsen, *supra* n. 82, p. 512.

168 Beti Hohler, *Responsibility of International Organisations: The Element of Attribution in the Context of Peacekeeping Operations* (Overview of normative framework and Manifestation in practice), Paper presented at the 2nd Global International Studies Conference, University of Ljubljana, Faculty of Social Science, Ljubljana, 23–26 July 2008, available at: www.wiscnetwork.org/ljubljana2008/papers/WISC_2008-363.doc.

169 Hirsch, *supra* n. 154, p. 77; See. Bell, *supra* n. 85, p. 544.

170 Ibid.

171 See Sari, *supra* n. 13, pp. 167–168.

172 Among them, the ERRC application regarding the Roma poisoning case in North Mitrovica. See ERRC, Press Release "European Court of Human Rights has no Jurisdiction in Kosovo Lead Poisoning Case", 3 April 2006, available at: www.errc.org. Yet one should look at the recent case ECtHR, *Grudić v. Serbia*, judgement of 24 September 2012, which involved applicants of Bosniak origin who lived in Kosovo but allegedly moved to Novi Pazar (Serbia) for the purpose of realising their rights to a disability pension. Like all

In 2013, it turned down a complaint lodged by Stichting Mothers of Srebrenica against the Netherlands.[173] The complaint was rejected as it was found to be manifestly ill founded on the ground that the UN enjoyed immunity from national courts' jurisdiction. Once again, it rejected attempts to question what it would take for an international organisation to be legally accountable for its conduct.[174]

Similarly, the domestic courts in several countries have refused to review cases that involved human rights violations committed by both Member states acting under UN authority and the United Nations as an international organisation, taking the same stand as the ECtHR but not specifically referring to the *Behrami and Saramati* decision.

Kosovan citizens, the Grudić couple (wife and husband) had not received their pension since 1999 and 2000. The Serbian authorities claimed that pensions could no longer be paid to the applicants because the Serbian authorities had stopped collecting insurance contributions in Kosovo as of its placement under international administration in 1999. However, in 2005 the applicants decided to acquire a residence in the nearest town in Serbia, Novi Pazar, where they initiated proceedings before the domestic courts in Serbia proper. Soon after, they lodged an application with the Strasbourg authorities, relying on Article 1 of Protocol No. 1 (protection of property) and Article 14 (prohibition of discrimination), complaining that the state was unwilling to continue paying their pensions, as well as about discrimination against them because of their ethnic minority status. Interestingly, besides Serbian laws a subject of the Court's examination appears to have been not only UNMIK's regulations, but also the legal acts issued by the Kosovo Assembly (namely regulations 2001/35; 2005/20; see Section III (The Relevant Law)). Recently, the ECtHR was once again challenged with regard to the applicability of the ECHR on the territory of Kosovo in the case of *Ali Azemi v. Serbia (Appl1209/2009)*. The applicant, who is a Kosovan citizen, lodged an application against Serbia regarding non-execution of the employment-related decision issued by the Municipal Court of Ferizaj in Kosovo on 11 January 2002. The applicant alleged that the violation had occurred prior to the arrival of UNMIK (he was unlawfully dismissed from his job in the early 1990s) and that the impugned decision was based on Serbian legislation which had been inherited by UNMIK. The Court held that even if the respondent state exercised "jurisdiction" as regards Serbia's actions prior to UNMIK's arrival 10 June 1999, these complaints would be incompatible *ratione temporis* in accordance with Article 35 §§ 3 (a) and 4 of the Convention, due to the fact that the state of Serbia became party to the Convention on 3 March 2004. See ECtHR, *Ali Azemi v. Serbia*, Second Section Decision issued on 5 November 2013.

173 *Stichting Mothers of Srebrenica and Others against the Netherlands*, App. No. 65542/12, ECtHR Decision, 11 June 2013. The Court was asked to decide whether the Netherlands had violated the applicants' right of "access to a court", as guaranteed by Article 6 of the Convention, by granting the United Nations immunity from domestic jurisdiction. In addition, pursuant to Article 13 it was asked to assess whether the granting of immunity to the United Nations allowed the Netherlands State to evade its liability towards the applicants. See Press release issued by the Register of the Court, ECHR 194, 27 June 2013, available at: http://hudoc.echr.coe.int/sites/eng-press/pages/search.aspx?i=003-4416460-5307356#{%22itemid%22:[%22003-4416460-5307356%22]}.

174 See Press release issued by the Register of the Court, ECHR 194, 27 June 2013, available at: http://hudoc.echr.coe.int/sites/eng-press/pages/search.aspx?i=003-4416460-5307356#{%22itemid%22:[%22003-4416460-5307356%22]}.

Two court proceedings before courts in the Netherlands were initiated by the relatives of the Srebrenica victims. One was the case *Mothers of Srebrenica Association et al. v. the Netherlands and the United Nations*,[175] which concerned responsibility for the failure of both UN and Dutchbat to prevent the genocide in Srebrenica. The other was the case *Nuhanović and Mustafić v. the Netherlands*,[176] which aimed to prove the responsibility of Dutchbat for the death of three individuals, Rizo Mustafić, an electrician who was providing maintenance and repair work to Dutchbat, and the Nuhanović couple, parents of Hasan Nuhanović, an interpreter working for the United Nations military observers.[177]

While the Supreme Court of the Netherlands dismissed the appeal in cassation in the *Mothers of Srebrenica Association et al. v. the Netherlands and the United Nations* case, reaffirming that it had no jurisdiction vis-à-vis the UN, in the Nuhanović judgment it held the state of the Netherlands responsible for the death of the three individuals. The first judgment shows that the immunity of the United Nations prevailed, whereas the second suggests that the exercise of effective control was possible only within the Dutchbat compound, which automatically excluded the troops having responsibility outside the military compound.

Nevertheless, it has been noted that the Dutch courts refused to follow the reasoning of the ECtHR in *Behrami and Saramati*. The "ultimate authority and control" test that was launched in the *Behrami and Saramati* decision did not come into play.[178] While in the first instance the Court denied the claims on the ground that the acts of Dutchbat were attributable to the UN rather than to the state of the Netherlands, later the Appeal Court accepted that there was "the possibility that more than one party has 'effective control" over the alleged conduct. Yet it id did not focus on examining the type of control exercised by the UN.[179]

175 *Mothers of Srebrenica Association et al. v. the Netherlands and the United Nations*, Case No. 295247, Judgment, 10 July 2008, available at the following website: www.rechtspraak.nl.

176 *Mustafić and Hasan Nuhanović versus the State of the Netherlands*, District Court the Hague, Case Nos. 265618 and 265615, Judgment, 10 September 2008, available at: www.rechtspraak.nl.

177 During the siege of Srebrenica, all three victims were allowed to stay in the Dutchbat military compound but as soon as the situation deteriorated they were given the order to leave the military premises, which resulted in their subsequent death together with thousands of other Bosnian Muslims.

178 "In a sense, then, the Dutch court in the Srebrenica cases and the ECHR in *Al-Jedda* approached *Behrami* from different sides: In the Dutch/Bosnian case, the UN mission was already over, which meant that the effective control of the sending state was revived, whereas in *Al-Jedda*, the mission had begun before the involvement of the UN, which meant that the UN would not have acquired effective control. See Tobies Thienel, Issues *of Attribution in Al-Jedda and Srebrenica: The Cases Compared*, available at the following website: http://invisiblecollege.weblog.leidenuniv.nl/2011/08/28/issues-of-attribution-in-al-jedda-and-sr/.

179 Nuhanović Appeals Court Judgment, *supra* n. 176, § 5.9. The reason it decided not to examine the degree of control exercised by the UN was to avoid the complexities arising from the legal implications of the immunity of the United Nations.

The reasoning in the *Behrami and Saramati* decision did not influence the House of Lords in the United Kingdom when it had to decide in the case of *Al-Skeini and Al-Jedda*.[180] The House of Lord did not even see an analogy between the situation of military troops and civilian structures operating in Kosovo (KFOR and UNMIK) and the situation of British troops operating in Iraq.[181] But the reasoning of the Appeal Court in the *Nuhanović and Mustafić v. the Netherlands* case to a certain extent resembled the reasoning of the UK's House of Lords decision in *Al-Skeini*. While deliberating on the UK's jurisdiction in the given case, the House of Lords found that only one applicant, Mr. Mousa, fell within the UK's jurisdiction as a military detention facility had a special status, comparable to an embassy.[182]

In this regard, one may draw the conclusion that in a peacekeeping operation human rights obligations are only valid within the military compound of the peacekeeping troops and that as such the possibility of attribution of conduct outside a military compound is entirely precluded, despite the fact that the military troops may be in charge of an entire area.

Nevertheless, in the meantime considerable hope has been placed in the adoption of the ILC Draft Articles on Responsibility of International Organizations[183] in the expectation that they might provide an adequate clarification of this matter. But it has been observed that in the Sixth Committee of the General Assembly, which at that time was dealing with the ILC's work on the responsibility of international organisations, a number of states opportunistically invoked *Behrami* and called upon the ILC to take into consideration the Court's decision.[184] Despite such pressure, the ILC decided to incorporate the multiple attribution rule into its work. Yet scholars remain not very optimistic. They note that although this implies the possibility of a multiple attribution of conduct, it will not be easy to develop these rules without an extensive body of practice, as was previously done with the Articles on State Responsibility, which became the product of existing rules and in many cases codified customary law. The international Law

180 *R (Al-Skeini) v. Secretary of State for Defence* (2007) UKHL 26, available at the following website: www.refworld.org/docid/4672880a2.html.

181 Lord Bingham stated: "The analogy with the situation in Kosovo breaks down, in my opinion, at almost every point". See Opinions of the Lords of Appeal for Judgment in the Case, *R(on application of Al-Jedda) (FC) (Appellant) v. Secretary of State for Defense (Respondent)*, Lord Bingham and Baroness Hale of Richmond, para 124.

182 In light of this, Lord Brown stated: "For the sixth case, I for my part would recognise the UK's jurisdiction over Mr. Mousa only on the narrow basis found established by the Divisional Court, essentially by analogy with the extra-territorial exception made for embassies (an analogy recognised too in Hess v. United Kingdom (1975) 2 DR 72, a Commission decision in the context of a foreign prison which had itself referred to the embassy case of X v. Federal Republic of Germany". See *R (Al-Skeini) v. Secretary of State for Defence* (2007) UKHL 26, para 97 (per Lord Carswell), para 132 (per Lord Brown), available at the following website: www.refworld.org/docid/4672880a2.html.

183 The Draft Articles on the Responsibility of International Organizations were adopted by the International Law Commission at its sixty-third session in 2011.

184 Milanovic and Papic, *supra* n. 83, p. 273.

Commission is not in possession of a compendium of the general practice of international organisations on which it can base its work.[185] Generally speaking, the Court has affirmed in the *Behrami and Saramati* decision that it has no power to review acts of the ITA authority. Instead of providing a further clarification as to what Member Responsibility involves it simply insisted on "distinction between cases", and as such worsened the ambiguity surrounding this issue.[186] Subsequently, complaints of those that have suffered violations of their human rights by ITA do not form the object of judicial review before any judicial body, be it national or international.

Conclusion

The foregoing discussion demonstrates that the obligations arising from international human rights instruments do not apply automatically in a situation where member states undertake a joint operation under the umbrella of the United Nations.

The only possible option, that of the extraterritorial application of human rights, lacks clarity as to which conditions apply for an individual to be considered to be "within the jurisdiction" of a member state. Despite abundant case law, the issue remains controversial. Yet even if clarified one day, it will only bring a partial solution, since it will only include the Council of Europe countries.

As may be noted, the substantial body of case law of ECtHR jurisprudence has dealt with the spatial model of jurisdiction, which involves the application of human rights treaties based on a state's effective control. The outcome of this reasoning makes it evident that there is an inconsistency of reasoning in the Court's decisions when it comes to the determination of effective control.

Although the Court opened the door to the possibility of establishing a jurisdictional link through a mix of spatial and personal models of jurisdiction (*Al-Skeini v. UK*), it failed to provide clear grounds as to what the concept of public power meant.

The existing case law makes it evident that the ECtHR is reluctant to deal with wrongful conduct by the UN.

The famous "ultimate overall control" test that emerged from *Behrami and Saramati* case has diminished the chances of a transfer of responsibility to the troop-sending state in the future. This was the only option that promised to achieve some notion of justice. The Court misconstrued its own case law established in this area.

185 E. Kristen, New Direction in Responsibility: Assessing the International Commission's Draft Articles on the Responsibility of International Organizations, *The Yale Journal of International Law Online*, Vol. 37, Spring 2011, p. 9.

186 The Court draw a sharp line between B*ehrami and Saramati* and *Bosphorus case*, stating "the present cases are therefore clearly distinguishable from the Bosphorus case in terms both of the responsibility of the respondent States under Article 1 and of the Court's competence ratione personae". *See Bosphorus Hava Yollarim Torizm ve Ticaret Anonim Sirketi v. Ireland*, *supra* n. 111. Para 151. See also, Ryngaert, *supra* n. 136, pp. 1007–1008.

In *Behrami and Saramati*, the ECtHR narrowed the door to the extraterritorial application of human rights treaties and consequently set a dangerous precedent for justice.

Though it succeeded in establishing both institutional and control connections between alleged violations and the UN, it remained vague on which bodies and institutions were responsible for carrying out the enforcement of accountability that would remedy the wrongful conduct of UN agencies.

The debate on whether ITAs can provide new grounds for the development of customary international law through their own practice, which may in time acquire the character of customary law, be it general or specific rules that will only apply in the circumstances when UN undertakes the role of the state, proves to be unconvincing and even contrary to the promotion and protection of human rights in practice. The numerous shortcomings that accompanied UN practice in Kosovo and East Timor provide sufficient evidence that such practice would not be beneficial for a custom as it is clearly inconsistent with the spirit of human rights law.

The most appropriate solution to the problem of the accountability of international organisations would therefore be to make it a standard procedure for them to become parties to human rights conventions in their own capacity.

General conclusions

UNMIK's conduct can be figuratively compared with the Roman god Janus, god of beginning and transitions. Like Janus, UNMIK had the ability to look forward and back at the same time, symbolising change and transition, such as progression of past to future, adapting itself to one condition or another, or going from one vision to another.[1] As the protector of its governed population, UNMIK was required to protect their wellbeing, their doors, gates, and roads.

The association of Janus with UNMIK becomes visible if we look at the ability of UNMIK to play a game between two points, notably the preservation of the sovereignty of the original sovereign and the desire of the majority population for independence. The path that connected these two points was thorny and as such had to be cautiously approached.

In the introduction we stated that due attention would be given to arguments that tend to associate today's international territorial administrations with those of colonial administrations, as well as other forms of territorial domination. In this context, two parallels can be drawn. When it comes to UNMIK's legitimacy, despite the complexity surrounding its establishment it did not lack legitimacy. UNMIK was established through a UNSC resolution as well as the consent of the host state.

In comparison to United Nations territorial administrations, colonial administrations are self-imposed and were mainly undertaken for the purposes of exploration and the fulfilment of economic or military interests, and were based on racist ideas regarding the colonial population.

As noted earlier in this research, the potential analogy between UNMIK and colonial administration arises from a sort of colonial mentality that one may sense in the conduct of activities as well as in the behaviours of certain international actors. These include the absolute power of the SRSG, the privileges of UNMIK's officials, the division between international and local actors, the intrusiveness in imposing decisions and the labels used to differentiate the local population, for example "democrats" from "extremists" (under colonialism, people would be divided into higher and lower class).

1 More information about the god Janus is available at the following website: www.crystalinks.com/janus.html.

The same explanation would stand for the opinion that regards UNMIK as a form of modern occupation. Taking into account the unique character of the UN's legal personality, it is difficult to accept this assertion.

Thus generally speaking, it is difficult to assert that UNMIK's activities fully mirror any one form of territorial dominion. Looking at UNMIK's activities overall, I would say rather that UNMIK's performance merely reflects a complex enterprise consisting of the transplantation of various ad hoc tools borrowed from past experiments, which enabled the consolidation and survival of its own power on the ground.

What is the final result of the evaluation of UNMIK's overall engagement on the ground? The answer to this question may lead to an answer to the principal question of this research, which seeks to establish whether an ambitious UN administration is capable of responding to the needs of the governed population, above all, protecting its fundamental rights.

Generally speaking, a measure of UNMIK's success would be its capacity to achieve the goals for which its mandate holds it responsible. So did UNMIK fulfil the goals enshrined in its mandate of establishment, namely UNSC Resolution 1244?

UNMIK's mandate comprised several requirements, including maintaining law and order, the creation of provisional institutions, the transfer administrative powers to local institutions and facilitating the political process that would determine the final status of the country.

Looking at the overall performance of its responsibilities, namely those related to establishing basic civilian administrative functions and to maintaining law and order, as well as the creation of provisional institutions, one may note that they were partially fulfilled.[2]

The UNMIK authorities could only maintain law and order and establish provisional institutions in the area where they did not encounter rejection. This raises a question as to what would have been the consequences if UNMIK's administration had been rejected on a larger scale. How would UNMIK have fulfilled its mandate? Could UNMIK have escaped from the obligations enshrined in its mandate by invoking an "inability" to ensure public order and safety on the ground? What would be a proper policy and a legal response to such situation? Would a power-sharing option solve the problem?

The situation in the northern part of the territory has the features of a failed state paradigm. So was international territorial administration allowed to fail its tasks assigned by the Security Council's mandate? And if yes, who could have saved it from its failure?[3]

2 "The major powers simply were not willing or did not have any stomach for a fight to establish authority in the north". Interview with a high-level UNMIK official, 10 May 2011.

3 Would an advisory opinion of the International Court of Justice be an option? For instance to follow the example of the ICJ's advisory opinion regarding the South-West Africa (renamed Namibia in 1968) when an advisory opinion was issued with regard to the UNSC Resolution 276 (1970) of 30 January 1970. On 29 July 1970, the Security Council, requested an

The UNMIK experience demonstrates that the biggest danger to human rights protection resides as much in what authorities refrain from doing as in what they do.

So was UNMIK capable of protecting the human rights of the population it governed? What is a common standard for measuring performance? Can the quality of its legal framework and its implementation in practice serve as a unit of measurement? Or alternatively its independent judicial mechanisms for protecting and remedying human rights violations? And above all, when does the UNMIK mission end and who is responsible for termination of UNMIK's mandate?

The adequacy of UNMIK's legislation

In discussing the adequacy of UNMIK's legislation for protecting and promoting human rights, it is important to underline the positive achievements in this regard. The overall legislation enacted under the auspices of UNMIK provides a sufficient basis for the protection of human rights. Yet it should be emphasised that the failure to establish a body that would measure the quality of the legislation, in particular to determine the compatibility of adopted laws with international legal instruments, has caused controversy, difficulties, and delays in the implementation of these laws in practice. An ad hoc mechanism comprising human rights experts would have been an appropriate tool to review past laws. Hence, the establishment of a Special Chamber for reviewing UNMIK's laws was of the utmost importance. It is difficult to understand why it was never put into practice.

The adequacy of the judicial mechanisms

Throughout this research, concern was expressed about the weakness of the judicial system arising from the centralisation of the powers into a sole authority, the SRSG. In light of this, one may ask whether such centralisation could have been avoided? Perhaps yes, if one of the pillars of UNMIK had taken overall responsibility for the judicial system. It would have eliminated, or at least minimised, the interference of the SRSG. In this context, I argue that sharing and dividing of powers among three diverse administrative pillars could have minimised excessively concentrated governance. The existence of fragile, thin, or simply confused lines of separation of powers threatens the efficiency and efficacy of the system.

However, the effectiveness of the UNMIK judiciary is brought into question by its inability to make justice accessible to everyone. Access to justice is an important element of human rights protection and promotion. By failing to establish

---

advisory opinion on "the legal consequences for States of the continued presence of South Africa in Namibia, notwithstanding the UNSC Resolution 276". The Court issued an advisory opinion declaring the continued presence of South Africa is illegal and advised its immediate withdrawal from Namibia. See, ICJ, Advisory Opinion of 21 June 1971. South West Africa (Namibia).

a court structure in the northern part of the territory, it has prevented the entire population of this area from having their rights recognised and enforced.

Human rights mechanisms

The existing internal human rights oversight mechanisms, such as the Ombudsperson and the Human Rights Advisory Panel (HRAP), despite contributing much towards promoting and protecting human rights, lacked sufficient institutional capacity to act as a real watchdog over of the UNMIK administration. Similar to the hybrid courts, they lacked basic safeguards that could ensure their independence in practice. In addition, the lack of enforcement powers hindered their ability to respond adequately to human rights violations. As it was already stressed by the members of the panel in their final report "the biggest failure of the entire HRAP experience was the fact that UNMIK did not follow the Panel's recommendations".[4]

The most significant flaw that accompanied UNMIK's authorities was their mindset, which make them unaware of the fact that they were performing state-like functions and not merely representing the United Nations. The lack of a clear and coherent legal framework contributed towards such a lack of understanding. UN officials who are assigned to a job in the UN need clear guidance from the start. They should not be allowed to follow their own perceptions of how to respond to an immediate situation on the ground. As indicated in this research, an "ad hoc functioning formula" may not adequately secure and protect the rights and freedoms of people.

Most importantly, United Nations actors should accept the fact that they are not infallible and as such cannot be absolved from being accountable for their wrongdoings.

The accountability deficit of international territorial administrations will, unfortunately, remain so as long as an international court does not establish a precedent on how to maintain a correct balance between the importance of not impeding the course of justice and the interests of preserving organisational immunity. In this situation, the immunity and privileges granted to an international organisation will continue to pose a stumbling block to the accountability of international organisations. The Srebrenica case was a missed opportunity for the ECtHR to provide a proper balance and establish premises that would finally end the culture of impunity for UN officials.

Yet this should not discourage scholars and practitioners from continuing their struggle in searching for paths that lead towards accountability for international actors.

To sum up, for all its shortcomings, UNMIK has not been worse than most governments around the world. This implies that the United Nations as well

4 HRAP Final Report, para 241, issued on 30 June 2016. Available at: www.unmikonline.org/hrap/Eng/pages/Annual-report.aspx.

as other international institutions should continue to exercise surrogate state administration whenever this is deemed appropriate.

As the underlying problem of such an endeavour has proved to be the lack of a clear mandate, for an ITA to handle its functions effectively the following elements should be included in its constitutive document.

As noted, today's peacekeeping operations comprise two contrasting components, civilian and military. This dual nature makes the undertaking complex and involves three distinct entities, namely the United Nations, NATO, and troop-sending countries. Although these two contrasting components are established simultaneously, they act under separate rules and are placed under distinct authorities. Consequently, problems arise once the peacekeepers act in violation of the human rights of the population they are deployed to protect. In this regard, it becomes difficult to determine which component is ultimately responsible for human rights violations.

This would require the enactment of a comprehensive mandate with clear mission objectives, as well as specifying a system of command and control. Additionally, it should establish a clear division of powers among the civil structures that assume governmental powers. It should be emphasised that this endeavour requires a specific human rights-based approach.

Long-lasting mandate: ending the Security Council resolutions

Studies show the duration of UN peacekeeping missions is becoming longer. While an average mission in the 1990s lasted 26 months, today, peacekeeping missions can last decades.[5]

UNMIK marks 19 years of its existence in Kosovo. Although its mandate has been gradually squeezed after the proclamation of independence yet the Resolution 1244 continues to play a consistent framework for both the UNMIK administration and the EULEX. Moreover, the Resolution provides a legal foundation for the NATO-led security force that has an exclusive role in securing Kosovo.

For difference of other peacekeeping mission UNMIK's mandate has not been subject to any revision. From 2008 on the political circumstances have been changed but UNMIK's mandate remained in line with UNSC Resolution 1244.[6] The Security Council did not envisage a timeframe for validity of the resolution 1244. In this regard sets of questions emerged. What is the durability of peacekeeping operation? Why would UN administration that has completed the main tasks of its mission stay on? These are important but, to date, under-studied legal issues?

5 Jessica Di Salvatore and Andrea Ruggeri, *Effectiveness of Peacekeeping Operations*, Oxford Research Encyclopedia of Politics, September 2017.

6 If we turn to UN mission in Sierra Leone one may noticed that the UN mandate has been subject to revision twice. See UNSC Resolutions: 1270, 1289 and 1829.

The international law stays silent on the issues that involve the termination or revision of the UNSC resolutions. Article 27 of the United Nations Charter provides that Council decisions require "an affirmative vote of nine members including the concurring votes of the permanent members". The UNSC has the sole authority to decide to either suspend or terminate the resolution. Yet this would require the unanimity of great powers, meaning that any disagreement among the permanent members may prevent Council from arriving at any substantive decision. Resolutions termination/revision -related cases have been absent from the international courts as well. As a result of this weak legal response it remains unclear what are the conditions for termination or revision of UNSC resolutions. This has stifled rather than sharpened the academic debates on that issue. It thus is important to explore when and how Council members might seek a legal ground to initiate terminations or revision of Council's resolutions. This is particularly important in the case when UNSC did not specify conditions of termination of the given resolution, or did not authorise an actor other than the Council to terminate all or part of the resolution? In this regard, the lack of clarity regarding the termination of resolutions may lead to arbitrariness and can navigate the tensions between big powers. Taking UNSC Resolution 1244 o as an example where the Council failed to envisage a timeframe for validity of the resolution it turned this very resolution into a deal in a way that guarantee the very existence of both UNMIK and Kosovo as a new state. The proclamation of independence in February 2008 did not trigger termination of the resolution although this very act has been seen by some scholars as an attempt to establish a new constitutional order and as such overturn the legally constituted order, established pursuant to the UNSC resolution 1244.[7] Yet even it has brought a change both in a domestic legal and political area however, in the eyes of the ICJ judges such an act did not take effect on the Resolution 1244's legal order.[8] It has been underlined that since the resolution does not contain a clause providing for termination and neither has been repealed, the UN administration, namely the SRSG continues to exercise his functions.[9] So as it may be seen the factual situation did not affect the formal side of the resolution. On the other side there is a hope among both UN officials as well as scholars that the future political settlement between Serbian and Kosovar government may trigger the end of the 1244 Resolution.[10] However, for the time being it is crystal clear, the 1244 Resolution cannot be undone due to the absence of clear legal provision and the political settlement can possibly trigger the termination if interpreted as a call for sunsetting the resolution, since it will expire as a matter of law. The up today practice shows that any permanent member may block the termination of the resolution in particular if it strongly favours the existing resolution, especially if its prolongation may bring

7 Martina Spernbauer, *EU Peace-Building in Kosovo and Afghanistan: Legality and Accountability*, Martinus Nijhoff Publishers, 2014, p. 66.

8 ICJ Advisory Opinion on Kosovo, 22. July 2010, para 493–94.

9 Ibid., para 92.

10 Interview with UNMIK official, conducted on 14 August 2018 in Prishtina, Kosovo.

some side deals.[11] From the international community's perspective, an eventual stance on the issue of Kosovo and the achievement of consensus among their respective member states might facilitate the revision or termination of UNSCR 1244 which would be in compliance with the contemporary circumstances in Kosovo. Nevertheless for the time being it is necessary to keep Resolution in force even if it does not produce the same legal effect. The UN administration in Kosovo shows that a peacekeeping operation should stay on and continue as long as it appears to be beneficial for both sides, and ensure the achievement of a just and comprehensive peace in the country.

The following can be suggested

The international law is meant to serve peace.[12] In the words of Lauterpacht "International law should be functionally oriented towards both the establishment of peace between nations and the protection of human rights".[13] In doing so the international law should be ready to respond to the variety of challenges that afflict the international community, such as, human rights abuses, consequences caused by armed conflicts, terrorism, environmental degradation and etc. However, this assumption should follow the fact that international law operates on consent- based legal norms and this makes international law less operational as states may always object to any proposed rule.

An effective response requires a collaborative effort by many states. Yet the collaboration is not easy to be achieved.[14]

This undermines the international actors 'capacity to fulfil their own obligation to follow the law. Consequently, it causes lack of faith in international law and the ability of international actors to solve problems.

It is generally known that international law has a range of common interests that have been styled pursuant to some common values. Yet one may note that those common values always reflect "egocentric interest" of the states which are often resulting from "coinciding individual interests".[15] On the other hand, despite such attitudes, though, there were situations where egocentric interests of the states have been challenged. The concept of human rights protection has played an important role in challenging existing international law rules. One may

11 Reason why termination of the UNSC Resolution 1244 has not been initiated yet is because of the fear that such an initiative might be blocked by the Russia. See the interview of Florian Bieber and Tim Judah given to the daily newspaper B92, "Deal to cancel Resolution 1244, But Russia won't let it?, available at: www.b92.net/eng/news/politics.php?yyyy=2018&mm=07&dd=20&nav_id=104679.

12 Christina Voigt, Delineating the common interest in International law, in Wolfgang Benedek, Koyen de Feyter, Mathias C. Ketterman, Christina Voight (eds.), *The Common Interest in International Law*, Intersentia, 2014, p. 9.

13 Ibid., quoted on page 9.

14 Guzman Andrew, *The Consent Problem in International Law, Berkley Program in Law, Economics*, Working Paper Series, 03 October 2013.

15 Ibid., p. 11.

freely say that international law has passed and is still going through evolutionary process thanks to human rights challenges. It is still "a work in progress" that searches for new modalities to promote and protect human rights by reshaping existing rules and practice as well as introducing new rules and review bodies. In this context, mobilisation about reframing international law and human rights is focused on "concern" rather than interest, since "concern" entails strong imperative than "interest".[16] This has been proven in the past on several occasions, for instance the intervention in Kosovo and East Timor which has been undertaken based on an ad hoc designed principle named "'humanitarian intervention" and most recently, a newly emerged norm named "responsibility to protect" provided legal justification for the intervention in Libya, Côte d'Ivoire, South Sudan, Yemen and Syria. This shows the ability of international law to adapt to the needs and different circumstances, to reconnect itself with some important issues of global justice.[17]

This could imply that importance of an issue lies in the "importance of the values at stake," namely the interest and the commitment of international community to translate its interest and concern into legal instrument.[18]

With this in mind I turn to the issue of accountability of international actors that includes international administration. In this regard, one may wonder are states ready to undertake some concrete steps towards meaningful international governance or rather continue to run around the notion of state supremacy, immunity and political interest. Although I do not believe that there is willingness at the moment to do so, however I would like to underline that current framework of international human rights law – if it is to be promoted and respected – must adapt to the needs of the population which happen to be governed by the international organisations. Along these lines, the adoption of human rights instruments by the ITA should become a standard procedure. Upon its establishment, the ITA should undergo the formal procedure for accession to human rights instruments. Subsequently, this would require the establishment of a hybrid Human Rights Chamber, composed of both international and national judges, with the mandate to examine alleged human rights violations committed by the ITA authorities. Such an endeavour would put in place law and justice and create a safe space for both the ITA authorities and the governed population. In this regard, the ITA authorities would themselves abide by the law, while the governed population would enjoy their rights.

As to the military component, although placed under the operational command of the UN each troop-contributing country should retain responsibility for its own troops. The liability for any violations arising from military conduct

16 Ibid., p. 12.

17 Richard Falk, *Balakrishnan Rajagopal, Jacqueline Stevers, Third World Quarterly*, Vol. 27, No. 5, Routledge, 2006, p. 711.

18 Christina Voigt, Delineating the Common Interest in International Law, in Wolfgang Benedek, Koyen de Feyter, Mathias C. Ketterman and Christina Voight (eds.), *The Common Interest in International Law*, Intersentia, 2014, pp. 12–13.

should be subjected to the military tribunals of the troop-sending country. In this context, the government of the troop-sending country would be required to sign an agreement with the ITA authorities, in this case the SRSG. This agreement should specify that the troop-sending country retains responsibility for any human rights abuses by its military troops. This includes the responsibility to provide recourse and redress to the victims of the human rights violations. Moreover, the responsible troop-sending country should ensure access to information and transparency regarding proceedings.

The dilemmas arising from the fear that such an undertaking would expose a contributing state to enormous expense can be minimised by adopting preemptive measures to prevent military troops from committing wilful misconduct. In this regard, the contributing state should set up adequate guidelines for its contingent. It should ensure that they are properly trained in and aware of human rights standards as provided in human rights instruments. Particular attention should be given to the process of hiring individuals for participation in peacekeeping operations. In this context, their background should be of crucial importance. Thus, the risk of misconduct will be diminished and, most importantly, the contributing country will be prevented from escaping from its human rights obligations.

Another solution to this problem albeit less effective could be if the Security Council would take the responsibility to devise an instrument in frame of its competence to -maintain international peace and security- and thus expand its competence in the area of peacebuilding. In this context, the UNSC could directly require that all contributing states when establishing an ITA should accept the liability in the human rights law applicable to them for human rights violations occurring pursuant to the given mandate. Nevertheless, taking into consideration that such solution will require both coordination and toleration among international actors for the time being it looks unrealistic due to the fact that majority of international actors behave in anarchical and pluralistic way of functioning subordinating themselves only to the interest of their sending states.

Furthermore, future ITAs should avoid a one-person model of exercising public power and instead turn to a temporary power-sharing model. Self-centred mechanism may lead to arbitrariness. Power should be exercised by the representatives of both the national and international actors, who can jointly and cooperatively make decisions. The exclusion of local actors from participating in institution-building processes will limit the ability of international actors to conduct thoughtful assessments of the causes and dynamics of the problems in the governed society. The UN cannot embark on a mission based on past experiences, because every single involvement is unique and will therefore require a specific approach. This can only be achieved with the close cooperation of local actors.

Both should be involved in developing solutions that will serve in the long term. Through a power-sharing model, they will teach national actors the principles of democracy and the rule of law. It is a common prerogative of international protagonists to teach and encourage local actors to adopt a power-sharing model (a model that includes power sharing among different groups in society). However, instead of teaching and encouraging it would be more appropriate to show them through their own example how to do it.

This can play a positive role in the country. The lessons learned from the "international-national" power-sharing model can be used for "inter-group power-sharing" and as such can help to balance the claims of the different groups within a society. This will buttress newly created states against possible collapse and a renewal of ethnic hostilities.

Bibliography

Books and articles

Abraham, E., The Sins of the Saviour: Holding the United Nations Accountable to International Human Rights Standards for Executive Order Detentions in Its Mission in Kosovo, *American University Law Review*, Vol. 52, No. 1291, 2003.

Addo, M.K., *The Legal Nature of International Human Rights*, Martinus Nijhoff Publishers, 2010.

Aird, S., History of Human Rights Crisis, Part One of the Two Series on Kosovo Crisis, *Human Rights Brief*, Vol. 6, No. 2, Brief 30, 1999.

Akande, D., The International Court of Justice and the Security Council: Is There a Room for Judicial Control of Decision of Political Organs of United Nations?, *International Comparative Law Quarterly*, Vol. 46, No. 2, 1197.

Akande, D. and Shah, S., Immunities of State Officials, International Crimes and Foreign Domestic Courts, *The European Journal of International Law*, Vol. 21, No. 4, 2011.

Allott, P., The Concept of International Law, *European Journal of International Law*, Vol. 10, 1999.

Allott, P., *Eunomia: New Order for a New World*, Oxford: Oxford University Press, 2001.

Alston, P. (ed.), *Non-State Actors and Human Rights*, Oxford: Oxford University Press, 2005.

Alston, P., The UN's Human Rights Record: From San Francisco to Vienna and Beyond, *Human Rights Quarterly*, Vol. 16, No. 2. 1994.

Altman, F.L., The Status of Kosovo, in D. Triantaphyllou (ed.), *What Status for Kosovo?*, EU-ISS Chaillot Paper No. 50, October, Paris, 2001.

Alvarez, J.E., *International Organisations as Law Makers*, Oxford: Oxford University Press, 2005.

Alvarez, J.E., Methods for the Identification of Customary International Law in the International Court of Justice's Jurisprudence: 2000–2009, *International and Comparative Law Quarterly*, Vol. 60, No. 3, 2011.

Amerasinghe, C.F., Accountability of International Organizations for Violations of the Human Rights of Staff, in J. Wouters, E. Brems, S. Smiss and P. Schmitt (eds.), *Accountability for Human Rights Violations by International Organizations*, Intersentia, 2010.

Andenas, M. and Fairgrieve, D., Judicial Independence and Accountability, National Traditions and International Standards, in Independence: Accountability, and the

Judiciary, *The British Institute of International and Comparative Law*, London, 2006.

Anghie, A., Colonialism and Birth of International Institutions: Sovereignty, Economy, and the Mandate System of the League of Nations, *International Law and Politics*, Vol. 34, No. 513, December, 2002.

Anghie, A., Finding the Peripheries: Sovereignty and Colonialism in Ninetieth Century International Law, *Harvard International Law Journal*, Vol. 40, No. 1, Winter, 1999.

Anghie, A., The Heart of My Home: Colonialism, Environmental Damage, and the Nauru Case, *Harvard International Law Journal*, Vol. 34, No. 2, 1993.

Applbaum, A.A., Legitimacy in Bastard Kingdom, Working Paper, Centre for Public Leadership, John F. Kennedy School of Government, Center for Public Leadership Working Papers, Spring, Cambridge, 2004.

Arajarvi, N., Customary International Law and the Principle of Legality in International Criminal Courts, Tilburg Law Review, *Journal of International and European Law*, Vol. 15, No. 2, 2011.

Arajarvi, N., From State Centrism to Where? The Formation of Customary International Law and Non-State Actors, available at: http://ssrn.com/abstract=1599679.

Arraiza, J.M. and Moratti, M., Getting the Property Question Right Legal Policy Dilemmas in Post-Conflict Property Restitution in Kosovo (1999–2009), *International Journal of Refuge Law*, Vol. 21, No. 3, 2009.

Aznar-Gomez, M.J., Some Paradoxes on Human Rights Protection in Kosovo, Volkerreccht als Wertordnung, in F.C. Tomuschat (ed.), *Common Values in International Law*, Kehl: N.P. Engel Verlag, 2006.

Ballard, M.J., Post Conflict Property Restitution: Flawed Legal and Theoretical Foundations, *Berkley Journal of International Law*, Vol. 28, No. 2, 2010.

Bangamwabo, F.X., Right to an Independent and Impartial Tribunal: A Comparative Study of Namibian Judiciary and International Judges, available at the following website: www.kas.de/upload/auslandshomepages/namibia/Independence_Judiciary/bangamwabo.pdf.

Barnett, H., *Constitutional and Administrative Law*, Ninth Edition, New York: Routledge, 2011.

Baskin, M., Between Exit and Engagement: On the Division of Authority between International and Domestic Institutions in Transitional Administration, *Global Governance*, Vol. 10, 2004.

Baylis, E., Parallel Courts in Post Conflict Kosovo, *The Yale Journal of International Law*, No. 2, 2007.

Beatty, D.M., *The Ultimate Rule of Law*, New York: Oxford University Press, 2004.

Beauvais, C.J., Benevolent Despotism: A Critique of UN State Building in East Timor, *International Law and Politics*, 2000–2001, Vol. 33, No. 4, Summer, 2001.

Bederman, D.J., Acquiescence, Objection and the Death of Customary International Law, *Duke Journal of Comparative International Law*, Vol. 21, No. 221, 2010.

Belhabib, Ch., *The United Nations Trusteeship System, 1945–1961*, A Bell & Howell Company, 1994.

Bell, C. and Evans, B., Post-Interventionary Societies: An Introduction, *Journal of Intervention and Statebuilding*, Vol. 4, No. 4, December, 2010.

Bell, S.S., *Administration of Colonies by Great Britain*, Longman, Brown, Green, Longmans and Roberts, 1859.

Bellamy, R., The Political Form of the Constitution, the Separation of Powers, Rights and Representative Democracy, in R. Bellamy (ed.), *The Rule of Law and the Separation of Powers*, Ashgate/Dartmouth, 2005.

Bellamy, R., *The Rule of Law and the Separation of Powers*, Farnham: Ashgate, 2005.

Ben Naftali, O., *International Humanitarian Law and International Human Rights Law*, Oxford: Oxford University Press, 2011.

Bennett, T.W. and Powell, C., The State as Trustee of Land, *S. African Journal on Human Rights*, Vol. 16, No. 601, 2000.

Benzing, M., Midwifing a New State: The United Nations in East Timor, *Max Planck Yearbook of United Nations Law*, Vol. 9, 2005.

Berdal, M., Lessons Not Learned: The Use of Force in 'Peace Operations in the 1990', *International Peacekeeping*, Vol. 7, No. 4, 2000.

Berdal, M. and Caplan, R., The Politics of International Administration, *Global Governance*, Vol. 10, 2004.

Berman, N., In the Wake of Empire, the Grotius Lecture Series, *American University International Law Review*, Vol. 14, No. 6.

Betts, W.S., Carlson, S. and Giswold, G., The Post Conflict Transitional Administration in Kosovo and the Lessons Learned in Efforts to Establish a Judiciary and Rule of Law, *Michigan Journal of International Law*, Vol. 22, 2001.

Biddle, S., Friedman, J.A. and Long, S., Civil War Intervention and Problem of Iraq, *International Studies Quarterly*, Vol. 56, 2012.

Binnendijk, H., Barry, C., Cordero, G., Nussbaum, L.P. and Sinclair, M., *Solution for Northern Kosovo: Lessons Learned in Mostar, Eastern Slavonia and Brcko*, Centre for Technology and National Security Policy, August, 2006.

Blocker, N., Beyond Dili: On the Power and Practice of International Organisations, in G. Kreijen, M. Brus, J. Duursma, E. De Vos and J. Dugard (eds.), *State, Sovereignty, and International Governance*, Oxford: Oxford University Press, 2002.

Boddy-Evans, A., Mandates in Africa, African History, available at the following website: http://africanhistory.about.com/od/eracolonialism/p/MandateAfrica.htm.

Bongiorno, C., A Culture of Impunity, Applying International Human Rights Law to the United Nations in East Timor, Columbia, *Human Rights Law Review*, Vol. 33, 2002.

Boon, K., Legislative Reform in Post-Conflict Zones: Jus Post Bellum and the Contemporary Occupant's Law-Making Powers, *Michigan Law Journal*, Vol. 50, 2005.

Boothby, D., The Political Challenges of Administering Eastern Slavonia, *Global Governance*, Vol. 10, 2004.

Bothe, M. and Marauhn, T., UN Administration in Kosovo and East Timor, Concept, Legality, and Limitations of Security Council-Mandated Trusteeship Administration, in F.C. Tomuschat (ed.), *Kosovo and the International Community: A Legal Assessment*, Kluwer Law International, 2002.

Bowdenm, B., The Colonial Origins of International Law, European Expansion and the Classical Standard of Civilisation, *Journal of International Law*, Vol. 23, 2005.

Bowett, D.W., *United Nations Forces: A Legal Study of United Nations Practice*, London: Stevens & Sons Ltd, 1964.

Boyle, K., Overview of a Dilemma, in C. Sandra (ed.), *Striking a Balance, Hate Speech, Freedom of Expression and Non-Discrimination*, International Centre against Censorship and Human Rights Centre, University of Essex, 1992.

Bradley, C. and Gulati, M., Customary International Law and Withdrawal Rights in an Age of Treaties, *Duke Journal of Comparative International Law*, Vol. 21, No. 221, 2010.

Braithwaite, J., On Speaking Softly and Carrying Big Sticks: Neglected Dimension of a Republication Separation of Powers, *University of Toronto Law Journal*, Vol. 47, No. 305, 1997.

Brand, M., The Development of Kosovo Institutions and the Transition of Authority from UNMIK to Local Self Government, Cluster of Competence, in *The Rehabilitation of Warn Torn Societies*, Centre for Applied Studies in International Negotiations (CASIN), 2003.

Brand, M., Institution-Building and Human Rights in Kosovo in the Light of UNMIK Legislation, *Nordic Journal of International Law*, Vol. 70, 2001.

Brand, M., Kosovo under International Administration, Statehood, Constitutionalism and Human Rights (PhD dissertation on file with the University of Vienna), 2002.

Brannen, D.E., Jr., *Constitutional Role of the Executive Branch, Checks and Balances: The Branches of the American Government*, USA: Thomson & Gale, 2005.

Breitegger, A., Sacrificing the Effectiveness of the European Convention on Human Rights on the Altar of the Effective Functioning of Peace Support Operations: A Critique of Behrami and Saramati and Al-Jedda, *International Community Law Review*, Vol. 11, 2009.

Brennan, F.G., The State of the Judicature, *Australian Law Journal*, Vol. 72, 1998.

Brooks, R.E., Failed States, or the State as Failure, *University of Chicago Law Review*, Vol. 72, No. 4, 2005.

Brooks, R.E., The New Imperialism, Violence, Norms, and the 'Rule of Law', *Michigan Law Review*, Vol. 101, June, 2003.

Brown, M.J. and Brooks, B., Recommendations for Preventing Lead Poisoning among the Internally Displaced Roma Population in Kosovo, The Centres for Disease Control and Prevention, Atlanta, GA, 27 October, 2007.

Brownlie, I., *Principles of Public International Law*, Fifth Edition, Oxford: Clarendon Press, 1998.

Buchahan, A., *Human Rights: Legitimacy and Use of Force*, Oxford: University Press, 2010.

Burbank, S. and Friedman, B., *Judicial Independence at the Crossroad: An Interdisciplinary Approach*, Sage Publications, 2002.

Burri, T., The Kosovo Opinion and Succession: The Sounds of Silence and Missing Links, *German Law Journal*, Vol. 11, No. 8, 2010.

Callahan, M.D., *A Sacred Trust: The League of Nations, and Africa 1929–1946*, Portland, Oregon: Sussex Academic Press, 2004.

Cameron, L., Accountability of International Organisations Engaged in the Administration of Territory, *University Centre for International Humanitarian Law*, February, Vol. 90, No. 871, 2006.

Cameron, L., Does the Law of Occupation Preclude Transformational Developments by the Occupying Power, in M. Vuijlsteke and F. Olteanu (eds.), *Current Challenges to the law of Occupation*, Collegium No. 34, Special Edition, 2006.

Cameron, L., Human Rights Accountability of International Civil Administrations to the People Subject to Administration, *Presentation for the International Conference: Accountability for Human Rights Violations by International Organizations*, Brussels, 17 March, 2007. Human Rights International Discourse, Vol. 2, Conference Reader.

Caplan, R., *International Governance of War-Torn Territories, Rule and Reconstruction*, Oxford: Oxford University Press, 2005.

Caplan, R., Who Guards the Guardians? International Accountability in Bosnia and Hercegovina, available at the following website: www.dur.ac.uk/resources/law/LCD/Caplan-Durhamwebsite.pdf.

Cappelletti, M., Who Watches the Watchmen? A Comparative Study on Judicial Responsibility, *American Journal of Comparative Law*, Vol. 13, No. 1, 1983.

Carey, J. 'The United Nations' Double Standard on Human Rights Complaints, *American Journal of International Law*, Vol. 60, No. 4, 1966.

Carlowitz, L., Settling Property Issues in Complex Peace Operations/The CRPC in Bosnia and Herzegovina and the HPD/CC in Kosovo, *Leiden Journal for International Law*, Vol. 17, 2004.

Carlson, S.N., Betts, W.S. and Gisvold, G., The Post-Conflict Traditional Administration of Kosovo and Lessons Learned in Efforts to Establish Judiciary and Rule of Law, *Michigan Journal of International Law*, Vol. 22, No. 33, Spring, 2001.

Carss-Frisk, M., A Guide to the Implementation of Article 1 of Protocol 1 to the European Convention of Human Right, *Human Rights Handbook*, Vol. 4, 2001.

Cassese, A., The Nicaragua and Tadic Test Revisited in Light of the ICJ Judgment on Genocide in Bosnia, *European Journal of International Law (EIL)*, Vol. 18, 2007.

Cerone, J., Out of Bounds? Considering the Reach of International Human Rights Law, Working Paper, Center for Human Rights and Global Justice, NYU School of Law No. 5, 2, New York, 2006.

Chan, J., State Succession to Human Rights Treaties, Hong Kong and International Covenant on Civil and Political Rights, *International and Comparative Law Quarterly*, Vol. 45, No. 4, October, 1996.

Chandler, D., *Bosnia: Faking Democracy after Dayton*, Second Edition, London: Pluto Press, 2000.

Chandler, D., *From Kosovo to Kabul and Beyond: Human Rights and International Intervention*, London: Pluto Press, 2006.

Charlesworth, H., The Constitution of East Timor, *International Journal of Constitutional Law*, Vol. 1, 2003.

Cheng, B., 'United Nations Resolutions on Outer Space', Instant International Customary Law, *International Journal of International Law*, Vol. 5, 1965.

Chesterman, S., Justice under International Administration, Kosovo, East Timor and Afghanistan, *International Peace Academy*, September, New York, 2002.

Chesterman, S., The United Nations as Government: Accountability Mechanisms for Territories under UN Administration, *International Peace Academy Paper*, 2002, available at: www.ipacademy.org.

Chesterman, S., *You the People: The United Nations, Transitional Administration, and State-Building*, Oxford: Oxford University Press, 2004.

Chinkin, M.C., NATO's Kosovo Intervention: Kosovo: A 'Good' or 'Bad' War?, *American Journal of International Law*, Vol. 93, No. 841, 1999.

Chopra, J., Building State Failure in East Timor, *Development and Change*, Vol. 33, No. 5.

Chopra, J., The UN's Kingdom of East Timor, *Survival*, Vol. 42, No. 2, Autumn, 2000.

Chowdhuri, R.N., *International Mandates and Trusteeship Systems: A Comparative Study*, The Hague: Martinus Njihoff, 1995.

Cias, M., Justice gaps in Kosovo Legal System, Graduate Student Workshop, 8–9 February, 2002, Kokalis programme, Kennedy School of Government, Harvard University.

Clapham, A., *Human Rights Obligations of Non-State Actors*, Oxford: Oxford University Press, 2006.

Cohen, L.J., Post Federalism and Judicial Changes in Yugoslavia: The Rise of Ethno Political Justice, *International Political Science Review*, Vol. 13, No. 3, 1992.

Colonialism in Africa, *Africa an Encyclopaedia for Students*, Vol. 1, Charles Scribner's Sons, 2002.

Colon-Rios, J., The Legitimacy of the Juridical, Constituent Power, Democracy and the Limits of the Constitutional Reform, *Osgoode Hall Law Journal*, Vol. 48, 2010.

Cooke, J.F., Some Reflection on International Trusteeship System, with Particular Impact on the Government and People of the Trust Territories, *International Organisation*, Vol. 13, No. 3, Summer, 1959.

Covey, J., Dziedzic, M. and Hawley, L., *The Quest for Visible Peace, International Intervention and Strategies for Conflict Transformation*, US Institute for Peace Press, 2005.

Craig, P., The Common Law, Shared Power and Judicial Review, *Oxford Journal of Legal Studies*, Vol. 24, No. 2, 2004.

Craig, P., Legislative Intent and Legislative Supremacy: A Reply to Professor Allan, *Oxford Journal of Legal Studies*, Vol. 24, No. 4, 2004.

Cranston, R., *Legal Ethics and Professional Responsibility*, Oxford: Clarendon Press, 1996.

Crawford, J.R., *The Creation of States in International Law*, Oxford: Clarendon Press, 1979.

Cuhna, A., Eulex Inside UNMIK, Too Late? Observatorie Balcanie Caucaso, available at the following website: www.balcanicaucaso.org/eng/Regions-and-countries/Kosovo/EULEX-inside-UNMIK-too-late-41332.

D'Amato, A., Human Rights as a Part of Customary International Law: A Plea for Change of Paradigms, Faculty Working Paper, Northwestern University School of Law Scholarly Commons, 2010.

D'Amato, A., Trashing International Customary Law, *American Journal of International Law*, Vol. 101, 1987.

Danilenko, G.M., Implementation of International law in CIS States, Theory and Practice, *European Journal of International Law*, Vol. 10, 1999.

Dann, P. and Al-Ali, Z., The Internationalised Pouvoir Constituent-Constitution-Making under External Influences in Iraq, Sudan and East Timor, *Max Planck Yearbook of United Nations Law*, Vol. 10, 2006.

Dannenbaum, T., Translating the Standard of Effective Control Into a System of Effective Accountability: How Liability Should Be Apportioned for Violations of Human Rights by Member State Troop Contingents Serving as United Nations Peacekeepers, *Harvard International Law Journal*, Vol. 51, Winter 70:80, 2010.

Da Rocca Ferreira, A., Formation and Evidence of Customary International Law, *UFRGS Model United Nations Journal*, Vol. 1, 2013.

Davis, L.E., *Peacekeeping and Peacemaking after Cold War*, RAND Summer Institute, 1993.

De Brabandere, E., The Kosovo Advisory Proceedings and the Court's Advisory Jurisdiction as a Method of Dispute Settlement, The Hague Justice Portal, 2010.

De Brabandere, E., *Post Conflict Administrations in International Law*, Martinus Nijhoff Publishers, 2009.

De Brabandere, E., State Centrism and Human Rights Obligations, Challenging 'Stateless' Approaches towards Direct Corporate Responsibility, *International Law Association, Research Seminar on Non State Actors*, 26–28, 2009, Leuven, Belgium.

De Coste, F.C., Redeeming the Rule of Law: Constitutional Justice: A Liberal Theory of the Rule of Law, *Alberta Law Review*, Vol. 39, No. 1004, 2002.

De Groot-van Leeuwen, L.E. and Rombouts, W. (eds.), *Separation of Powers in Theory and Practice: An International Perspective*, Nijmegen: Wolf Legal Publications, 2010.

De Hoogh, J.J.H.A., Attribution or Delegation of Legislative Power by the Security Council: The Case of the United Nations Administration in East Timor (UNTAET), in M. Bothe and B. Kondoch (eds.), *International Peacekeeping, Yearbook of International Peace Operation*, Kluwer Law International, 2002.

Delcourt, B. and Nina Wilen, N., International Administration of Foreign Territories and Sovereignty: An Impossible Equitation? *Finish Yearbook of International Law*, Vol. 18, 2007.

De Schutter, O., The Accountability of Multinationals for Human Rights Violations in European Law, Center for Human Rights and Global Justice, Working Paper No. 1, 2004, New York University School of Law, New York, 2004.

De Schutter, O., Human Rights, Globalization and Jurisdiction: Lessons from the European Convention on Human Rights, *Baltic Yearbook of International Law*, Vol. 6, 2006.

De Wet, E., *The Chapter VII Powers of the United Nations Security Council*, Oxford and Portland, Oregon: Hart Publishing, 2004.

De Wet, E., The Governance of Kosovo, Security Council 1244 and Establishment and Functioning of the EULEX, *The American Journal of International Law*, Vol. 103, No. 83, 2009.

De Wet, E., The International Constitutional Order, *International and Comparative Law Quarterly*, Vol. 55, 2006.

Diehl, P.F., *The Politics of Global Governance: International Organizations in an Interdependent World*, Boulder: Lynne Rienner, 2005.

Dimitrijevic, V., Customary Law as an Instrument for the Protection of Human Rights, *Isituto per gli Studi di Politica Internazionale*, WP 7, 2006.

Dinstein, Y., *The International Law of Belligerent Occupation*, Cambridge: Cambridge University Press, 2009.

Dinstein, Y., Legislation under Article 43 of the Hague Regulations Belligerent Occupation an and Peace-Building, *Occasional Program on Humanitarian Policy and Conflict Research*, Harvard University, Papers Series No. 1, 2004.

Duffield, M. and Hewitt, V. (eds.), *Empire Development and Colonialism: The Present in the Past*, James Currey, 2009.

Dumbuya, P.A., *Tanganyika under International Mandate 1919–1946*, 10 October, Maryland: University Press of America, 1995.

Dupuy, P.M., Constitutional Dimension of the Charter of the United Nations Revisited, *Max Planck Yearbook of United Nations Law*, Vol. 1, 1997.

Eclavea, R.P., Erkman, L.J., Espring, E.K. and Farell, T.B., *Force and Effect of International Law: American Jurisprudence*, Second Edition, The Lawyers Co-operative Publishing Co., 2010.

Edelstein, M.D., *Occupational Hazards*, Ithaca: Cornell University Press, 2008.

Elias, T.O., *Africa and the Development of International Law*, edited by Richard Akinjide, Martinus Nijhof Publisher, 1988.

Ely, J.H., *Democracy and Distrust: A Theory of Judicial Review*, Cambridge: Harvard University Press, 1980.

Emmet, E., The Mandate over South-West Africa, *Journal for Comparative Legislation and International Law*, Vol. 9, No. 3, 1927.

Ervin, S.J., Separation of Powers: Judicial Independence, *Law and Contemporary Problems*, Vol. 35, 1970.

Estreicher, S., Rethinking the Binding Effects of Customary International Law, *Virginia Journal of International Law*, Vol. 33, 2003.

Evans, L.H., The General Principles Governing the Termination of Mandate, *American Society of International Law*, Vol. 26, No. 4, 1932.

Evans, M.D. (ed.), *International Law*, Oxford: Oxford University Press, 2006.

Everly, R., Reviewing Governmental Acts of United Nations in Kosovo, *German Law Journal*, Special Issue, What Future for Kosovo, Vol. 8, No. 1, 2007.

Eyre, D. and Wittkowski, A., The Political Economy of Consolidating Kosovo: Property Rights: Political Conflict and Stability, 2002, available at: http://library.fes.de.

Falk, R., Agora: The ICJ's Kosovo Advisory Opinion: The Kosovo Advisory Opinion: Conflict Resolution and Precedent, *American Society of International Law*, Vol. 105, No. 1, 2011.

Falk, R. and Strauss, A., On the Creation of a Global People's Assembly: Legitimacy and the Power of Popular Sovereignty, *Stanford Journal of International Law*, Vol. 36, 2000.

Fassbender, B., The United Nations Charter as Constitution of the International Community, *Columbia Journal of Transnational Law*, Vol. 36, 1998.

Fausey, J.K., Does the United Nations' Use of Collective Sanctions to Protect Human Rights Violate Its Own Human Rights Standards?, *Connecticut Journal of International Law*, Vol. 10, 1994.

Fearon, J.D. and Laitin, D.D., Neotrusteeship and the Problem of Weak States, *International Security*, Vol. 28, 2004.

Fellmeth, A.X., Negative and Positive Human Rights, *Athens Institute for Education and Research 8th Annual International Conference on Law*, Athens, Greece, 18–21 July, 2011.

Ferejohen, J.A. and Kramer, L.D., Independent, Dependent Judiciary: Institutionalising Judicial Restraint, *New York University Law Review*, Vol. 77, 2002.

Ferraro, T., Occupation and Other Forms of Administration of Foreign Territory, Report, Expert Meeting, International Committee of the Red Cross, p. 4, available at: www.icrc.org/eng/assets/files/publications/icrc-002-4094.pdf.

Fetherston, A.B., *Towards a Theory of United Nations Peacekeeping*, Palgrave Macmillan, 1994.

Fitzpatrick, D., Developing Legal System in East Timor, Some Issues of UN Mandate and Capacity, *Austrian Review of International and European Law*, Vol. 5, 2000.

Fitzpatrick, D., Land Policy in Post-Conflict Circumstances: Some Lessons from East Timor, UNHCR Working Paper No. 58, 2002, available at: www.unhcr.ch.

Fleck, D., Civil and Military Administration in Peacekeeping Operations, Focus on Kosovo, in M. Bothe and B. Kondoch (eds.), *International Peace keeping: The Yearbook of International Peace Operations*, Vol. 7, Kluwer Law International, 2002.

Fleck, D., *The Handbook of International Humanitarian Law*, Second Edition, Oxford: Oxford University Press, 2008.

Fletcher-Cooke, J., Some Reflections on the International Trusteeship System, with Particular Reference to its Impact on the Governments and Peoples of the Trust Territories, *International Organization*, Vol. 13, No. 3, 1959.

Ford, C.E. and Oppenheim, B.A., Neotrusteeship or Mistrusteeship? The 'Authority Creep' Dilemma in United Nations Transitional Administration, *Vanderbilt Journal of Transnational Law*, Vol. 41, No. 1, January, 2008.

Forowicz, M., *The Reception of International Law in the European Court of Human Rights*, Oxford: Oxford University Press, 2010.

Fortna, V.P., Does Peacekeeping Keep Peace? International Intervention and the Duration of Peace after Civil War, *International Studies Quarterly*, Vol. 48, 2004.

Franck, T., The Emerging Right to Democratic Governance, *American Journal of International Law*, Vol. 86, 1992.

Franck, T., *Fairness in International Law and Institutions*, Oxford: Clarendon Press, 1995.

Friedrich, C.J., *Constitutional Government and Democracy: Theory and Practice in Europe and America*, Boston: Ginn and Company, 1946.

Friedrich, C.J., *Constitutional Government and Politics*, New York: Harper & Row, 1937.

Friedrich, C.J., *Limited Government: A Comparison*, London: Prentice-Hall and Englewood Cliffs, 1974.

Friedrich, C.J., *Transcendent Justice: The Religious Dimensions of Constitutionalism*, Durham: Duke University Press, 1964.

Friedrich, C.J., UNMIK in Kosovo; Struggling with Uncertainty, *Max Planck Yearbook of United Nations Law*, Vol. 9, 2005.

Frohlich, M., Keeping Track of UN Peacekeeping-Suez, Srebrenica, Rwanda and Brahimi Report, in J. Frowein and R. Wolfrium (eds.), *Max Planck Yearbook of International Law*, Vol. 5, Kluwer Law International, 2001.

Fuduli, J., Kosovo and Bosnia: Different Products of Yugoslavia's Disintegration, in L. Wentz (ed.), *Lessons from Kosovo: The KFOR Experience*, DoD Command and Control Research Programme, CCRP Publication Series, 2002.

Gaillard, E. and Pingell-Lenuzza, I., International Organisations and Immunity from Jurisdiction: To Restrict or to Bypass, *International and Comparative Law Quarterly*, Vol. 51, 2002.

Galluci, G., North Mitrovica and 'Returns', available at the following website: http://outsidewalls.blogspot.com/search/label/construction.

Gillard, E., and Lenuzza, I.P., International Organisations and Immunity from Jurisdiction: To Restrict or to Bypass, *International and Comparative Law Quarterly*, Vol. 51, 2002.

Ginsburg, T., Economic Analysis of the Design of Constitutional Courts, *Global Jurist Frontiers*, Vol. 1, No. 2, Art. 2, 2001, available at: www.bepress.com/gj/frontiers/vol1/iss2/art2.

Ginsburg, T., *Judicial Review in New Democracies: Constitutional Courts in Asian Cases*, New York: Cambridge University Press, 2003.

Glennon, M.J., Kosovo and the United Nations Charter, in *Limits of Law, Prerogatives of Power Interventionism after Kosovo*, New York: Palgrave, 2001.

Glopen, S., Gargarella, R. and Skaar, E., (eds.), *Democratization and the Judiciary: The Accountability Function of Courts in New Democracies*, London: Frank Cass Publishers, 2004.

Goldstone, A., UNTAET with Hindsight: The Peculiarities of Politics in an Incomplete State, *Global Governance*, Vol. 10, 2004.

Goodman, R., Human Rights Treaties, Invalid Reservations, and State Consent, *American Journal of International Law*, Vol. 96, 2002.

Goodwin, M., From Province to Protectorate to State? Speculation on the Impact of Kosovo's Genesis upon the Doctrines of International Law, *German Law Journal*, Vol. 80, No. 1, 2007.

Gordon, R.E., Saving Failed States: Sometimes a Neocolonialist Notion, *American University Journal of International Law & Policy*, Vol. 12, 1997.

Gordon, R.E., Some Legal Problems with Trusteeship, *Cornell International Law Journal*, Vol. 301, 1195.

Grant, D.T., East Timor, the UN system, and Enforcing Non-Recognition in International Law, *Vanderbilt Journal of Transnational Law*, Vol. 33, No. 2, March, 2000.

Grant, R.W. and Keohane, R.O., Accountability and Abuses of Power in World Politics, *American Political Science Review*, Vol. 99, 2005.

Greenwood, C., Humanitarian Intervention: Case of Kosovo, *Finish Yearbook of International Law*, Vol. 10, 1999.

Grenfell, L., Legal Pluralism and the Rule of Law in Timor Leste, *Leiden Journal of International Law*, Vol. 19, 2006.

Grover, S.C., *The European Court of Human Rights as a Pathway to Impunity for International Crimes*, Springer-Verlag, Berlin, Heidelberg, 2010.

Hall, H.D., *Mandates, Dependencies and Trusteeship*, London: Stevens & Sons Limited, 1948.

Hall, H.D., The Trusteeship System, *British Yearbook of International Law*, Vol. 34, 1947.

Handlin, O. and Handlin, M., *The Popular Sources of Political Authority: Documents on the Massachusetts Constitution 1780*, Cambridge: Harvard University Press, 1966.

Harland, D., Legitimacy and Effectiveness in International Administration, *Global Governance*, Vol. 10, 2004.

Harrington, A.R., A Tale of Three Nations? The Role of United Nations Peacekeeping and Missions on the Concept of Nations-State, Nationalism, and Ownership of the State in Lebanon, the Democratic Republic of Congo, and Kosovo, *The Connecticut Journal of International Law*, Vol. 21, No. 213, University of Connecticut School of Law, 2006.

Harris, G.T., The Era of Multilateral Occupation, *Berkley Journal of International Law*, Vol. 24, 2006.

Hartmann, M., International Judges and Prosecutors in Kosovo, Special Report 112, United States Institute of Peace, 2003.

Hayden, R.M., *Bosnia Ten Years after 'Independence': The Dictatorship of the Protectorate under Civicist Self-Management*, East European Studies Special Report Woodrow Wilson International Center, 2002.

Hayek, F.A., *The Political Ideal of the Rule of Law*, Cairo: National Bank of Egypt. Cairo N.B.E. Printing Press, 1955.

Hayek, F.A., *The Road to Serfdom*, Chicago: University of Chicago Press, 1994.

Heininger, J.E., *Peacekeeping in Transition: The United Nations in Cambodia*, New York: The Twenty Century Fund Press, 1994.

Helfer, L., Constitutional Analogies in the International Legal System, *Loyola Los Angeles Law Review*, Vol. 37, 2004.

Helman, G.B. and Ratner, S.R., Saving Failed States, *Foreign Policy*, Vol. 89, 1993.

Helmke, G. and Rosenbluh, F., Regimes and the Rule of Law, Judicial Independence in Comparative Perspective, *The Annual Review of Political Science*, Vol. 12, 2009.

Henry, S., Philip, P. and Goodman, R., *International Human Rights in Context: Law, Politics, Morals*, Third edition, Oxford: Oxford University Press, 2008.

Herring, E., From Rambouillet to the Kosovo Accords: NATO' War Against Serbia and Its Aftermath, in K. Booth (ed.), *The Kosovo Tragedy: The Human Rights Dimension*, The International Journal of Human Rights, Special Issue, Vol. 4, No. 3/4, Autumn/Winter, London, 2000.

Heun, W., Supremacy of the Constitution, Separation of Powers, and Judicial Review in Nineteenth-Century German Constitutionalism, *Ratio Juris: International Journal of Jurisprudence, and Philosophy of Law*, 2003.

Heyns, C.H. and Viljoen, F., The Impact of the Human Rights Treaties on the Domestic Level, *Human Rights Quarterly*, Vol. 23, No. 3, 2001.

Higgins, R., The United Nations and Law Making, *The American Journal of International Law*, Vol. 64, No. 4, 1970.

Hill, N.L., The Individual in International Organizations, *American Political Science Review*, Vol. 28, No. 2, 1934.

Hirsch, M., *The Responsibility of International Organizations Toward Third Parties: Some Basic Principles*, Dordrecht: Martinus Nijhoff, 1995.

Hitoshi, N., *Peacekeeping in Perspective: A Study of Article 40 of the UN Charter*, Martinus Nijhoff Publishers, 2009.

Hohler, B., Responsibility of International Organisations: The Element of Attribution in the Context of Peacekeeping Operations, (Overview of Normative Framework and Manifestation in Practice), Paper presented at the *2nd Global International Studies Conference*, University of Ljubljana, Faculty of Social Science, Ljubljana, 23–26 July, 2008, available at: www.wiscnetwork.org/ljubljana2008/papers/WISC_2008-363.doc.

Hoof, G.J.H., *Rethinking Sources of International Law*, The Netherlands: Kluwer Academic Publisher, 1983.

Hooker, M.B., *Legal Pluralism: An Introduction to Colonial and Neo-Colonial Laws*, Oxford: Clarendon Press, 1975.

Hosmer, S.T., *The Conflict over Kosovo, Why Milosevic Decided to Settle When He Did*, RAND, 2001.

Howard, C., *Civil Resistance in Kosovo*, London: Pluto Press, 2000.

Howse, R. and Teitel, R., Delphic Dictum: How Has the ICJ Contributed to the Global Rule of Law by Its Ruling on Kosovo? *German Law Journal*, Vol. 11, No. 8, 2010.

Igarashi, M., Jan Smut's Mandate Plan: A Precursory Idea of Peace Building by International Organization, *Hokkaido Journal of New Global Law and Policy*, Vol. 3, 2009.

Ingimundarson, V., Pitting Democratic Standards against Sovereign Rights: The Nature of International Rule in Kosovo, *New Balkans Politics*, No. 7/8, 2003.

Ingravallo, I., UN Territorial Administrations: Between International Humanitarian Law and Human Rights Law, in R. Kolb and G. Gaggioli (eds.), *Research Handbook on Human Rights and Humanitarian Law*, UK: Edward Elgar Publishing, 2013.

Irmscher, T.H., The Legal Framework for the Activities of the United Nations Interim Administration Mission in Kosovo: The Charter, Human Rights, and the Law of Occupation, *German Yearbook of International Law*, Vol. 44, 2001.

Jackson, R., International Engagement in War-Torn Countries, *Global Governance*, Vol. 10, 2004.

Janaby, G.M. and Bashir, K.R., The Right of Individuals to Take Judicial Action against International Persons: The Case of NATO's Intervention in Libya, *Cambridge Journal of International and Comparative Law*, Vol. 1, No. 3, 2012.

Jarstad, A.K., From War to Democracy, in A.K. Jarstad and T.D. Sisk (eds.), *Dilemmas of Peacekeeping*, Cambridge: Cambridge University Press, 2008.

Jayasuriya, K., Globalization, Law and the Transformation of Sovereignty: The Emergence of Global Regulatory Governance, *Indiana Journal of Global Legal Studies*, Vol. 6, 1999.

Jennings, R. and Watts, A., *Oppenheim's International Law*, Vol. 1, Ninth Edition, Oxford: Oxford University Press, 2008.

Joerges, C., Sand, I.-J. and Teubner, G. (eds.), *Transnational Governance and Constitutionalism*, Oxford: Hart, 2004.

Johnson, A.R., East European Studies Special Report, An Assessment of the Decade of Western Peace-Keeping and Nation-Building in the Balkans, Woodrow Wilson International Center, Washington, 2003.

Jones, S.G., Wilson, J.M., Rathmell, A. and Rilley, K.J., *Establishing Law and Order after Conflict*, Rand, 2005.

Kahn, P.W., The Question of Sovereignty, *Stanford Journal of International Law*, Vol. 40, 2004.

Karadjava, M., Property Restitution in Eastern Europe: Domestic and International Human Rights Law Responses, *Central and East European Law Review*, Vol. 29, No. 3, Martinus Nijhoff, 2004.

Karnavas, M., Creating the Legal Framework of the Brčko District of Bosnia and Herzegovina: A Model for the Region and Other Post Conflict Countries, *American Journal of International Law*, Vol. 97, 2003.

Kaufman, I.R., The Essence of Judicial Independence, *Columbia Law Review*, Vol. 80, No. 4, 1980.

Kelly, F.B.W., An Independent Judiciary the Core of the Rule of Law, International Justice for Criminal Law Reform and Criminal Justice Policy, available at: www.icclr.law.ubc.ca/Publications/Reports/An_Independant_Judiciary.pdf.

Keohane, R., Commentary on the Democratic Accountability of Non-Governmental Organizations, *Chicago Journal of International Law*, Vol. 3, 2002.

Keohane, R. and Nye, J., Democracy, Accountability, and Global Governance, Harvard University John F. Kennedy School of Government, Politics Research Group Working Papers on International Relations No. 01–4, 2001, available at: www.ksg.harvard.edu/prg/nye/ggajune.pdf.

Kern, F., *Kingship and Law in the Middle Ages*, New York: Harper Torch Books, 1956.

Kerwiin, G.J., The Role of United Nations General Assembly Resolutions in Determining Principles of International Law in United States Courts, *Duke Law Journal*, 1983, pp. 876–899.

King, I. and Mason, W., *Peace at any Price: How the world failed Kosovo*, London: Hurst, 2006.

Kirgis, F.L., Security Council Governance of Post-Conflict Societies: A Plea for Good Faith and Informed Decision Making, *American Journal of International Law*, Vol. 95, 2001.

Klabbers, J., Constitutionalism Lite, *International Organizations Law Review*, Vol. 1, 2004.

Klabbers, J., The Life and Times of the Law of International Organisations, *Nordic Journal of International Law*, Vol. 70, 2001.

Klabbers, J., Possible Islands of Predictability: The Legal Thought of Hannah Arendt, *Leiden Journal of International Law*, Vol. 20, 2007.

Knoll, B., Beyond the Mission Civilisatrice: The Properties of a Normative Order within an Internationalized Territory, *Leiden Journal of International Law*, Vol. 19, 2006.

Knoll, B., From Benchmarking to Final Status? Kosovo and the Problem of an International Administration's Open-Ended Mandate, *European Journal of International Law*, Vol. 16, No. 637, 2005.

Knoll, B., *The Legal Status of Territories Subject to Administration by International Organizations*, Cambridge: Cambridge University Press, 2008.

Knoll, B., Legitimacy and UN-Administration of Territory, *German Law Journal*, Vol. 80, 2007.

Knoll, B., UN Imperium: Horizontal and Vertical Transfer of Effective Control and the Concept of Residual Sovereignty in 'Internationalized' Territories', *Austrian Review of International and European Law*, Vol. 7, 2002.

Knudsen, T.B. and Lautsten, C.B., *Kosovo between War and Peace, Nationalism, Peace-Building and International Trusteeship*, Oxford: Routledge, 2007.

Kohn, M., Colonialism, *The Stanford Encyclopedia of Philosophy*, edited by E.N. Zalta, Fall, 2011 Edition, available at: http://plato.stanford.edu/entries/colonialism/.

Kondoch, B., Human Rights Law and UN Peace Operations in Post-Conflict Situations, in N. White and D. Klaasen (eds.), *The UN, Human Rights and Post-Conflict Situations*, Manchester University Press, 2005.

Kondoch, B., The Responsibility of Peacekeepers, Their Sending States, and International Organizations, in T. Gill and D. Fleck (eds.), *The Handbook of the International Law and Military Operations*, Oxford: Oxford University Press, 2010.

Korhonen, O., International Governance in Post Conflict Situations, *Leiden Journal of International Law*, Vol. 14, No. 03, 2001, pp. 495–529.

Koskenniemi, M., Solidarity Measures: State Responsibility as a New International Order? *British Yearbook of International Law*, Vol. 72, No. 1, 2001.

Kreijen, G. (ed.), *State, Sovereignty, and International Governance*, Oxford: Oxford University Press, 2002.

Krieger, H., *The Kosovo Conflict and International Law: An Analytical Documentation 1974–1999*, Cambridge: Cambridge University Press, 2001.

Kristen, E., New Direction in Responsibility: Assessing the International Commission's Draft Articles on the Responsibility of International Organizations, *The Yale Journal of International Law*, Vol. 37, Spring, 2011.

Krug, P. and Price, M.E., A Module for Media Intervention/Content Regulation, in Post Conflict Zones, in *Forging Peace, Intervention, Human Rights, and Management of Media Space*, Indiana University Press, 2002.

Ku, C. and Jacobson, H. (eds.), *Democratic Accountability and the Use of Force in International Law*, Cambridge: Cambridge University Press, 2003.

Kuperman, A., Suicidal Rebellions and Moral Hazard of Humanitarian Intervention, Ethnopolitics, *Formerly Global Review on Ethnopolitics*, Vol. 4, No. 2, June, 2005.

Ladley, A., Peacekeeper Abuse, Immunity and Impunity: The Need for Effective Criminal and Civil Accountability on International Peace Operations, *Politics and Ethics Review*, Vol. 1, 2005.

Lakshminarayan, C.V., Analyses of the Principles and System of International Trusteeship in the Charter: A Study of the Origin, Principles and Application in International Law, Thesis No 80, University of Geneva, Geneva.

Lantschner, E., Marko, K. and Petrucusic, A., *European Integration and Its Effects on Minority Protection in South Eastern Europe*, EURAC Research (band 12).

Larkins, C.M., Judicial Independence and Democratization: A Theoretical and Conceptual Analyses, *American Journal of Comparative Law*, Vol. 44, 1994.

Larsen, M.K., Attribution of Conduct in Peace Operation: The Ultimate Authority Control Test, *The European Journal of International Law*, Vol. 19, No. 3, 2008.

Leck, C., International Responsibility in United Nations Peacekeeping Operations: Command and Control Arrangements and the Attribution of Conduct, *Melbourne Journal of International Law*, Vol. 10, 2009.

Lemay-Hebert, N., State Building from the Outside-In: UNMIK and Its Paradox, *Journal of Public and International Affairs*, Vol. 20, 2009.

Le Mon, C.J., Unilateral Intervention by Invitation in Civil Wars: The Effective Control Tested, *International Law and Politics*, Vol. 35, 2003.

Lim, C.L. and Olufemi, E., Withdrawing from Custom and the Paradox of Consensualism in International Law, *Duke Journal of Comparative and International law*, Vol. 21, 2010.

Mackenzie, R. and Sands, P., International Courts and Tribunals and the Independence of the International Judge, *Harvard International Law Journal*, Vol. 44, No. 1, 2003.

Madison, J., Federalist 47, in K. O'Regan (ed.), Checks and Balances Reflections on the Development of the Doctrine of Separation of Powers under the South African Constitution, *PER/PELJ*, Vol. 8, No. 1, 2005.

Mageahan, P., The Role and Independence of Prosecutors, Conference Paper, Cairo, 2005, available at: www.pogar.org/publications/ruleoflaw/cairo/pmageean.pdf.

Mahoney, P., Right to Fair Trial in Criminal Matters, under Article 6 of the ECHR, *Judicial Studies Institute Journal*, Vol. 4, No. 2, 2004.

Malanczuk, P., *Akehurst's Modern Introduction to International Law*, Seventh Edition, Routledge, 1997.

Malcolm, N., *Kosovo: A Short History*, London: New York University Press, 1998.

Malleson, K., System for Appointing Judges Undermining International Courts, *The Guardian UK*, available at the following website: www.guardian.co.uk/law/2010/sep/08/law-international-court-justice-legal.

Mani, R., Rebuilding the Rule of Law in the Aftermath of Complex Political Emergencies, *International Peacekeeping*, Vol. 5, No. 3, Autumn, 1998.

Manson, K., The Forgotten Agenda: Human Rights Protection and Promotion in Cold Was Peacekeeping, *Journal of Conflict & Security Law*, Vol. 10, No. 3, Oxford University Press, 2005.

Mansson, K., Implementing the Concept of Protection of Civilian in the Lights of Humanitarian Law and Human Rights Law: The case of Monuc, in R. Arnold and N. Quiniver (eds.), *International Humanitarian Law and Human Rights Law: Towards New Merger of International Law*, Martinus Nijhoff Publisher, 2008.

Mantouvalou, V., Extending Judicial Control in International Law: Human Rights Treaties and Extra Territoriality, *International Journal of Human Rights*, Vol. 9, No. 2, 2005.

Markovic, R., *Ustavno Pravo i Politicke Institucije*, Sluzbeni Glasnik, 1998.

Marphy, S.D., Reflection on ICJ Opinion on Kosovo, Interpreting Security Council Resolution 1244, in M. Wood and M. Milanovic (eds.), *The Law and Politics of the Kosovo Advisory Opinion*, Oxford: Oxford University Press, 2015.

Marshall, D. and Inglis, S., The Disempowerment of Human Rights-Based Justice in the United Nations Mission in Kosovo, *Harvard Human Rights Journal*, Vol. 16, 2003.

Martinez, M.M., *National Sovereignty and International Organizations*, The Hague: Kluwer Law International, 1996.

Matheson, M.J., United Nations Governance of Post Conflict Societies, Symposium: State Reconstruction after Civil Conflict, *The American Journal of International Law*, Vol. 95, No. 76, 2001.

Matz, N., Civilization and the Mandate System under the League of Nations as Origin of Trusteeship, *Max Plank Yearbook of United Nations Law*, Vol. 9, 2005.

McCoubrey, H. and White, N.D., *The Blue Helmets: Legal Regulation of United Nations Military Operations*, Dartmouth Pub, 1996.

Megret, F. and Hoffman, F., Fostering Accountability: An Ombudsman for the United Nations, *Global Governance*, Vol. 11, 2005, pp. 43–63.

Megret, F. and Hoffman, F., The UN as a Human Rights Violator? Some Reflections on the United Nations Changing Human Rights Responsibilities, *Human Rights Quarterly*, Vol. 25, No. 2, 2002.

Meron, T., Judicial Independence and Impartiality in International Criminal Tribunals, *The American Journal of International Law*, Vol. 99, 2005.

Mertus, J., Reconsidering the Legality of Humanitarian Intervention: Lesson from Kosovo, *William and Mary Law Review*, Vol. 41, 2000.

Miko, S., Al-Skeini v. United Kingdom and Extra-Territorial Jurisdiction under the European Convention for Human Rights, *Boston Colleague International and Comparative Law Review*, Vol. 35, No. 3, 2013.

Milano, E., Security Council Action in the Balkans: Reweaving the Legality of Kosovo's Territorial Status, *European Journal of International Law*, Vol. 14, 2003.

Milano, E., *Unlawful Territorial Situations in International Law: Reconciling Effectiveness, Legality and Legitimacy*, Leiden: Nijhoff, 2006.

Milanovic, M. and Papic, T., As Bad as It Gets: The European Court of Human Rights' Behrami and Saramati Decision and General International Law, *International and Comparative Law Quarterly*, Vol. 58, No. 2, 2009.

Miller, A., UNMIK: Lessons from Early Phase, *New England Law Review*, Vol. 39, 2004.

Miller, S., Revisiting Extraterritorial Jurisdiction: A Territorial Justification for Extraterritorial Jurisdiction under the European Convention, *The European Journal of International Law*, Vol. 20, No. 4, 2010.

Mole, N., Who Guards the Guards: The Rule of Law in Kosovo, in *European Human Rights Law Review*, Vol. 6, London: Sweets and Maxwell, 2001.

Moliterno, J.E., What the ICJ's Decision Means for Kosovars, *German Law Journal*, Vol. 11, No. 8, 2010.

Momirov, A., *Accountability of International Organizations in Post-Conflict Governance Missions*, Den Haag: Boom Juridische Uitgevers, 2005.

Momirov, A., *Accountability of International Territorial Administrations: A Public Law Approach*, Eleven International Publishing, 2011.

Momirov, A., Dutch Courts and Srebrenica Ascribing Responsibility and Defining Legal Relevant Relationships, *Netherlands Yearbook of International Law*, Vol. 43, 24 June, 2013.

Momirov, A., The Individual Right to Petition in Internationalized Territories: From Progressive Thought to an Abandoned Practice, *Journal of the History of International Law*, Vol. 9, 2007.

Montesquieu, *The Spirit of Laws*, Cambridge: Cambridge University Press, 1989.

Morais, H.V., The Quest for International Standards: Global Governance vs. Sovereignty, *University of Kansas Law Review*, Vol. 50, 2002.

Morrow, J. and White, R., The United Nations in Transitional East Timor: International Standards and the Reality of Governance, *Australian Yearbook of International Law*, Vol. 22, 2002.

Morse, B.W. and Woodman, G.R., *Indigenous Law and the State*, Dordrecht: Foris, 1988.

Mortimer, E., International Administration of War-Torn Societies, *Global Governance*, Vol. 10, 2004.

Mowbray, A., *The development of Positive Obligations under the European Convention on Human Rights by the European Court of Human Rights*, Oxford and Portland, Oregon: Hart Publishing, 2004.

Mujezinovic Larsen, K., Attribution of Conduct in Peace Operation: The Ultimate Authority Control Test, *The European Journal of International Law*, Vol. 19, No. 3, 2008.

Muller, S., *International Organizations and Their Host States: Aspects of Their Legal*, Kluwer Law International, 1995.

Murati, G.B., Can Identity Cleansing be Negotiated, Prishtina Insight, Balkan Investigative Reporting Network (BIRN) No. 63, 6 May, 2011.

Mutua, M., Justice under Siege: The Rule of Law and Judicial Subservience in Kenya, *Human Rights Quarterly*, Vol. 23, 1991.

Naidoo, V., A Human Rights Perspective on Policy Implementation Process: Observation from the South African Public Service, *Democracy and Governance*, Human Sciences Research Council, 2003.

Newman, E., Peacebuilding as Security in Failing and Conflict-Prone States, *Journal of Intervention and Statebuilding*, Vol. 4, No. 3, September, 2010.

Oberg, M.D., The Legal Effects of Resolutions of the UN Security Council and General Assembly in the Jurisprudence of the ICJ, *The European Journal of International Law*, Vol. 16, No. 5, 2006.

Ochoa, C., Disintegrating Customary International Law: Reactions to Withdrawing from International Customs, *Duke Journal of Comparative& International Law*, Vol. 21, 2010, pp. 207–220.

O'Connell, M.E., Responsibility to Peace: A Critique of R2P, *Journal of Intervention and Statebuilding*, Vol. 4, No. 1, March, 2010.

O'Conor, V. and Rausch, C. (eds.), *Model Codes for Post Criminal Justice, Peace Building and Rule of Law*, United States Institute of Peace, 2007.

O' Flaherty, M., *The Human Rights Field Operation: Law Theory and Practice*, Ashgate, 2007.

Oisin, T., *Regime-Building: Democratisation and International Administration*, Oxford Studies in Democratisation, Oxford: Oxford University Press, 2009.

O'Neil, W., *Kosovo: An Unfinished Peace*, Boulder, Co: Lynne Reinner Publisher, 2002.

Oosthuizen, G.H., Playing the Devil's Advocate: The United Nations Security Council Is Unbound by Law, *Leiden Journal of International Law*, Vol. 12, 1999.

Orrico, D.G., Security Council Resolutions under Chapter VII, Design Implementation and Accountabilities, Fride, 2009.

Pantuliano, S., *Uncharted Territorry: Land Conflict and Humanitarian Action*, Humanitarian Policy Group Policy Briefs 39, Oversees Development Institute, London, 2009.

Parenti, M., *To Kill a Nation: The Attack on Yugoslavia*, Verso, 2000.

Paris, R., *At War's Ends: Building Peace after Civil Conflict*, Cambridge: Cambridge University Press, 2004.

Paris, R., International Peacebuilding and 'Mission Civilisatrice', *Review of International Studies*, Vol. 28, 2002.

Parker, T., The Ultimate Intervention: Revitalizing the UN Trusteeship Council for the 21st Century, Rapport/ Report Centre for European and Asian Studies, Norwegian School of Management, BI, 2003.

Parmer, N., Clark, Ph. and Cranville, D., *Critical Perspective in Transitional Justice*, Intersentia, 2012.

Pasquee, D. and Dewulf, S., International Territorial Administrations and the Rule Of Law: The Case of Kosovo, *Essex Human Rights Review*, Vol. 4, No. 1, February, 2007.

Pattision, J., *Humanitarian Intervention and the Responsibility to Protect: Who Should Intervene?*, Oxford: Oxford University Press, 2010.

Pejic, J., The European Court of Human Right's Al-Jedda Judgment: The Oversight of the International Humanitarian Law, *International Review of the Red Cross*, Vol. 93, No. 883, September, 2011.

Pellet, A., The Opinions of the Badinter Arbitration Committee a Second Breath for the Self-Determination of Peoples, *European Journal of International Law*, Vol. 3, 1992.

Perriello, T. and Wierda, M., Lessons from the Deployment of International Judges and Prosecutors in Kosovo, *The International Centre for Transitional Justice*, March, 2006.

Perritt, H.H., Providing Judicial Review for Decisions by Political Trustees, *Duke Journal of Comparative & International Law*, Vol. 15, No. 1, 2004.

Perritt, H.H., *The Road to Independence for Kosovo: A Chronical of Ahtisaari Plan*, Cambridge: Cambridge University Press, 2010.

Perritt, H.H., Structures and Standards for Political Trusteeship, *Journal of the International Law and Foreign Affairs*, Vol. 8, 2003.

Persson, T., Roland, G. and Tabellini, G., Separation of Powers and Accountability, *The Quarterly Journal of Economics*, Vol. 112, No. 4, 1997.

Petersen, N., Customary Law without Custom? Rules, Principles, and the Role of State Practice in International Norm Creation, *American University International Law Review*, Vol. 3, No. 2, 2008.

Philpott, D. and Powers, G.F., *Strategies of Peace, Transforming Conflict in a Violent World*, Oxford: Oxford University Press, 2010.

Pittman, B., Nations, *The American Political Science Review*, Vol. 16, No. 4, 1992.

Polansky, P., Roma Children Dying of Lead Poisoning, *New Kosova Report*, 17 November, 2008, available at the following website: www.newkosovareport.com/200811171411/Views-and-Analysis/roma-children-dying-of-lead-poisoning.html.

Préfontaine, D.C., Q.C. and Lee, J., The Rule of Law and the Independence of the Judiciary, The International Centre for Criminal Law Reform and Criminal Justice Policy, Working Paper prepared for *World Conference on Universal Declaration of Human Rights*, Montreal, 7–9 December, 1998.

Prettitore, P., The Right to Housing and Property Restitution in Bosnia and Herzegovina: A Case Study, Working Paper No. 1. Organisation for Security and Cooperation in Europe (OSCE), April, Vienna, 2003.

Quaye, C.O., *Liberation Struggles in International Law*, Philadelphia: Temple University Press, 1991.

Rachel Smit, A.R., Housing and Property Restitution and IDP Return in Kosovo, *Journal Compilation: IOM International Migration*, Vol. 44, No. 3, Blackwell Publishing Ltd, 2006.

Rajagopal, B., *International Law from Below: Development, Social Movement and Third World Resistance*, Cambridge: Cambridge University Press, 2003.

Ratner, S., Foreign Occupation and International Territorial Administration: The Challenges of Convergence, *European Journal of International Law*, Vol. 16, No. 4, 2005.

Ratner, S., *The New UN Peacekeeping: Building Peace in Lands of Conflict after the Cold War*, New York: St. Martin's Press, 1996.

Rawski, F., Wave or Not to Wave, *Connecticut Journal of International Law*, Vol. 18, 2002.

Reif, L.C., *The Ombudsman, Good Governance and the International Human Rights System*, Leiden and Boston: Martinus Nijhoff, 2004.

Reinisch, A., Developing Human Rights and Humanitarian Law Accountability of the Security Council for the Imposition of Economic Sanctions, *American Journal of International Law*, Vol. 95, 2001.

Reinisch, A., Securing the Accountability of International Organizations, *Global Governance*, Vol. 7, 2001.

Reinisch, A. and Weber, A.U., In the Shadow of Waite and Kennedy, *International Organizations Law Review*, Vol. 1, 2004.

Reka, B., *UNMIK as an International Governance in Post-War Kosova: NATO's Intervention, UN Administration and Kosovar Aspirations*, Shkup: Logos, 2003.

Richardson, H.J., III, Failed States, Self Determination, and Preventive Diplomacy: Colonialist Nostalgia and Democratic Expectations, *Temple International and Comparative Law Journal*, Vol. 10, 1994.

Riesman, M., Reflection on State Responsibility for Violations of Explicit, Protectorate, Mandate and Trusteeship Obligation, *Michigan Journal of International Law*, Vol. 10, No. 231, 1989.

Risch, I., Some Practical Issues Concerning the Development of the Judicial System in Kosovo, New Approaching in International Criminal Justice Kosovo, Sierra Leone and Cambodia, Max Planck Institute fur auslandernes und internationals strafrecht, Heidelberg, 2003.

Roberts, A.E., Traditional and Modern Approaches to Customary International Law: A Reconciliation, *American Journal of International Law*, Vol. 95, 2001.

Roberts, A.E., Who Killed Article 38 (1) (B)? A Reply to Bradly and Gulati, *Duke Journal of Comparative International Law*, Vol. 21, No. 221, 2010.

Romano, C. and Ingadottir, Th., *The Financing of the International Criminal Court, Project on International Courts and Tribunals (PICT)*, The Center on International Cooperation, New York University, New York.

Romeu, F.R., The Establishment of Constitutional Courts: A Study of 128 Democratic Constitutions, *Review of Law and Economics*, Vol. 2, No. 1, 2006.

Rosand, E., The Security Council as Global Legislator Ultra Vires or Ultra Innovative?, *Fordham International Law Journal*, Vol. 28, No. 3, 2004.

Rothert, M., UN Intervention in East Timor, *Columbia Journal of Transnational Law*, Vol. 39, 2000.

Rucker, J., Former UNMIK SRSG (2006–2008), Kosovo Today, Presentation at the University of Oxford, St. Anthony's College, January, 2009, available at: www.joachim-ruecker.de/PresentationOxford%2026Jan09.pdf.

Ruffert, M., The Administration of Kosovo and East Timor, *International and Comparative Law Quarterly*, Vol. 50, 2001.

Ryngaert, C., Clarifying the Extra-Territorial Application of the European Convention on Human Rights, *Utrecht Journal of International and European Law*, pp. 57–60, available at: http://dx.doi.org/10.5334/ujiel.ba.

Ryngaert, C., Responsibility of Member States, in Connection with Acts of International Organisations: Assessing the Recent Case Law of the European Court of Human Rights, *International and Comparative Law Quarterly*, Vol. 16, October, 2011.

Sari, A., Status Forces and Status Mission Agreements under ESDP, the EU's Evolving Practice, *European Journal of International Law*, Vol. 19, No. 1, 2008.

Sarooshi, D., Conferrals by States of Powers on International Organizations: The Case of Agency, *The British Year Book of International Law*, Vol. 74, No. 291, 2004.

Sarooshi, D., The Essentially Contested Nature of the Concept of Sovereignty: Implications for the Exercise by International Organizations of Delegated Powers of Government, *Michigan Journal of International Law*, Vol. 25, No. 1107, 2004.

Sarooshi, D., *International Organizations and Their Exercise of Sovereign Powers*, Oxford: Oxford University Press, 2005.

Sarooshi, D., The Nature of the Concept of Sovereignty: Implications for the Exercise by International Organizations of Powers of Government, *Michigan Journal of International Law*, Vol. 25, No. 1107, 2004.

Sarooshi, D., The Role of the UN Secretary-General in UN Peace-Keeping, *Australian Yearbook of International Law*, Vol. 20, No. 279, 2000.

Sarooshi, D., The UN and the Establishment of Peace, *Current Legal Problems*, Vol. 53, No. 621, 2000.

Sarooshi, D., *The United Nations and the Development of Collective Security: The Delegation by the Security Council of Its Chapter VII Powers*, Oxford: Oxford University Press, 2000.

Sayre, F.B., *Experiments in International Administration*, New York: Harper & Brothers, 1919.

Schachter, O., The Sources of Human Rights Law, Custom, Jus Cogens, and General Principles, in Bruno Simma and Philip Alston (eds.), *Australian Yearbook of International Law*, Vol. 85, No. 12, 1988–1989.

Scheffer, D.J., Beyond Occupation Law, *American Journal of International Law*, Vol. 97, 2003.

Scheiper, S., *Negotiating Sovereignty and Human Rights, International Society and the International Criminal Court*, Manchester University Press, 2009.

Schermers, H.G., *International Institutional Law*, The Netherlands: Sijthoff and Noordhoff, 1980.

Schoenbroad, D., Separation of Powers and Powers That Be: The Constitutional Purposes of Delegation Doctrine, *The American University Law Review*, Vol. 36, 1987.

Shaw, M., *International Law*, Sixth Edition, Cambridge: Cambridge University Press, 2008.

Sheeran, S. and others, UN Peace Keeping and the Model of Status Forces Agreement, United Nations Peace-Keeping, Law Reform Project, Essex School of Law, February 2011, available at the following website: www.essex.ac.uk/plrp/.
Shelton, D., Normative Hierarchy in International Law, *The American Journal of International Law*, Vol. 100, No. 2, April 2006.
Shelton, D., *Remedies in International Human Rights Law*, Oxford: Oxford University Press, 2005.
Shetreet, S. and Deschenes, J. (eds.), *Judicial Independence: The Contemporary Debate*, Dordrecht: Martinus Nijhoff Publishers, 1985.
Shraga, D., The United Nations as an Actor Bound by International Humanitarian Law, in L. Condorelli et al. (eds.), *The United Nations and International Humanitarian Law*, Paris: Editions Pedone, 1996.
Shraga, D., UN Peacekeeping Operations: Applicability of International Humanitarian Law and Responsibility for Operations-related Damage, *American Journal of International Law*, Vol. 94, 2000.
Siers, H., Separation of the Judiciary and Judicial Independence in Bangladesh, 2004, available at: dhaka.net/School_Library/senior%20Projects/04_Hadley_judiciary.pdf.
Simma, B. and Alston, P., The Sources of Human Rights Law, Custom, Jus Cogens, and General Principles, *Australian Yearbook of International Law*, Vol. 85, No. 12, 1988–1989.
Simmons, B., Civil Rights in International Law, Compliance with Aspects of International Bill of Rights, *Indian Journal of Global Legal Studies*, Vol. 16, No. 2, Summer 2009.
Singer, M., Jurisdictional Immunity of International Organisations: Human Rights and Functional Necessity, *Virginia Journal of International Law*, Vol. 46, No. 53, 1995–1996.
Slaughter, A., Sovereignty and Power in a Networked World Order, *Stanford of International Law*, Vol. 40, 2004.
Smith, J.H., Independent Judiciary, the Colonial Background, *University of Pennsylvania Law Review*, Vol. 1105, 1975–1976.
Smitt, A.R., Housing and Property Restitution and IDP Return in Kosovo, *International Migration*, Vol. 44, No. 3, 2006.
Smuts, J.C., *The League of Nations: A Practical Suggestion*, London: Hodder & Stoughton, 1918.
Smyrek, D.S., *Internationally Administered Territories: International Protectorates? An Analysis of Sovereignty over Internationally Administered Territories with Special Reference to the Legal status of Post-War Kosovo*, Berlin: Duncker & Humblot, 2005.
Spijkers, O., Immunity of the United Nations in Relation to the Genocide in the Eyes of the Dutch District Court, *Journal of International Peace Keeping*, Vol. 13, 2009.
Spijkers, O., The Netherlands' and the United Nations' Legal Responsibility for Srebrenica before the Dutch Courts, *Military Law and the Law of War Review*, Vol. 50, No. 3–4, 2011.
Stahn, C., Accountability and Legitimacy in Practice: Lawmaking by Transitional Administrations, *International Peacekeeping*, Vol. 11, available at: www.esil-sedi.org/english/pdf/Stahn.PDF.
Stahn, C., Constitution without State? Kosovo under the United Nations Constitutional Framework for Self Government, *Leiden Journal of International Law*, Vol. 14, 2001.

Stahn, C., The Geometry of Transitional Justice: Choices of Institutional Design, *Leiden Journal of International Law*, Vol. 18, 2005.

Stahn, C., International Territorial Administration in the Former Yugoslavia: Origins, Developments and Challenges ahead, *Zeitschrift für Ausländisches Öffentliches Recht und Völkerrecht*, Vol. 61, No. 105, 2001.

Stahn, C., Justice under Transitional Administration: Contours and Critique of a Paradigm, *Houston Journal of International Law*, Vol. 27, 2004–2005.

Stahn, C., *The Law and Practice of International Territorial Administration*, Cambridge: Cambridge University Press, 2008.

Stahn, C., The United Nations Transitional Administration in Kosovo and East Timor: A First Analyses, *Max Planck Yearbook of United Nations Law*, Vol. 5, *Kluwer Law International*, 2001.

Stavileci, E., Which Laws Should Be Drafted for the New Administration in Kosova?, *Published in Kosova Law Review*, Vol. 4, No. 4, Winter 1999.

Steele, M.T., Judicial Independence, *Widener Law Journal*, Vol. 18, No. 2, 2009.

Stein, P., *Roman Law in European History*, Cambridge: Cambridge University Press, 1999.

Steinberg, R.H., Who Is Sovereign, *Stanford Journal of International Law*, Vol. 40, No. 2, Summer 2004.

Stephan, P.B., Accountability and International Lawmaking: Rules, Rents and Legitimacy, *Northwestern Journal of International Law & Business*, Vol. 17, 1997.

Stephan, P.B., Disaggregating Customary International Law, *Duke Journal of Comparative and International Law*, Vol. 21, No. 191, 2010.

Stevens, R., A Loss of Innocence? Judicial Independence and the Separation of Powers, *Oxford Journal of Legal Studies*, Vol. 9, No. 3, 1999.

Strobel, M., *Ustavno Pravo SFR Jugoslavije*, Casopisni Zavod Uradni List S.R Slovenije, 1986.

Strohmeyer, H., Collapse and Reconstruction of a Judicial System: The United Nations Missions in Kosovo and East Timor, *American Journal of International Law*, Vol. 95, 2001, pp. 46–63.

Stromseth, J., Post Conflict Rule of law Building, Need For a Multi-Layered, Synergic Approach, *William and Mary Law Review*, Vol. 49, No. 4.

Swaine, E.T., Bespoke Custom, *Duke Journal of Comparative & International Law*, Vol. 21, 2010, 207–220.

Tamanaha, B.Z., *On the Rule of Law*, Cambridge: Cambridge University Press, 2004.

Tansey, O., Kosovo: Independence and Tutelage, *Journal of Democracy*, Vol. 20, No. 2, 2009.

Tansey, O., *Regime Building: Democratisation and International Administration*, Oxford: Oxford University Press, 2009.

Tavil, E., Property Rights in Kosovo: A Haunting Legacy of Society in Transition, Occasional Papers Series, *International Centre for Transitional Justice*, February 2009.

Thakur, R., *The United Nations, Peace and Security, from Collective Security to Responsibility to Protect*, Cambridge: Cambridge University Press, 2006.

Thienel, T., Issues of Attribution in Al-Jedda and Srebrenica: The Cases Compared, available at the following website: http://invisiblecollege.weblog.leidenuniv.nl/2011/08/28/issues-of-attribution-in-al-jedda-and-sr/.

Thomas, D.C., International NGOs, State Sovereignty and Democratic Values, *Chicago Journal of International Law*, Vol. 2, 2001.

Thullen, G., Problems of the Trusteeship System: A Study of Political Behaviour in the United Nations, *Geneve Librairie Droz, India Quarterly*, Vol. 22, No. 3, 1964, pp. 295–296.

Thurer, D., Current Challenges to the Law of Occupation, in M. Vuijlsteke and F. Olteanu (eds.), *Current Challenges to the law of Occupation*, Special Edition, Collegium, No. 34, 2006.

Thurer, D., The Failed State and International Law, *International Review of the Red Cross*, No. 836, p. 1999.

Tilly, R. and Welfens, P.J.J., *Economic Globalization, International Organizations and Crisis Management*, Heidelberg: Springer, 2005.

Tittimore, B., New from the International Criminal Tribunals: ICTY, available at the following website: www.pict-pcti.org/publications/ICC_paprs/FinancingICC.pdf.

Tomushat, C., Yugoslavia Damaged Sovereignty over the Province of Kosovo, in G. Kreijen, M. Brus, J. Duursma, E. De Vos and J. Dugard (eds.), *State, Sovereignty, and International Governance*, Oxford: Oxford University Press, 2002.

Tonchi, V., Lindeke, W.A. and Grotpeter, J.J., *Historical Dictionary of Namibia*, Second Edition, Scarecrow Press, 2012, p. 296.

Trachtman, J.P., Persistent Objectors, Cooperation, and the Utility of Customary International Law, *Duke Journal of Comparative International Law*, Vol. 21, No. 221, 2010.

Traub, J., Inventing East Timor, *Foreign Affairs*, Vol. 79, 2000.

Trechsel, S. and Summers, S., *Human Rights in Criminal Proceedings*, Oxford: Oxford University Press, 2005.

Tremblay, L.B., General Legitimacy of Judicial Review and the Fundamental Basis of Constitutional Law, *Oxford Journal of Legal Studies*, Vol. 23, No. 4, 2003.

Trimble, P.R., A Revisionist View of Customary International Law, *UCLA Law Review*, Vol. 33–665, 1986.

Tsagourias, N., Security Council Legislation Article 2(7) of the UN Charter and the Principle of Subsidiary, Working Papers, Series, 2011:05, Adam Smith Research Foundation.

Turk, D., Recognition of States: A Comment, *European Journal of International Law*, Vol. 4, 1993.

Turner, R.V., *Magna Carta through the Ages*, Harlow: Pearson Education Limited, 2003.

Tushnet, M., The Political Institutions of Rights-Protection in *The Legal Protection of Human Rights: Sceptical Essays*, in T. Campbell, K.D. Ewing and A. Tomkins (eds.), Oxford: Oxford University Press, 2011.

Udwadia, S., Corporate Responsibility for International Human Rights Violations, *Southern California Interdisciplinary Law Journal*, Vol. 13, No. 359, 2004.

Upthegrove, C.L., *Empire by Mandate: A History of the Relations of Great Britain with the Permanent Mandate Commission of the League of Nations, Bookman Associates*, New York, The ANNALS of the American Academy of Political and Social Science, Vol. 296, No. 1, 1954, pp. 204–205.

Urquhart, B., The United Nations, Collective Security, and International Peacekeeping, in M. Goulding (ed.), *The Evolution of United Nations Peacekeeping*, International Affairs, Royal Institute of International Affairs 1944, Vol. 69, No. 3, July 1993.

Vagle, B. and de Medina-Rosales, F., An Evaluation of the Housings and Property Directorate in Kosovo, NORDEM Report 12, 2006.

Van Banning, T.R.G., *The Human Right to Property Antwerpen*, Cambridge: Intersentia, 2002.

Van Boven, T., Distinguishing Criteria of Human Rights, in H.J. Steiner, P. Alston, R. Goodman (eds.), *International Human Rights in Context, Law: Politics, Morals*, Third Edition, Oxford: Oxford University Press, 2008.

Ventura, M. and Akande, D., Mothers of Srebrenica: The Obligation to Prevent Genocide and Jus Cogens-Implication for Humanitarian Intervention, Comments on EJIL Talk, 6 September 2013, available at the following website: www.ejiltalk.org/ignoring-the-elephant-in-the-room-in-mothers-of-srebrenica-is-the-obligation-to-prevent-genocide-jus-cogens/.

Verdirame, G., A Normative Theory of Sovereignty Transfer, *Stanford Journal of International Law*, Vol. 49, No. 2, 2013.

Verdirame, G., *The UN and Human Rights, Who Guards the Guardians*, Cambridge: Cambridge University Press, 2011.

Verschuur, R.C., Independence of the Judiciary, Conference Paper, 2 June 2007, Belgrade, available at: www.medel.bugi.web.com.

Voeten, E., The Politics of International Judicial Appointments, Evidence from the European Court of Human Rights, *International Organization*, Vol. 61, 2007.

Voigt, C., The Role of General Principles in International Law and Their Relationship to Treaty Law, *Retfaerd Argang*, Vol. 31, No. 2/121, 2008.

Von Carlowitz, L., UNMIK Law Making between Effective Peace Support and Internal Self-Determination, *Archiv des Volkerrechts*, Bd. 41, 2003.

Vradenburgh, A.M., The Chapter VII Powers of the United Nations Charter: Do They 'Trump' Human Rights Law?, *Loyola of Los Angeles International and Comparative Law Journal*, Vol. 14, 1991.

Walker, N. (ed.), *Sovereignty in Transition*, Oxford: Hart Publishing, 2003.

Waters, C.P.M., "Kosovanizing" the Ombudsperson: Implication for Kosovo and Peacekeeping, *International Peacekeeping*, Vol. 15, No. 5, 2008.

Watkins, J., Responsibility in Context, *Oxford Journal of Legal Studies*, Vol. 26, No. 3, 2006.

Wellens, K., *Remedies against International Organizations*, Cambridge: Cambridge University Press, 2002.

Weller, M., The Rambouillet Conference on Kosovo, *International Affairs*, Vol. 75, No. 2, April 1999.

Weymouth, A. and Hening, S. (eds.), *The Kosovo Crisis: The Last American War in Europe*, Reuters and Pearson Education, 2001.

Widner, J., Courts and Democracy in Post-Conflict Transitions: A Social Scientist's Perspective on the African Case, *American Journal of International Law*, Vol. 95, 2001.

Wilde, R., Advancing the Effectiveness of International Law: Is U.N. Reform Necessary? Enhancing Accountability at the International Level: The Tension between International Organisation and Member State Responsibility and the Underlying Issue at Stake, *ILSA Journal of International & Comparative Law*, Vol. 12, No. 395, 2006.

Wilde, R., From Danzing to East Timor and Beyond: The Role of the International Territorial Administration, *American Journal of International Law*, Vol. 95, No. 3, 2001.

Wilde, R., International Territorial Administration and Human Rights, in N. White and D. Klaasen (eds.), *The UN, Human Rights and Post-Conflict Situations*, Manchester University Press, 2005.

Wilde, R., *International Territorial Administration, How Trusteeship and Civilizing Mission Never Went Away*, Oxford: Oxford University Press, 2008.

Wilde, R., *Quis Custodiet Ipsos Custodes?* Why and How UNHCR Governance of Development Refugee Camps Should Be Subject to International Human Rights Law, *Yale Human Rights & Development Law Journal*, Vol. 1, 1998.

Wilde, R., Representing International Territorial Administration: A Critique of Some Approaches, *European Journal of International Law*, Vol. 15, No. 1, 2004.

Williams, J., Al Skeini: A Flawed Interpretation of Bankovic, *Wisconsin International Law Journal*, Vol. 23, No. 4.

Williams, P., Earned Sovereignty: The Road to Resolving Conflict over Kosovo Status, *Denver Journal of International Law, and Policy*, Vol. 31, No. 3, 2003, pp. 387–403.

Williams, P.R. and Pecci, F.J., Earned Sovereignty: Bridging the Gap between Sovereignty and Self-Determination, *Stanford Journal of International Law*, Vol. 40, 2004.

Williams, R.C., Post-Conflict Property Restitution in Bosnia: Balancing Repatriations and Durable Solutions in the aftermath of displacement, Tesev, International Symposium on 'Internal Displacement in Turkey and Abroad', Istanbul, 5 December 2006.

Willner-Reid, M., *Post Colonial Governments of Leading Strings: The Legitimacy and Accountability of International Transitional Administrations*, Coimbra University, Portugal, 2005–2006.

Woelk, J., Palermo, F. and Marko, J., *Tolerance through Law, European Academy Bozen*, Bolzano: Bill Nijhoff, 2007.

Wood, N., In Kosovo, Newspapers Exposes of War Criminals Led to Murder, *The Guardian*, 21 June 2000.

Woodman, G.R., Legal Pluralism and the Search for Justice, *Journal of African Law*, Vol. 40, No. 152, 1996.

Wouters, J., Brems, E., Smiss, S. and Schmitt, P (eds.), *Accountability of International Organizations for Violations of the Human Rights of Staff*, Intersentia, Cambridge, 2010.

Wouters, J. and de Man, P., International Organizations as Law Makers, Working Paper No. 21, March 2009, Leuven Centre for Global Governance Studies, Catholic University of Leuven.

Wouters, J. and Van Dries, E., Giving Effect to Customary International Law through European Community Law, Working Paper No. 25, The Institute for International Law, K.U Leuven, June 2002.

Wright, Q., *Mandates Under the League of Nations*, Chicago: Chicago University Press, 1930.

Wright, Q., Some Recent Cases on Status of Mandate Areas, *The American Journal of International Law*, Vol. 20, No. 4, 1926.

Wright, Q., Sovereignty of the Mandates, *The American Journal of International Law*, Vol. 17, No. 4, 1923.

Wright, Q., Status of the Inhabitants of Mandated Territory, *American Journal of International Law*, Vol. 18, No. 2, 1924.

Yannis, A., The Concept of Suspended Sovereignty in International Law and Its Implications in International Politics, *European Journal of International Law*, Vol. 13, No. 5, 2003.

Yannis, A., The UN as Government in Kosovo, *Global Governance*, Vol. 10, No. 1, January 2004.
Ydit, M., *Internationalised Territories*, Leiden: A.W. Sythoff, 1961.
Young, A.I., Deconstructing International Organization Immunity, *Georgetown Journal of International Law*, Vol. 44, 2012.
Zegveld, L., *Armed Opposition Groups in International Law: The Quest for Accountability*, Cambridge: Cambridge University Press, 2000.
Zimmermann, A. and Stahn, C., Yugoslav Territory, United nations Trusteeship or Sovereign State? Reflections on the Current and Future Legal Status of Kosovo, *Nordic Journal of International Law*, Vol. 71, No. 4, 2002.
Zoethout, C., Tang, G.V.D. and Akkermans, P. (eds.), *Control in Constitutional Law*, Dordrecht: Nijhoff. 1993.
Zurn, M., Democratic Governance beyond the Nation-State: The EU and Other International Institutions, *European Journal of International Relations*, Vol. 6, 2001.
Zwanenburg, M., Legal Interoperability in Multinational Forces: A Military Necessity, in M. Vuijlsteke and F. Olteanu (eds.), *Current Challenges to the Law of Occupation*, Special Edition, Collegium, No. 34, College of Europe 2006.

League of Nations

Covenant of the League of Nations, adopted on 28 April 1919.
Treaty of Versailles, signed on 28 June 1919.

United Nations documents

Convention against Torture and Other Cruel, Inhuman or Degrading Treatment and Punishment, adopted on 10 December 1984.
Convention on the Elimination of All Forms of Racial Discrimination, adopted on 21 December 1965.
Convention on the Privileges and Immunities of the United Nations, 13 February 1946, 1U.N.T.S. 15.
Covenant on Economic, Social and Cultural Rights, adopted on 16 December 1966.
Geneva Convention 'for the Amelioration of the Condition of the Wounded and Sick in Armed Forces in the Field', adopted on 12 August 1949.
Geneva Convention 'for the Amelioration of the Condition of Wounded, Sick and Shipwrecked Members of Armed Forces at Sea', adopted on 12 August 1949.
Geneva Convention 'relative to the Protection of Civilian Persons in Time of War', adopted on 12 August 1949.
Geneva Convention 'relative to the Treatment of Prisoners of War', adopted on 12 August 1949.
Hague Convention Respecting the Laws and Customs of War on Land (Hague IV), 18 October 1907.
International Covenant on Civil and Political Rights, 19 December 1966.
Protocol I Additional to the Geneva Conventions, adopted on 8 June 1977
Protocol III Additional to the Geneva Conventions, adopted on 8 December 2005.
United Nations Charter, signed on 26 June 1945.
Vienna Convention on Diplomatic Relations, 18 April 1961, 500 U.N.T.S. 95.
Vienna Convention on the Law of Treaties, 23 May 1969, 1155 U.N.T.S. 331.

Regional human rights documents

African Charter on Human and Peoples' Rights, adopted 27 June 1981.
American Convention on Human Rights, adopted 22 November 1969.
European Convention on Human Rights 4, adopted November 1950.

Council of Europe

Council of Europe: The European Charter on the Statute for Judges, Adopted by the Committee of Ministers on 13 October 1994.
Council of Europe: Kosovo: Commissioner Hammarberg Calls for Stop of Forced Returns and Immediate Evacuation of Roma from Lead-Contaminated Camps, News Item, 15 February 2010.
Council of Europe, Parliamentary Assembly, Resolution 1417 (2005), issued on 25 January 2005.
Council of Europe: Recommendation No. R (94) 12 of the Committee of Ministers to Member States on the Independence, Efficiency and Role of Judges, 13 October 1994.
Council of Europe: Report of the Council of Europe Commissioner for Human Rights' Special Mission to Kosovo(1), Doc. CommDH (2009) 23, 2 July 2009.
Council of Europe: Resolution 1708 (2010) of the Parliamentary Assembly of the Council of Europe on Solving Property Issues of Refugees and Displaced Persons.
European Commission for Democracy through Law (Venice Commission): Opinion No. 403/2006, 22 June 2007.
European Commission for Democracy through Law (Venice Commission): 'Opinion on Human Rights in Kosovo: Possible Establishment of Review Mechanisms', 8–9 October 2004, 60th Plenary Session.

UN Security Council resolutions

UNSC Resolution 855, issued on 9 August 1993 (On the refusal of the authorities of the FRY to allow a CSCE special mission into Kosovo).
UNSC Resolution 1160, issued on 31 March 1998 (On the imposition of an arms embargo on Yugoslavia).
UNSC Resolution 1199, issued on 23 September 1998 (On the situation in Kosovo).
UNSC Resolution 1203, issued on 24 October 1998 (On agreements for the verification of compliance with the provisions of resolution 1199).
UNSC Resolution 1207, issued on 17 November 1998 (On the failure of Yugoslavia to execute arrest warrants issued by the International Tribunal for the Former Yugoslavia).
UNSC Resolution 1239, issued on 14 May 1999 (On relief assistance to Kosovo refugees and internally displaced persons in Kosovo, the Republic of Montenegro and other parts of the Federal Republic of Yugoslavia).
UNSC Resolution 1244, issued on 10 June 1999 (On the deployment of international civil and security presences in Kosovo).
UNSC Resolution 1272, Establishing the UNTAET Administration in East Timor, adopted on 25 October 1999.
UNSC Resolution 1373, adopted on 28 September 2001 (On Threats to International Peace and Security Caused by Terrorist Acts).
UNSC Resolution 1540 Regarding the Non-Proliferation of Weapons of Mass Destructions, adopted on 28 April 2004.

UN agreements/documents

Agreement between the United Nations Interim Administration Mission in Kosovo and the Council of Europe on Technical Arrangements Related to the European Convention for the Prevention of Torture and Inhuman or Degrading Treatment or Punishment, 23 August 2004.

Agreement between the United Nations Interim Administration Mission in Kosovo (UNMIK) and the Council of Europe on Technical Arrangements Related to the Framework Convention for the Protection of National Minorities, 23 August 2004.

Agreement on the Principles (Peace Plan) to Move towards a Resolution of the Kosovo Crisis Presented to the Leadership of the Federal Republic of Yugoslavia by the President of Finland, Martti Ahtisaari, Representing the European Union, and Viktor Chernomyrdin, Special Representative of the President of the Russian Federation (included as an Annex to the Letter dated 7 June 1999 from the Permanent Representative of Germany to the United Nations Addressed to the President of the Security Council), U.N. Doc. S/1999/649.

Comprehensive Proposal for Kosovo Status Settlement. Accessed on 6 June 2007 from the Website of the United Nations Office of the Special Envoy for Kosovo, available at: www.unosek.org/unosek/en/statusproposal.html.

Framework Agreement between the United Nations Interim Administration Mission in Kosovo (UNMIK), Acting for and on Behalf of the Provisional Institutions of Self-Government in Kosovo and the European Investment Bank Governing the Bank's Activities in Kosovo, 3 May 2005.

Other international documents

Handbook on United Nations Multidimensional Peacekeeping Operations, Published by Peacekeeping Best Practice Unit, Department of Peacekeeping Operations, United Nations 2003.

International Bar Association Code of Minimum Standards of Judicial Independence, adopted in 1982.

International Law Commission (ILC) Articles on Responsibility of States for Internationally Wrongful Acts, Annex to UNGA Resolution 56/83 (2002), and Commentaries; ILC 53rd Session, November 2001.

Office of the High Commissioner of Human Rights (OHCHR): A Manual on Human Rights for Judges, Prosecutors and Lawyers, in Cooperation with International Bar Association, Professional Training Series, 9, United Nations 2003.

The Pinheiro Principles (The Principles on Housing and Property Restitution for Refugees and Displaced People), adopted by the UN Sub-Commission on the Protection and Promotion of Human Rights, adopted 28 of June 2005.

UN Basic Principle on the Independence of the Judiciary, adopted by General Assembly Resolutions 0/32 of 29 November 1985 and 40/146 of 13 December 1985.

Domestic legislation

Executive Decision 2004/1, Setting Aside of a Decision of the Municipal Assembly of Prishtine/Pristina of 30 December 2003, 18 February 2004.

Executive Decision 2004/22, Setting Aside a Decision of 5 July 2004 of TM Board of Directors, 7 October 2004.

Executive Decision EC/2001/04 On Extending Temporary Media Code of Conduct, issued on 20 Marc 2001.

Executive Decision EC/2001/07 On Extending Temporary Media Code of Conduct, issued on 20 March 2001.

Executive Decision EC/2001/13 on Extending Temporary Media Code of Conduct, Issued on 7 December 2001.

Executive Decision ED/2000/2 'on the Closing of Offices of Dita Newspaper', issued on 2 June 2000.

Executive Decision ED/2003/11 'Setting Aside a Decision of the Municipal Assembly of Fushe Kosove/Kosovo Polje', issued on 27 August 2003.

Executive Decision ED/2004/25 'Mobikos Tender', issued on 20 October 2004.

Executive Decision No. 2000/21.

Law Amending UNMIK Regulation 2006/50 'on the Resolution of Claims Relating to Private Immovable Property, Including Agricultural and Commercial Property', enacted on 13 June 2008.

Law on the Action of Republican Organs Special Circumstances, the Work on Termination of Work of SAPK and the Executive Council of the Assembly of SAPK.

Law on Basic Property Relations (Official Gazette of SFRY No. 6/80).

Law on Construction of Annexes to Buildings and Conversion of Common Premises into Apartments (Official Gazette of SAP Kosovo No 14/88).

Law on Construction of Facilities for Investment-Commercial Purposes (Official Gazette of SAP Kosovo No 5/86).

Law on Co-Ownership of an Apartment (Official Gazette SAP Kosovo No 43/80 and 22/87).

Law on Expropriation (Official Gazette SAP Kosovo No. 21/78 and 46/86).

Law on Expropriation (Official Gazette of SAP Kosovo No. 37/71).

Law on Forests (Official Gazette SAP Kosovo No 46/86 and 10/87).

Law on Housing Relations (Official Gazette SAP Kosovo No. 11/83, 29/86 and 42/86).

Law on Labor Relations under Special Circumstances, the University Law.

Law on Land for Construction (Official Gazette SAP Kosovo No. 14/80 and 42/86).

Law on Registration of Real Properties in Social Ownership (Official Gazette SAP Kosovo No 37/71).

Law on Transfer of Real Property (Official Gazette of SAP Kosovo No.45/81 and 28/88).

Law on Transfer of Real Property (Official Gazette SAP Kosovo No 45/81, 29/86 and 28/88).

Ligji mbi Gjykatat e Rregullta, Gazeta Zyrtare e Krahines Socialiste Autonome e Kosoves (Law on Regular Courts, Official Gazette of the Socialist Autonomous Province of Kosovo), No. 21, promulgated on 28 April 1978.

Ligji mbi Zyren e Prokurorit, Gazeta Zyrtare e Krahines Socialiste Autonome e Kosoves (Law on Prosecutor's Office Gazeta Zyrtare e Krahines Socialiste Autonome e Kosoves), No. 32/76, 52/77, 49/79, 44/84, 18/87 and No. 18/88.

The Provisional Criminal Code, enacted on 6 July 2003.

Regulation 2000/47, 1999 'On Privileges and Immunities of International Presences in Kosovo', enacted on 18 August 2000.

UMIK Regulation 1999/16 'on the Establishment of Central Fiscal Authority of Kosovo and Other Related Matters', enacted on 6 November 1999.

UNMIK Administrative Direction 2001/16 'On the Registration of Contracts for the Sale of Real Property in Specific Geographical Areas on Kosovo', enacted on 29 March 2002.

UNMIK Administrative Direction No. 2002/4 Implementing UNMIK Regulation No. 2001/17 'On the Registration of Contracts for the Sale of Real Property in Specific Geographical Areas of Kosovo', enacted on.

UNMIK/REG/2006/12 'On the Establishment of the Human Rights Advisory Panel', enacted on 23 March 2006.

UNMIK Regulation 1999/7 'on the Appointment and Removal from Office of Judges and Prosecutors', enacted on 7 September 1999.

UNMIK Regulation 1999/10 'on repeal of Discriminatory Legislation Affecting Housing and Rights in Property', enacted on 13 October 1999.

UNMIK Regulation 1999/23 'On the Establishment of the Housing and Property Directorate and the Housing and Property Claim Commission'.

UNMIK Regulation 1999/24 December 12, 1999 'on the Applicable Law' as amended by UNMIK Regulation 2000/59 October 27, 2000.

UNMIK Regulation 2000/38 'on the Establishment of Ombudsperson Institution in Kosovo', enacted on 30 June 2000.

UNMIK Regulation 2000/59 'Amending UNMIK's Regulation 1999/24 on Applicable Law in Kosovo', enacted on 27 October 2000.

UNMIK Regulation 2000/60 'On Residential Property Claims and the Rules of Procedure and Evidence of the Housing and Property Directorate and the Housing and Property Claims Commission', enacted on 31 October 2000.

UNMIK Regulation 2001/2, 'Amending UNMIK Regulation 2000/6, on the Appointment and Removal of International Judges and Prosecutors', enacted on 12 January 2001.

UNMIK Regulation 2001/9 'on a Constitutional Framework for Provisional Self-Government', enacted on 15 May 2001.

UNMIK Regulation 2001/10 'on the Prohibition of Unauthorised Border/Boundary Crossing', enacted on 10 May 2001.

UNMIK Regulation 2001/17 'on the Registration of Contracts for the Sale of Real Property', enacted on 22 August 2001.

UNMIK Regulation 2001/17 'on the Registration of Contracts for the Sale of Real Property in Specific Geographical Areas of Kosovo', enacted on 22 August 2001.

UNMIK Regulation 2001/18 'on the Establishment of Detention Review Commission for Extra-Judicial Detentions Based on Executive Orders', enacted on 25 August 2001.

UNMIK Regulation 2001/19, enacted on 13 September 2001.

UNMIK Regulation 2001/19 'on the Executive Branch of the Provisional Institutions of Self Government in Kosovo', enacted on 13 September 2001.

UNMIK Regulation 2006/06 'on the Establishment of Ombudsperson Institution', enacted on 16 February 2006.

UNMIK Regulation 2006/10.

UNMIK Regulation 2006/12, 23 March 2006.

UNMIK Regulation 2006/50 'on the Resolution of Claims Relating to Private: Immovable Property, Including Agricultural and Commercial Property', enacted on 16 October 2006.

UNMIK Regulation No. 1999/01 on the Authority of the Interim Administration in Kosovo as amended by UNMIK Regulation No. 1999/25, December 12, 1999 and UNMIK Regulation No. 2000/54 September 27, 2000.

UNMIK Regulation No. 2002/22 'On the Establishment of an Immovable Property Rights Register', enacted on 20 December 2002.

UNMIK Regulation No. 2003/13 'On the Transformation of the Right of Use to Socially-Owned Immovable Property', amended by the Regulation No. 2004/45, enacted on 9 May 2003.

UNMIK Regulation No. 2003/26 'On the Provisional Criminal Procedure Code of Kosovo', issued 6 July 2003.

UNMIK Regulation No. 2004/4 'On the Promulgation of the Law on Cadastre', enacted on 18 February 2004.

UNMIK Regulation No. 2005/13 'On the Long-Term Allocation of Socially-Owned Immovable Property Managed by the Municipalities in Kosovo', enacted on 4 March 2005.

UNMIK Regulation No.2005/54 On the Framework and the Guiding Principles of the Kosovo Police Service and Administrative Direction 2006/9 Implementing UNMIK Regulation No.2005/54 On the Framework and the Guiding Principles of the Kosovo Police Service.

United Nations Transitional Administration in East Timor (UNTAET)

UNTAET Regulation 1999/1, On the Authority of the Transitional Administration, enacted on 27 November 1999.

UNTAET Regulation 1999/2, On the Establishment of a National Consultative Council, enacted on 2 December 1999.

UNTAET Regulation 1999/3, On the Establishment of a Transitional Judicial Service, enacted on 27 November 1999 Commission, 3 December 1999.

International Court of Justice (case law)

ICJ, Advisory Opinion, Difference Relating to Immunity from Legal Process of a Special Rapporteur of the Commission on Human Rights, 29 April 1999.

ICJ, Advisory Opinion 'in Reparations for Injuries Suffered in the Service of the United Nations', I.C.J. Reports 1949.

ICJ, Advisory Opinion on Access to, or Anchorage in, the Port of Danzing of Polish War Vessels, Advisory Opinion, 11 December 1931 Series A/B, No 43.

ICJ, Advisory Opinion on the Applicability of Article VI, Section 22, of the Convention on the Privileges and Immunities of the United Nations (Known as Mazilu Case), issued on 15 December 1986.

ICJ, Advisory Opinion on 'the Legal Consequences for States of the Continued Presence of South Africa in Namibia, Notwithstanding the UNSC Resolution 276', of 21 June 1971, South West Africa (Namibia).

ICJ, Advisory Opinion on Unilateral Declaration of Independence in Respect of Kosovo, 22 July 2010.

ICJ Advisory Opinion, South West Africa, ICJ Report 1950.

ICJ Judgement, Bosnia and Herzegovina v. Serbia and Montenegro, 26 February 2007.

ICJ Judgement, North Sea Continental Shelf, ICJ Reports, 1969, paras. 74 and 77.

ICJ Judgement, the Teheran Hostages Case, the United States v. Iran, Case Concerning United States Diplomatic and Consular Staff in Teheran, judgement 24 May 1980.

ICJ Military and Paramilitary Activities, Nicaragua. v. U.S., 1986, 14 June 27.
ICJ, Report, Reservations to the Convention on the Prevention and Punishment of the Crime of Genocide, 19, 1951.

European Court of Human Rights (case law)

ECtHER, Ilaşcu and Others v. Moldova, App. No. 48787/99, Judgment of 8 July 2004.
ECtHR, Agim and Bekim Behrami v, France App. No. 71412/01 and Ruzhdi Saramati v. France Germany and Norway App. No. 78166/01 (Behrami and Saramati), Admissibility Decision of 2 May 2007.
ECtHR, Akdeniz and Others v. Turkey, App. No. 25165/94, Judgment 31 May 2001.
ECtHR, Aksoy v. Turkey, App. No.21987/93, Judgment, 18 December 1996.
ECtHR, Ali Azemi v. Serbia, App. No. 11209/09, Second Section Decision issued on 5 November 2013.
ECtHR, Al-Jedda v. United Kingdom, App. No. 27021/08, Judgment 7 July 2011.
ECtHR, Al-Skeini and Others United Kingdom, App. No. 55721/07, Judgment of 7 July 2001.
ECtHR, Assanidze v. Georgia, App. No.71503/01, Judgment of 8 April 2004.
ECtHR, Axen v. Federal Republic of Germany, Judgment of 8 December 1983.
ECtHR, Bankovic et al v. Belgium et al., Grand Chamber, Decision 12 December 2001.
ECtHR, Bosphorus Hava Yollarim Torizm ve Ticaret Anonim Sirketi v. Ireland, App. No. 45036/98, Judgement of 30 June 2005.
ECtHR, Campbell and Fell v. the United Kingdom, App. No.7819/77, Judgment, 28 June 1984.
ECtHR, Çıraklar v. Turkey, App. No. 19601/92, Judgement, of 28 October 1998.
ECtHR, Cyprus v. Turkey, App. No. 25781/94, Judgement of 10 May 2001.
ECtHR, Daktaras v. Lithuania, App. No. 42095/98, ECtHR, Judgment of 10 October 2000.
ECtHR, Decision, Stichting Mothers of Srebrenica and Others against the Netherlands, App. No. 65542/12, 11 June 2013.
ECtHR, Dokic v. Bosnia and Hercegovina, App. No 6518/04, Judgement of 27 May 2010.
ECtHR, Ergi v. Turkey, App. No. 23818/94, Judgment of July1998.
ECtHR, Findlay vs. United Kingdom, App. No. 22107/93, Judgement of 25 February 1997.
ECtHR, Hakkansson and Sturesson v. Sweden, App. No.11855/85, Judgement of 21 February 1990.
ECtHR, Hornsby v. Greece, App. No. 18357/91, Judgment of 19 March 1997.
ECtHR, I.A. v. France, App. No. 28213/95, Judgment of 23 September 1998.
ECtHR, Incal v. Turkey, App. No. 22678/93, Judgement of 25 February 1997.
ECtHR, Issa and Others v. Turkey, App. No. 31821/96, Judgement, 16 October 2004.
ECtHR, Judgement, Döry v. Sweden, No. 28394/95, § 37, Judgment of 12 November 2002.
ECtHR, Kelly and Others v. United Kingdom, Judgment of 4 August 2001.

ECtHR, Kelly v. United Kingdom, App. No. 30054/96, Judgment of 4 August 2001.
ECtHR, Khan v. United Kingdom, App. No. 35394/87, Judgment 12 May 2000.
ECtHR, Lavents v. Latvia, App. No. 58442/20, Judgment of 28 November 2002.
ECtHR, Loizidou v. Turkey, App. No. 15315/89, Judgement of 18 December 1996.
ECtHR, Lundevall v. Sweden, No. 38629/97, § 39, Judgment of 12 November 2002.
ECtHR, Mago and Others v. Bosnia and Hercegovina, Apps. Nos. 12959/05, 19724/05, 47860/06, 8367/08, 9872/09 and 11706/09, Judgement of 24 September 2012.
ECtHR, M and Co v. Federal Republic of Germany, App. No. 13258/77, Decision on Admissibility, 9 February 1990.
ECtHR, Matthews v. the United Kingdom, App. No. 24833/94, Judgement of 18 February 1999.
ECtHR, Morris v. UK, App. No. 68416/01, Judgement 26 February 2002.
ECtHR, Nachova and Others v. Bulgaria, App. No. 43577/98 and 43579/98, Judgement of 6 July, 2005.
ECtHR, N.C. v. Italy, App. No. 24952/94, Judgment of 11 January 237.
ECtHR, Önen v. Turkey, App. no. 22876/93, Judgment of 14 May 2002.
ECtHR, Orhan v. Turkey, App. No. 25656/94, Judgment 18 June 2002.
ECtHR, Osman v. United Kingdom, Judgement of 28 October 1998, para 115.
ECtHR, Padovani v. Italy, App. No. 13396/87, Judgment of 26 February 1993.
ECtHR, Piersack v. Belgium, App. No.8692/79, Judgment of 1 October 1982.
ECtHR, Posokhov v. Russia, App. No. 63486/00, Judgment of 4 March 2003.
ECtHR, Pretto and Others v. Italy, App. No. 7984/77, Judgment of 8 December 1983, Series A no. 71.
ECtHR, Pursiheimo v. Finland, App. No. 57795/00, Judgment of 25 November 2003.
ECtHR, Scolo v. Italy, App. No. 19133/91, Judgment of 28 September1995, para. 26.
ECtHR, Sovtransavto Holdings v. Ukraine, App. No. 48553/99, Judgment of 25 July 2002.
ECtHR, Sremek v. Austria, App. No. 8790/79, Judgment of 22 October 1986.
ECtHR, Stichting Mothers of Srebrenica and Others v. the Netherlands, App. No. 65542/12, 11 June 2013.
ECtHR, Tahsin Acar v. Turkey, App. No. 26307/95, Judgment of 8 April 2004.
ECtHR, Tierce and Others v. San Marino, App. No. 24954/94, 24971/94, 24972/94, Judgment of 25 July 2000.
ECtHR, Van de Hurk v. the Netherlands, App. No. 16034/90), Judgment of 19 April 1994.
ECtHR, Waite and Kennedy v. Germany, Application No. 26083/94, Judgment, 18 February 1999.
ECtHR, Winterwerp v. the Netherlands, App. No. 6301/73, Judgment of 24 October 1979.

International Tribunal of Former Yugoslavia (case law)

ICTY Judgment, Milan Milutinović et al., No. IT-05-87-T, 26 February 2009.
ICTY Judgment, Vlastimir Đorđević, No. IT-05-87//1-8, 23 February 2011.
ICTY, Prosecutor v. Dusko Tadic, Appeals Chambers, Judgement 15 July 1999.

ICTY, Prosecutor v. Dusko Tadic, Jurisdiction Appeal, No. IT-94-1-AR72, 2 October 1995.

ICTY, Prosecutor v. Dusko Tadic Trial Chambers II, Opinion and Judgement, 7 May 1997.

Domestic case law

District Court the Hague, the Netherlands, Mustafić and Hasan Nuhanović versus the State of the Netherlands, Case Nos. 265618 and 265615, Judgment, 10 September 2008, available at: www.rechtspraak.nl.

District Court of the Hague, the Netherlands, Mothers of Srebrenica Association et al. v. the Netherlands and the United Nations, Case No. 295247, Judgment, 10 July 2008, available at the following website: www.rechtspraak.l.

House of Lords, R (Al-Skeini) v. Secretary of State for Defence (2007) UKHL 26.

Indictment No. PP 57–1, issued on 31 May 2007, (Kurti case).

R (on application of Al-Jedda) (FC) (Appellant) v. Secretary of State for Defense (Respondent), Lord Bingham and Baroness Hale of Richmond.

Human Rights Advisory Panel (HRAP)

HRAP, Decision, Balaj et al. v. UNMIK, (Case No. 04/07), Decision on admissibility, 6 June 2008.

HRAP, Decision, Balaj et al. v. UNMIK, (Case No. 04/07), Second Decision on admissibility, 31 March 2010.

HRAP, Decision, Case No. 26/08, N.M. et al. v. UNMIK, Decision on admissibility, 5 June 2009.

HRAP, Decision, N.M and Others v. UNMIK, (Case No. 26/08), Second Decision 31 March of 2010.

HRAP, Opinion, Shaip Canhasi v. UNMIK, (Case No. 04/08), 12 November 2008.

Human rights mechanisms

The European Committee for the Prevention of Torture and Other Cruel and Inhuman and Degrading Treatment (CPT): Report to International Interim Administration in Kosovo (UNMIK) on the visit to Kosovo, 21–29 March 2007, CPT/Inf, 2009/03, published on 20 January 2009.

Human Rights Committee (HRC): Concluding Observations, 14 August 2006, CCPR/C/UNK/CO/1.

Human Rights Committee (HRC): Concluding Observations of Committee on Economic, Social and Cultural Rights documents submitted by UNMIK, 1st December 2008.

Human Rights Committee (HRC): Consideration of Country Report, UNMIK in Kosovo Initial Report 14 July–28 July 2006.

Human Rights Committee (HRC): Consideration of Country Report, the United Nations Interim Administration of UNMIK, Initial Report 87th Session Geneva, 10 July–28 July 2008.

UNMIK: (ACFC/2005/003), Report Submitted by the United Nations International Administration Mission in Kosovo (UNMIK) Pursuant to Article 2.2 of the

Agreement between UNMIK and the Council of Europe Related to the Framework Convention for the Protection of National Minorities (30 May 2005 received in Strasbourg 2 June 2005).

UNMIK: (CCPR/C/UNK/1) Report Submitted by the United Nations Interim Administration Mission in Kosovo to the Human Rights Committee on the Human Rights Situation in Kosovo Since June 1999 (13 March 2006).

Ombudsperson Institution (OIK)

Ombudsperson Institution in Kosovo (OIK): Annual Report 2001–2002.

Ombudsperson Institution in Kosovo (OIK): Annual Report 2003–2004.

Ombudsperson Institution in Kosovo (OIK): Annual Report 2004–2005.

Ombudsperson Institution in Kosovo (OIK): Annual Report 2005–2006.

Ombudsperson Institution in Kosovo (OIK): Annual Report 2007–2008.

Ombudsperson Institution in Kosovo (OIK): Jusuf Gashi and Others against HPD, issued on 16 November 2004.

Ombudsperson Institution in Kosovo (OIK): Report, Afrim Zeqiri against UNMIK, issued on 30 May 2003.

Ombudsperson Institution in Kosovo (OIK): Report, Cele Gashi against United Nation Mission in Kosovo (UNMIK), Registration No. 256/1.

Ombudsperson Institution in Kosovo (OIK): Report, Cele Gashi, Avdyl Behluli and Jusuf Veliu, issued on 12 September 2001.

Ombudsperson Institution in Kosovo (OIK): Report, Ismet Ukqa and Others against HPD, issued on 12 November 2004.

Ombudsperson Institution in Kosovo (OIK): Report, N. Korca against HPD, issued on 24 September 2004.

Ombudsperson Institution in Kosovo (OIK): Report, Osman Kozmaqi, Avni Kumnova, Fatmir Dragaj, Hamdi Zenelaj and Asim Rragoni against the HPD, issued on 11 February 2005.

Ombudsperson Institution in Kosovo (OIK): Report, Hatixhe Rexhaj, Avdyli against the HPD, issued on 11 February 2005.

Ombudsperson Institution in Kosovo (OIK): Special Report No. 1 On the Compatibility with Recognized International Standards of UNMIK Regulation No. 2000/47 'On the Status and Privileges and Immunities of KFOR and UNMIK and Their Personnel in Kosovo and on the Implementation of the above Regulation', 2001.

Ombudsperson Institution in Kosovo (OIK): Special Report No. 3 On Conformity of Deprivation of Liberty under Executive Orders with Recognized International Standards, 2001.

Ombudsperson Institution in Kosovo (OIK): Special Report No. 4, issued on 12 September 2001.

Organization for Security and Co-Operation in Europe (OSCE)

OSCE/LSMS: Mission in Kosovo, Background Report, Lead Contamination in Mitrovice/Mitrovica Affecting the Roma Community, February 2009.

OSCE/LSMS: Mission in Kosovo, Commitment relating to the Rule of Law, Copenhagen Document 1990.

OSCE/LSMS: Mission in Kosovo, Parallel Structure in Kosovo 2006–2007.

OSCE/LSMS: Mission in Kosovo, Parallel Structure in Kosovo, Report, January 2007.

OSCE/LSMS: Mission in Kosovo, Report, the Implementation of Kosovo Assembly Laws, Report II, December 2005.

OSCE/LSMS: Mission in Kosovo, Report, Property Rights in Kosovo, January, 2002.

OSCE/LSMS: Mission in Kosovo, Report, Review of Criminal Justice System, Themes: Legal Representation: Detention Trafficking and Sexually Related Crimes Municipal and Minor Offence Courts, October 2001.

OSCE/LSMS: Mission in Kosovo, Report, a Review of Kosovo Justice System, September 2000–28 February 2001.

OSCE/LSMS, Mission in Kosovo, Report, as Seen as Told, October 1998–June 1999.

OSCE/LSMS: Mission in Kosovo, Report, the System of Kosovar Judiciary, July 2000.

OSCE/LSMS: Report No. 3, Observations and Recommendations of the OSCE Legal System Monitoring Section, Expiration of the Detention Period for Current Detainees.n.org/en/peacekeeping/missions/past/etimor/etimor.htm.

OSCE/LSMS: Report, Mission in Kosovo, Report, Review of the Criminal Justice System in Kosovo, 2001–2002.

OSCE/LSMS: Report, Privatization in Kosovo, Judicial Review of Kosovo Trust Agency Matters by the Special Chamber of the Supreme Court of Kosovo, May 2008.

OSCE, Press Release, UNMIK's Police-KFOR, Briefing, 9 January 2002, available at the following website: http://reliefweb.int/report/serbia/unmik-unmik-police-kfor-osce-press-briefing-9-jan-2002.

Human Rights Watch (HRW)

Humanitarian Law Centre (HLC): Press Release, 'Albin Kurti Found Guilty for Organising a Protest in Prishtina in February 2007', 17 June 2010.

Human Rights Watch (HRW): Kosovo: EU Should Ensure International Mission Is Accountable Success Will Depend on Effective Scrutiny of Human Rights Record, March 2008, available at the following website: www.commondreams.org/news2008/0310-02.htm; see.

Human Rights Watch (HRW): Report, Better Late Than Never: Enhancing the Accountability of International Institution in Kosovo, June 2007.

Human Rights Watch (HRW): Report 'Better Late Than Never', Number 2, June 2007, OIK, First Annual Report, 18 July 2001 and Second Annual Report 10 July 2002.

Human Rights Watch (HRW): Report, Kosovo: Poisoned by Lead, a Health and Human Rights Crisis in Mitrovica's Roma Camp, June 2009.

Amnesty International

Amnesty International: 'Human Rights Protection in Post-Status Kosovo/Kosova: Amnesty International's Recommendations Relating to Talks on the Final Status of Kosovo/Kosova', 24 July 2006, EUR 70/008/2006.

Amnesty International: KFOR and UNMIK Fail to Uphold Human Rights Standards in Mitrovica AI INDEX:EUR 70/14/00 13 March 2000.

Amnesty International: Kosovo: No Justice for the February 2007 Killings, Public Statement, AI Index: EUR 70/001/2009, 9 February 2009.

Amnesty International: Kosovo (Serbia): The UN in Kosovo: A Legacy of Impunity, EUR 70/015/2006, November 2006.

Amnesty International: 'Kosovo (Serbia and Montenegro) "So Does It Mean We Have the Rights?" Protecting the Rights of Women and Girls Trafficked for Forced Prostitution in Kosovo', 6 May 2004, AI Index: EUR 70/010/2004, available at the following website: http://web.amnesty.org/library/print/ENGEUR700102004.

Amnesty International: Serbia (Kosovo): The Challenge to Fix a Failed UN Justice Mission, EUR 70/001/2008, January 2008.

International Crisis Group (ICG)

International Crisis Group (ICG): Balkan Report, Starting from Scratch in Kosovo, Nr 83, 13 December 1999.

International Crisis Group: (ICG): Breaking the Kosovo Stalemate: Europe's Responsibility, 2007.

International Crisis Group (ICG): Collapse in Kosovo, Report No. 155, 22 April 2004, available at the following website: www.crisisgroup.org/en/regions/europe/balkans/kosovo/155-collapse-in-kosovo.aspx (last accessed 5th November 2013).

International Crisis Group (ICG): Finding the Balance: The Scales of Justice in Kosovo, ICG Balkans Report No. 134, Pristina-Brussels: 12 September 2002.

International Crisis Group (ICG): International Crisis Group, Bridging Kosovo's Mitrovica Divide, Europe Report No. 165, 13 September 2005.

International Crisis Group (ICG): International Crisis Group, Kosovo: Toward Final Status, Europe Report No. 161, 24 January 2005.

International Crises Group (ICG): North Kosovo, Dual Sovereignty in Practice, Report No. 211, 14 March 2011.

International Crisis Group (ICG): Waiting for UNMIK: Local Administration in Kosovo, Balkans Report, No. 79, 1999.

Miscellaneous reports and press releases

ABBACEELI, Judicial Reform Index, for Kosovo, April, 2002, American Bar Association.

Asian Human Rights Commission (AHRC): Rule of Law and Human Rights in Asia, 2006.

The Balkan Insight, Kosovo Police Pull Back from Serb Border, 26 July 2011.

Balkan Insight: Blood Testing to Begin for Roma Lead Camp Children, 24 November 2010, available at: www.balkaninsight.com/en/article/roma-children-to-test-lead-blood-contamination.

Bota Sot: Kosovo Daily Newspapers, Article Avni Gjakova jep doreheqje, 14 April 2010.

Centre for Balkan Development: History of the War in Kosovo, April 1999.

ECtHR: Press Release Issued by the Register of the Court, 194, 27 June 2013, available at: http://hudoc.echr.coe.int/sites/eng-press/pages/search.aspx?i=003-4416460-5307356#{%22itemid%22:[%22003-4416460-5307356%22]}.

European Committee for the Prevention of Torture and Other Cruel and Inhuman and Degrading Treatment (CTR): Report to International Interim Administration in Kosovo (UNMIK) on the Visit to Kosovo, Carried Out by the European Committee for the Prevention of Torture and Other Cruel and Inhuman and Degrading Treatment (CPT) from 21to 29 March 2007, CPT/Inf, 2009/03, published on 20 January 2009.

European Roma Rights Centre (ERRC): Press Release 'European Court of Human Rights Has No Jurisdiction in Kosovo Lead Poisoning Case', 3 April 2006, available at: www.errc.org.

European Stability Initiative (ESI): Lessons Learned and Analysis of the EU Pillar of UNMIK ESI, De-Industrialization and Its Consequences: A Kosovo Story, Pristina-Berlin, March 2002.

Gazeta Express: UNMIK-u rrenon nje shtepi shqiptareve ne very, 18 July 2011, available at: www.gazetaexpress.com/index.php/artikujt/rubrika/C112/C6/gallery.php?cid=1,15,58369.

Human Advisory Rights Panel (HRAP): Annual Report 2010.

Independent International Commission on Kosovo (IICK): The Kosovo Report, Oxford University Press.

Institute for International Law and Justice (IILJ): Working Paper 2004/7, Accountability and Abuses of Power in World Politics (Global Administrative Law Series), 2004, at: www.iilj.org.

International Commission on Intervention and State Sovereignty (ICISS): 'Report, Responsibility to Protect, December 2011, p. 18 (section 2.33), available at: http://responsibilitytoprotect.org/ICISS%20Report.pdf.

International Commission on Intervention and State Sovereignty (ICISS): Report: The Responsibility to Protect, Ottawa: International Development Research Center, 2001.

International Independent Commission on Kosovo (IICK): Report Issued by the Commission, the Kosovo Report, Conflict, International Response, Lessons Learned, Oxford University Press, 2000.

International Law Association (ILA): Accountability of International Organisations, Final Report, Berlin Conference, 2004, p. 20.

International Law Commission (ILC): First Report on Responsibility of International Organizations, Mr. Giorgio Gaja, ILC 55th session, August 2003.

International Law Commission (ILC): Reports of the Committee on Accountability of International Organizations, London Conference 2000 & New Delhi Conference 2002 Reports.

Judicial Office, Royal Courts of Justice, Judiciary of England and Wales, the Principal of Judicial Accountability, London, available at the following website: www.judiciary.gov.uk.

Koha Ditore, Kosovo: Daily Newspapers, Article Avni Gjakova jep doreheqje, 14 April 2010.

Kosova Information Centre: Nekibe Kelmendi, Kosova under the Burden of Discriminatory Laws, 1992, New Kosova Report, UNMIK Blocking Return Process 5 November 2008, available at the following website: www.newkosovareport.com/200811051367/Politics/unmik-blocking-return-process.html.

Kosovar Stability Initiative: (KSI), Mitrovica: Two Realities, One City, Policy Brief, December 2009.

Kosovo, Bureau of Democracy, Human Rights and Labour: Human Rights Report, 8 April 2011, available at the following website: www.state.gov/g/drl/rls/hrrpt/2010/eur/154432.htm.

Levizja Vetëvendosje, the Case at the Human Rights Panel 2007–2010, available at the following website: www.Vetëvendosje.org/en/the-case-at-the-human-rights-advisory-panel/.

NATO Office for Information and Press: Dajena Kumbaro, Final Report, the Kosovo Crisis in International Law, Perspective, Self-Determination, Territorial Integrity and the NATO Intervention, 16 June 2001.

Office of High Commissioner for Human Rights (OHCHR): Rule of Law Tools for Post Conflict States, Maximizing the Legacy of Hybrid Courts, Report 2008, HR/PUB/08/02.

Panel on United Nations Peace Operations (PUNP), Report, UN Doc, A/55/305-S/2000/809, 21 August 2000, Known as the Brahimi Report.

Police Inspectorate of Kosovo (PIK): Second Annual Report, available at the following website: www.mpb-ks.org/repository/docs/Annual_Report_2007_Eng_Final.pdf.

Saint Group UNMIK Police, CIVPOL Language and Culture, available at the following website: www.saint-claire.org/resources/UNMIK%20Police.pdf.

The Sofia Echo: UN Mission Closes Roma Camp in Kosovo, 10 October 2010, available at: http://sofiaecho.com/2010/10/10/974136_un-mission-closes-roma-camp-in-kosovo.

STP Society for Threatened Peoples (STP): German Non-Governmental Organization, Dossier of Evidence Supporting the Call to Take Decisive Action to Implement Immediately an Emergency Evacuation and the Highest Level of Medical Treatment for All Roma, Ashkali and Kosovan-Egyptian Families in the Displaced Persons Camps of North Kosovo: www.gfbv.de/uploads/download/download/Dossier%20of%20Evidence.pdf.

Trusteeship Council (TC): Report, Protection of the City of Jerusalem and Its Inhabitants; A/544, 9 May 1948.

UNICEF: Integration Subject to Conditions, A Report on a Situation of Kosovan Roma, Ashkaly and Egyptian Children in Germany after Their Repatriation to Kosovo, UNICEF Kosovo, 2010.

United Nations: (Doc. 10393), Report of Special Rapporteur Tony Lloyd on Protection of Human Rights in Kosovo Presented to the Parliamentary Assembly of the Council of Europe, 6 January 2005, Doc. 10393.

United Nations: Millennium Report of the Secretary General of the United Nations, 'We the Peoples': The Role of the United Nations in the 21st Century at 50, UN Sales No. 00.I.16 (2000).

United Nations: Report on the Applicability of International Humanitarian Law and International Human Rights to UN Mandated Forces, from the Expert Meeting on Multinational Peace Operations: Geneva, 11–12 December 2003: Working Session II: The Applicability of the Law of Occupation to UN-Mandated Forces, October 2004.

United Nations: (S/1999/672), Report of the Secretary-General Pursuant to Paragraph 10 of Security Council Resolution 1244 (1999), 12 June 1999.

United Nations: (S/2001/926) Report of the Secretary-General on the United Nations Interim Administration Mission in Kosovo, October 2001.

UNMIK Division of Public Information: Brajshori M, UNMIK Active in North Mitrovica, Southeast European Times, Prishtina, 19, July 2011,

UNMIK Division of Public Information: Brayshow Ch, UNMIK's Police-KFOR-OSCE-Press Briefing, 9 January 2002, available at the following website: http://

reliefweb.int/report/serbia/unmik-unmik-police-kfor-osce-press-briefing-9-jan-2002.

UN Office of the Special Envoy for Kosovo (UNOSEK): Eide Report, 'The Situation in Kosovo. Report to the Secretary General of the United Nations, Summary and Recommendations' by Ambassador Kai Eide, Brussels, 15 July 2004.

UN Special Committee Peacekeeping Operations (UNSPO): And Its Working Group, Report, Second Resumed Session 18 December 2006, General Assembly, Official Records, Sixty-Fifth Session, Supplement No. 19.

U.S Agency for International Development: Guidance for Promoting Judicial Independence and Impartiality, Office for Democracy and Governance, Bureau for Democracy, Conflict, and Humanitarian Assistance, Washington, DC 20523–3100, Revised Edition, January 2002.

US State Department: Ethnic cleansing in Kosovo: An Accounting, Report, December 1999.

Wilton Park Conference: WP784, Promoting Good Governance and Development in Conflict-Affected Countries: The Role of Parliament and Government, 6–9 June 2005.

Wilton Park Conference: WPS05/1, Transitional Justice and the Rule of Law in Post Conflict Societies: The Role of International Actors, 24–26 January 2005.

World Health Organisation (WHO): Memorandum, Capillary Blood Lead Confirmation and Critical Lead-Related Health Situation of the Roma Camps Children, 22 October 2004, available at the following website: http://kosovoroma.files.wordpress.com/2008/05/who-report-october-2004.pdf.

World Health Organisation (WHO): Preliminary Report on Blood Lead Levels in North Mitrovica and Zvecan, Main Office Prishtina, Institute of Public Health, July 2004.

Interviews and email communication

Albin Kurti, interview conducted on 18 May 2008.

Albin Kurti, phone interview conducted on 15th June 2010.

Diane Post, ERRC lawyer, email communication.

Eli Koppel, International Prosecutor, interview conducted on May 2008.

Glauk Konjufca, member of the *Vetëvendosje* movement, interview conducted on November 2005.

Judge Rexhep Haxhimusa, interview conducted 28 October 2005, Office of the Supreme Court, Prishtine.

Marek Antoni Nowicki, Ombudsperson in Kosovo, interview conducted on 3 October 2005 in Prishtina.

Sami Kurteshi, Kosovo Ombudsperson, email communication 2 September 2011.

Thomas Monaghan, UNMIK Department of Justice, Interview conducted 28 October 2004.

Websites

Centre for Defence of Human Rights and Freedoms (CDHRF) a Kosovo-based NGO: www.cdhrf.org.

Council of Europe: www.coe.int.

East Timor Action Network: www.etan.org.

European Court of Human Rights: www.echr.coe.int.
Global Policy Forum: UN Policy Making Monitor: www.globalpolicy.org.
House and Property Directorate/Kosovo Property Agency: www.kpaonline.org/hpd/aboutus.htm.
The History of Namibia, available at the following website: www.my-beautiful-namibia.com/namibia history. html (last accessed April 2014).
Human Rights Advisory Penal (UNMIK): www.unmikonline/org/hrap.
ICL: International constitutional law: www.uni-wuerzburg.de/law.
Institute for International Law and Justice: www.iilj.org.
International Bar Association: www.ibanet.org.
International Commission of Jurists: www.icj.org.
International Commission on Intervention and State Sovereignty: www.iciss.ca/menuen.asp.
International Court of Justice: www.icj-cij.org.
International Criminal Tribunal for the former Yugoslavia: www.un.org/icty.
International Crisis Group: www.crisisgroup.org/home/index.cfm.
International Law Association League of Nations Covenant: www.yale.edu/lawweb/avalon/leagcov.htm.
International Law Association: www.ila-hq.org/html/layout_about.htm.
International Law Commission: www.un.org/law/ilc/convents.htm.
International Peace Academy: www.ipacademy.org.
Kosovo Force (KFOR): www.nato.int/kfor.
Kosovo Helsinki Monitor: www.ihf-hr.org.
Kosovo JIAS: www.unmikonline.org/1styear/jias.htm.
Kosovo Transitional Council: www.unmikonline.org/1styear/ktc.htm.
Ombudsperson Institution in Kosovo: www.ombudspersonkosovo.org.
Organization for Security and Co-Operation in Europe Mission in Kosovo: www.osce.org/kosovo.
UN Interim Administration Mission in Kosovo: www.unmikonline.org.
United Nations Peace-building Commission: www.un.org/peace/peacebuilding/qanda.shtml.
United Nations: www.un.org.
UN Mission of Support in East Timor: www.un.org/Depts/dpko/missions/unmiset/index.html.
UN Transitional Administration in East Timor: www.un.org/peace/etimor/etimor.htm.
UN Transitional Authority in Eastern Slavonia, Baranja and Western Sirmium. UN peacekeeping website: www.un.org/Depts/dpko/dpko/co_mission/untaes.htm.
UN Treaty Database: http://untreaty.un.org/english/series/UNTS.asp.
UN Trusteeship Council: www.un.org/documents/tc.htm.
Venice Commission: www.venice.coe.int/WebForms/pages/?p=01_Presentation.
Vetëvendosje movement: www.levizjaVetëvendosje.org.
Woodrow Wilson International Center: East European Studies page: http://wwics.si.edu/index.cfm.

Index

For Product Safety Concerns and Information please contact our EU representative GPSR@taylorandfrancis.com
Taylor & Francis Verlag GmbH, Kaufingerstraße 24, 80331 München, Germany

www.ingramcontent.com/pod-product-compliance
Ingram Content Group UK Ltd.
Pitfield, Milton Keynes, MK11 3LW, UK
UKHW011001180926
475701UK00004B/507

* 9 7 8 1 0 3 2 2 3 6 2 0 9 *